Microsoft SQL Server 2008 R2 Administration Cookbook

Over 70 practical recipes for administering a
high-performance SQL Server 2008 R2 system

Satya Shyam K Jayanty

[PACKT] enterprise

PUBLISHING

professional expertise distilled

BIRMINGHAM - MUMBAI

Microsoft SQL Server 2008 R2 Administration Cookbook

First published: May 2011

Production Reference: 2230811

Published by Packt Publishing Ltd.
Livery Place
35 Livery Street
Birmingham B3 2PB, UK

ISBN 978-1-849681-44-5

www.packtpub.com

Cover Image by Artie Ng (artherng@yahoo.com.au)

Credits

Author
Satya Shyam K Jayanty

Reviewers
Vinod Kumar M

Ravikanth C

Venkatesan Prabu Jayakantham

Acquisition Editor
Kerry George

Development Editor
Maitreya Bhakal

Technical Editor
Shreerang Deshpande

Copy Editor
Laxmi Subramanian

Project Coordinator
Vishal Bodwani

Proofreader
Jacqueline McGhee

Indexer
Rekha Nair

Graphics
Geetanjali Sawant

Production Coordinator
ArvindKumar Gupta

Alwin Roy

Cover Work
ArvindKumar Gupta

Alwin Roy

About the Author

Satya Shyam K Jayanty is an Independent Consultant working as Principal Architect & Director for D Bi A Solutions Limited based in Europe. He has consulted in a wide range of industries, including the stock exchange, insurance, tele-communications, financial, retail, and manufacturing sectors, among others. Satya's SQL specialty is performance tuning, data platform review, and designing high availability database solutions.

He graduated with a Master's degree in Economics and Commerce from Osmania University, Hyderabad (India) and earned an MBA—Systems from the University of West England.

In 1992, Satya started his career in the IT industry as a computer operator and assistant programmer, and then in 1996 transformed his career as a SYBASE DBA. He has been working with SQL Server (beginning from version 4.2) for more than 15 years and is an accomplished Microsoft SQL Server MVP since 2006. He is a regular speaker and SME volunteer at major technology conferences such as Microsoft Tech-Ed (Europe, India, and North America), SQL PASS (Europe and North America), SQL Bits—UK, and manages the Scottish Area SQL Server user group based in Scotland. He is also a moderator in most web-based SQL Server forums (Microsoft Technet and `www.sql-server-performance.com`), a writer, a contributing editor, and blogs at `www.sqlserver-qa.net`, `www.sql-server-performance.com`, and `www.beyondrelational.com`.

Acknowledgment

Knowledge sharing, learning, and dedication gave me strength to deliver this book, not to mention about the coordinated efforts of editors at Packt Publishing and support from my friends and well-wishers.

I would like to start thanking my friend and fellow MVP Hemant Goswami who referred me to Packt Publishing and pulled this product together.

I would like to extend my gratitude to the wonderful bunch of professionals at Packt Publishing.

Kerry George, Acquisition Editor, for helping me to improve my writing skills and challenging me to explain every aspect of content in concise.

Vishal Bodwani, Project Coordinator, who supported me all along and kept me on track and on schedule.

Maitreya Bhakal, Development Editor, for professional support and help during edit and proof-reading phases.

Shreerang Deshpande, Technical Editor, who supported me at the final stages of book in formatting the book and testing the technical aspects of the recipes.

A special thanks and kudos to my technical reviewers and their feedback:

Vinod Kumar M, Technical Evangelist at Microsoft, who has helped me uncover the additional technical content for SQL Server and highlighting many tips.

Ravikanth Chaganti, SharePoint MVP, for support and helpful references in technical content.

Venkatesan Prabhu J, SQL Server MVP, for support and help in testing the code, suggested improvements for the implementation steps.

About the Reviewers

Vinod Kumar M has worked with SQL Server extensively since joining the industry over a decade ago. Working on various versions from SQL Server 7.0, Oracle, and other database technologies, he now works with Microsoft Technology Center (MTC) as a Technical Architect. With extensive database, BI, and application background, he currently helps customers maximize on their investments on technologies to solve real business and technology problems. He has worked in various roles and projects involving development, migration, deployment, networking, architecture, testing, packaging, R&D, and much more. He holds close to 26+ Microsoft Certification on various technologies. He is also a known speaker at Technical conferences such as Microsoft TechEd, MSDN, TechNet, and so on. Before working with Microsoft, he was a Microsoft MVP—Server for 3+ years.

Vinod has worked for more than 11 years in computers and database systems since earning his Engineering degree from the College of Engineering, Guindy, Chennai. He has published numerous articles in SQL Server on multiple sites and currently writes most of his learning onto his site and blog at `Blogs.ExtremeExperts.com`.

Ravikanth C has more than ten years of experience in the IT industry. At the beginning of his career, he worked at Wipro InfoTech managing Windows, Solaris servers, and Cisco network equipment. He currently works at Dell Inc. as a lead engineer in the SharePoint solutions group. As a part of his work, he authored several whitepapers on MOSS 2007 and SharePoint 2010 that provide guidance around infrastructure elements of a SharePoint deployment. His work also involves performance testing and sizing of SharePoint workloads on Dell servers and storage.

He is passionate about automation, and apart from his work he writes regularly on his blog at `http://www.ravichaganti.com/blog` about topics related to Windows PowerShell, Microsoft SharePoint, and Windows Server virtualization. In 2010, he received Microsoft's Most Valuable Professional (MVP) award in Windows PowerShell. You can also hear him speak regularly at BITPro (`http://bitpro.in`) user group meetings and other in-person events in Bangalore, India.

Venkatesan Prabu Jayakantham is a Microsoft SQL Server MVP for the year 2008, 2009, and 2010 and the founder of KaaShiv Info Tech (www.Kaashivinfotech.com), a company that is dedicated to delivering software and training solutions in Chennai, India. He has authored more than 500 articles guiding at least 400 developers per day from 250 countries all over the world. He is also passionate towards corporate training and has trained more than 400+ IT professionals and guided 3000+ IT students in India towards job opportunities. Venkat lives in Chennai with his wife Subashini S and his son Krishiv. You can check his technical blog http://venkattechnicalblog.blogspot.com/.

www.PacktPub.com

Support files, eBooks, discount offers and more

You might want to visit www.PacktPub.com for support files and downloads related to your book.

Did you know that Packt offers eBook versions of every book published, with PDF and ePub files available? You can upgrade to the eBook version at www.PacktPub.com and as a print book customer, you are entitled to a discount on the eBook copy. Get in touch with us at service@packtpub.com for more details.

At www.PacktPub.com, you can also read a collection of free technical articles, sign up for a range of free newsletters and receive exclusive discounts and offers on Packt books and eBooks.

PACKTLiB©

http://PacktLib.PacktPub.com

Do you need instant solutions to your IT questions? PacktLib is Packt's online digital book library. Here, you can access, read and search across Packt's entire library of books.

Why Subscribe?

- Fully searchable across every book published by Packt
- Copy and paste, print and bookmark content
- On demand and accessible via web browser

Free Access for Packt account holders

If you have an account with Packt at www.PacktPub.com, you can use this to access PacktLib today and view nine entirely free books. Simply use your login credentials for immediate access.

Instant Updates on New Packt Books

Get notified! Find out when new books are published by following @PacktEnterprise on Twitter, or the *Packt Enterprise* Facebook page.

To my adorable wife, Hima, who supported me through late nights and odd working hours to make my dream come true. To my children, Abhinav and Anjali, who give me joy and worthwhile time. To my parents, whose guidance helped me shape my life.

Table of Contents

Preface

Microsoft SQL Server is a powerful relational database engine, widely used to store and maintain data in Enterprises of various levels—be they small, medium, or large. SQL Server delivers a rich set of integrated services and reporting features that enable you to do more with your data such as query, search, synchronize, report, and analyze. SQL Server 2008 R2 accelerates the capabilities to scale database operations and is a highly scalable data platform.

This practical cookbook will show you the advanced administration techniques for managing and administering a scalable and high-performance SQL Server 2008 R2 system. It contains over 70 practical, task-based, and immediately useable recipes covering a wide range of advanced administration techniques for administering a high-performance SQL Server 2008 R2 system and solving specific administration problems. It shows how the SQL Server 2008 R2 system can be taken further.

Packed with reusable, real-world recipes, the book starts by providing an overview of the server and specialized editions of SQL Server 2008 R2 technologies, features, and solutions. Next, it covers database administration and management principles with real-world examples. The book then dives deep into topics such as administration of core Business Intelligence Services, management of core SQL Server 2008 R2 technologies, availability, security and programmability, implementing new manageability features and practices, and maintenance and monitoring, among others.

What this book covers

Chapter 1, Getting Started with SQL Server 2008 R2, begins with SQL Server 2008 R2 version's new features and enhancements such as master data services, data-tier applications, and adding the service pack features using Slipstream technology. We will run through the designing best practice approach in upgrading to SQL Server 2008 R2 and take advantage of federated servers enhancements.

Chapter 2, Administrating the Core Database Engine, covers the new SQL Server 2008 R2 feature utility administration and enhancements within DBA tasks such as availability, security, performance monitoring, tuning, and automated administration practices. The recipes also emphasize the usage of SQL Server Agent scheduled jobs for ETL and replication processes.

Chapter 3, Managing the Core Database Engine, enables the user to produce a resilient data platform, which is possible with new features of SQL Server 2008 R2 such as Utility Control point, multi-server management, and implementing central management feature enhancements. The recipes cover the key best practices that combine a streamline of services for deployment, migration, and management of data platform.

Chapter 4, Administering core Business Intelligence Services, emphasizes on the process and procedures in preparing, installing, and implementing scale-out deployment of core business intelligence services—Analysis Services (AS), Reporting Services (RS), and Integration Services (IS), and finally key practices in managing the ETL process efficiently.

Chapter 5, Managing Core SQL Server 2008 R2 Technologies, dives into the implementation phases of SQL Server 2008 R2 new features and essential steps in planning and implementing self-service BI services, SQLAzure connectivity, StreamInsight technologies, and deploying the master data services feature. These recipes involve the planning, design, and implementation of features that are important to the management of the core technologies.

Chapter 6, Availability and Programmability Enhancements, is the biggest among all the chapters, and it covers the key SQL Server 2008 R2 availability enhancements within failover clustering, database mirroring, log shipping, and replication. The recipes also highlight the programmability enhancements such as compressed storage feature, data partitioning solutions, sparse columns, spatial data storage methods, and management of data-tier applications.

Chapter 7, Implementing New Manageability Features and Practices, spotlights the new manageability features and practices such as auditing, security, compression, change tracking, policy-based management, transparent data encryption, implementing best practices analyzer, and PowerShell for SQL Server features.

Chapter 8, Maintenance and Monitoring, is based on the typical day-to-day tasks of a DBA. It will go through the the aspects of maintenance and monitoring the best practices with real world examples. The recipes will help the DBAs to adopt best methods with available technologies to keep up the database functionality at peak performance.

Chapter 9, Troubleshooting, covers the brainier task of administration which helps the users to solve the problems proactively, and this chapter spotlights the essential chores of troubleshooting. The recipes begin with monitoring methods and various available features such as filtered indexes, table hints, and query hints, and perform parallel query processing methods by taking advantage of hardware and system resources.

Chapter 10, Learning the tricks of the trade, emphasizes on the important aspects of configuration, administration, and management of the core data platform.

Appendix, More DBA Manageability best practices, contains a list of DBA Best Practices that are important to handle day-to-day tasks of the SQL Server 2008 R2 environment.

SQL Server 2008 R2 Prologue

The different editions of SQL Server 2008 R2 adapt the unique performance, runtime, and price requirements of organizations and individuals. The SQL Server 2008 R2 data platform meets the need of handling structured data (transactional consistency) and offers relational capabilities to unstructured data by providing a solution that can store and manage many types of data, including XML, e-mail, calendar, media files, documents, geospatial, and many more, which provides a rich set of services to interact with the data and built-in capabilities of search, query, data analysis, processing, reporting, and integration from different data sources. The data accessibility feature is unlimited, whereby it accesses information on creation to archiving on any device, from a global data-center server to desktop or mobile devices.

A new version of SQL Server is related as "Release To Manufacturing" (RTM) version [(Microsoft SQL Server 2008 R2 (RTM) –10.50.1600] that comprises various enhancements as an end-to-end solution area for data platform. The key to the success of any database platform is dependent upon cost-effective and scalable database solutions. SQL Server 2008 R2 helps achieve these goals to deliver an enterprise class data platform to improve efficiency through better resource utilization, and build confidence in end users to scale out the application solutions.

To commence a scalable and high performance database platform design, identifying which SQL Server features are needed is a key aspect of design decision. The SQL Server installation wizard provides a feature tree for installation of various SQL Server components that includes management tools and connectivity components. The different services for SQL Server are independent of each other and run as dedicated services on a system. It is important to know the different services that are running on the core operating system:

- **Database Engine**: SQL Server and SQL Server Agent are core database engine components that run as services.
- **SQL Server service**: The Server service is useful for data management. It finds services to store and manipulate data based on the application requirement with a variety of backup and restore solutions. The database engine contains advanced security capabilities to lockdown, protect, and audit the data, in parallel with services to ensure high availability is achieved. For high performance and scalability arrangements, the SQL Server service is accountable to host a relational model service, which facilitates any changes to the data to keep up the transactional consistency to ensure that database will revert to a known consistent state in the event of a server or database failure.

- **SQL Server Agent**: To automate essential administrative tasks, SQL Server Agent is essential. This service manages the information about scheduled jobs, monitors SQL procedures (performance objects), and processes alerts.

- **SQL Server Browser**: Browser service works as a listener service to peruse a list of available servers and connects to a correct server instance. SQL Server Browser uses port 1434 to cater to a client request to SQL Server by sending a User Datagram Protocol (UDP) message; the task replies with TCP/IP or named-pipes protocol of installed instances. This is a key service to be used in emergency situations such as connecting to a SQL Server instance using Dedicated Administrator Connection (DAC) endpoints.

- **SQL Server Integration Services**: Extract, Transform, and Load (ETL) activities are highly manageable and programmable using SQL Server Integration Services (SSIS). This service is capable of performing a variety of tasks to enable packages to import or export data from various file sources, manipulate files in operating system folders, or perform complex calculations inside database tables. A set of specialized tasks such as copy SQL Server objects or perform database backups or database maintenance operations can be designed as out of the box solutions using Visual Studio tools for Applications or the Business Intelligence Development Studio tool.

- **SQL Server Reporting Services**: To design and manage a flexible platform for reports and data-distribution, SQL Server Reporting Services (SSRS) and tools are available. It creates a standardized methodology and builds complex reports so that the end user can obtain reports rapidly without having any knowledge of programming language or trying to understand the underlying complexity of the RDBMS platform. The SSRS is capable of configuring a report subscription to set up a schedule to execute the report and send it (by e-mail) to the preferred user distribution channel with their prescribed format specifications. The rendering capability to Portable Document Format (PDF) or Excel (XLS) format or Word format (.DOCX) is a highly advantageous feature for a DBA as it takes advantage of two main components—a report server and report designer.

- **SQL Server Analysis Services**: Decision Support Systems can manage high volumes of data. Blending Business Intelligence features to the system can help us to manage data warehousing issues. The SQL Server Analysis Services (SSAS) is best used to cater the data needs of business users and the ability for IT to manage data efficiently. SQL Server 2008 R2 is built upon highly scalable systems to provide Online Analytical Processing (OLAP) and Data Mining capabilities. The data mart feature with SSAS extends the business analysis to allow the users to find patterns and predictions for their business values by utilizing several built-in mining algorithms.

- **Full-Text Search Service**: Full-Text Search (FTS) consists of full-text indexing and a search engine, which is integrated into the core database engine. FTS is essential to perform a variety of tasks such as gathering data and sending it to the filter-daemon host for processing to 'tokenize' by a full-text gatherer. Once this is completed, SQL Server receives results to index them as an inverted index structure for optimized performance during a search function.

Built on core SQL Server 2008 technologies, the SQL Server 2008 R2 delivers these enhancements by advancing the efficiency to end users on the areas of high availability, enterprise security, enterprise manageability, data warehousing, reporting, scalability, and performance.

SQL Server 2008 R2 new enhancements

SQL Server 2008 R2 meets the large-scale requirements with first-hand enhancements such as two new premium editions and comprehensive additions to existing server editions. The new additions to server and specialized editions of SQL Server 2008 R2 can accommodate the requirement from the lowest level to the highest level of Enterprise needs by offering manageability and straightforward monitoring capabilities.

The installation requirements vary based on the application requirements, and the different editions of SQL Server 2008 R2 which support different features independent to other editions. They offer rich functionality to support mission-critical transactional (OLTP) and Business Intelligence (OLAP) analytical workloads that can be synchronized to access from any type of device. The newest service provision in SQL Server 2008 R2 is SQL Azure, which is a cloud-based relational database service built on SQL Server technologies.

To develop a data management solution to offer performance, scalability, and availability, the selection of SQL Server edition is essential. Though SQL Server 2008 R2 is classified as a marginal change to SQL Server 2008 version, the new editions meet the needs of large-scale data centers and data warehouse deployment. The existing core server edition is coupled with robust and enhanced offerings to enable the highest service levels for mission-critical data loads and provide optimized results. SQL Server editions are classified into three categories: Other, Core, and Premium editions.

1. The Other category of editions is as follows:

    - SQL Server 2008 R2 Express and Express with Advanced Services (free and lightweight to use)

    - SQL Server 2008 R2 Compact (standalone and mobile devices)

    - SQL Server 2008 R2 Workgroup (to host branch applications and provide remote synchronization capability)

    - SQL Server 2008 R2 Web (secure and scalable platform for websites)

    - SQL Azure (cloud-based offering with relational data model)

    - SQL Server 2008 R2 Developer (equivalent to Enterprise edition for builds and test purpose only)

2. The Core category of editions is as follows:

    - SQL Server 2008 R2 Standard (reliable data management and BI offering for small and medium-sized organizations)

       ❑   SQL Server 2008 R2 Enterprise (comprehensive data management solution with end-to-end BI solutions for large organizations)

3. The 'new' Premium category of editions is as follows:

       ❑   SQL Server 2008 R2 Datacenter (highest levels of scalability for mission-critical applications in large-scale data centers)

       ❑   SQL Server 2008 R2 Parallel Data Warehouse (accelerate data processing by using Massive Parallel Processing (MPP) technology)

SQL Server 2008 R2 DataCenter

The DataCenter edition is designed to distribute the high-performance data platform for mission-critical application workloads, and leverage the maximum OS memory limits and physical server resources to cater to maximum virtualization platform support that is essential for database infrastructure consolidation with maximum ROI.

The key effectiveness of this edition is Application and Multi-Server Management (Utility Control Point) for managing multiple instances (up to 25) of SQL Server services. The DataCenter edition offers key levels of scalability with a support of more than eight processors and up to 256 logical processors and memory support limits up to Operating System maximum.

The ROI on consolidation and virtualization is high with a support on memory limits up to the Operating System maximum. The latest supplement for this edition is StreamInsight, which enables you to process a large volume of events across multiple data-streams with low latency and an advantage of mining the KPIs from the historical data for business effectiveness.

SQL Server 2008 R2 Parallel Data Warehouse

The SQL Server 2008 R2 Parallel Data Warehouse (PDW) is built upon a data warehouse technology that takes advantage to improve the reliability and performance of the instance that is highly scalable and built on a Massive Parallel Processing (MPP) and Symmetric Multi-processing (SMP) architecture to enable better administration, scalability of predictable performance, and reduced risk and lower cost per terabyte storage support with major hardware partner compatibility.

PDW provides the scalability and query performance by running independent servers in parallel, which means adding a CPU or memory capacity to the server is a straightforward process. SMP offers the ease of administration and MPP offers linear improvement in processing power, which is the scalability. To achieve scalable query performance, the appliance distributes data across multiple servers and SQL Server instances, and then uses its massive parallel processing (MPP) engine to execute queries in parallel.

The advanced data warehouse capability and standards of Star Join Queries, Change Data Capture, and integration with other Business Intelligence services such as SQL Server Integration Services (SSIS) and SQL Server Reporting Services (SSRS) are additional benefits. Appliance hardware is a multi-rack system with one control rack that controls appliance operations, and one or more data racks that store user data on multiple compute nodes. When designing your own appliance, you can scale out query performance and expand storage capacity by adding data racks.

SQL Server 2008 R2 Core Editions Enhancements

The Enterprise Edition is classified as a comprehensive data platform to meet the high demands of online transactional processing and data warehouse capabilities for all kinds of Enterprise-wide solutions.

There are new additions to these two core editions, which revolutionize the comprehensive solutions within the areas of availability, business intelligence, and scalability having built-in security features.

- **Application and Multi-server management**: This feature from the DataCenter edition is a new edition to the Enterprise Edition, which provides a drill-down capability of resources utilization of applications and instances. It provides the user with a central control to set up and enroll instances for policy evaluation and trend analysis of applications and instances to streamline the consolidation efforts management, which supports up to 25 instances.

- The Business Intelligence capability within Enterprise Edition includes the following key add-ins:
  - PowerPivot add-in for Excel provides users to create effective BI solutions by supporting the seamless sharing of data models and reports through Microsoft Office SharePoint 2010 server.
  - SQL Server Reporting Services Reporting Builder 3.0 is an ad hoc reporting client to accelerate the consistent process from report creation to collaboration to enable the rapid assembly of common business reports using the shared components, for a better scale-out deployment.
  - SharePoint 2010 Operations Dashboard enables the users to monitor access and utilization of server resource usage, manage the right security privileges, and the ability to develop user-generated solutions.
  - PowerPivot for SharePoint contributes to the ability to analyze the large volumes of data with a seamless integration with SharePoint Server 2010 to monitor and manage effectively.

- **Master Data Services**: It is a representation of a single version of data across the Enterprise. The master data hub facilitates the centralized approach to define, deploy, and manage master data efficiently in a consistent manner to enable a solution to create, manage, and circulate changes from a single-master view of multiple business entities.

- **Unified Dimension Model**: It is used to integrate and consolidate data from heterogeneous datasources such as SQL Server, DB2, SAP, Oracle, and Teradata.

- **Scale-up and Scale-out**: It features with an advantage of 64-bit technologies, which enables greater scalability with support for non-uniform memory access (NUMA) hardware without any application configuration changes. Hot-Add memory and CPU capability of Windows Server 2008 to scale up without having to stop SQL Server services.

- Improvements to Reporting Services with easier authoring and ad hoc reporting support for more data types, better control, and management of reports.

- **StreamInsight**: It processes large volumes with less latency; reduces the development and management costs to the benefit of near real-time event processing as a
  large-scale data platform. This feature is available for 64-bit and 32-bit platforms as a server and client packages with two different methods of installations—attended and un-attended.

- **Live Migration**: Windows Server 2008 R2 Hyper-V provides greater flexibility with Live Migration. Live Migration is integrated with Windows Server 2008 R2 Hyper-V and Microsoft Hyper-V Server 2008 R2. If the physical host that the VM is migrated to, is already clustered, then the VM will be automatically configured to be highly available and ready for Live Migration. See `http://download.microsoft.com/download/4/4/D/44DB08F7-144B-4DF6-860F-06D30C6CE6E4/SQL%20Server%202008%20R2%20Virtualization%20Whitepaper.docx` for more details.

- The new capabilities of the Standard Edition are as follows:

  - Backup compression from Enterprise edition is now supported on every SQL Server 2008 R2 edition, with a limitation such as compressed and uncompressed backups cannot co-exist in a media set and previous versions cannot read the compressed backups.

  - The Standard Edition can be a managed instance for application and multi-server management capabilities.

What you need for this book

- Operating System:

  - Windows Server 2008 R2

  - Windows 7 or Windows Vista

- ► Software: Install the following tools and services:
    - ❏ SQL Server (SQL Server 2008)
    - ❏ SQL Server (SQL Server 2008 R2)
    - ❏ SQL Server 2008 R2 Management Studio
    - ❏ SQL Server 2008 R2 Reporting Services
    - ❏ SQL Server 2008 R2 Business Intelligence Development Studio
    - ❏ SQL Server Configuration Manager
    - ❏ SharePoint 2010 Services

Who this book is for

If you are an experienced database administrator and database architect who wants to design, administer, and manage a scalable and high-performance SQL Server 2008 R2 system then this book is for you. The book assumes that you have a good understanding of database management systems, and specific experience in Microsoft SQL Server 2008 administration.

Conventions

In this book, you will find a number of styles of text that distinguish between different kinds of information. Here are some examples of these styles, and an explanation of their meaning.

Code words in text are shown as follows: "We can include other contexts through the use of the `include` directive."

A block of code is set as follows:

```
create table test (
    x int not null,
    y char(896) not null default (''),
```

Any command-line input or output is written as follows:

```
DISKPART> select volume=<drive-number>
```

New terms and important words are shown in bold. Words that you see on the screen, in menus or dialog boxes for example, appear in the text like this: "clicking the Next button moves you to the next screen".

Warnings or important notes appear in a box like this.

Tips and tricks appear like this.

Reader feedback

Feedback from our readers is always welcome. Let us know what you think about this book—what you liked or may have disliked. Reader feedback is important for us to develop titles that you really get the most out of.

To send us general feedback, simply send an e-mail to feedback@packtpub.com, and mention the book title via the subject of your message.

If there is a book that you need and would like to see us publish, please send us a note in the SUGGEST A TITLE form on www.packtpub.com or e-mail suggest@packtpub.com.

If there is a topic that you have expertise in and you are interested in either writing or contributing to a book, see our author guide on www.packtpub.com/authors.

Customer support

Now that you are the proud owner of a Packt book, we have a number of things to help you to get the most from your purchase.

Downloading the example code

You can download the example code files for all Packt books you have purchased from your account at http://www.PacktPub.com. If you purchased this book elsewhere, you can visit http://www.PacktPub.com/support and register to have the files e-mailed directly to you.

Errata

Although we have taken every care to ensure the accuracy of our content, mistakes do happen. If you find a mistake in one of our books—maybe a mistake in the text or the code—we would be grateful if you would report this to us. By doing so, you can save other readers from frustration and help us improve subsequent versions of this book. If you find any errata, please report them by visiting http://www.packtpub.com/support, selecting your book, clicking on the errata submission form link, and entering the details of your errata. Once your errata are verified, your submission will be accepted and the errata will be uploaded on our website, or added to any list of existing errata, under the Errata section of that title. Any existing errata can be viewed by selecting your title from http://www.packtpub.com/support.

Piracy

Piracy of copyright material on the Internet is an ongoing problem across all media. At Packt, we take the protection of our copyright and licenses very seriously. If you come across any illegal copies of our works, in any form, on the Internet, please provide us with the location address or website name immediately so that we can pursue a remedy.

Please contact us at copyright@packtpub.com with a link to the suspected pirated material.

We appreciate your help in protecting our authors, and our ability to bring you valuable content.

Questions

You can contact us at questions@packtpub.com if you are having a problem with any aspect of the book, and we will do our best to address it.

1

Getting Started with SQL Server 2008 R2

In this chapter, we will cover:

- ▶ Adding SQL Server R2 Service Pack features using Slipstream Technology
- ▶ Designing a best practice approach in upgrading to SQL Server 2008 R2
- ▶ Working with Data-Tier applications
- ▶ Designing and adopting SQL Server 2008 R2 solutions
- ▶ Designing applications to use federated servers

Introduction

Microsoft SQL Server 2008 has opened up a new dimension within data platforms and SQL Server 2008 R2 has been developed on the areas of core Database Platform and rich Business Intelligence. On the core database environment, SQL Server 2008 R2 advances the new enhancements as a primary goal of scalability and availability for highly transactional applications on enterprise-wide networks. On Business Intelligence platforms, the new features that are elevated include **Master Data Management (MDM)**, **StreamInsight**, **PowerPivot for Excel 2010, and Report Builder 3.0**. The SQL Server 2008 R2 Installation Center includes system configuration checker rules to ensure the deployment and installation completes successfully. Further, the SQL Server setup support files will help to reduce the software footprint for installation of multiple SQL instances.

This chapter begins with SQL Server 2008 R2 version's new features and enhancements, and adding the service pack features using Slipstream technology. Then an explanation towards how best the master data services can help in designing and adopting key solutions, working with data-tier applications to integrate development into deployment, and an explanation of how best the federated servers enhancement can help to design highly scalable applications for data platforms.

Adding SQL Server 2008 R2 Service Pack features using Slipstream technology

The success of any project relies upon the simpler methods of implementation and a process to reduce the complexity in testing to ensure a successful outcome. This can be applied directly to the process of SQL Server 2008 R2 installation that involves some downtime, such as the reboot of servers. This is where the Slipstream process allows other changes to the databases or database server. This method offers the extension of flexibility to upgrade the process as an easier part, if there are minimal changes to only those required for the upgrade process. The following recipe is prepared to enable you to get to know Slipstream.

Slipstream is the process of combining all the latest patch packages into the initial installation. The major advantage of this process is time, and the capability to include all the setup files along with service pack and hotfixes. The single-click deployment of Slipstream helps us to merge the original source media with updates in memory and then install the update files to enable multiple deployments of SQL Server 2008 R2.

Getting Ready

In order to begin adding features of SQL Server using Slipstream, you need to ensure you have the following in place:

> ▶ **.NET Framework 3.5 Service Pack 1**: It helps improvements in the area of data platform, such as ADO.NET Entity Framework, ADO.NET data services, and support for new features of SQL Server 2008 version onwards.
>
> You can download .NET Framework 3.5 Service Pack 1 from `http://www.microsoft.com/downloads/en/details.aspx?FamilyID=ab99342f-5d1a-413d-8319-81da479ab0d7&displaylang=en`.
>
> ▶ **Windows Installer 4.5**: It helps the application installation and configuration service for Windows, which works as an embedded chainer to add packages to a multiple package transaction. The major advantage of this feature enables an update to add or change custom action, so that the custom action is called when an update is uninstalled.

You can download Windows Installer 4.5 redistributable package from `http://www.microsoft.com/downloads/en/details.aspx?FamilyID=5A58B56F-60B6-4412-95B9-54D056D6F9F4`.

- ▸ **SQL Server setup support files**: It installs SQL Server Native Client that contains SQL OLEDB provider and SQL ODBC driver as a native dynamic link library (DLL) supporting applications using native code APIs to SQL Server.

How to do it...

Slipstream is a built-in ability of the Windows operating system and since the release of SQL Server 2008 Service Pack 1, it is included.

The best practice is to use Slipstream Service Pack as an independent process for Service pack installation, Cumulative Update patching, and Hotfix patching. The key step to Slipstream success is to ensure the following steps are succeeded:

1. The prerequisite steps (mentioned in the earlier sections) are completed.
2. In case of multiple language instances of SQL Server, we need to ensure that we download the correct service pack language from `http://www.microsoft.com/downloads/en/` that suits the instance.
3. The Service Pack files are independent to each platform to download, such as X86 for 32-bit, X64 for 64-bit, and IA64 for Itanium platform.

To perform the Slipstream Service Pack process, you need to complete the following steps:

1. Create two folders on the local server: `SQL2K8R2_FullSP` and `SQL2K8R2SP`.
2. Obtain the original SQL Server 2008 R2 setup source media and copy to `SQL2K8R2_FullSP` folder.
3. Download the Service Pack1 from Microsoft Downloads site to save in `SQL2K8R2SP` folder, as per the platform architecture:
   - ❏ `SQLServer2008SP1-KB968369-IA64-ENU.exe`
   - ❏ `SQLServer2008SP1-KB968369-x64-ENU.exe`
   - ❏ `SQLServer2008SP1-KB968369-x86-ENU.exe`

4. Extract the package file using Windows Explorer or using a command prompt operation, as shown in the following screenshot:

```
C:\Windows\system32\cmd.exe

Microsoft Windows [Version 6.1.7600]
Copyright (c) 2009 Microsoft Corporation.  All rights reserved.

C:\Users\ssqa.net>            C:\SQL2K8R2SP\SQLServer2008SP1-KB968369-IA64-ENU.exe
 /x:c:\SQLServer2008_FullSP1\PCU
```

5. In case the platform consists of multiple SQL instances with different architectures, for instance SQL Server 2008 R2 Enterprise Edition 64-bit as a default instance and SQL Server 2008 R2 Standard Edition as a named instance, then make sure you download the relevant architecture file `http://www.microsoft.com/downloads/en/` as stated previously and extract to relevant folders.

6. This is the first checkpoint to proceed further and the key to ensuring the original setup media is updated correctly.

7. Copy the executable and localized resource file from the extracted location to the original source media location using `robocopy` utility, which is available from Windows Server 2008 onwards:

```
C:\Windows\system32\cmd.exe

Microsoft Windows [Version 6.1.7600]
Copyright (c) 2009 Microsoft Corporation.  All rights reserved.

C:\Users\ssqa.net>            robocopy C:\SQLServer2008R2_FullSP1\PCU
 c:\SQLServer2008R2_FullSP1 Setup.rll
                             robocopy C:\SQLServer2008R2_FullSP1\PCU
 c:\SQLServer2008R2_FullSP1 Setup.exe
```

8. Copy all the files except the module program file that is executed by various programs and applications in Windows operating systems.

```
C:\Windows\system32\cmd.exe

Microsoft Windows [Version 6.1.7600]
Copyright (c) 2009 Microsoft Corporation.  All rights reserved.

C:\Users\ssqa.net>              robocopy C:\SQLServer2008R2_FullSP1\pcu\ia64
 C:\SQLServer2008_FullSP1R2\ia64 /XF Microsoft.SQL.Chainer.PackageData.dll
```

9. It is important to ensure the correct architecture files are copied, such X64 and X86 related files.

10. In addition to the initial checkpoint, this additional checkpoint is required in order to ensure the correct path is specified that will be picked up by Slipstream during the setup of SQL Server 2008 R2 and Service Pack installation.

11. The defaultsetup.ini is the key to guide the Slipstream process to install the RTM version and Service Pack files. The file can be located within the SQL2K8R2_ FullSP folder as per the architecture.

12. From Windows Explorer, go to the SQL2K8R2_FullSP folder and open the defaultsetp.ini file to add the correct path for the PCUSOURCE parameter.

```
DefaultSetup - Notepad

File  Edit  Format  View  Help

;SQLSERVER2008 Configuration File
[SQLSERVER2008]
PID="GYF3T-H2V88-GRPPH-HWRJP-QRTYB"
```

13. The file can be located from the SQL Server setup folder location for the processor, for instance, the 32-bit platform the file is available from \\servername\directory\ SQL Server 2008 R2\X86 folder.

14. The previous screenshot represents the file existence within the server, to ensure that the matching SQL Server Product ID (license key) is supplied.

15. There is more attached to the process if the file does not exist, there is no harm to the Slipstream process, the file can be created at the original folder defined in the following steps.

16. It is essential that the license key (product ID) and PCUSource information is included as follows:

```
;SQLSERVER2008 Configuration File
[SQLSERVER2008]
PID="??"
PCUSOURCE=??
```

17. Now, the PCUSOURCE value should consist of the full path of Service pack files that are copied during the initial step, the entry should be as follows:

```
add PCUSOURCE="{Full path}\PCU".
```

18. The full path must include the absolute path to the PCU folder, for instance, if the setup files exist in local folder the path must be as follows:

```
<drivename>\SQLServer2008R2_FullSP
```

19. If that folder is shared out, then the full path must be:

```
\\MyServer\SQLServer2008_FullSP1
```

20. The final step of this Slipstream process is to execute the setup.exe from SQL2K8R2_FullSP folder.

How it works...

The Slipstream steps and installation process are a two-fold movement. Slipstream uses the **Remote Installation Services** (**RIS**) technology of Windows Server services to allow configuration management to be automated. The RIS process is capable of downloading the required files or images from the specific path to complete the installation process.

The SQL Server 2008 R2 setup runs a pre-check before preceding the installation. The **System Configuration Check** (**SCC**) application scans the computer where the SQL Server will be installed. The SCC checks for a set of conditions that prevent a successful installation of SQL Server services.

Before the setup starts the SQL Server installation wizard, the SCC executes as a background process and retrieves the status of each item. It then compares the result with the required conditions and provides guidance for the removal of blocking issues.

The SQL Server Setup validates your computer configuration using a System Configuration Checker (SCC) before the Setup operation completes using a set of check-parameters that will help to resolve the blocking issues. The sample list of check-parameters is as follows:

Check item	Description	User action
RebootRequiredCheck	Checks if a pending computer restart is required. A pending restart can cause a Setup to fail.	A computer restart is required. You must restart this computer before installing SQL Server.
OsVersionCheck	Checks if the computer meets the minimum operating system version requirements.	Ensure that the operating system version meets the minimum requirements for this product.
ThreadHasAdminPrivilegeCheck	Checks if the account running SQL Server Setup has administrator rights on the computer.	Ensure that the account that is running SQL Server Setup has administrative rights on the computer.
WmiServiceStateCheck	Checks if the WMI service has been started and is running on the computer.	Ensure that the Windows Management Instrumentation (WMI) service is running.
FacetPowerShellCheck	Checks if Windows PowerShell is installed. Windows PowerShell is a pre-requisite of SQL Server 2008 R2 Express with Advanced Services.	For installations of Microsoft SQL Server 2008 Express with Advanced Services, ensure that Windows PowerShell is installed.
FacetWOW64PlatformCheck	Determines if the Setup program is supported on the operating system platform.	This rule will block unsupported installations on the 64-bit platform.
SqlUnsupportedProductBlocker	Checks whether SQL Server 7.0 or SQL Server 7.0 OLAP Services is installed.	Remove SQL Server 7.0 or install SQL Server 2008 R2 on a different computer.

The following are some of the additional checks that SCC performs to determine if the SQL Server editions in an in-place upgrade path are valid:

- Checks the system databases for features that are not supported in the SQL Server edition to which you are upgrading
- Checks that neither SQL Server 7.0 nor SQL Server 7.0 OLAP Services is installed on the server

SQL Server 2008 or higher versions are not supported on the server that has SQL Server 7.0.

- Checks all user databases for features that are not supported by the SQL Server edition
- Checks if the SQL Server service can be restarted
- Checks that the SQL Server service is not set to `Disabled`
- Checks if the selected instance of SQL Server meets the upgrade matrix requirements
- Checks if SQL Server Analysis Services is being upgraded to a valid edition
- SCC checks if the edition of the selected instance of SQL Server is supported for 'Allowable Upgrade Paths'

There's more...

As the prerequisite process of Slipstream is completed, we need to ensure that the installation of SQL Server 2008 R2, Service Pack, and Hotfixes patches are applied with the setup steps. To confirm the workflow process is followed correctly from the folder `SQL2K8R2_FullSP`, double-click on `setup.exe` file to continue the installation of RTM version, Service Pack, and required hotfix patches.

While continuing the setup at the **Installation Rules** screen, the SCC rule checks for **Update Setup Media Language Compatibility** value, which should be **passed** in order to proceed, as shown in the following screenshot:

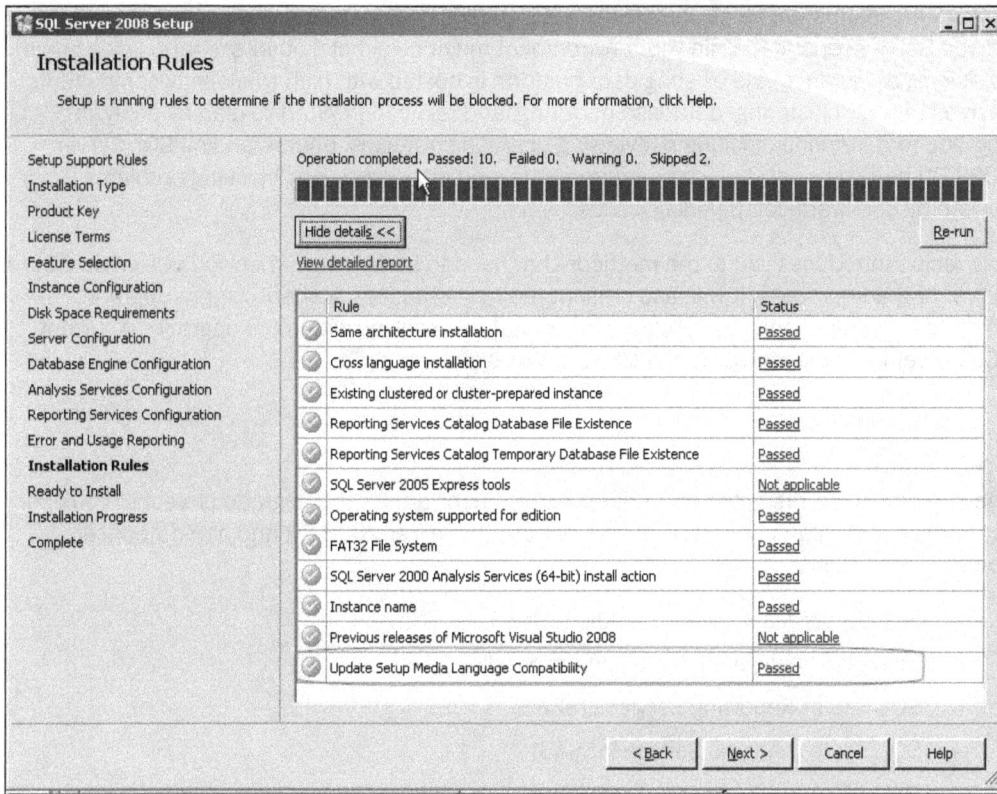

If you have failed to see the update setup media language rule, then the same information can be obtained once the installation process is completed. The complete steps and final result of setup are logged as a text file under the folder: `C:\Program Files\Microsoft SQL Server\100\Setup Bootstrap\Log`. The log file is saved as `Summary_<MachineName>_Date_Time.txt`, for example, `'Summary_DBiA-SSQA_20100708_200214.txt'`.

Designing a best practice approach to upgrading to SQL Server 2008 R2

The upgrade is the most important aspect of the SQL Server 2008 R2 platform management. To prepare for an upgrade, begin by collecting information about the effects of the upgrade and the risks it might involve. When you identify the risks upfront, you can determine how to lessen and manage them throughout the upgrade process.

Upgrade scenarios will be as complex as your underlying applications and instances of SQL Server. Some scenarios within your environment might be simple, other scenarios may prove complex. For instance, the existing data platform is hosted with high availability components such as failover clustering, database mirroring, and replication. Start to plan by analyzing upgrade requirements, including reviewing upgrade strategies, understanding SQL Server 2008 R2 hardware and software requirements, and discovering any blocking problems caused by backward-compatibility issues.

This recipe introduces you to the methods that need to be followed when you design an SQL Server upgrade process. It will also present the best practices scenario for pre-upgrade, during the upgrade, and post-upgrade tasks that are involved within the upgrade of current SQL Server instance to SQL Server 2008 R2 version.

Getting Ready

The upgrade is not restricted to databases. It is important for the upgrade project to consider the various tools, components, and services of SQL Server 2008 R2 and non-database components, such as:

- SQL Server Management Studio (SSMS)
- Business Intelligence Development Studio (BIDS)
- SQL Server Reporting Services (SSRS)
- SQL Server Analysis Services (SSAS)
- Data Mining
- Linked Server configuration
- Log Shipping servers
- Database Mirroring pair
- SQL Server Replication
- SQL Server Agent jobs
- DTS Packages
- SQL Server Integration Services (SSIS)
- Microsoft Desktop Engine (MSDE) or SQL Server Express edition

Further to the list of tools, components, and services, you need to include technical issues (if any) and decisions that are involved in an upgrade to SQL Server 2008 R2, in addition to recommendations for planning and deploying an upgrade. The upgrade processes include upgrade strategies (pre/during/post), test, and rollback considerations and upgrade tools.

The windows architecture upgrade is also essential such as an upgrade from a 32-bit to a 64-bit platform. Additionally, the upgrade from a Standalone server to Microsoft Clustering services is required:

▶ **Upgrading from SQL Server 2005**: Run the upgrade from the command prompt on each failover cluster node, or by using the Setup UI to upgrade each cluster node. If Full-text search and Replication features do not exist on the instance being upgraded, then they will be installed automatically with no option to omit them.

▶ **Upgrading from SQL Server 2000**: This is similar to upgrading from SQL Server 2005. You can run the upgrade from the command prompt on each failover cluster node, or by using the Setup UI to upgrade each cluster node. It's supported for 32-bit scenarios only. Failover cluster upgrades from SQL Server 2000 (64-bit) are not supported.

Before you install SQL Server 2008 R2, we should also run the SQL Server **Best Practices Analyzer** (**BPA**) against your current legacy instances of SQL Server. If bad or questionable practices exist, you can then address them before the upgrade, moving the fixes through test and into production. The BPA tool installation is a straight-forward process and this diagnostic tool performs the following functions:

▶ Gathers information about a server and installed SQL Server instances

▶ Determines if the configurations are set in accordance with the best recommended practices

▶ Produces a report on all configurations that indicates settings that differ from recommendations

▶ The report consists of any potential problems in the installed instance of SQL Server and recommends solutions to potential problems

No configuration settings or data is changed when you execute this tool.

How to do it...

The following steps are classified as the best practices approach in preparing the environment for an upgrade:

1. To obtain the relevant Best Practices Analyzer (BPA) tool that suits your legacy instances of SQL Server, refer to the following links:

   ❑ For SQL Server 2000 version download from `http://www.microsoft.com/downloads/en/details.aspx?FamilyID=b352eb1f-d3ca-44ee-893e-9e07339c1f22&displaylang=en`.

   ❑ For SQL Server 2005 version download from `http://www.microsoft.com/downloads/en/details.aspx?FamilyID=DA0531E4-E94C-4991-82FA-F0E3FBD05E63`.

> ❏ For SQL Server 2008 and SQL Server 2008 R2 version download from `http://www.microsoft.com/downloads/en/details.aspx?FamilyID=0fd439d7-4bff-4df7-a52f-9a1be8725591`.

2. To install SQL Server 2008 R2 BPA tool the following tools are required:

> ❏ PowerShell V2.0: review the requirements and download it from `http://support.microsoft.com/kb/968929`.
>
> ❏ Microsoft Baseline Configuration Analyzer (MBCA) V2.0: review the requirements and download from `http://www.microsoft.com/downloads/en/details.aspx?displaylang=en&FamilyID=1b6e9026-f505-403e-84c3-a5dea704ec67`.

3. Start the installation process for BPA tool by double-clicking on the downloaded file.

4. Upgrade strategies include two fundamental methods, they are: 'side-by-side' and 'in-place'. It's worth mentioning about additional conventional methods of upgrade, such as using **Copy Database Wizard** and **manual Schema rebuild** method with scripts.

> ❏ Using the side-by-side upgrade requires the user to move all or some data from an instance of SQL server 2000, or SQL Server 2005, or SQL Server 2008 to a separate instance of SQL Server 2008 R2. The variations in this strategy include, one-server—the new instance exists on the same server as target instance); and two-servers—the new instance exists on a different server than the target instance.
>
> ❏ Using the in-place upgrade will involve a direct upgrade of the previous version of SQL Server to SQL Server 2008 R2, where the older instance is replaced.
>
> ❏ Using Copy Database Wizard to upgrade an SQL Server 2000 or SLQ Server 2005 database, offers the advantage for the database to be available immediately, which is then upgraded automatically.
>
> ❏ Using the Schema rebuild method with scripts is a manual operation, which requires individual script files to create database, tables, logins, users, and scheduled jobs. Additionally, these external components also require scripting, such as SSIS packages, Linked Server information, and database maintenance plans.

5. Documentation is the key to a successful upgrade. Everyone should work as part of a team. The planning process will begin with a document that stands as a communication to involve all the stakeholders and teams to complete the data platform upgrade process.

6. In case of any specific requirement from Business teams within the upgrade process, that information must be documented in an Upgrade document along with their contact information.

7. Using the documentation acts as a base to execute the upgrade during the deployment phase. The plan should be as detailed as possible, and you should store the resulting document or documents by using some form of change control, such as a source control system. In the rest of this section, we will detail these steps.

8. Finally, within that planning documentation, include the upgrade requirements in addition to the rationale for choosing an upgrade strategy (refer step 3) for each instance or class of instances. Use the rest of the plan to detail remaining issues.

9. Detail the steps required for taking the systems offline for a period of time and bringing them back online.

10. Upgrade the Advisor tool:

    ❑ Upgrade Advisor is available in the `\X86 (or x64, ia64) \redist\Upgrade Advisor` folder of the SQL Server installation media.

    ❑ The tool is also available from Microsoft SQL Server 2008 R2 Feature pack page: `http://www.microsoft.com/downloads/ en/details.aspx?FamilyID=ceb4346f-657f-4d28-83f5- aae0c5c83d52&displaylang=en`.

Within this feature pack page choose the appropriate file that suits to the environment, `X86`, `X64`, or `IA64`.

11. Run the SQL Server 2008 Upgrade Advisor to determine potential blocking issues:

    ❑ Deprecated features

    ❑ Discontinued features

    ❑ Breaking changes

    ❑ Behavior changes

It analyzes objects and code within legacy instances to produce reports that detail upgrade issues, if there are any, organized by SQL Server component.

The resulting reports show detected issues and provide guidance about how to fix the issues, or work around them. The reports are stored on disk, and we can review them by using Upgrade Advisor or export them to Microsoft Excel for further analysis.

In addition to analyzing data and database objects, Upgrade Advisor can analyze Transact-SQL scripts and SQL Server Profiler/SQL Trace traces. Upgrade Advisor examines SQL code for syntax that is no longer valid in SQL Server 2008 R2.

Whether you choose an 'in-place' upgrade or a 'side-by-side' upgrade, you can still run Upgrade Advisor on your legacy systems. We can run Upgrade Advisor from a local or remote server. To execute from a Command Prompt window, we require a configuration file name as an input parameter as follows:

```
C:\Program Files\Microsoft SQL Server 2008 R2 Upgrade Advisor\
UpgradeAdvisorWizardCmd.exe" -ConfigFile "C:\Documents and
Settings\SSQA.net\My Documents\SQLServer 2008 R2 Upgrade Advisor
Reports\MyServer\Config.xml"
```

How it works...

As we discussed, the best practices approach for a server instance or database upgrade process, it is essential to understand how the process works when you adopt any two upgrade choices that are available in SQL Server 2008 R2 and their characteristics.

 ▸ **In-place upgrade**: Using the SQL Server 2008 Setup program to directly upgrade an instance of SQL Server 2000, or SQL Server 2005 to SQL Server 2008 results in the older instance of SQL Server being replaced. The number of servers used in 'In-place' upgrade is 1, which implies that all the steps within an upgrade are performed on the same server.

 ▸ **Side-by-side upgrade**: Using steps to move all or some data from an instance of SQL Server 2000 or SQL Server 2005 to a separate instance of SQL Server 2008. Inside the side-by-side upgrade strategy, we have two variations of how upgrade is processed:

  ❑ **One server**: The new instance exists on the same server as the target instance

  ❑ **Two servers**: The new instance exists on a different server than the target instance

Characteristics of an In-Place Upgrade vs. a Side-by-Side Upgrade are as follows:

Process	In-Place Upgrade	Side-by-Side Upgrade
Number of resulting instances	One only	Two
Number of physical servers involved	One	One or more
Data file transfer	Automatic	Manual
SQL Server instance configuration	Automatic	Manual
Supporting tool	SQL Server Setup	Several data transfer methods

The important process of the upgrade is a collection of database objects required from the previous versions of SQL Server. During the upgrade process, Transact-SQL code objects are essentially passive. Whether the process of an 'in-place' upgrade or a 'side-by-side' upgrade is chosen, the end result will be the same as far as your Transact-SQL code is concerned.

> If in case any external scripts required on the user database are not associated within Stored Procedures or Functions, then they will remain unchanged by a direct upgrade process. You must apply these scripts manually to ensure that the post-upgrade tasks for the user databases can be classified as completed.

Based upon the new server or existing server upgrade, it is a best practice to move any Transact-SQL external scripts to a new server, or correct references within your database to those scripts.

The Post Upgrade process is also equally important and it is easy to analyze how the new SQL Server 2008 R2 instance performs compared with your original SQL Server 2000, SQL Server 2005, or SQL Server 2008 instance. Download the RML Utilities for SQL Server from `http://go.microsoft.com/fwlink/?LinkId=133157` under the Microsoft download site. These utilities stand as a suite of tools for load testing, workload replay, and performance analysis.

As soon as you have completed the upgrade tasks, you need to perform two important steps to ensure that the initial process of SQL Server upgrade is accepted. The two steps are:

1. Integrate the new SQL Server instance into the application and database server environment.

2. Application testing process, such as: Change connectivity settings to the new server, if a side-by-side upgrade is chosen.

3. Change authentication mode of upgraded SQL Server instance.

   ❑ **Linked servers**: The current system might depend on linked server relationships and definitions that must be applied for an upgrade. The application might fail, if those linked servers are not defined and tested correctly.

   ❑ **Logins**: All the required logins and users with relevant privileges on the database must be applied for an upgrade of databases. By using `Transfer Logins` task from SSIS, the logins can be transferred between a source and a destination SQL Server instance.

   ❑ **Scheduled jobs**: The routine administrative tasks are coupled as jobs that are executed using SQL Server Agent service, which are stored in `msdb` system database, which may not be part of the usual upgrade method. In such cases, it is essential to script all the scheduled jobs on the source server and execute them on the destination server.

> ❑ **Imports and exports**: The legacy database system might receive data imports and can become the source of data exports. These imports and exports might use DTS, converted to SSIS, or use other tools. You have to isolate these requirements and make sure of the resulting upgraded instance's correct participation.

> ❑ **Components referring to older SQL Server versions**: If the user is selectively transitioning legacy SQL Server instances, make sure that the resulting instance of SQL Server 2008 has components that can still connect successfully to the older SQL Server versions.

> ❑ **Drivers required for changing to a 64-bit version of SQL Server**: These required drivers might include drivers for accessing other database systems and mainframes from a 64-bit server.

> ❑ **Patches, hotfixes, and cumulative updates**: After you upgrade to SQL Server 2008 from another edition of SQL Server, you must reapply any hotfix or service pack updates to the upgraded SQL Server instance. The process of Slipstream helps here to avoid spending time installing hotfixes or service pack patch upgrades.

4. Determine whether the upgrade was successful by using the following methods:

> ❑ Upgrade to support SQL Server 2008.

> ❑ Change connectivity settings.

> ❑ Change authentication mode.

> ❑ Accept the upgrade, and how it will make the "go/no-go" decision:

5. Verify tests to ensure applications using the upgraded database servers run as expected and required.

6. If available, enlist the support of the QA team to develop appropriate acceptance tests.

7. Determine exactly when and how a rollback to the legacy SQL Server might be required.

8. Test the rollback plan.

If the application connectivity tests are successful, then the next step is to test the reporting section. For instance, if the installation includes custom report items, assemblies, or extensions, you must re-deploy the custom components. If you deployed and used any custom extensions, or custom assemblies for reports with SSRS 2000 or SSRS 2005, you need to redeploy the extensions or assemblies for use with SSRS 2008 R2.

These two steps need not necessarily be sequential. For example, you might apply some acceptance criteria immediately to obtain a go/no-go decision. This could then be followed by integrating the new instance and applying the remaining set of acceptance tests.

Update statistics include:

- Rebuild indexes on user database tables
- Re-organizing indexes if it is a very large database
- Rebuild cubes
- Reconfigure log shipping
- Database mirroring
- Test a failover cluster
- Verify that SQL Server Agent jobs run correctly

Backward Compatibility—Deprecate & Discontinued features

Backward compatibility with earlier versions of SQL Server was a high priority from SQL Server 2008 version onwards. So in most cases, applications will behave as in the past. There are several features from SQL Server 2008 version onwards that are marked for removal in the next version of SQL Server.

After you upgrade, you should remove the usage of these features from existing applications and avoid them in new development work. Several features from earlier versions of the SQL Server Database Engine are not supported in SQL Server 2008 and SQL Server 2008 R2, so you must use replacement features for these.

With an in-place upgrade, the upgrade process handles all aspects of the upgrade, automatically by upgrading the metadata for each database found in SSAS 2005. However, for SQL Server 2000, the upgrade process will not automatically reprocess the upgraded databases. Each database must be fully processed after the upgrade to ensure users can access the data that is contained in each database.

If there is a frequent upgrade failure, then the easiest resolution is to reinstall SSAS 2000. Restore the installation to the state before the upgrade process was started. This ensures that all the data and configuration information that is needed to restore the existing installation is available

The manual transfer of database objects needs to be performed with utmost care due to the nature of all database objects (inclusive within database and exclusive of database). The outer objects of SQL Server are also important for databases, such as the objects that you must transfer, which include the following:

- Data files
- Database objects
- SSAS cubes
- Configuration settings
- Security settings
- SQL Server Agent jobs
- SSIS packages

There's more.

The following Upgrade checklist will be a useful resource while upgrading the SQL Server platform:

Planning for Upgrade		
Documentation	1.	Obtain all the necessary leads pertaining to the SQL Server data platform (hardware), web and application environment (software) to document high-level and detailed information.
	2.	Highlight all the important resources required for pre-upgrade, during-upgrade, and post-upgrade tasks.
	3.	Highlight all the required application testing and business escalation resources.
	4.	Document implementation steps including the back-out plan tasks.
Requirements	1.	Hardware and Software requirements for SQL Server 2008 R2.
	2.	Hardware considerations—existing and new.
	3.	Application compatibility—essential for third-party applications.
	4.	Ready with required environment for thorough testing at pre-upgrade and post-upgrade implementation.
Strategic Decision	1.	Determine whether In-place or Side-by-side upgrade method is being used.
	2.	In case of failover clustering and/or database mirroring environment:
		❑ Establish backup and recovery plan.
		❑ Establish roll-back and roll-forward plan.
Pre-Upgrade		
Environment	1.	In case of side-by-side upgrade, ensure that the required databases, jobs, logins, packages, and linked-server information are restored.
	2.	Ensure no errors are reported on environment (OS, SQL Server, and application).
	3.	Download and execute SQL Server 2008 R2 Upgrade Advisor.
	4.	Download and execute SQL Server Best Practice Analyzer tool for 2000, 2005, and 2008 R2 versions.
	5.	Perform basic connectivity testing from the application.

The Upgrade

Documentation	1.	Ensure to list out all the steps that will be implemented, a screenshot of each screen is an ideal concept to perform the upgrade by any user.
	2.	Make sure to include all the checkpoints that will control the GO or NO-GO decision.
	3.	Every checkpoint should insist on the point of referring to relevant log files including SQL Server error logs.
	4.	Action a roll-forward plan by troubleshooting the issue wherever possible.
	5.	In case of serious issue of environment, invoke the no-go step to implement the back-out plan.
Environment	1.	Obtain necessary passwords from safe.
	2.	Perform a health check on OS and SQL Server.
	3.	Perform the upgrade using SQL Server installation center tool.
	4.	Perform the system and user database backups, once the upgrade is completed successfully.

Post-Upgrade

Acceptance	1.	Determine the application acceptance by performing end-to-end testing.
	2.	Integrate the new instance to connect the live application.
	3.	Apply required security patches and hotfixes.
	4.	Review security settings and execute Best Practice Analyzer tool for SQL Server 2008 R2.
	5.	Review event viewer and SQL server error logs.
	6.	Perform
Documentation	1.	Document any new steps and modify the existing steps wherever necessary.
	2.	Perform failover and failback tasks to ensure Disaster Recovery provision is not compromised.

Working with Data-Tier applications

Data-Tier Applications (DAC) is the newest addition in SQL Server 2008 R2 data management and Visual Studio 2010 development system. The DAC helps users to develop, deploy, and manage the data-tier portion of the applications in a flexible manner and more efficiently than ever before. The key output of DAC is automation and facilitation of database objects and SQL Server instance level objects within the lifecycle of database systems.

Database objects that fall under this category include:

▸ Object permissions

▸ Role membership (mappings between users and database roles)

▸ Extended properties

▸ Statistics

▸ Diagrams

▸ Plan guides

SQL Server instance-level objects in this category include:

▸ Linked servers

▸ SQL jobs

▸ Certificates

▸ Endpoints

▸ Credential objects

▸ User-defined policies and conditions

▸ Role membership (mappings between logins and server roles)

This recipe gives an insight of the DAC process, how to install it, and use it to deploy within the network.

Getting ready

The self-contained unit of deployment is the first step for the DAC process that enables the Developers and Database Administrators (DBA) to package the SQL Server objects, such as database and instance objects into a single-entity called Data-Tier Applications (DAC) package.

The official representation of DAC is represented by Microsoft as follows:

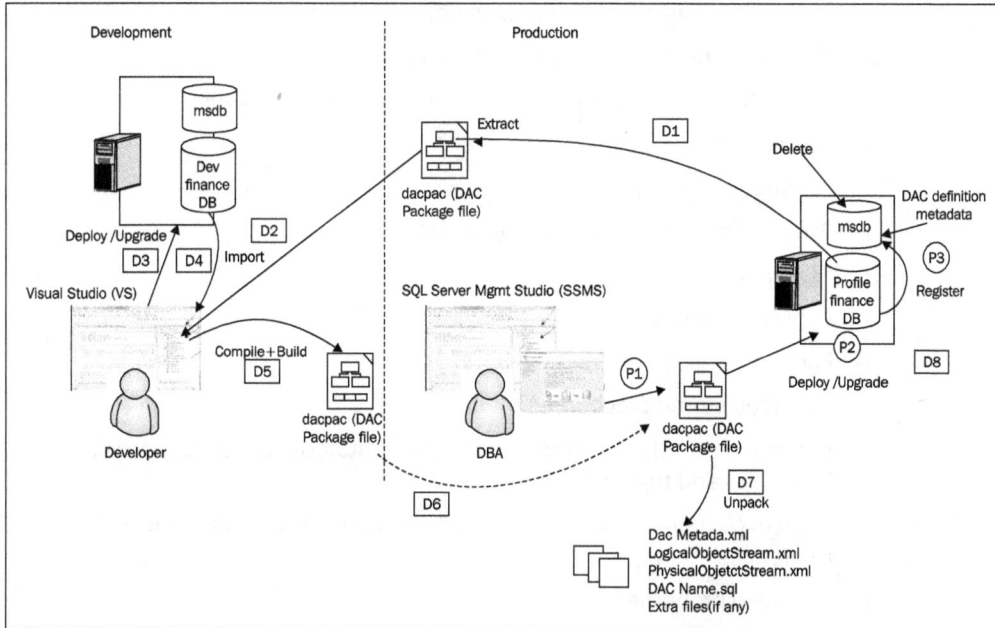

For the ease of understanding the Production deployment and Development extract process, it is represented with numbers—P1 for production and D1 for Development.

The build process of the DAC package can be accomplished using Data-Tier application project system in Visual Studio application. The data management process of the DAC package can be accomplished by using SQL Server Management Studio (SSMS).The DAC deployment installs a new database on the instance, creates the database objects, and creates the logins associated with the users of the database. If a previous version of the DAC is already available, then the DAC package can be used to upgrade the existing DAC instance to a newer version.

The following are few of the best practice items provided for DAC package deployment and extraction that are directed for Independent Software Vendors (ISV) and Internet (Web hosting) Service Providers (ISP):

- The database should contain up to a few gigabytes of data (for example, up to 10 GB).
- There are certain limitations and support restrictions for data-tier applications, such as the common database objects. They are:
    - Objects marked for deprecation, including defaults, rules, and numbered stored procedures

- ❏ CLR objects and data types (such as Spatial, Geography, Geometry, Hierarchy ID data types, SQL assemblies, CLR stored procedures, and functions)
- ❏ User-defined aggregates and user-defined CLR types
- ❏ Partition schemes and partition functions
- ❏ XML schema collections, XML indexes, and spatial indexes
- ❏ Service broker objects
- ❏ FileStream columns
- ❏ Symmetric keys, asymmetric keys, and certificates
- ❏ DDL triggers
- ❏ Application roles
- ❏ Full-text catalog objects
- ❏ Extended stored procedures
- ❏ Encrypted objects (for example, encrypted stored procedures, views, functions, and triggers)
- ❏ Objects containing cross-database dependencies and linked server references
- ❏ Extended properties
- ❏ Linked Servers
- ❏ Synonyms

- ▸ The Data-Tier Application is wrapped with schema and metadata.
  - ❏ The schema consists of tables, views, constraints, stored procedures, users, logins, and file group
  - ❏ The metadata consists of management policies and failover policies that map a database having a direct relationship with the relevant .dacpac definition file

- ▸ There are no specific hardware or software requirements for data-tier applications. However, to manage the data-tier applications through the SQL Server Utility, users must consider the limitations imposed by the utility and managed instances.

- ▸ Though the data-tier applications can be used to work with existing databases, or implement them as new releases, we need to know how to create data-tier applications in existing systems to register each database as a data-tier application.

- The build process of the DAC package can be accomplished by using Data-Tier application project system in Visual Studio application.

- The data management process of the DAC package can be accomplished by using SQL Server Management Studio (SSMS). The DAC deployment installs a new database on the instance, creates the database objects, and creates the logins associated with the users of the database.

- If a previous version of the DAC is already available, the DAC package can be used to upgrade the existing DAC instance to a newer version.

How to do it...

The Extract Data-tier application process creates a DAC package from a database. To extract a DAC package, perform the following steps:

1. Register the instance of SQL Server. In the **Object Explorer** pane, click on **Connect** and follow the instructions in the **Connect to Server** dialog box.

2. In **Object Explorer**, select the node of the instance from which you want to extract a data-tier application and expand its **Databases** node.

3. Select the database for the extraction. Right-click the databases node, point to **Tasks**, and then click **Extract Data-tier Application** to launch the Extract Data-tier Application Wizard.

4. On the **Set Properties** page (shown in the next screenshot), review or change the properties and then click on **Next**. These properties are displayed in Visual Studio and in SQL Server Management Studio and are used as follows:

   - **Application Name**: It identifies the application. For example, if a database called `FinanceDB` serves the Finance application, the application name should be set to Finance. The application name is used when a data-tier application is upgraded. In order to upgrade a DAC V1 to a DAC V2, the application names of V1 and V2 must be identical.

   - **Version**: It's the version of the data-tier application. By default, the version number is 1.0.0.0.

   - **Description**: Optional.

> ❑ **Save to DAC package file**: It specifies the filename and path for the DAC package file. This file must end with the `.dacpac` extension.

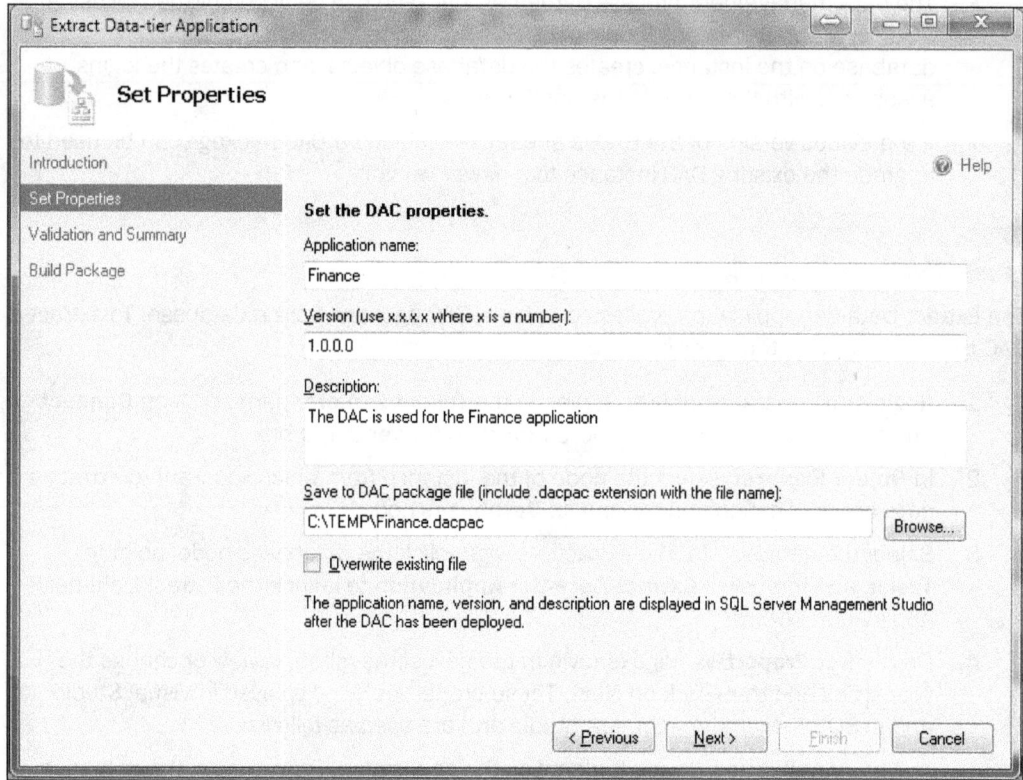

5. This is where the retrieval of database objects and relevant logins with checks of DAC package can be created with a validation process.

6. The validation process ensures that all database objects are supported by a DAC, and all dependent objects are available in the database. For example, if a view depends on a table and the latter was dropped from the database, a DAC cannot be extracted.

7. When the validation completes, all issues and errors that prevent the creation of a DAC package appear in the summary tree (refer to the next screenshot). If there are no issues with the validation report, then click **Next** to create and save the DAC package file.

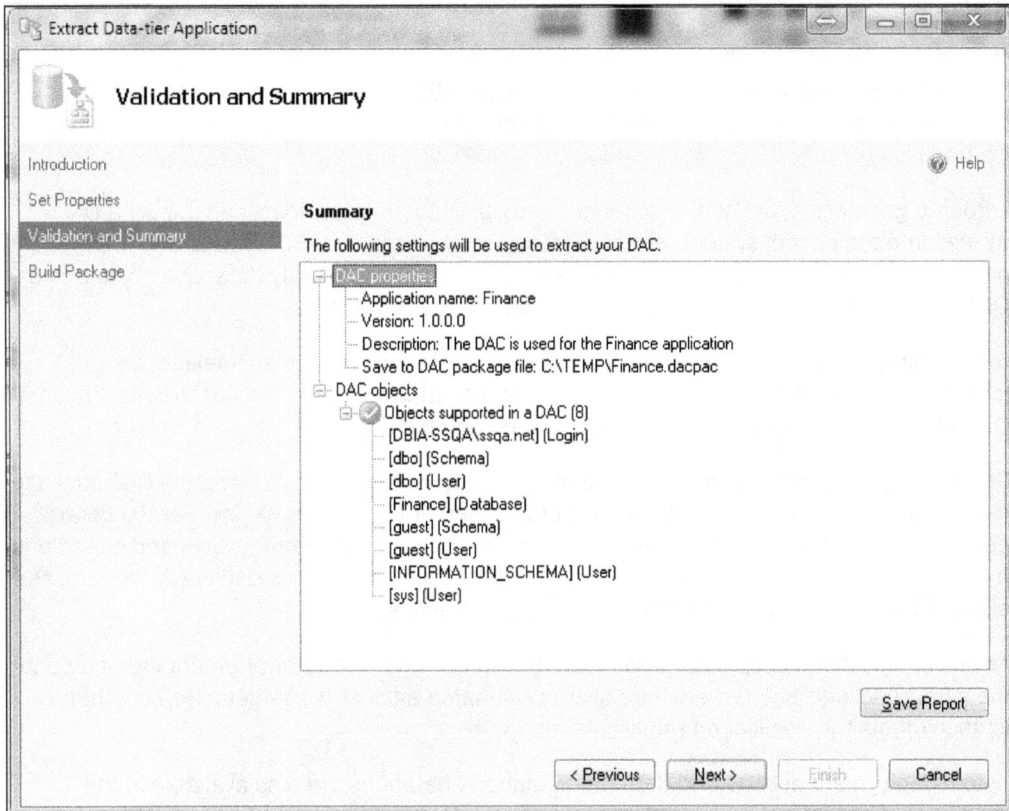

8. On the **Build Package** page, review the status of building the DAC package file. When the build is finished, click **Finish** to close the wizard. Finally, verify that a new DAC package file was created in the path you specified in step 4.

9. The extracted DAC package file can now be imported to a Data-tier Application project in Visual Studio. In addition, the DAC package can also be deployed to create a new data-tier application on an instance of SQL Server, or to upgrade an older version of an existing data-tier application.

> In an ISV-based environment, if the referred .dacpac file is received from a third-party or an unknown source, then it is essential to review the file contents that contain the pre and post schema change scripts. The default practice must include verification of the package file contents with an anti-virus scanner.

How it works...

There are three key components of a data-tier application project initiation—SQL Server objects, a server selection policy, and custom scripts (sometimes referred to as additional or extra files).

In order to get started, define the schema of an application. Developers can import a DAC package into the project system, or they can select an instance of SQL Server and import objects from an existing database. Then, users can create and modify database objects and SQL Server instance objects that are associated with the database.

Programming users can utilize advanced code editing features (such as IntelliSense technology, auto-completion, code snippets, and the Transact-SQL compiler) to write Transact-SQL code for stored procedures, functions, users, and logins.

After adding tables to the data-tier application projects, developers can create a DAC package and deploy the project to a target instance of SQL Server to test the release. For the control deployments, a server selection policy enables developers to set prerequisites and conditions on the target instance of SQL Server where the data-tier application is deployed. This process helps to dictate prerequisite conditions on target instances.

The server selection policy helps developers to express and dictate deployment intents. Each time a DAC package is deployed, the policy is evaluated against the target to ensure that the instance meets the application requirements.

Custom deployment actions and data manipulation operations are also available in the data-tier application project through custom scripts. Users can provide Transact-SQL scripts and include them in the DAC package. While the system does not automatically execute or reason over custom scripts, users can manually execute these scripts during DAC deployment or upgrade.

The unpack functionality is provided to let users view the content of a DAC package and generate the Transact-SQL script that corresponds to the deployment or upgrade of a data-tier application. The best practice is to use the unpack feature before you deploy or upgrade a DAC package in production, to review the code and compare or identify changes.

There's more...

In order to simplify the management of SQL Server environments, the health of DAC resources (for example, CPU, and disk space) across multiple computers and instances can be viewed in a central interface called the Utility Explorer in SQL Server Management Studio.

The Utility Explorer displays aggregated data and information, enabling DBAs to easily obtain utilization reports and statistics for their SQL Server installations. Furthermore, in order to customize CPU and disk space performance reports, DBAs can use Utility Health Policies to tune and control views showing the DAC resource consumption.

Designing and adopting SQL Server 2008 R2 solutions

The design of a solution needs guidance and planning, that has a series of collection consisting of information such as infrastructure planning, design, and implementation process which leads the sequence of core decision points. Designing the SQL Server 2008 R2 is no different to the key steps mentioned preciously. It also provides a means of validation to design and deploy the key business decisions to ensure that the solution meets the near-to-clear requirements for both technology and business stakeholders.

The design and adoption program must include technologists, such as Architects, to have an operational grasp of the technology to make the best use of new features. Also, the business team involvement is a high-level need to ensure that they understand the technology decisions being made for development and support. This can affect the business.

Getting ready

SQL Server 2008 R2 contains new features within the Business Intelligence stack such as PowerPivot, StreamInsight, and Master Data Services. A series of technology adoption program needs to be designed from an IT and Business perspective. A step beyond the traditional technology provision and SQL Server 2008 R2, consists of a series of best practices to implement the real-world BI solutions to leverage the best use of technologies.

The adoption programs should be designed to help users understand how the new SQL Server features interact with established technologies such as SQL Server Analysis Services, or SQL Server Integration Services, or SQL Server Reporting Services. In this recipe, we will go through the required process in designing and adopting the SQL Server 2008 R2 solutions.

The guidance must include the activities of planning a design, understanding new features, and implementing them effectively. In this case, SQL Server 2008 R2 new features. The critical design elements of planning are project scope determination, roles of people (such as dividing the technology and business decision-maker levels and infrastructure adoption of SQL Server 2008 R2 technologies), core database engine, integration services, analysis services, reporting services, and master data services.

Each user and stakeholder's needs should be classified taking the following considerations into account:

▶ Organizations that are implementing SQL Server for a specific application

▶ Organizations that are implementing SQL Server to provide a business intelligence platform for managers and decision makers to conduct data integration, reporting, and analysis

> ▸ Organizations that are implementing SQL Server as a service that is expected to be available to multiple business units

> ▸ Organizations that are upgrading an existing SQL Server implementation by migrating to new hardware

How to do it...

The following set of processes is involved in designing and adopting specific SQL Server 2008 R2 solutions:

1. In a typical application fetching data from a database server approach, the SQL Server infrastructure is designed to support a specific application.

2. This approach involves gathering the requirements about the application, determining which SQL Server roles will be required, and optimizing the server design for those specific applications.

3. Another approach is to design Database as a Service that makes the easy availability of new features for general platform usage.

4. Now the important aspect of design: Before proceeding to the implementation of database infrastructure, the aspect of storage and performance requirements will need to be gathered.

5. So the core service for storing, processing, and securing data is catered through the database engine that supports both relational (OLTP) and analytical (OLAP) methods for desktop requirements to data warehouse databases.

6. If the application being implemented requires one or more OLTP databases, then the same process of collection of performance requirement must be repeated.

Other services that may be selected in later tasks could determine the need for the Database Engine, such as:

> ▸ **Reporting Services**: It requires access to SQL Server-based database server to store metadata; this metadata database can be on the same server as Reporting Services, or on another database server. Integration Services can store packages in the msdb database–which is the system database–or on the filesystem.

> ▸ **Storage location**: It will be determined by the outcome of the decision of whether or not a database may be required for Integration Services. The inner process of Integration Services are required, such as:

>> ❑ Merge data from heterogeneous data sources

>> ❑ Populate data warehouses and data marts

>> ❑ Cleanse and standardize data

>> ❑ Automate administrative functions and data loading

For Data Warehouse, SQL Server Analysis Services (SSAS) supports OLAP (online analytical processing) and data mining functionalities. This allows a database administrator to design and create multidimensional structures that contain data aggregated from other data sources, such as relational databases.

Analysis Services may be needed if the organization needs to rapidly access reports with varying degrees of granularity (for example, yearly totals, monthly totals, quarterly totals, and individual transactions) and requires that the yearly totals appear just as quickly as the daily totals.

An online transaction processing (OLTP) system would have to add up these values, while an SSAS system, in many cases, will already have the answers pre-calculated.

SQL Server Reporting Services (SSRS) delivers enterprise reporting functionality for creating reports that gather content from a variety of data sources, publishing the reports in various formats, and centrally managing their security and subscriptions. Reports can be delivered on a scheduled basis to users, accessed through a web interface from SharePoint, or from custom applications including Windows Forms applications that call through web services.

Reporting Services can be used to generate reports on OLTP databases, SSAS cubes, data warehouses, data marts, or third-party data sources such as flat files, Oracle databases, or web services.

How it works...

There are potential reasons why a database might not be located within an existing instance:

- **Regulatory requirements**: Corporate policies or government regulations may require separate storage for certain types of data or for certain parts of the organization.
- **Memory isolation**: There may be a database application with a memory leak. It's therefore desirable to place it in its own instance and cap the memory available to this instance to protect other databases on the server from being affected.
- **Fault tolerance**: Clustering is on the instance level; thus, it will be necessary to place a database in an instance with similar fault-tolerance requirements.
- **Authentication**: Authentication is set at the instance level to be either an SQL Server authentication or a Windows authentication. The new database's authentication requirements need to be compatible with the instance's authentication setting.
- **Security concerns**: Total database encryption can be used to add security to a database. The service master key is for all databases in an instance. To minimize exposure, if a key is compromised, it may be desirable to place the database in a separate instance.
- **Support requirements**: The vendor or developer may require that the database runs in a separate instance.

- ▶ Two factors that may change the number of servers running SQL Server are:

    - ❑ Whether or not scaling out will be implemented
    - ❑ Whether fault tolerance will be implemented at the database level or instance level

Scaling out is the process of distributing an SQL Server load across multiple servers; thus, the decision to scale out will increase the number of servers required. Multiple scale-out options are available, and this section will provide a brief overview. Scale-out options require design changes that occur at the database level and are outside the scope of this guide. It is expected that any decisions relative to scaling out should be made in conjunction with the database administrator.

> Note that a new server, by definition, is a new instance.

There's more...

The detailed information on the installation and configuration process is discussed in *Chapter 5, Management of core SQL Server 2008 R2 technologies* recipes:

- ▶ *Designing Data Integration Solution for Master Data Management*
- ▶ *Designing and Deploying framework to use Master Data Services*
- ▶ *Troubleshooting SQL Server Master Data Services*

Designing applications to use federated servers

The high level of performance is an immediate requirement in current application database systems. In this scenario, to manage an application as 'high-available' and establish a load balancing of processing load for each task across multiple servers is called **Federated Servers**. Adding a federation of database servers to a highly-available system offers the flexibility to manage the resources for mission-critical processes efficiently.

Getting ready

The application system that is always available (high-availability) is a key ingredient for the success of every enterprise which establishes a federation of database servers, thereby distributing the processing load across a group of servers by horizontally partitioning the data in an SQL Server database. These servers are managed independently, but cooperate to process requests on the database.

The Federated Server is made up of two systems; a 'program'—to access data and a 'database structure'—to store the data. Similarly, to achieve the high levels of performance required by a client-server application or a website on a 24/7 basis, then a multi-tier system is needed that can typically balance the processing load for each tier across multiple servers.

By design, SQL Server features can share the database processing load across a group of servers by horizontally partitioning the data in a database. These servers are managed independently, but cooperate to process the database requests from the applications; for example, a cooperative group of servers is called a federation.

Designing and implementing structured storage within the database–which is called **partition**–is the first step to planning a federated database design. To accomplish the concept of database partition, we should create the underlying objects, such as **partition function** and **partition scheme**. The partition function handles the mapping of the rows of a table to the set of partitions based on certain column values, which are called **partitioning columns**. A partition scheme handles the mapping of each partition specified by a partition function to a file group.

The important choice for partitioning column values can be determined by the extent to which the data is grouped logically. Grouping by date is an adequate approach for managing subsets of data. For example, the `SalesHistory` and `SalesHistoryArchive` tables are partitioned by the `TransactionDate` field. Each partition consists of one month, which enables the `SalesHistory` table to maintain the year's worth of transactions as current and the `SalesHistoryArchive` table to maintain the data older than one year. By partitioning the tables in this way, the database engine can offer the scalability to transfer the old data quickly and efficiently.

How to do it...

Once we have decided the partition function and partition scheme, the implementation of the partitioned table or index is the key step. The steps for creating a partitioned table or index using Transact-SQL are as follows:

1. Create partition function (rules) that specify how a table or index is partitioned:

```
CREATE PARTITION FUNCTION partition_function_name(input_parameter_
type)
AS RANGE [ LEFT | RIGHT ]
FOR VALUES ( [boundary_value [ ,...n ] ] )
[ ; ]
```

2. From the previous syntax, the key value is RANGE, you have to choose between RANGE RIGHT and RANGE LEFT. CREATE PARTITION FUNCTION [dbo].[PF_ SalesMonths] (datetime) as RANGE RIGHT FOR VALUES ('20110201','20110 301','20110401','20110501','20110601','20110701','20110801','20110 901','20111001','20111101','20111201');

3. The following list represents how an underlying table would be partitioned:

Partition	1	2	12
Values	SalesDate<February 1, 2011	SalesDate>= February 1, 2011 AND SalesDatel<March 1, 2011	SalesDate>= December 1, 2011

> If no RANGE option is mentioned, then RANGE LEFT is the default.

4. Create a partition scheme that specifies the placement of partitions of a partition function on file groups:

    ```
    CREATE PARTITION SCHEME PS_SalesRange AS PARTITION PF_SalesMonths
    TO ([PRIMARY],[FEBRUARY],[MARCH],[APRIL],[MAY],[JUNE],[JULY],[AUGU
    ST],[SEPTEMBER],[OCTOBER],[NOVEMBER],[DECEMBER])
    ```

5. The scheme defines the function of where to put the partition data. This step enables the partition of the `SalesHistory` table based on the Date by month range.

6. Create a table or index using the defined partition scheme.

    ```
    CREATE TABLE SalesHistoryPartitionedTable (
    TransactionIDint PRIMARY KEY,
    SalesDate DATETIME,
    ProductIdint) on PS_SalesRange(ID)
    ```

These steps can be achieved using SQL Server Management studio:

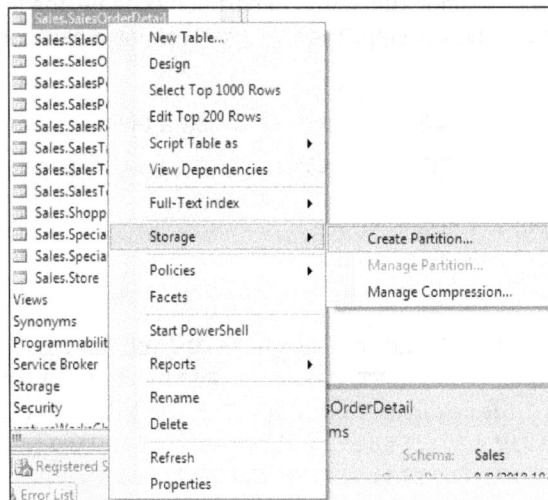

The partitioned table approach is a common solution. The pattern of data and the relationship of such tables are important to route the federation.

To accomplish this task, it is essential to develop a list of the SQL statements that will be executed by the application during typical processing periods. The process of developing a list can be accomplished as follows:

- Differentiate the list into SELECT, UPDATE, INSERT, and DELETE categories
- Order the list in each category by the frequency of execution
- If the SQL statements reference the stored procedures, then use the base SELECT, INSERT, UPDATE, and DELETE statements from the stored procedure
- If you are partitioning an existing SQL Server database, you can use SQL Server Profiler to obtain such a list

The frequency of such SQL statements can be determined to sustain a reasonable estimate for an OLTP system where distributed partitioned views work best. Such systems are characterized by having individual SQL statements that retrieve relatively small amounts of data when compared to the types of queries in a decision support, or an OLAP system.

When each SQL statement references a small amount of data, just studying the frequency of each statement yields a reasonable approximation of the data traffic in the system.

However, many systems have some groups of SQL statements that reference a lot of data. You may want to take the additional step of weighing these queries to reflect their larger data requirements.

The routing rules must be able to define which member server can most effectively process each SQL statement. They must establish a relationship between the context of the input by the user and the member server that contains the bulk of the data required to complete the statement.

The applications should be able to take a piece of data entered by the user, and match it against the routing rules to determine which member server should process the SQL statement.

High-level performance cannot be achieved simply by deploying the Federated Server process; the database design and table normalization is essential to keep up the performance and scalability.

This is referred to as collocating the SQL statement with the data required by the statement, it is the key to design a partitioning scheme to be clear about what data belongs to each member table. The partitioning scheme can be designed as follows:

- The original table is replaced with several smaller member tables
- Each member table will have the same number of columns matching as the original table

> ▸ Each column will have the same attributes as the column in the original table where the attributes, such as data type and collation must be matched

How it works...

> ▸ The process of federated servers is implemented with the design architecture of the User/Business/Data services tier.

> ▸ The initial tier of User Services is a set of thin clients that focus on managing the application user interface.

> ▸ The User Services tier calls the next tier to perform the business functions needed to support user requests.

> ▸ So the Business Services Tier consists of a set of 'COM+' components that encapsulate the business logic of the organization. The Business Services tier uses the next tier for any permanent data storage that has to be performed.

> ▸ The final stage of storage is the Data Services Tiers, such as SQL Server databases, which can store data in a permanent medium. This is also referred to as **persisting the data**.

2
Administrating the Core Database Engine

In this chapter, we will cover:

- ▶ Designing automated administration practices
- ▶ Implementing Security feature enhancements
- ▶ Implementing Availability feature enhancements
- ▶ Implementing Monitoring and Tuning for performance
- ▶ Administering SQL Server workloads with Resource Governor
- ▶ Designing SQL Server Agent scheduled jobs for ETL processes
- ▶ Troubleshooting multi-server instances with utility administration
- ▶ Administering SQL Server Replication processes

Introduction

SQL Server administration is one of the key responsibilities for every DBA to keep up the availability, performance, and scalability of the data platform. This chapter will cover all the aspects of database administration.

SQL Server 2008 R2 features include important elements as part of a toolkit to automate the core database development and administration functionalities. To be a competent Developer and Database Administrator, the user needs to have a firm understanding of the tools, features and architecture of the system.

In this chapter, we will look at the automated administration practices such as the implementation of security, availability, performance monitoring, and tuning features of SQL Server 2008 R2. We will also look at the concepts related to scheduling aspects of the SQL ServerAgent to handle the **Extract-Transform-Load** (**ETL**) processes, and administering the replication process to trouble shooting multi-server instances using the new utility administration tool from **SQL Server Management Studio** (**SSMS**).

Designing automated administration practices

The automation of administrative tasks is essential when the data platform turns to more complex systems and larger databases. The key task for the Database Administrator is to be able to automate the routine tasks and develop proactive maintenance to ensure that data availability and integrity is maintained without any interruption. The life-cycle of automated processes for SQL Server administration is a large topic, and it's not possible to cover all of them in this recipe alone. Hence, the key aspects of automation have been enlisted. In order to accomplish the automated administration, the SQL Server Services must be setup with startup accounts with necessary privileges that will help to harden the SQL Server platform at the time of deployment.

The evolving business needs and application requirements have made the Database Administrator's role more challenging. Prior to SQL Server 2008, a great deal of time was spent performing routine administrative tasks such as backup/restore operations and monitoring the SQL Server instances. The key ingredient for this recipe is to understand the windows operating system service and account privileges to implement the SQL Server platform's automation methods.

Getting ready

The SQL Server setup wizard follows the process of a windows installer-based installation that provides a single-tree feature to select or de-select SQL Server tools and components. The various components that can be selected are the SQL Server Database Engine, Analysis Services, Reporting Services, Integration Services, Replication, and Management tools. Each of the above services in SQL Server represents a set of processes to manage the authentication of server operations with Windows services, as seen in the following screenshot:

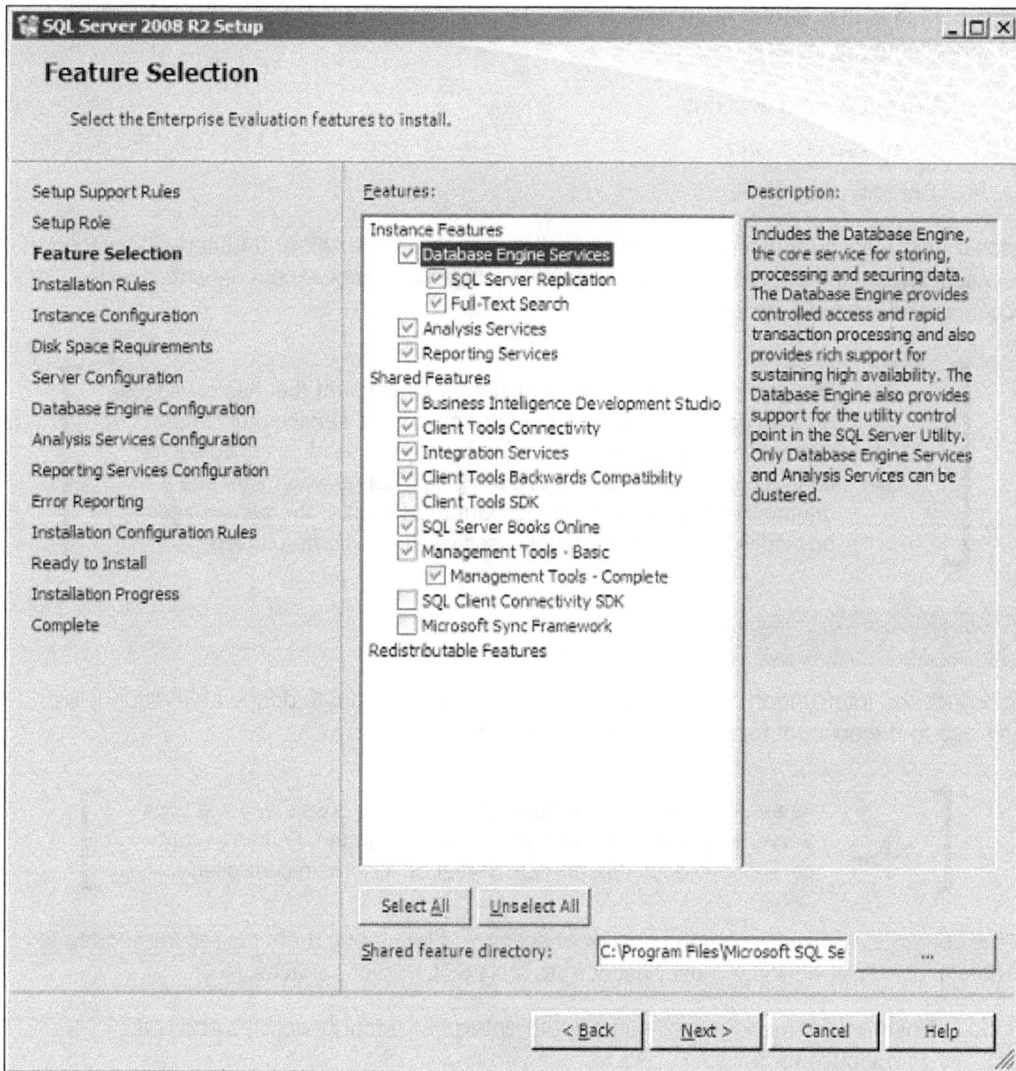

Depending upon the selected component that you decide to install, SQL Server setup will install the following services by default:

- ▶ SQL Server Database Services—relational core database engine
- ▶ SQL Server Agent—scheduling service to manage jobs, fire alerts, and the automation of some administrative tasks

Each service in SQL Server must have an account configured during the installation. The various account types are:

- ▶ Built-in system account
- ▶ Local user accounts
- ▶ Domain user accounts

Each of these account types has various privileges on the local server and network execution services. The built-in system accounts are the local service account, the network service account, and the local system account.

> The domain user account is a local server account that has privileges on a domain network. As a best practice, if the service must interact with network services such as file share or be used as linked server connections to other servers running SQL Server, you might use a minimally-privileged domain account to safeguard the system against any individual services or processes which are compromised.

How to do it...

To reduce the interruption on administrative tasks, it is essential to define an indispensible privilege to the account for instance-aware services.

> As an administrative best practice, wherever possible, use a Local Server account for a new SQL Server installation. From a security perspective *do not install* SQL Server on a domain controller.

If the server is a new installation or no local account is available, then it is recommended to create a local user or domain user account to start SQL Server services.

1. Ensure that the password suffices the enterprise security policies and is a strong password.
2. As seen in the following screenshot, create the local user account without Windows Administrator privileges:

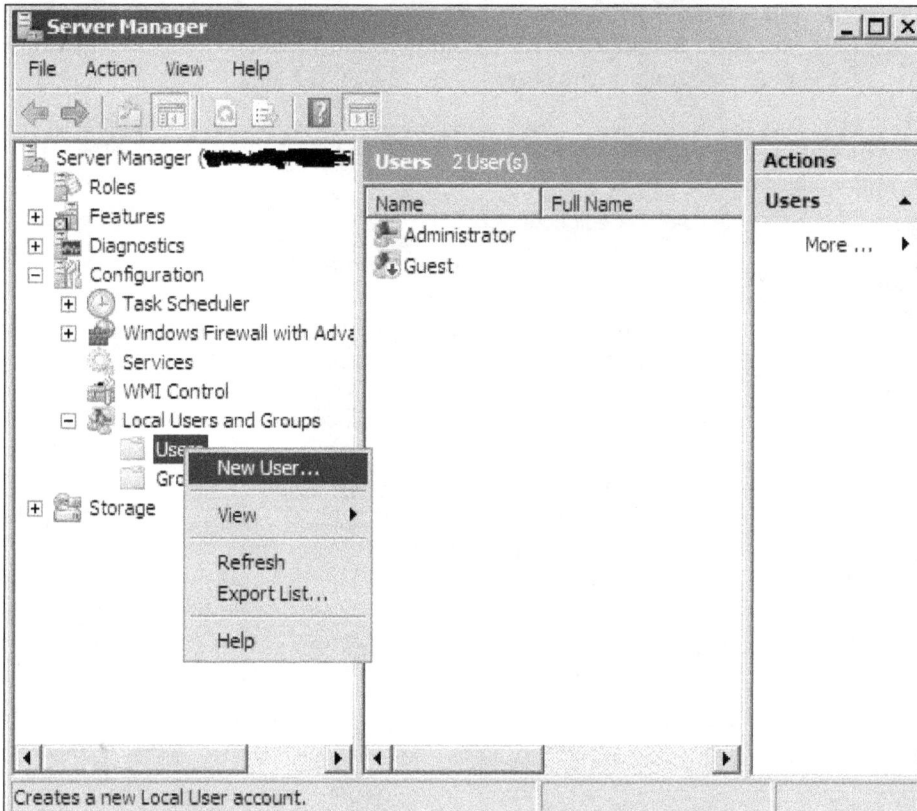

3. If only the SQL Server service must interact with the network services or have access to domain resources then create the domain user account, which should be pre-created by the domain administrator with necessary privileges.

4. Once the account is created, it is essential to grant privileges for that account on SQL Server. You can accomplish this in two ways:

    ❏ Denote the account name and password while performing the setup (as shown in the next screenshot) or

□ Update the SQL Server services using SQL Server Configuration Manager from **SQL Server 2008 R2 | Configuration Tools** and select the appropriate program group on the server

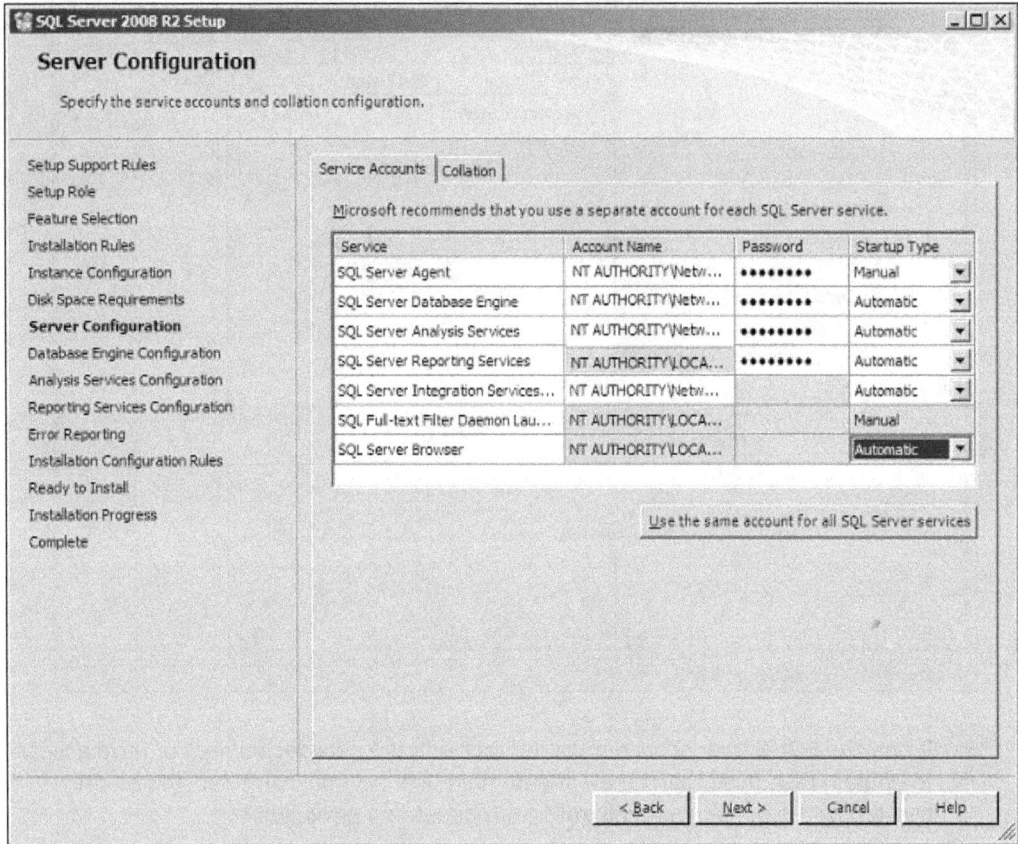

Always use SQL Server Configuration Manager to attempt any password changes to the SQL Server services account. The advantage is the password for the account is updated immediately and will take effect as soon as the specified service is restarted.

5. Similarly the best practice is to use a local service account with Administrator privileges on SQL Server and a Local server to perform the necessary tasks on Administration.

How it works...

The role of the SQL Server Agent is to handle the scheduling of tasks and communicate the results to relevant alert resources.

For the purpose of our recipe, the key functionality of SQL Server Agent service is classified as relics, which can be used to combine the alerts and communication to facilitate proactive administration. The SQL Server Agent service is the key control. First, we must understand the functionality of how these relics are governed by the service and then begin the process of configuring the service for automated administration.

The security context of a job step execution has a specific entity. For instance, if the job step specifies a proxy, the job step then runs in the security context of the credential of the proxy. If no proxy account is defined on the SQL Agent, then the default execution of that job step runs in the context of the SQL Server Agent service account. To facilitate the proactive administration methods, the agent functionality is differentiated into jobs, schedules, operators, alerts, and proxies, as shown in the following screenshot:

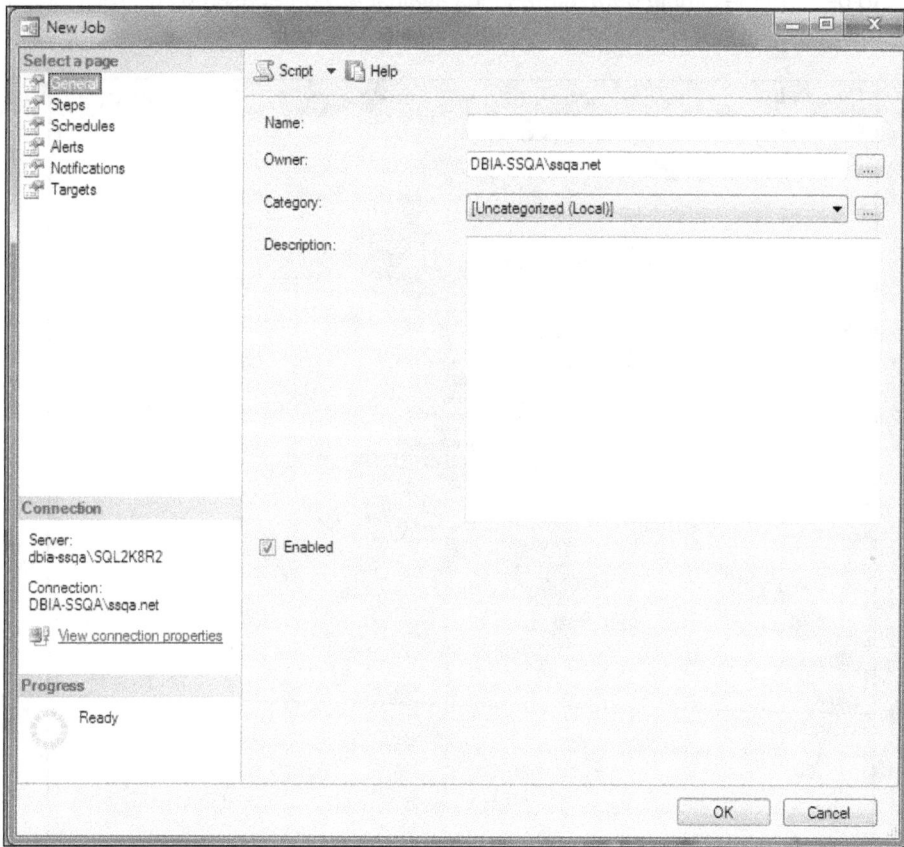

Inside a 'new job' and the 'job steps' there are different execution methods that are used to achieve the administrative tasks on SQL Server.

The different types of job steps are:

▸ Analysis Services tasks

▸ Executable programs

▸ Integration Services packages

▸ Microsoft ActiveX scripts

▸ Operating System commands

▸ PowerShell Scripts

▸ Transact SQL (TSQL) statements

For this recipe, we will use the following types of execution methods:

▸ `Transact-SQL (TSQL)`: The default execution type selected is Transact-SQL script. To perform the simple data interactions against any database object, TSQL steps are the most efficient way to handle them. See the following screenshot:

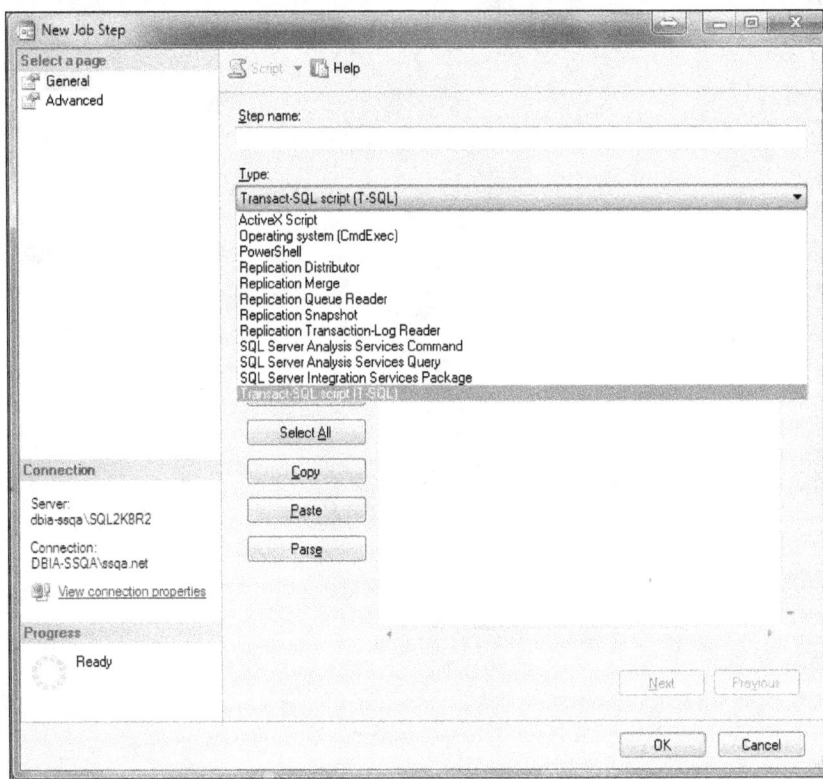

- ▸ `ActiveX Script`: This is useful when you need to execute a task using scripting languages such as VBScript or JScript. This type is more useful when you need to perform operations using SQL Server Management Object (SMO) that is designed for programming all aspects of management.

- ▸ `CmdExec —Operating System`: By the name this is useful to execute any shell commands within SQL Server environments.

- ▸ `PowerShell`: This is a substitute scripting method for both `CmdExec` and `ActiveX` scripts. It's a useful scripting shell that automates the administrative and application deployment activities.

MultiServer administration enables automated administration on multiple servers, which are called **target servers**. In a MultiServer environment, the jobs will be processed on all target servers that are first defined on a master server and then downloaded to the target servers. The security is addressed by default by the full SSL encryption and certification validation, which is enabled for the connection between master server and target server. To create a MultiServer environment, we can use Master Server wizard from SSMS using SQL Server Agent and point to MultiServer Administration.

Schedules allow the SQL Server Agent to execute the single or multiple job steps at defined intervals. The schedule can be used to automate routine administrative tasks as a single-step execution or as a recurring execution of desired steps, such as data ETL operations. The execution schedule can be any one of the following:

- ▸ One-time—to execute the job step(s) at that particular defined time only
- ▸ Recurring—to execute the job step(s) repeatedly, based on a defined time interval

There's more...

To automate the administrative tasks, it is important to set up the job step execution. To do this, you need to complete the following steps:

- ▸ One-time
- ▸ Recurring
- ▸ Execute the job step when SQL Server Agent service starts
- ▸ Execute the job step when CPU is idle

See Also

The *Designing SQL Server Agent scheduled jobs for ETL processes* recipe covers the usage of 'how to manage the alerts of automated administrative tasks effectively while executing SSIS packages.'

Implementing Security feature enhancements

Any data platform or database that stores sensitive information needs a robust infrastructure to control the data access in a secure manner. SQL Server 2008 R2 has inherited the 'secure-by-default' features (with several configurable features) in the areas such as platform (Operating System), architecture (32-bit and 64-bit), database objects (data layer), and application (connectivity).

In case the data is related to the financial services sector, then certain levels of criteria certification are essential for the verification of extensive security to access the layers of SQL Server, which is called **Common Criteria Certification**. The objective within Common Criteria Certification covers the evaluation of Information Technology (IT) products to improve security, availability, and efficiency. The various levels of security can be implemented on authentication, access privileges, database permissions, and data encryption.

The security architecture internals are classified into authentication, validation, and rights management. All of these internals are managed by three other internal objects that are called as **logical entities**—Principals, Permissions, and Securable:

> ▶ **Principals**: They are the key objects that grant permissions on a database user, database role, or application role.

> ▶ **Permissions**: They define the access rights for the Principal (or grantor) for DCL operations.

> ▶ **Securable**: A database user is a database-level securable contained within the database that is its parent in the permission hierarchy. Principals that have CONTROL permission on a securable can grant permission on that Securable.

Further, the authentication levels on instance level database security can be managed by using logical namespace which are schemas. SQL Server 2008 R2 has a new security feature called **Extended Protection** (**EP**), which enhances the protection and handling of credentials when authenticating the network connections using **Integrate Windows Authentication** (**IWA**). This feature is introduced on Windows Server 2008 R2 and Windows 7 Operating Systems. This feature is only supported by SQL Server 2008 R2 version onwards by the **SQL Server Native Client** (**SQLNCLI**), but is not supported by the other SQL Server client providers.

The required action to implement this feature is to perform changes to the specific server and client applications, which use IWA to ensure that they opt in to this new technology. Upon installation, **Extended Protection for Authentication** (**EPA**) is controlled on the client through the use of registry keys and on the server configuration it is specific to the application. In this recipe, we will cover the elements of SQL Server security internals that will play an important role in designing the security model for your SQL Server 2008 R2 installation and multiple instance management.

Getting ready

To implement the EPA feature on an SQL Server 2008 R2 instance, it is easy to set using SQL Server Configuration Manager from the SQL Server 2008 R2 program group on the server. In order to use the EPA features on service-binding and channel-binding, the SQL Server Connection settings must be used. The configuration settings data changes when you implement this feature.

How to do it...

The following steps show how to ensure that the EP feature is used effectively on both the server and client application connections. To enable Extended Protection for the SQL Server Database engine, complete the following steps:

1. Go to the **Start** menu, choose **All Programs** and point to **Microsoft SQL Server 2008 R2**.
2. Open **Configuration tools** and click **SQL Server Configuration Manager**.
3. Expand the **SQL Server Network Configuration** option, which will present the protocols for installed instances.
4. Select the **SQL Server 2008 R2** instance and then right-click on the **Protocols for <SQL Server 2008 R2>** instance to choose properties, as seen in the following screenshot:

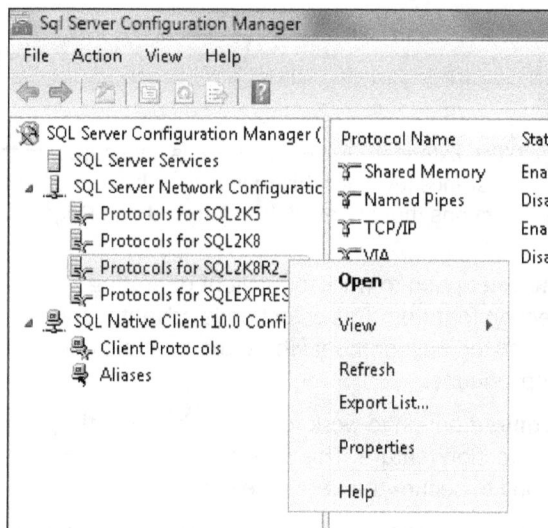

The previous operation presents the properties for the selected SQL Server 2008 R2 instance. In this recipe, our aim is to set the Extended Protection feature on the instance.

5. As we see in the following screenshot, go to the **Advanced** tab to select the appropriate security feature setting:

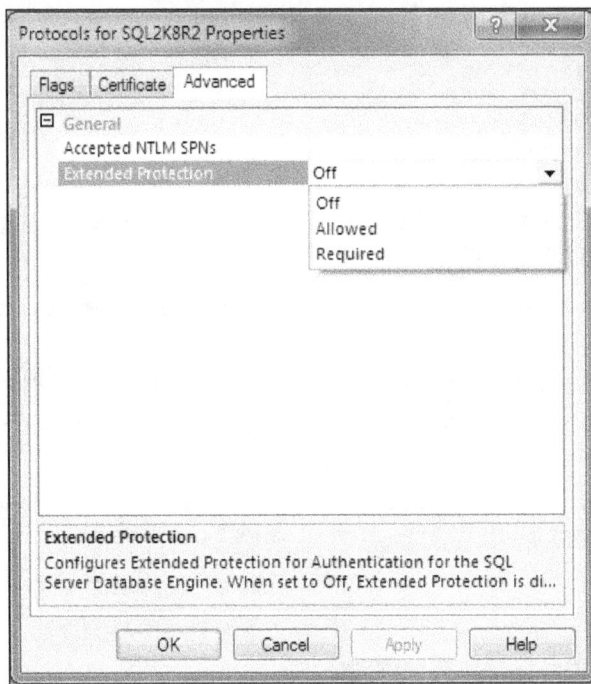

> The Extended Protection value is configured on the instance level, for this recipe we will choose the two options that are available: **Allowed** and **Required**.

6. Choose the **Allowed** option to work for a client operating system that supports extended protection features. This selection is advantageous if the network is equipped with a mixed environment where the multiple operating systems are used by the client applications.

7. Choose the **Required** option to work for the client operating system that supports the extended protection feature. This selection is used to develop the most secure connection setting to secure the database server.

8. From the protocol's properties, click on the **Flags** tab. Select **Yes** to set **Force Encryption**. This option sets a self-signed certificate process that will increase security, but it does not provide protection against identity spoofing by the server.

9. All data transmitted across a network between SQL Server and the client application will be encrypted using the self-signed certificate.

As seen in the preceding screenshot, the two feature options – which are advanced settings to set both service-binding and channel-binding – will be affected when the selected instance is restarted.

How it works...

The Extended Protection (EP) feature is managed using the Windows Operating System's **User Access Control** (**UAC**) methods. The UAC reduces the number of programs that run with elevated privileges, thereby helping to prevent users from accidentally changing the system settings that reduce any unprecedented attacks by unknown sources. In order to manage the security validations, security internals will authenticate three areas, namely: Principals, Securables, and Permissions.

> By default, the improvements from SQL Server 2008 and Windows Server 2008 operating system decrease the surface and the attack area from SQL Server with an artifact of 'least privileged' policy and additional separation of Windows Administrators and SQL Server System Administrator (SA).
>
> By default, the local Windows group BUILTIN\Administrator is no longer allowed to access the SQL Server instance with an elevated privilege of sysadmin with that of a fixed server role on the new SQL Server 2008 R2 installations.

To avoid any interruption to the application functionality, which depends on the elevated privileges on SQL Server 2008 R2 instance using BUILTIN\Administrator local group, you must grant the permission explicitly after the installation is finished, or add the required Windows Administrators group login during the setup at the point of the **Account Provisioning** tab, as shown in the next screenshot:

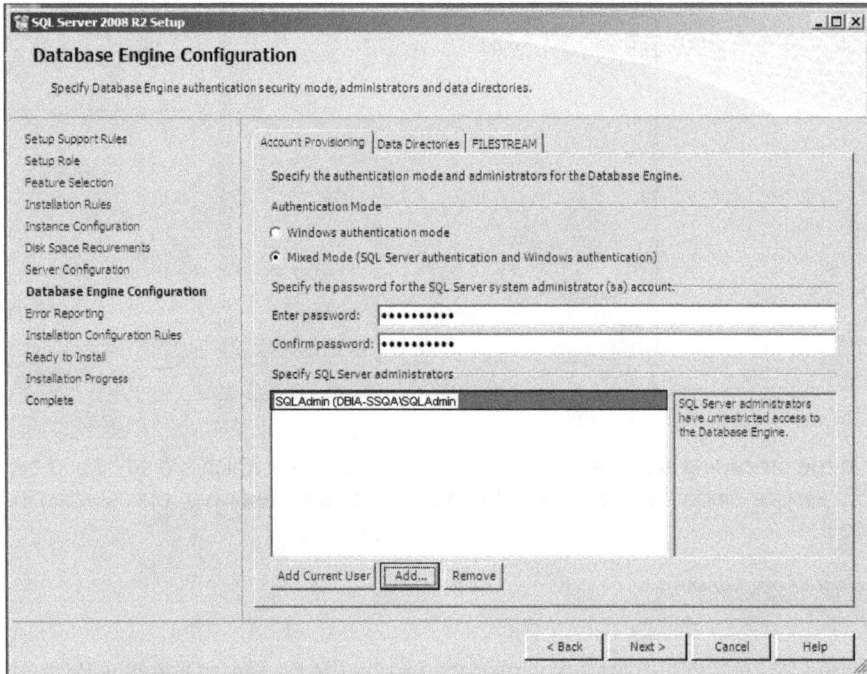

The Extended Protection feature is enabled by default. The feature of Extended Protection for Authentication is handled by the Operating System that enhances the protection to handle the credentials when authenticating network connections by using Integrated Windows Authentication. By default, SQL Server supports the service-binding and channel-binding that reduces the service attacks.

See Also

The Policy Based Management Framework can be used by referring to the Server Protocol Settings facet. Refer to the *Implementing Policy-based management features* as mentioned in *Chapter 7, Implementing new Manageability features and practice.*

Implementing Availability feature enhancements

Data recovery is a key step in providing availability to the systems. Hardware and software play a vital role in helping the system to minimize the downtime. The more complex and larger a database application, the more important it is to automate administrative tasks with proactive maintenance tasks to ensure data is available. The key factors for hardware and software solutions are cost, implementation, and feature support, which has its own advantages and disadvantages.

Any high-availability solution must have provisions for hardware availability and data availability. These two provisions must work in parallel to build an effective, high-availability strategy, which requires planning and implementation at the SQL Server instance configuration level. SQL Server 2008 R2 has no new features with regard to Availability; with the only enhancements in this area being the performance improvements to database mirroring, replication, and database backup strategies. This recipe covers the specific availability performance improvements to Database Mirroring from SQL Server 2008 R2 version, which includes the configuration of endpoints, post configuration, and failover process settings.

Database Mirroring (DBM) is the software solution for increasing the database availability, where all the bulk operations are fully logged. The main benefits of database mirroring are:

- ► Increased data protection
- ► Increased database availability
- ► Automated failover support, which provides minimized downtime for the rolling upgrade of databases

Before we begin with this recipe, it is essential to highlight the authentication options that are required for the three SQL Server instances, which are referred to as **partners: Principal**, **Mirror**, and **Witness** to communicate with one another.

The partner that owns Principal role stands as the main database. For hot standby provision, the partner that owns Mirror role holds a copy of the database. The third partner in database mirroring is called Witness that supports automatic failover by verifying whether or not Principal server is functioning. It does not store any database information. By taking SQL Server 2008 R2 new performance enhancements, it is ideal to set up database mirroring pairs on a dedicated network adapter, as network configuration plays an important role in the performance and transactional safety.

By default, the DBM endpoint requires the encryption of data that is sent over DBM connections, which contains a bit of a performance lag. Unless you obtain a guarantee that both the mirroring partners' network is secure, you should not disable the encryption to gain performance.

The method of improving the performance and reliability of the storage depends on the configuration of drives, which implies the way data is divided between disks to distribute load, or mirrored to recover from disk failure. The implementation of RAID-based solutions is beyond the scope of this chapter. However, such a solution has been presented in the *Chapter 10, Troubleshooting* in this book.

> Although, the core functionality of database mirroring has not changed, SQL Server 2008 R2 does introduce data stream compression and automatic page recovery. These improvements don't require changes to the existing syntax.

Getting ready

The databases that are involved in mirroring, must have the database recovery model at full to ensure the mirror will fully execute all bulk operations. The Mirror database must be prepared with a restore from the primary server's full database backup copy. Also, the server instances that are involved in DBM should have a dedicated network adapter. The endpoint configuration is important as it allows the database mirroring services to interact with each other. The configuration must be applied on the Principal server, Mirroring, and Witness server (if included) as per the relevant database mirroring mode. To configure a dedicated network line, the server must have two network interface cards with two different IP addresses. For the recipe, let us assume the configuration for Principal server and Mirror server is as follows:

- Principal Instance Configuration:
    - **Server Name**: DBIA-SSQA
    - **SQL Server Name**: DBIA-SSQA\SQL2K8R2
    - **Edition**: Enterprise Edition
    - **NIC 1**: 161.19.70.01
    - **NIC 2**: 161.19.70.02

- Mirror Instance Configuration:
    - **Server Name**: DBIA-SSQA
    - **Edition**: Enterprise Edition
    - **SQL Server Name** : DBIA-SSQA\SQL2K8
    - **NIC 1**: 161.19.70.03
    - **NIC 2**: 161.19.70.04

- Witness Instance Configuration:
    - **Server Name**: DBIA-SSQA\SQLEXPRESS
    - **Edition**: SQLEXPRESS Edition

▶ Isolate the network connection between NIC2 of Principal instance and NIC2 of Mirror instance.

Now, we are ready to implement the database mirroring endpoint configuration as a dedicated mirroring session.

How to do it...

The endpoint configuration setup is possible using the **Configure Database Mirroring Security** from **SQL Server Management studio**. For this recipe, we will create endpoints to configure dedicated DBM sessions using TSQL methods, and also show you how it looks when you configure with the wizards. The CREATE ENDPOINT command is used to create the mirroring endpoints. The syntax that applies to database mirroring is as follows:

```
CREATE ENDPOINT endPointName [ AUTHORIZATION login ]
STATE = { STARTED | STOPPED | DISABLED }
AS TCP (LISTENER_PORT = listenerPort )
FOR DATABASE_MIRRORING (
[ AUTHENTICATION = {WINDOWS [ { NTLM | KERBEROS | NEGOTIATE } ] |
CERTIFICATE certificate_name
} ][ [ , ] ENCRYPTION = { DISABLED |SUPPORTED | REQUIRED }
[ ALGORITHM { RC4 | AES | AES RC4 | RC4 AES } ]
][,] ROLE = { WITNESS | PARTNER | ALL })
```

To create the endpoints using the Wizard, you will need to complete the following steps:

1. Expand the database pane and select the desired database to be chosen for database mirroring.
2. Right-click on the database and select either the **Mirror** or the **properties** option.
3. If the properties option is selected, then click on **Mirroring** on the left-hand side of the database properties screen.
4. On the right-hand screen from the status column we can see the value **This database has not been configured for mirroring**.
5. Click on the **Configure Security** button to open up the configuration. This is where we begin to setup the **Endpoint configuration** and **data encryption** option for database mirroring pairs.
6. On the PRINCIPAL instance, execute the following from the query editor:

```
CREATE ENDPOINT Mirroring
    STATE=STARTED
    AS TCP (LISTENER_PORT=5022,LISTENER_IP=(161.19.70.02))
 FOR DATABASE_MIRRORING (ROLE=PARTNER)
```

7. The following screenshot is presented to set the listener port and data encryption when using the wizard for the PRINCIPAL instance:

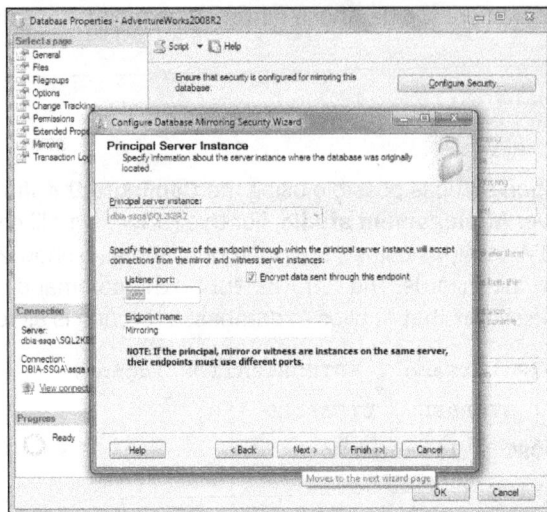

8. On the MIRROR instance, execute the following:

```
CREATE ENDPOINT Mirroring
    STATE=STARTED
    AS TCP (LISTENER_PORT=5023,LISTENER_IP=(161.19.70.04))
    FOR DATABASE_MIRRORING (ROLE=PARTNER)
```

9. The following screenshot illustrates the listener port and data encryption when using the wizard for the MIRROR instance:

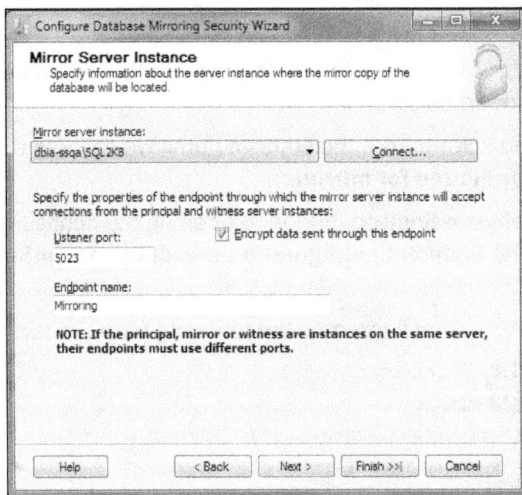

10. On the WITNESS instance, execute the following (see the next screenshot):

```
CREATE ENDPOINTMirroring
    STATE=STARTED
    AS TCP (LISTENER_PORT=5024,
    FOR DATABASE_MIRRORING (ROLE=WITNESS)
```

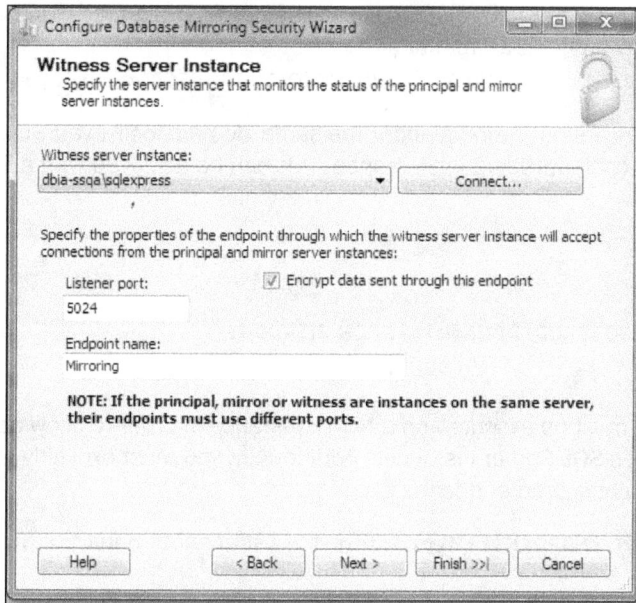

It is possible to SUSPEND a mirroring session and later RESUME it. If the mirroring is suspended for an extended period of time then, ensure sufficient disk space is available on the drive where the transaction log file is located.

The WITNESS is an essential instance of SQL Server that enables the mirror server in a high-safety mode session to recognize whether to initiate automatic failover, when no user data is stored on the witness server.

To enable Database Mirroring between two dedicated network adapters that is, between NIC2 of the Principle and NIC2 of the Mirror, we need to have a **Full Qualified Domain Name(FQDN)** for each of those instances. To perform this, complete the following steps:

1. Add the corresponding FQDN of NIC2 on the host file of each server.

2. The host file is located in the `C:\Windows\System32\drivers\etc` folder. Append the IP address of the corresponding instance and FQDN at the end of the host file:

```
161.19.70.02        DBM-MIRO.DBIA-SSQA.com
161.19.70.04        DBM-PRIM.DBIA-SSQA.com
```

Now, restart the Principal instance and Mirror instance to avoid any connectivity issues between the instances.

3. Set the partner for the MIRROR instance using the below script:

```
ALTER DATABASE <DatabaseName>
    SET PARTNER = 'TCP://DBM-PRIM.DBIA-SSQA.com:5022'
 Set the partner for PRINCIPAL instance using below script:
ALTER DATABASE <DatabaseName>
    SET PARTNER = 'TCP://DBM-MIRO.DBIA-SSQA.com:5023'
```

If the DBM instances are not running under the same 'domain login', you will need to create a windows login on each participating instance. This can be achieved with a TSQL script as follows:

```
USE master
GO
CREATE LOGIN [SSQAPROD\DBMAdmin] FROM WINDOWS
GO
```

The previous script must be executed on a Mirror instance in order to allow access to the principal and witness SQL Server instances. Additionally, you must explicitly grant the remote login access to the configured endpoints.

```
GRANT CONNECT ON ENDPOINT::Mirroring TO [SSQAPROD\DBMAdmin]
GO
```

How it works...

Connection management for database mirroring is based on endpoints. An endpoint is also treated as one of the server objects that enables SQL Server to communicate over the network.

For database mirroring, a server instance requires a dedicated database mirroring endpoint to receive database mirroring connections from other server instances. The database mirroring endpoint of a server instance is associated with the port on which the instance listens for database mirroring messages. Each database mirroring endpoint server listens on a unique TCP port number.

The wizard or TSQL method will configure the endpoints including granting permissions to a service account to communicate using the endpoint, as per the CREATE ENDPOINT syntax. Each SQL Server instance can have only one database mirroring endpoint. All databases in that instance – that are involved in database mirroring – must use the same endpoint. If the principal, mirroring, or witness instances exist on the same physical server then you are required to use different port numbers on their individual endpoints.

The next step for a database mirroring endpoint requires the encryption of data that is sent over mirroring connections. In this case, the endpoint can connect only to endpoints that also use encryption. Database mirroring endpoints support two encryption algorithms—RC4 and AES.

The final step is to ensure that the mirroring endpoint is created and configured correctly. The verification settings can be accomplished by querying the sys.database_mirroring_ endpoints system catalog view. The following query confirms the name of the endpoint, the state (whether or not it has started) and other mirroring related attributes:

```
SELECT  d.name, d.database_id, m.mirroring_role_desc,
m.mirroring_state_desc, m.mirroring_safety_level_desc,
m.mirroring_partner_name, m.mirroring_partner_instance,
m.mirroring_witness_name, m.mirroring_witness_state_desc
FROM    sys.database_mirroring m JOIN sys.databases d
ON      m.database_id = d.database_id
WHERE   mirroring_state_desc IS NOT NULL
```

There's more...

In order to continue the transactions from the primary server to the mirror server, it is ideal to restore the transaction log backup (which has been taken after the full database backup) on the mirror server. It is also essential that no transactions should occur on the primary database until the transaction log is restored on the mirror server.

Restoring a user database doesn't bring along the necessary SQL or Windows logins to the server containing the mirrored database. Any SQL or Windows logins mapped to database users in the principal database should also be created on the mirrored SQL Server instance. These logins should be ready in the event of a failover; when the mirror database takes over the role as the principal. If the logins are not on the mirror database SQL Server instance, the database users within the mirrored database will be orphaned (the database users, without any associated logins will not be able to be access the database).

See Also

For more information on SQL Server Database Mirroring feature enhancement such as automatic page recovery, refer to the *Implementing Database Mirroring features and performance enhancements* section of *Chapter 6, Availability and Programmability enhancement.*

Implementing, Monitoring, and Tuning for performance

SQL Server performance tuning and monitoring requires a multi-layered approach. The proper configuration of the resources (hardware) is the primary area of focus. This ensures that SQL Server will retain adequate resources that are tuned for performance and fault tolerance as a foundation for an optimized data platform.

The important ingredient in performance tuning is planning an appropriate baseline and benchmarking the data platform. Such planning requires an understanding of storage architecture and indexing of data tables. The process of baseline and benchmarking will enable better monitoring aspects.

In this recipe, we will cover the best usage of the **Dynamic Management Views (DMV)**, which is important when fine tuning the database performance and implementing monitoring methods.

Getting ready

Whenever you are seeking help to fine tune the performance, the response will always be 'it depends', as it is purely dependent upon the individual environment and configuration settings on hardware and software. To keep up the performance, the statistics on the table must be updated regularly as this will decide how best to execute the query. SQL Server may choose a less-than-optimal plan, if it is basing its execution decisions on stale statistics. In order to fine tune the performance it is important to capture and evaluate the currently executed statements on the SQL Server. The internal query architecture will save a plan for every statement that is executed on SQL Server.

To monitor a query process, the Profiler tool is used. It is a resource-intensive application that might cause additional problems, if the current environment is already hampered with the slow performance of queries. Hence, it's best to use TSQL based on capture using Dynamic Management View (DMVs), which returns the snapshot of the current system state without causing any overhead to the SQL Server.

How to do it...

To get started, you need to complete the following steps:

1. **Connect to the SQL Server** instance and open the query editor by clicking on the **New Query** button on SSMS.

2. To obtain a snapshot of the current running queries run the following TSQL:

   ```
   SELECT r.session_id, r.status, r.start_time, r.command,
   s.textFROMsys.dm_exec_requests r
   ```

Chapter 2

```
CROSSAPPLYsys.dm_exec_sql_text(r.sql_handle) s
WHERE r.status='running'
```

3. In addition to that process, let us obtain an extended version of queries that are executed in batches along with statistical information by executing the following TSQL statement:

```
SELECT s2.dbid,s1.sql_handle,(SELECTTOP 1SUBSTRING(s2.
text,statement_start_offset / 2+1 ,((CASEWHEN statement_end_
offset =-1          THEN (LEN(CONVERT(nvarchar(max),s2.text))* 2)
ELSE statement_end_offset END)- statement_start_offset)/ 2+1))
AS sql_statement,    execution_count,     plan_generation_num,
last_execution_time,       total_worker_time,      last_worker_
time,    min_worker_time,     max_worker_time,total_physical_
reads,      last_physical_reads,      min_physical_reads,       max_
physical_reads,       total_logical_writes,     last_logical_writes,
min_logical_writes,     max_logical_writes
FROMsys.dm_exec_query_statsAS s1
CROSSAPPLYsys.dm_exec_sql_text(sql_handle)AS s2
WHERE s2.objectid isnull
ORDERBY s1.sql_handle, s1.statement_start_offset, s1.statement_
end_offset;
```

> The results of the previous query will help you to understand the execution context such as physical reads, logical writes, and worker threads.
>
> To display the execution plan (detailed) for an SQL statement or batches, use the following statements at the top of the query: SET SHOWPLAN_ALL, SET SHOWPLAN_TEXT, and SET SHOWPLAN_XML.
>
> Here is the code example to show the way SQL optimizer analyzes and optimizes the use of indexes in queries:
>
> ```
> USE AdventureWorks2008R2;
> GO
> SETSHOWPLAN_ALLON;
> GO
> SELECT Person.Contact.ContactID, Person.Contact.
> FirstName, Person.Contact.LastName,
> Person.Contact.EmailAddress, HumanResources.Employee.
> Gender, HumanResources.Employee.BirthDate
> FROM HumanResources.EmployeeINNERJOIN Person.Contact
> ON HumanResources.Employee.ContactID= Person.Contact.
> ContactID
> GO
> SETSHOWPLAN_ALLOFF;
> GO
> ```

4. SQL Server 2008 R2 tools and system internal commands will be useful to identify and narrow down the problem. The first source of information you need to obtain is the resource usage such as executing threads and waits.

5. Using the `sys.dm_os_wait_stats` DMV, we can obtain the wait stats encountered by threads that are executed. The aggregate result of this DMV will help to diagnose the performance of specific queries and batches execution:

```
SELECT TOP 10
wait_type, wait_time_ms
FROM sys.dm_os_wait_stats
WHERE wait_type NOTIN
('LAZYWRITER_SLEEP','SQLTRACE_BUFFER_FLUSH',
'REQUEST_FOR_DEADLOCK_SEARCH','LOGMGR_QUEUE',
'CHECKPOINT_QUEUE','CLR_AUTO_EVENT','WAITFOR',
'BROKER_TASK_STOP','SLEEP_TASK','BROKER_TO_FLUSH')
ORDER BY wait_time_ms DESC
```

	wait_type	wait_time_ms
1	SQLTRACE_INCREMENTAL_FLUSH_SLEEP	4640579
2	XE_TIMER_EVENT	4620922
3	FT_IFTS_SCHEDULER_IDLE_WAIT	4560035
4	PAGEIOLATCH_SH	8252
5	PREEMPTIVE_OS_CREATEFILE	6461
6	BROKER_EVENTHANDLER	4701
7	PREEMPTIVE_OS_LIBRARYOPS	3509
8	SLEEP_DBSTARTUP	3303
9	PREEMPTIVE_OS_GENERICOPS	3070

> In order to view the Server-scoped dynamic management views and functions, the relevant login requires VIEW SERVER STATE permission on the server. Similarly, for database-scoped dynamic management views and functions, the login requires VIEW DATABASE STATE permission on the database

How it works...

The `sys.dm_exec_requests` DMV returns information about each request that is executing within SQL Server instance. The `sys.dm_exec_requests` DMV execution is a two-fold process, which joins within another system catalog to obtain the information on a command execution. The column names that are used in DMV are self-explanatory. Select the session ID, status of the query, start time, command type, (such as **SELECT/INSERT/UPDATE/ DELETE/DBCC/BACKUP DB**) and actual text that is used in the execution.

The `sys.dm_exec_sql_text` function returns the text of the SQL batch that is identified with the `sql_handle` column. As you can see in the previous query, the function takes the `sql_handle` value from the `sys.dm_exec_requests` DMV with a `CROSS APPLY` join type to return associated SQL text. The final layer is the `WHERE` clause, which gives you the values for the status of the request which can be: `Background/Running/Runnable/Sleeping/Suspended`, and `cannot be null` to complete the execution. To obtain a current snapshot of the query execution, the following two DMVs `sys.dm_exec_sql_text` and `sys.dm_exec_requests` are used.

Understanding a query execution plan is essential to fix a poorly performing query to obtain a detailed execution plan in the form of graphical/text/XML format. The following information is visible from the query execution plan:

- Highest cost queries within a batch and highest cost operators within a query
- Index or table scans (accessing all the pages in a heap or index) against using seeks
- Missing statistics or other warnings
- Costly sort or calculation activities
- High row counts being passed from operator to operator
- Discrepancies between the estimated and actual row counts
- Implicit data type conversions

The output is provided with the plan information, without executing the query which allows you to adjust the query or indexes on the referenced tables before actually executing it. Each of these commands return the information in a different way. Further, within the query editor at the beginning of the query, using `SET SHOWPLAN_ALL` returns the estimated query plan in a tabular format, with multiple columns and rows. The `SET SHOWPLAN_TEXT` command returns the data in a single column, with multiple rows for each operation. You can also return a query execution plan in XML format using the `SET SHOWPLAN_XML` command. The syntax for each of these commands is very similar. Each command is enabled when set to `ON`, and disabled when set to `OFF`:

```
SET SHOWPLAN_ALL { ON | OFF}
```

```
SET SHOWPLAN_TEXT { ON | OFF}
```

```
SET SHOWPLAN_XML { ON | OFF}
```

The output includes information such as the estimated IO or CPU of each operation, estimated rows involved in the operation, operation cost (relative to itself and variations of the query), and the physical and logical operators used.

The output from the first query of `SETSHOWPLAN_ALL` will provide information about `PhysicalOperation`, `LogicalOperation`, `EstimateIO`, `EstimateCPU`, and `AvgRowSize`, as shown in the following screenshot:

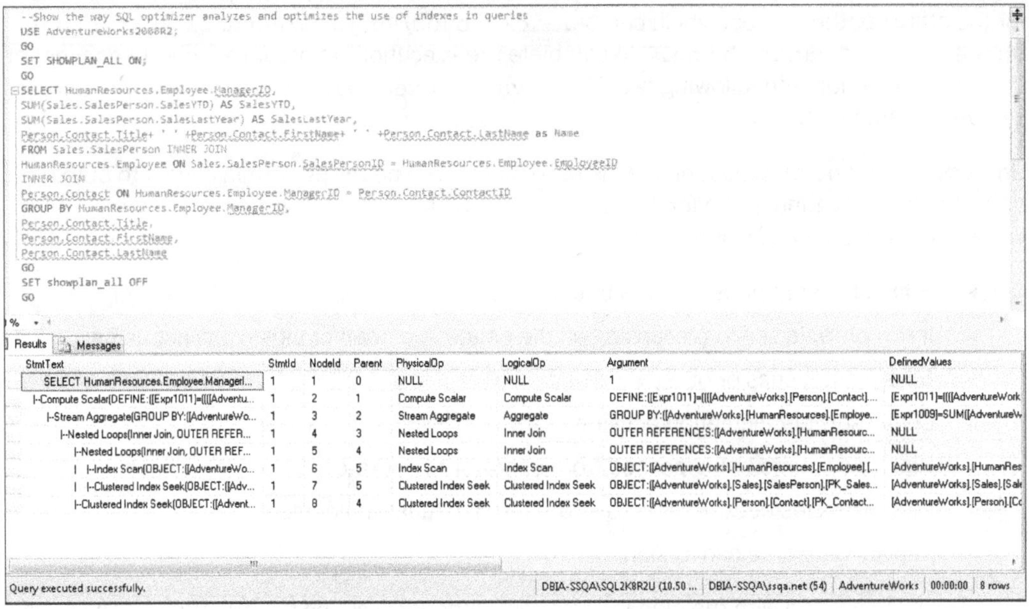

In addition to using the `SETSHOWPLAN_ALL` TSQL statement, you can use the `SET STATISTICS PROFILE` statement to obtain the executed query result set, followed by an additional result set that shows a profile of query executions. The additional information is as follows:

Column name	Description
Rows	Actual number of rows produced by each operator
Executes	Number of times the operator has been executed

The results are shown in the following screenshot:

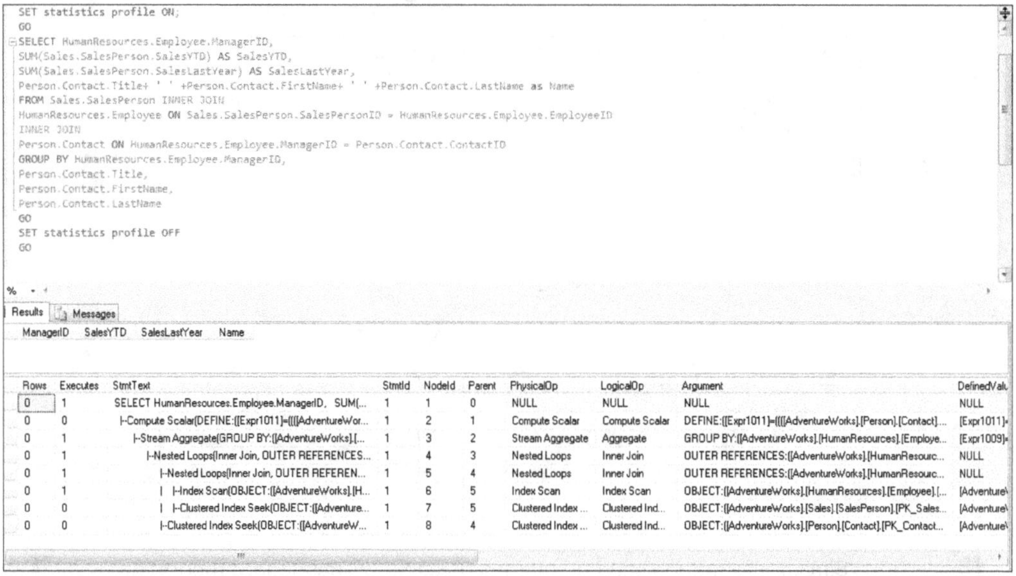

It should be observed that, there are additional commands that can be used to return the query and batch execution statistics information using SET STATISTICS IO, SET STATISTICS TIME, SET STATISTICS PROFILE, and SET STATISTICS XML statements. These are different to SHOWPLAN commands, which return the actual execution of statements and the SET STATISTICS IO command, which returns disk activity generated during the query execution. The SET STATISTICS TIME command returns the number of milliseconds taken to parse, compile, and execute each statement executed in the batch.

The resource usage information on 'threads' and 'waits' is obtained using `sys.dm_os_wait_stats` DMV. The results will be as shown in the following screenshot:

```
SQLQuery1.sql - dbia-ssqa\...\s...t (52))*   Utility Explorer Content
    SELECT TOP 2
    wait_type, wait_time_ms
    FROM sys.dm_os_wait_stats
    WHERE wait_type NOT IN
    ('LAZYWRITER_SLEEP', 'SQLTRACE_BUFFER_FLUSH',
    'REQUEST_FOR_DEADLOCK_SEARCH', 'LOGMGR_QUEUE',
    'CHECKPOINT_QUEUE', 'CLR_AUTO_EVENT','WAITFOR',
    'BROKER_TASK_STOP',| 'SLEEP_TASK', 'BROKER_TO_FLUSH')
    ORDER BY wait_time_ms DESC
```

	wait_type	wait_time_ms
1	FT_IFTS_SCHEDULER_IDLE_WAIT	336686834
2	SQLTRACE_INCREMENTAL_FLUSH_SLEEP	113082823

> Similar information can be obtained using SSMS dashboard reports on server-scope and database-scope. For instance, on server-scope, we can refer to **Performance | Batch Execution Statistics** or **Performance | Top queries by Average CPU**. On database-scope, refer to **Resource Locking Statistics by Objects** and **Object Execution Statistics**.
>
> As a part of baseline and benchmarking strategy, the historic information for query statistics and resource usage can be obtained using **Management Data Warehouse (MDW) | Data collector:Server Activity and Query Statistics report**.

From the results, the two wait types are presented, `FT_IFTS_SCHEDULER_IDLE_WAIT` which is used as a background task process by full-text search requests which indicates it is waiting for work to do.

At this point in time, we can safely ignore the outcome unless there are complaints from the users about application search functionality, which uses Full-text search service. Further information on detailed information and interpretation of these wait types can be obtained from SQL Server Books Online that are published by Microsoft. The results from `sys.dm_os_wait_stats` DMV produces another wait type `SQLTRACE_INCREMENTAL_FLUSH_SLEEP` value, which indicates the internal trace, SQL trace or PROFILER process with a high value in number, which can be related to corresponding I/O problems on the server.

> In order to get accurate information on the statistics of wait types based on the defined period of time, you can execute the DBCC SQLPERF ('sys. dm_os_wait_stats', CLEAR) statement on that SQL Server instance. This DBCC statement will reset the wait-statistics that will cause a significant change of information, which can be executed by SysAdmin privilege logins only on the Production instance.

Administering SQL Server workloads with Resource Governor

Controlling workloads and managing server resources using a tool is a definitive choice for every DBA. Resource Governor is a new technology introduced in SQL Server 2008 that enables the DBA to manage the SQL Server workload and resources by specifying the limits on resource consumption. To manage the multiple distinct workloads, the tool will allow DBAs to differentiate these workloads to define resource pools and allocate shared resources as they are requested. It's based on the specified limits such as minimum and maximum CPU task scheduling bandwidth and reserve memory.

Internally, SQL Server database engine manages the CPU and memory resources as pools, which are default and internal. The internal resource pool is restricted and cannot be modified, using the unrestricted resources for the exclusive usage of SQL Server processes. The default resource pool is reserved for connections to the server, which can be configured to eliminate any limitations present on the resources.

Resource Governor is an Enterprise Edition feature and creating your own resource pool is the first step in managing the server resources. Using the CREATE RESOURCE POOL command, you can create your own resource pool. By default, you can associate multiple work groups with a single resource pool, but a workload group cannot be associated with multiple resource pools.

In this recipe, we will go through the process of creating multiple resource pools to govern the SQL Server workloads, which are used by the Resource Governor Tool.

Getting ready

The Inventory application database server is used by the Manufacturing team (Team M) where the server will accept connections that must run consistently without causing any downtime to the application. The Sales application database is used by the marketing team (Team S) who run ad hoc queries and reports for their day to day work purpose.

In addition to the above two types of users, there are certain users from the Senior Management (Team SM) who require periodic information (by the way of reports) about the sales transactional activity and stock control reports that cause intermittent performance issues for the application. So at this juncture, your task is to keep up the performance for the application by helping the database engine to manage its resources efficiently during heavy usage.

Using the CREATE RESOURCE POOL command, you can create your own resource pool. The basic syntax for this command is as follows:

```
CREATE RESOURCE POOL pool_name
[ WITH
( [ MIN_CPU_PERCENT = value ]
[ [ , ] MAX_CPU_PERCENT = value ]
[ [ , ] MIN_MEMORY_PERCENT = value ]
[ [ , ] MAX_MEMORY_PERCENT = value ] )]
```

Using the CREATE WORKLOAD GROUP statement you can create the groups; the syntax is as follows:

```
CREATE WORKLOAD GROUP group_name
[ WITH
( [ IMPORTANCE = { LOW | MEDIUM | HIGH } ]
[ [ , ] REQUEST_MAX_MEMORY_GRANT_PERCENT = value ]
[ [ , ] REQUEST_MAX_CPU_TIME_SEC = value ]
[ [ , ] REQUEST_MEMORY_GRANT_TIMEOUT_SEC = value ]
[ [ , ] MAX_DOP = value ]
[ [ , ] GROUP_MAX_REQUESTS = value ] )]
[ USING { pool_name | "default" } ]
```

How to do it...

In this recipe, we will use Resource Governor to create separate user-defined resource pools on the SQL Server instances.

The first pool is classed as high-priority, which is created for the SM team to ensure that this pool reserves a good amount of CPU and memory resources at the time of the query connection.

1. Taking into consideration the syntax mentioned previously, let us create the resource pool and appropriate workload groups. To create the first pool for the SM team, reserve at least 30 percent of the CPU and memory and do not exceed 70 percent.

```
USE master
GO
```

```
CREATERESOURCEPOOL priority_Team_SM_queries
WITH (MIN_CPU_PERCENT = 30,
MAX_CPU_PERCENT = 70,
MIN_MEMORY_PERCENT = 30,
MAX_MEMORY_PERCENT = 70)
GO
```

2. Create the next resource pool that will be reserved for ad hoc queries to reserve maximum CPU and memory of these pools, at 25 percent, at the time of multiple query connections and high contention on the SQL Server instance.

```
CREATE RESOURCE POOL ad_hoc_queries
WITH ( MIN_CPU_PERCENT = 5,
MAX_CPU_PERCENT = 25,
MIN_MEMORY_PERCENT = 5,
MAX_MEMORY_PERCENT = 25)
GO
```

3. The resource pool values can be modified at any time using the ALTER RESOURCE POOL statement. Now it will be ideal to check if the settings are applied for these resource pools by querying the following system catalog:

```
SELECT pool_id,name,min_cpu_percent,max_cpu_percent,
min_memory_percent,max_memory_percent
FROMsys.resource_governor_resource_pools
```

The results should be as follows:

	pool_id	name	min_cpu_percent	max_cpu_percent	min_memory_percent	max_memory_percent
1	1	internal	0	100	0	100
2	2	default	0	100	0	100
3	258	priority_Team_SM_queries	25	75	25	75
4	259	ad_hoc_queries	5	25	5	25

As you can see from the results, the SQL Server internal resource pools and the user-defined resource pools govern the system resources. By using SSMS, we can view the created resource pools navigate to **Management node | Resource Governor** and choose **Resource Pools**.

Now that we have created the resource pools, the next thing we will do is create workload groups for the highest priority application connections. These connections must have high-importance on system resource usage and lowest importance application connections with less resource consumption capabilities:

```
--High priority applications
CREATEWORKLOADGROUP application_Sales
WITH
(IMPORTANCE = HIGH,
REQUEST_MAX_MEMORY_GRANT_PERCENT = 75,
REQUEST_MAX_CPU_TIME_SEC = 75,
REQUEST_MEMORY_GRANT_TIMEOUT_SEC = 60,
MAX_DOP = 8,
GROUP_MAX_REQUESTS = 8 )
USING priority_Team_SM_queries
GO


--Low importance applications
CREATEWORKLOADGROUP application_adhoc
WITH
( IMPORTANCE = LOW,
REQUEST_MAX_MEMORY_GRANT_PERCENT = 50,
REQUEST_MAX_CPU_TIME_SEC = 40,
REQUEST_MEMORY_GRANT_TIMEOUT_SEC = 540,
MAX_DOP = 1,
GROUP_MAX_REQUESTS = 4 )
USING ad_hoc_queries
GO
```

By default, we can assign one resource pool to a workload, even though that individual resource pool can serve multiple workload groups. In the above TSQL statement, we set the relative 'importance' of each workload group as HIGH or LOW.

Similarly, as we checked earlier to confirm user-defined resource pools were created, let's now check if workload groups are created by querying the following system catalog:

```
SELECT name, Importance impt,
request_max_memory_grant_percent max_m_g, request_max_cpu_time_sec max_
cpu_sec,
request_memory_grant_timeout_sec m_g_to, max_dop, group_max_requests
max_req, pool_id
FROMsys.resource_governor_workload_groups
```

The results are as follows:

	name	impt	max_m_g	max_cpu_sec	m_g_to	max_dop	max_req	pool_id
1	internal	Medium	25	0	0	0	0	1
2	default	Medium	25	0	0	0	0	2
3	application_Sales	High	75	75	60	8	8	258
4	application_adhoc	Low	50	40	540	1	4	259

1. Now, the important task is to create a classifier function that will be called for each new connection. Resource Governor supports user-defined functions, whose return values are used for classifying sessions that are then routed to the appropriate workload group.

2. This function's logic is to return the workload group where all connection requests will be sent.

3. The classifier function can use several different connection-related functions for use in the logic, including the system default HOST_NAME (), APP_NAME (), SUSER_ NAME (), SUSER_SNAME ().

4. The following code is used for this function that screens the login name and connection host name in order to see to which workload group that connection should be assigned as per the above WORKLOAD group settings:

```
USE master
GO
CREATE FUNCTION dbo.SalesApp_PROD_classifier()
RETURNS sysname
WITH SCHEMABINDING
AS
BEGIN
DECLARE @resource_group_name sysname
IF SUSER_SNAME() IN ('Login1','Login2')
SET @resource_group_name ='application_sales'
IF SUSER_SNAME() IN ('Login3','Login4')
SET @resource_group_name ='application_stock'
IF HOST_NAME() IN ('SalesAppHost1','SalesAppHost2')
SET @resource_group_name ='ad_hoc_queries'
-- If the resource group is still unassigned, use default
IF @resource_group_name ISNULL
SET @resource_group_name ='default'
RETURN @resource_group_name
END
GO
```

> The value for the `@resource_group_name` variable is `default`; there is a reason for this specification. If, in case, the Classifier function yields any invalid resource group then the specified login will be set as a `default` group.

5. The next step is to activate the defined classifier function and enable the configuration.

6. For both of these tasks, we will use the ALTER RESOURCE GOVERNOR statement:

```
-- Assign the classifier function
ALTER RESOURCE GOVERNOR
WITH (CLASSIFIER_FUNCTION = dbo.SalesApp_PROD_classifier)
GO

--Enable the configuration
ALTER RESOURCE GOVERNOR RECONFIGURE
GO
```

7. You then need to perform a final check to see whether the classifier function is enabled and working, by running the following statements:

```
SELECT*FROM sys.resource_governor_configuration
```

8. The result will be:

Classifier_function_id   is_enabled

1211151360   1

9. This step confirms that all the incoming application connections will be routed to the appropriate workload groups and this will allocate relevant resources as per the user-defined resource pools.

> In order to collect the statistics for all the incoming application connections, resource pools, and workload groups, you can query DMVs:
>
> `sys.dm_resource_governor_resource_pools`
> `sys.dm_resource_governor_workload_groups`

How it works...

The Resource Governor (RG) works on three fundamentals:

- Resource pools
- Workload groups
- Classification

Let's see how these RG components and their relationships work with each other as they exist in the database engine environment. The functions behind the resource governor will govern the system resource usage such as CPU and memory into separate resource pools that represent the physical resources of the server. A pool has two parts; one part does not overlap with other pools by maintaining a minimum (MIN) resource reservation. The other part is shared with other pools to support maximum (MAX) possible resource consumption.

A workload group serves as a container for session requests that are similar according to the classification criteria that are applied to each request. RG predefines two workload groups, the internal group and the default group. These workload groups can be managed by using DDL statements, such as CREATE, ALTER, and DROP statements that are transactional. However, the completion of these statements does not make the changes effective. You must execute the ALTER RESOURCE GOVERNOR RECONFIGURE statement to apply the changes.

A workload group allows the aggregate monitoring of resource consumption and the application of a uniform policy to all the requests in the group. A group defines the policies for its members.

Finally, the classification is based on a set of user-written criteria contained in a function. The logic within this function will control and enable the Resource Governor to classify sessions into existing workload groups. The only exception for this functionality is using the **Dedicated Administrative Console (DAC)** that shall bypass any allocation of the resource group.

> The internal workload group is populated with requests that are for internal use only. You cannot change the criteria used for routing these requests and you cannot classify requests into the internal workload group.

As per the previous recipe the function dbo.SalesApp_PROD_classifier() will apply the configuration changes, then RG classifier will use the workload groups application_Sales and application_adhoc returned by the function to send a new request to the appropriate workload group. The overall context of the classification process will begin with login authentication. This is done by associating a LOGON trigger execution and using the value returned by the function to send requests to appropriate workload groups.

The execution of the classifier function and LOGON triggers is exposed in sys.dm_exec_sessions and sys.dm_exec_requests. Refer to the recipe *Implementing Tuning and Monitoring performance* for more information on these DMVs.

There's more...

The new functionality within SQL Server 2008 R2 version allows the System Administrators and DBAs to obtain significant control over the SQL Server instances that will have varying workload requirements with limited system resources. The Microsoft SQL Server documentation refers to a simple flow chart described as follows:

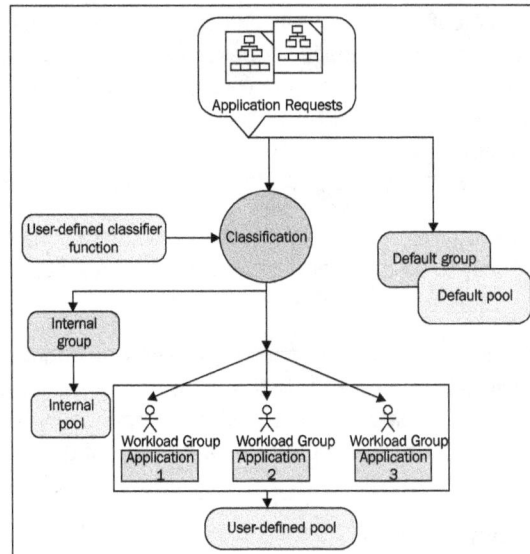

- ▸ The Session 1 of n is an incoming connection (workload), which is related to a Classification (user-defined classifier function)

- ▸ Session 1 of *n* workload is routed to a workload group

- ▸ The workload group uses the resource pool; it is associated with User-defined pool

- ▸ The resource pool provides (and limits) the resources required by the Application 1, Application 2 and Application 3

Designing SQL Server Agent scheduled jobs for ETL processes

Extracting, Transforming, and Loading (**ETL**) are key processes for any data management. ETL activities include an import and export of data from various data sources into an SQL Server table format. The data volume will vary from one row to billions of rows. To handle such import/export active ETL operations, a tool is essential. SQL Server Business Intelligence tools provide a strong foundation by the way of services (SSA) & tools (BIDS).

SQL Server provides many processes for the ETL management, such as BCP (Bulk Copy), BI (Bulk Insert), DTS (Data Transformation Services) and SSIS (SQL Server Integration Services). Since SQL Server 2005 DTS has been transformed into SSIS, which is a step ahead in terms of functionality providing more intuitive design and management for ETL operations, henceforth DTS functionality has been discontinued. SQL Server 2008 and SQL Server 2008 R2 enhances the native .NET execution environment to continue the ETL process with significant pipeline scalability enhancements such as persistent lookups, which is a significant improvement for data warehousing environment. The SQL Server Agent service manages many different objects on the server, each one responsible for its own function in the larger automation infrastructure. Mastering these objects is critical to implement an effective automation plan. For backward compatibility, SQL Server 2008 R2 supports the DTS packages. Using the command-line arguments, we can initiate the Import and Export wizard.

In this recipe, we will look at the SQL Server 2008 R2 tools and agent service capabilities to design an effective scheduled activity to handle critical ETL processes. SQL Server 2008 R2 consists of multiple windows services, for scheduling and automation activities. SQL Server agent service is useful, as it contains various artifacts such as jobs, schedules, operators, and alerts.

Getting ready

For ETL management within these job steps, the SQL Server Integration Service (SSIS) package is the key. Since these SSIS packages contain the corresponding administrative step, the entire package can be defined as a single-step to execute it within the job. Not only can we create the job steps from the SQL Server agent, we can also create the ETL processes using SQL Server Management Studio using SQL Server's import and export wizard. For desktop-based environments, the ETL activities can be accomplished using the SQL Server Express with the Advanced Services edition that consists of a basic installation of SQL Server Management Studio.

Although, SQL Server 2008 R2 extends the support to run DTS packages and Integration Services packages on the same server, the setup does not install the run-time support for DTS packages. You have to install this run-time support during the setup on the **Feature Selection** page by selecting **Integration Services** to install ActiveX script task and DTS package migration wizard and **Client Tools Backward Compatibility.** However, these components are not fully functional without the manual installation of additional, optional components that are not available during Setup.

Further, on a 64-bit environment, there is no 64-bit run-time support for DTS packages and Integration Services packages that run DTS packages, they can run only in 32-bit mode. To run packages in 32-bit mode outside BI Development Studio on a 64-bit computer, during Setup, select **Business Intelligence Development Studio** or **Management Tools | Complete.**

How to do it...

There are two ways to begin designing SQL Server Agent scheduled jobs for ETL processes.

1. For the **SQLExpress** environment, use **SQL Server Import and Export** wizard and for the server environment, use **SQL Server agent**.

2. There are two ways to open up the **SQL Server Import and Export** wizard, either using GUI tools or **command line** operations. Let us do this by using the command line operation:

   Open a command prompt window with Administrative privileges and type `dtswizard.exe`.

3. The file can be located within the `%\program files\Microsoft SQL Server\100\DTS\binn` folder, as shown in the following screenshot:

4. From your local machine, using the **Start** menu point to **All Programs**.

5. As per the following screenshot, point to Microsoft SQL Server 2008 R2 and click **Import and Export Data**.

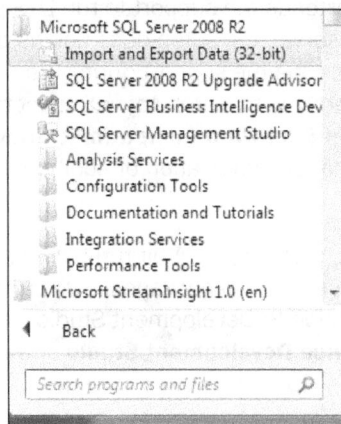

6. Similarly, using SQL Server 2008 R2 client tools, you can choose **SQL Server Management Studio (SSMS)** or **Business Intelligence Development Studio (BIDS)**.

7. Right-click the `SSIS Packages` folder and select the SSIS **Import and Export Wizard**.

8. Using BIDS tool, go to **Project** menu, choose the **SSIS Import and Export Wizard**.

9. For the ease of this recipe, we will skip to the screen where you need to save the package (see the next screenshot) as the Import and Export wizard, which has the self-explanatory screens to proceed.

10. We need to provide all the necessary information to create an import or export task and once we get to the save and Run Package screen, you need to choose **Run Immediately**, if it is a one-off requirement to perform ETL activities.

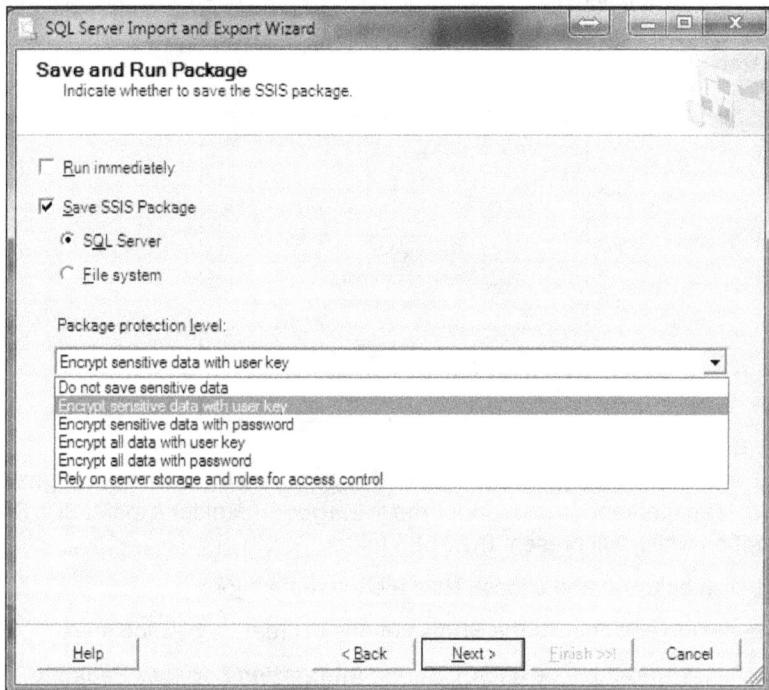

11. In case the referred ETL process is a continuous task to schedule for administrative processes, we need to choose the **Save SSIS package** option with two more options to choose from.

12. We can choose either to save a package in SQL Server (package) or File System (as a file) with a protection level of '**Encrypt data**' with a password/key, or rely on windows operating system roles for access control.

> The package store includes `msdb` database and folders in the filesystem, for the better administration of the ETL process using a backup strategy it is essential to save a copy of the package to SQL Server, which is saved to the `sysssispackages` table.

For this recipe, we chose to create a simple ETL process to export Department table data from `AdventureWorks2008R2` database to a Flat-file destination (text file) with a protection level of '**encrypt all data with password**' option. The package has been saved to SQL Server with the name **Export Department Data** (as shown in the next screenshot) and not chosen to '**Run immediately**'.

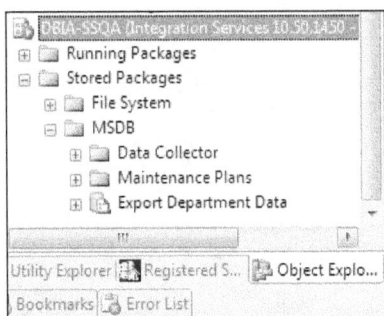

1. Now, we are at the stage where we need to schedule the saved package using SQL Server Management Studio. Under the `Management` folder expand SQL Server Agent, the option which will present the `Jobs` folder.

2. Right-click on `Jobs` and choose **New job** to create a job.

3. Name the job and choose the **Steps** options to create a new job step.

4. Now choose the step type as **SQL Server Integration Services Package**.

5. Choose the package source, which is **SQL Server** in our case.

6. Enter the SQL Server 2008 R2 instance name to choose the relevant package **Export Department Data**, as shown in the following screenshot.

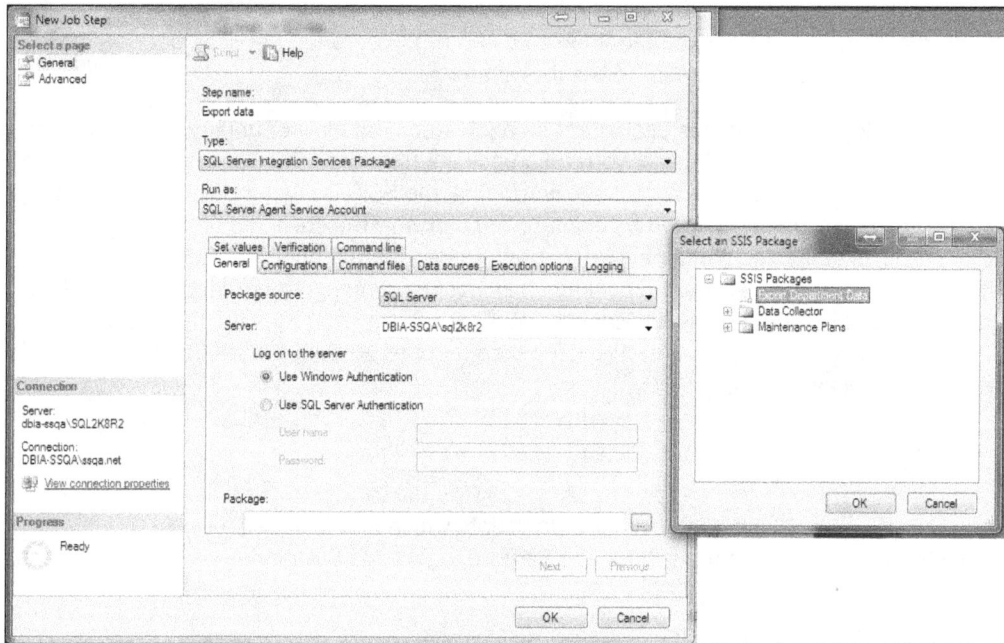

7. Now, let us look into how to automate the package execution for administrative purposes without choosing any other tool or process. This SSIS job step presents various execution options, such as **Configurations**.

8. SSIS service relies on a configuration, which stands as settings for all the packages on that SQL Server instance. By default, the configuration file is stored as an XML file, which can be located under the folder %ProgramFiles%\Microsoft SQL Server\100\DTS\Binn with the name MsDtsSrvr.ini.xml.

9. You need to modify the configuration file, if your packages are stored in a named instance, or a remote instance of the Database Engine, or in multiple instances of the Database Engine.

10. If the configuration file is moved to a different location other than the earlier specified default location, you have to modify the registry to specify the new location. The registry key can be located in: HKEY_LOCAL_MACHINE\SOFTWARE\Microsoft\ Microsoft SQL Server\100\SSIS\ServiceConfigFile.

How it works...

After you create the job, you must add at least one step and set the type of the step to the SQL Server Integration Services Package. A job can include multiple steps, each running a different package. An SQL Server Agent job step can run Integration Services packages that are saved to the `msdb` database, or to the filesystem.

Running an Integration Services package from a job step is similar to running a package using the **dtexec** and **DTExecUI** utilities. If you run a package from the SSIS Designer, the package always runs immediately. While a package is running, the SSIS Designer displays the progress of the package execution on the **Progress** tab. You can view the start and finish time of the package and its tasks and containers, in addition to information about any tasks or containers in the package that failed. After the package has finished running, the run-time information remains available on the **Execution Results** tab. The account that runs an Integration Services package as an SQL Server Agent job step requires all the permissions as an account that runs the package directly.

There's more

Using the `PowerShell` platform, we can run scripts which are designed for best administration needs, such as Backup and Restore, Agent Job Creation, Server Configuration, and Database Object Scripting tasks.

Troubleshooting multi-server instances with utility administration

Monitoring and managing multiple instances of SQL Server and databases is a very challenging task. SQL Server tools are easy to use and help to manage multi-server management through automated multi-server jobs, event forwarding and the ability to manage multiple instances from a single-machine console. Using SQL Server 2008 R2, database administrators can define and manage such tasks centrally using **Utility Control Point** (**UCP**).

UCP is a model that will represent the organization's SQL Server entities as a unified view. The viewpoints are key sectors to identify which applications use that instance. This can be handled using the SQL Server Management Studio (SSMS) tool. The following entities can be viewed using UCP tool:

- Instance names of SQL Server (multiple)
- Data-tier applications
- Database files
- Resource utilization dimension
  - CPU utilization

❑   Storage space utilization

▸   Storage volume information

This Utility architecture provides capabilities such as dashboard, viewpoints, and resource utilization policies, which can be classified as utility administration. Using SQL Server 2008 R2 Enterprise Edition UCP tool, we can manage 25 instances.

In this recipe, we will look at how to enroll multiple SQL Server instances and create a central dashboard view as a single-point troubleshooting tool.

Getting ready

Open up the SQL Server Management Studio (SSMS), next to **Object Explorer**, a new tab **Utility Explorer** will appear. Similarly, the **Utility Explorer** can be presented by navigating View—**Utility Explorer** option. On the right-hand side, towards **Object Explorer Details**, you will see multiple options that comprise the utility configuration steps (see the next screenshot).

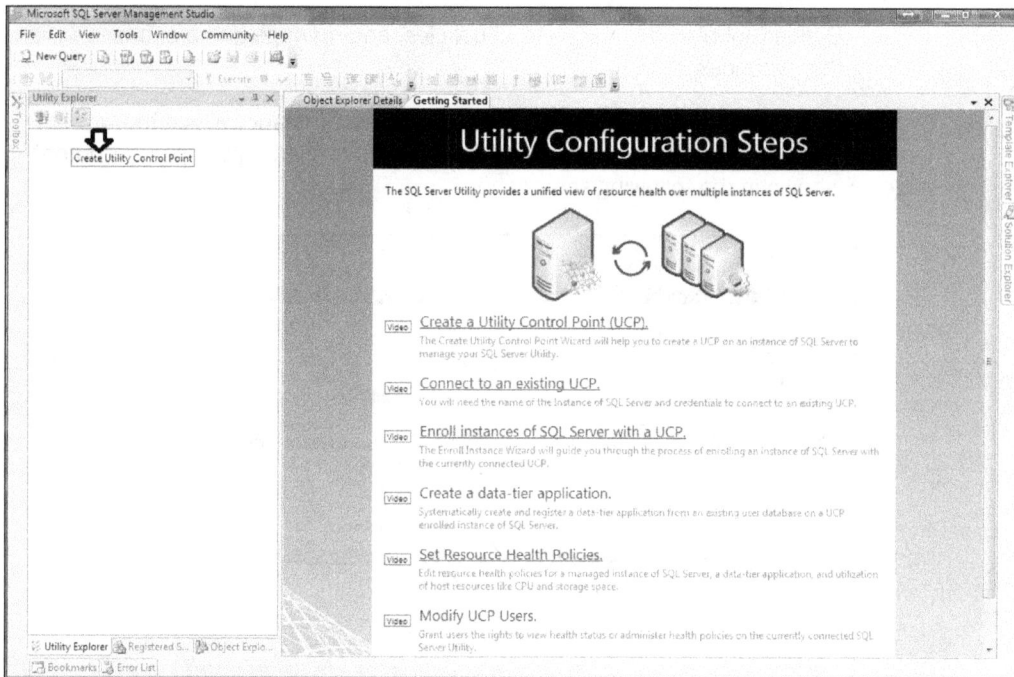

How to do it...

In order to begin enrolling multiple SQL Server instances and create a central dashboard view as a single-point troubleshooting tool, you will need to complete the following steps:

1. If you click on the **Create a Utility Control Point (UCP)**, it opens up the **Getting Started** window that includes shortcuts to wizards that you can use to set up a UCP.

2. This acts a single-point of server to manage other multiple servers in a centralized manner.

3. The primary step is to specify the SQL Server instance, which will be designated as a control point—UCP to host the central management servers.

4. Once the UCP is created, click on **Enroll instances of SQL Server with a UCP** to enroll additional server instances that will enable us to monitor and manage them efficiently.

5. Specify the SQL Server instance that is to be designated as a UCP and that will host the central system management data warehouse.

6. This data warehouse will record all the instance's resource utilization and health information. To set up the SQL Server Utility you need to:

   ❑ Create a UCP from the SQL Server Utility

   ❑ Enroll instances of SQL Server with the UCP

   ❑ Define Global and Instance level policies, and manage and monitor the instances

7. By default, the UCP instance itself becomes a managed instance. Once the wizard has successfully finished, the process will be directed to the Utility Explorer Content page, as shown in the following screenshot:

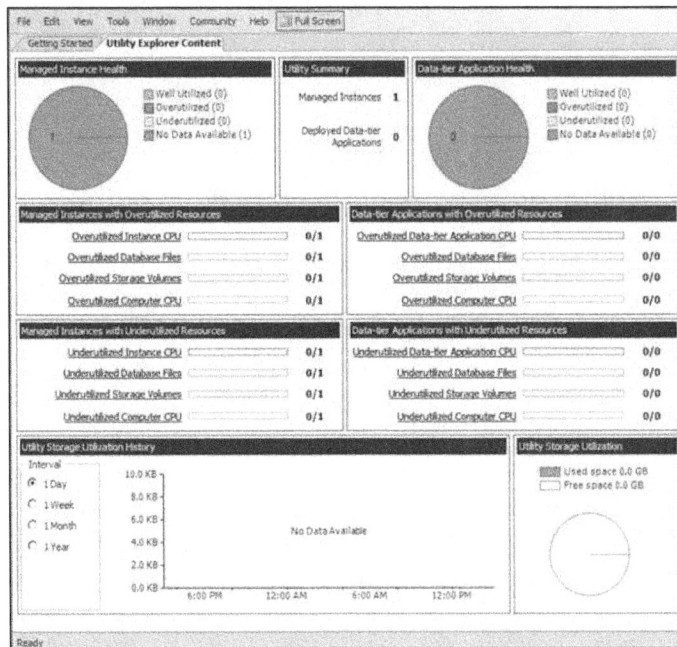

8. The Utility administration option page (as seen in the next screenshot) can be used to modify or view the global policy settings, which are effective across the SQL Server utility.

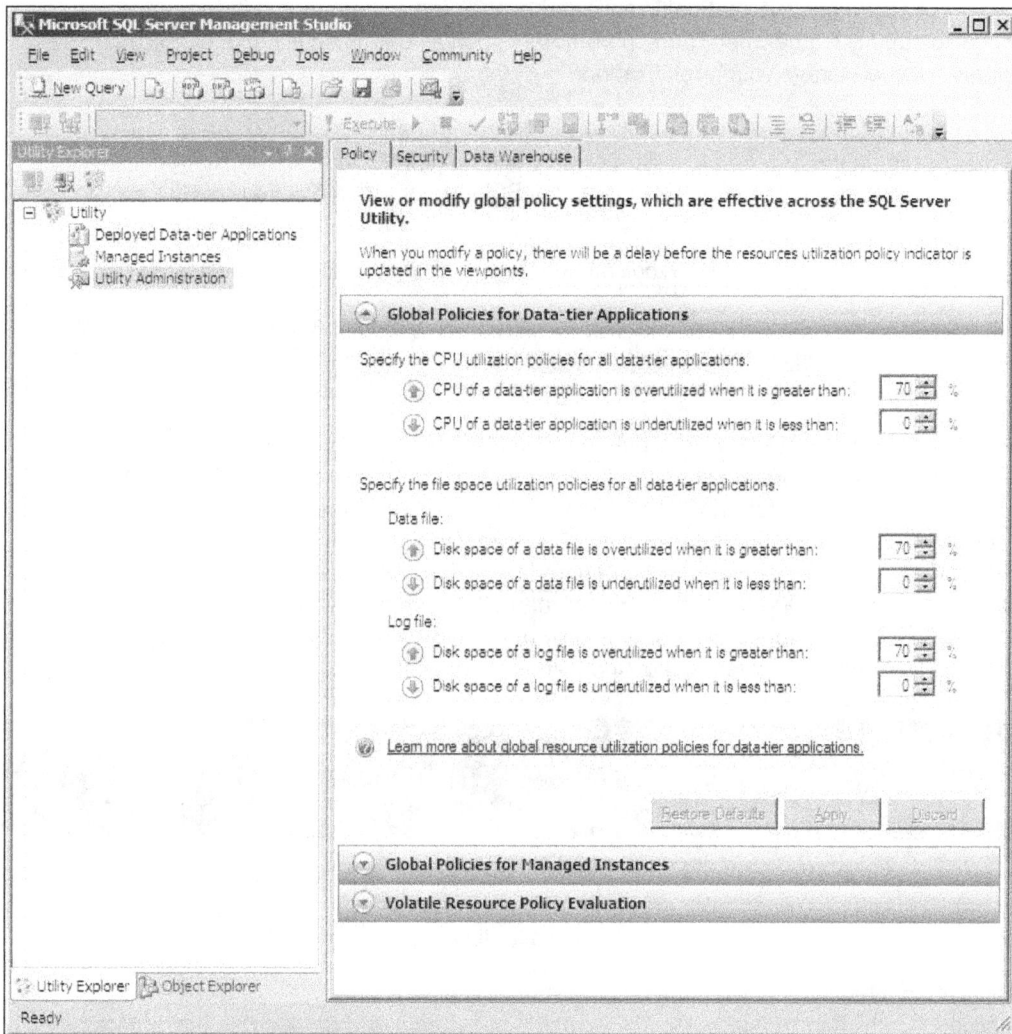

9. The **Utility Administration** page is very useful in defining the global policies for Data-tier applications, managed instances, and validation of the resource policy evaluation.

10. To enroll the multiple SQL Server instances, using the SSMS Utility Administration pane, right-click on **Managed Instances** and click **Add**.

How it works...

SQL Server Utility is instrumented to manage instances that are registered with a data collection set, which sends configuration and performance data to UCP every 15 minutes. DAC applications are automatically managed by UCP, if they belong to a managed instance. UCP also supports other monitoring parameters such as database file space utilization, CPU utilization, and storage volume utilization.

Health policies can be defined globally for all data-tier applications and managed instances of SQL Server in the SQL Server Utility, or they can be defined individually for each data-tier application and for each managed instance of SQL Server in the SQL Server Utility.

Using SQL Server 2008 R2 **SSMS** tool, an SQL Server 2008 instance can be enrolled with a **UCP**.

The evaluation time period and tolerance for percent violations are both configurable using the **Policy** tab settings in the **Utility Administration** node of Utility Explorer. You can also restore default values or discard changes using buttons at the bottom of the display.

The summary and detailed data is presented in Management Studio for each instance of SQL Server and data-tier application, SQL Server Utility dashboard in SSMS presents an at-a-glance summary of performance and configuration data for managed instance and data-tier application CPU utilization, database file utilization, storage volume utilization, and computer CPU utilization. Data displays provide separation of over-utilized and under-utilized resources, as well as graphs of CPU utilization and storage utilization over time. Each instance of SQL Server and data-tier application managed by the SQL Server Utility can be monitored based on global policy definitions, or based on individual policy definitions.

Administering SQL Server Replication processes

Replication is the oldest data distribution technique within RDBMS and has been supported by SQL Server since version 6.5. Replication's main purpose is to copy data from one server to another, which is used as a marginal high availability feature for certain types of applications.

Replication agents are the key handlers that carry out all the tasks associated with replication, which includes creating a snapshot of schema and data, detecting updates, detecting conflict updates, and propagating changes between servers. All the replication agents are run under SQL Server agent job steps and these executables can be called directly from a batch script, or command-line operation. Replication provides a default profile for each agent and additional pre-defined profiles for the log reader agent, distributor agent, and merge agent. The agent profile contains a set of parameters that are used each time an agent runs at the Distributor server instance.

Monitoring is a part of the administration procedure. Replication monitor allows the user to obtain information and perform tasks associated with each replication agent.

The various agents that are associated with publications in the replication monitor are:

- ▶ snapshot agent
- ▶ log reader agent
- ▶ queue reader agent

The two agents that are associated with subscriptions in the replication monitor are:

- ▶ distribution agent
- ▶ merge agent

In this recipe, we will look at the practices which define the procedures for replication topology administration, this is essential to follow after you have configured the replication. The recipe includes the administration process that should be implemented for all replication topologies.

Getting ready

The following administration practices should be implemented for all replication topologies:

- ▶ Backup and Restore strategy
- ▶ Scripting in replication
- ▶ Replication Monitor
- ▶ Thresholds and Alerts
- ▶ Performance tuning baselines

Configuring a replication method is not as simple as clicking through a few options of a wizard. A number of prerequisite steps must be fulfilled before a replication can be configured and implemented to administer the replication process. The prerequisite steps are:

1. The hosting instance replication folder needs enough free space to support the replication that has the snapshot files of the same size as the database.
2. The snapshot agent then locks the whole table when the data is copied from the publisher to the distributor. So you must choose the snapshot schedule and frequency carefully without causing any slowdown to the general application functionality.
3. The distribution database needs to have ample free disk space to support the transaction log. The log file growth is based on the frequency of the transactional replication model.
4. All the transactions are logged in a distributed database between the snapshots, and it will be cleared only when a new snapshot is created.

5. All the tables included in the transactional replication must have the primary key associated with the published table.

6. For peer-to-peer transactional replication, the distribution must be configured on each node first and then database schema must be initialized to perform snapshot processes.

> Before you can configure replication, you must install it into the servers that will participate in your replication topology.
>
> If you have not already installed replication on all participating servers, go back to the SQL Server Installation Center and add the replication feature to your servers. It will also make the process of configuring replication easier if you connect your Object Explorer in SSMS to all the Data Engine services that will participate in your replication model.

How to do it...

The following are the steps to administer the snapshot and transactional replication setup:

1. *Backup* the publication database at the Publisher.

2. *Backup* the distribution database at the Distributor.

3. *Backup* the subscription database at each Subscriber

4. *Backup* the `master` and `msdb` system database at the Publisher, Distributor and Subscriber.

5. All of these databases should be backed up at the same time. Backup settings for Transactional replication are as follows:

   - To check if sync with backup is set on your publication or distribution databases, execute the following command at the publisher or distributor server instance:

```
select databasepropertyex('db_name', 'IsSyncWithBackup')
```

   - If the value is 1, sync with the backup is set. If sync with backup is not set, enter the following TSQL command to configure it:

```
sp_replicationdboption @db_name = 'db_name',
@optname = 'sync with backup',
@value = 'true'
```

   - Let us work on restore strategies within snapshot replication and transactional replication. To restore publication database in snapshot replication, restore the latest backup of the publication database.

6. Determine if the publication database backup contains the latest configuration for all publications and subscriptions. If yes, then the restore is completed. If no, then go to the next step.

7. Remove the replication configuration using the `sp_removedbreplication` statement from the Publisher, Distributor, and Subscribers, and then recreate the configuration. The restore is completed.

8. To restore transactional replication with updated subscriptions, restore the latest backup of the publication database.

9. Run the Distribution Agent until all Subscribers are synchronized with the outstanding commands in the distribution database.

10. Verify that all commands are delivered to Subscribers by using the **Undistributed Commands** tab in Replication Monitor, or by querying the **MSdistribution_status** view in the distribution database.

11. If you are using queued updating subscriptions, connect to each Subscriber and delete all rows from the **MSreplication_queuetable** in the subscription database.

12. Run the Distribution Agent until all Subscribers are synchronized with the outstanding commands in the distribution database.

13. Verify that all commands are delivered to Subscribers by using the Replication Monitor or by querying the **MSdistribution_status** view in the distribution database.

14. Use the `tablediff` Utility or another tool to manually synchronize the Publisher with the Subscriber. This enables you to recover data from the subscription database that was not contained in the publication database backup.

> Script every component and configuration change in your replication. Use SSMS tool to create objects and script them, or only script them.

15. To script an object or multiple objects from Management studio, connect to the Distributor, Publisher, or Subscriber in Management Studio, and then expand the server node. Right-click the `Replication` folder and then click on **Generate Scripts**.

16. Specify options in the **Generate SQL Script | <ReplicationObject>** dialog box.

17. Click **Script to File**. Enter a file name in the **Script File Location** dialog box, and then click **Save**. Click **OK**, and then click **Close**.

18. The key aspect of administration practices is monitoring replication to ensure that it is up and running. Replication monitor displays the status information for publication and subscriptions. To view information for a publication, connect to the Publisher group in Management Studio, and then expand a publisher and select a publication.

19. To view and modify publication properties, right-click on **publication** to select **properties**.

20. To view information about subscriptions, click the **All Subscriptions** tab.

21. To view information about agents, click the **Agents** tab.

22. Click the **Warnings** tab to configure alerts from pre-defined replication alerts. This screen can be used to view information about agent warnings and thresholds.

23. Expand a Publisher group in the left pane, expand a Publisher, and then click on **publication**.

24. Click the **Warnings** tab. Enable a warning by selecting the appropriate checkbox. Warn if a subscription will expire within the threshold, or Warn if latency exceeds the threshold.

25. Set a threshold for the warnings in the Threshold column. For example, if you have selected Warn, if latency exceeds the threshold, you should select a latency of 60 seconds in the **Threshold** column.

26. Click **Save Changes**.

27. Again, Replication monitor gets the performance related values for replication. The key values to monitor are: **Current Average Performance** and **Current Worst Performance** columns.

The values are determined as follows:

- For transactional replication, performance quality is determined by the latency threshold. If the threshold is not set, a value is not displayed.

- For merge replication, Replication Monitor displays detailed statistics for each article processed during synchronization. Also the amount of time spent in each processing phase (uploading changes, downloading changes, and so on).

- The key areas to lookup for replication performance tuning are: latency, throughput, concurrency, duration of synchronization, and resource consumption.

How it works...

All the data validations and monitoring aspects of replication are managed by the core database engine. The validation works by calculating row count or checksum at the Publisher and then comparing those values to the row count or checksum calculated at the Subscriber.

While the calculations are performed, shared locks are placed temporarily on tables for which row counts or checksums are being run, but the calculations are completed quickly and the shared locks removed, usually in a matter of seconds. When binary checksums are used, 32-bit cyclic redundancy check (CRC) occurs on a column-by-column basis rather than a CRC on the physical row on the data page.

When replication is configured, a set of agent profiles is installed on the Distributor. An agent profile contains a set of parameters that are used each time an agent runs: each agent logs in to the Distributor during its startup process and queries for the parameters in its profile. For merge subscriptions that use Web synchronization, profiles are downloaded and stored at the Subscriber. If the profile is changed, the profile at the Subscriber is updated the next time the Merge Agent runs.

See Also

The detailed information about the configuration of distributor, publisher, and subscriber are discussed in the recipe *Managing SQL Server Replication processes* in *Chapter 3, Managing the Core Database Engine*, and *Implementing and Designing new Replication features* mentioned in *Chapter 5, Management of core SQL Server 2008 R2 technologies*.

3
Managing the Core Database Engine

In this chapter, we will cover:

- ▶ Implementing Central Management feature enhancements
- ▶ Designing Multi-server management from SQL Server 2008 R2
- ▶ Managing Utility Control Point data warehouse database
- ▶ Implementing Utility and Non-utility collection sets
- ▶ Designing and refreshing Scalable Share database features and enhancements
- ▶ Managing SQL Server Replication processes
- ▶ Implementing security for SQL Server Agent jobs management
- ▶ Using Utility Explorer to manage multiple instances

Introduction

The goal of this chapter is to design, implement, and manage an effective core database engine to produce a resilient data platform. The core database engine is the main platform for managing all of the business data for your organization–both archived and current–in a relational database management system. The physical and logical architecture we choose for SQL Server can have a dramatic impact on the system's ability to stand as mission-critical databases that are flexible and scalable. As a DBA and advanced user of SQL Server 2008 R2, you have to develop best practices that combine a streamline of services for deployment, migration, and management of your data platform.

SQL Server 2008 R2 has rich and intuitive GUI management tools, which lower the costs in data management by incorporating automation and delegation of administrative tasks. This chapter covers the SSMS features that are new and enhanced in SQL Server 2008 R2 to enable operational efficiency in developing the joint best practices and integrated solutions to derive a greater **Return On Investment** (**ROI**) and lower the **Total Cost Ownership** (**TCO**) for the data platform environment.

Implementing Central Management feature enhancements

Central Management Server (**CMS**) is a feature that enables the DBA to administer multiple servers by designating a set of server groups, which maintain the connection information for one or more instances of SQL Server. In this recipe, we will go through the implementation strategy for the CMS feature in your SQL Server data platform. Before we continue into the recipe, it is essential for you to understand the core functionality of this feature, which uses the multiple features from the SQL Server core database engine:

▶ SQL Server system repository

▶ Manage the SQL Server farm from one location

▶ Easy reporting about system state, configuration, and performance

Getting ready

As per the feature characteristics described previously, there are three important components in the system. These components are:

▶ Storage

▶ Execution

▶ Reporting

Storage is used to store the system repository, Execution manages the SQL Server instances, and Reporting shows the statistical information.

The CMS feature implementation is a dual-process (setup and configuration) making use of SQL Server components. The prerequisite of services is to install SQL Server 2008 R2 and Reporting Services. To support the extensive features of the core database engine Enterprise Edition, it is recommended that the CMS be a single point of resource to manage the multiple instances of SQL Server. However, for cost purposes, you can still make use of the Standard Edition.

CMS is introduced in SQL Server 2008, as earlier versions of SQL Server cannot be designated as a Central Management Server. The main characteristic of CMS is to execute TSQL and Policy-based management policies at the same time against these designated server groups.

How to do it...

To get started, we will need to complete the following steps to implement the central management server feature to the existing SQL Server data platform:

1. SQL Server Management Studio is the main tool to designate the CMS feature. Open **SQL Server Management Studio,** on the **View** menu, click **Registered Servers**.

2. In **Registered Servers**, expand **Database Engine**, right-click **Central Management Servers**, point to **New**, and then click **Central Management Servers**.

3. In the **New Server Registration** dialog box, register the instance of SQL Server that will be the central management server.

4. In **Registered Servers**, right-click the central management server, point to **New**, and then click **New Server Group**. Type a group name and description, and then click **OK**.

5. In **Registered Servers**, right-click the central management server group, and then click **New Server Registration.**

6. In the **New Server Registration** dialog box, register one or more instances of SQL Server that will be members of this server group, see the following screenshot:

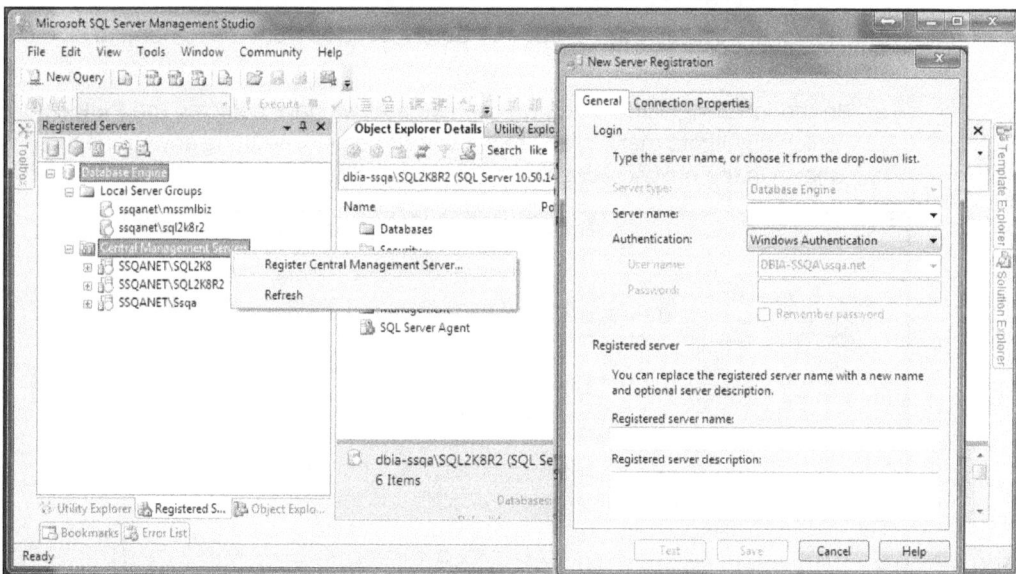

7. After you have registered a server, the Central Management Server (CMS) will be able to execute queries against all servers in the group at the same time.

[🔆 TSQL statements and Policy-based management policies can be executed at the same time against the server groups; CMS maintains the connection information for one of more instances of SQL Server. It is essential to consider the effective permissions on the servers in the server groups, which might vary; hence, it is best to use Windows Authentication in this case.]

8. To enable the single-point of resource to execute a single query on multiple CMS servers, it is easier to access the registration properties of a group of servers. Using that specific server group, there are multiple options of **new query**, **object explorer**, **evaluate policies**, and **import policies**.

[📝 The CMS feature is a powerful manageability feature and is easy to set up. However, it is potentially dangerous to implement a policy that may not be suitable for a set of server groups.]

9. Therefore, it is best to represent the CMS query editor with a specific color that can easily catch our eye to avoid any 'unintentional execution of queries or policies'. To enable such a representation follow these steps:

   ❑ Open SQL Server Management Studio, on the **Tools** menu, click on **Options**.

   ❑ In **Options**, select **Editor Tab** and **Status Bar**.

   ❑ Select the **Status Bar Layout and Colors section** from the right-hand side of the options window.

   ❑ In the following screenshot, we can see that we have selected the **Pink** color, which highlights that extra care is needed before executing any queries, as shown in the next screenshot:

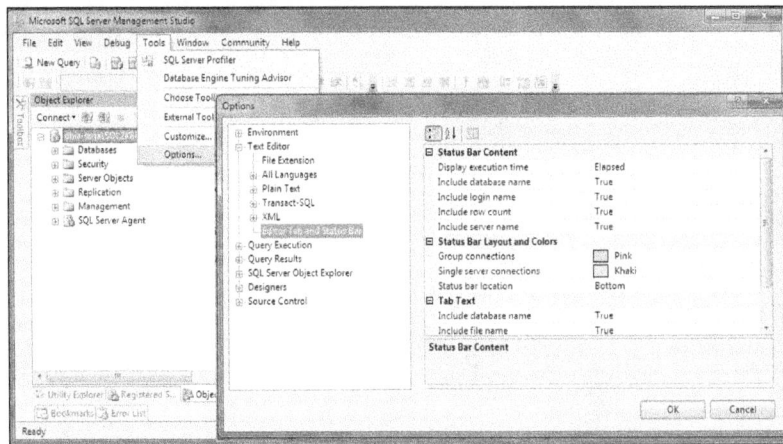

Now, let us evaluate how to create a CMS server group, evaluate policies, and execute queries on multiple servers.

1. Open SQL Server Management Studio; on the **View** menu, click on **Registered Servers**, expand Database Engine, right-click **Central Management Servers**, point to **New**, and then click **Central Management Servers**.

2. In the **New Server Registration** dialog box, register the instance of SQL Server that will be the Central Management Server.

3. In **Registered Servers**, right-click on **Central Management Server**. Point to **New** and click on **New Server Group**. Now type a group name and description, for instance, UAT or Production and click **OK**. See the following screenshot:

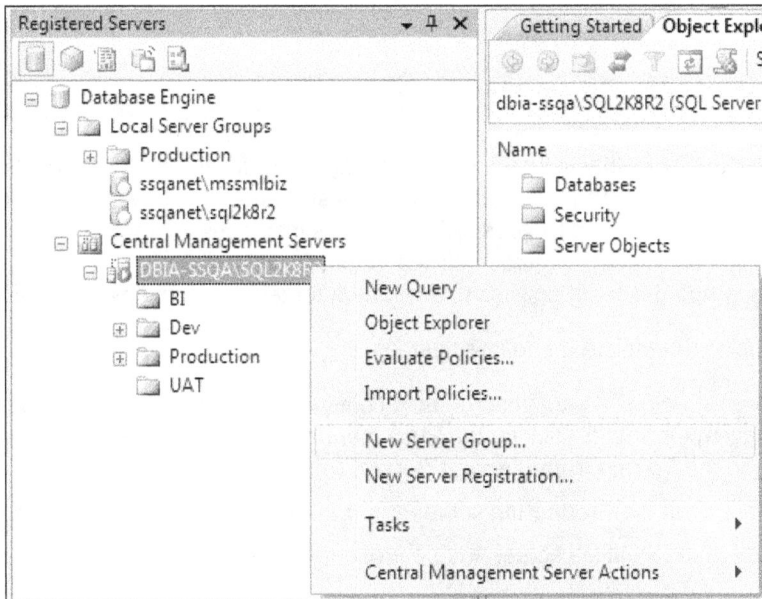

4. To register the servers to these individual server groups, in **Registered Servers** right-click on **Central Management Server Group** and then click **New Server Registration**.

5. In the **New Server Registration** dialog box, register one or multiple instances that are applicable to the relevant server groups, such as Development or Production.

As a best practice, it is ideal to create individual groups within CMS to enable a single-query execution against multiple servers as in the following screenshot:

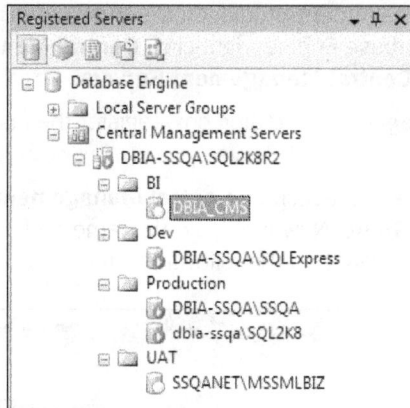

SQL Server 2008 R2 provides a 'Policy Based Management framework' that consists of multiple sets of policy files that you can import as best practice policies. You can then evaluate the policies against a target set that includes instances, instance objects, databases, or database objects. You can evaluate policies manually, set policies to evaluate a target set according to a schedule, or set policies to evaluate a target set according to an event.

To evaluate a policy complete the following steps:

1. To evaluate the policy against multiple configuration targets in the SQL Server Management Studio, click on the **View** menu to select **Registered Servers** and expand the **Central Management Server**.

2. Right-click on the **Production** server group and click on **Evaluate Policies**.

3. The **Evaluate Policies** screen will be presented as shown in the next screenshot.

4. Click on **Source** to **Choose Source**.

5. The relevant best practices policies are stored as XML files under `%:\ Program Files\Microsoft SQL Server\100\Tools\Policies\ DatabaseEngine\1033` directory, which is shown in the next screenshot:

> For this recipe, we have chosen to select the policy from SQL Server 2008 R2 Best Practices Analyzer that is downloaded from `http://www.microsoft.com/downloads/en/ details.aspx?FamilyID=0fd439d7-4bff-4df7- a52f-9a1be8725591`and installed on the server.

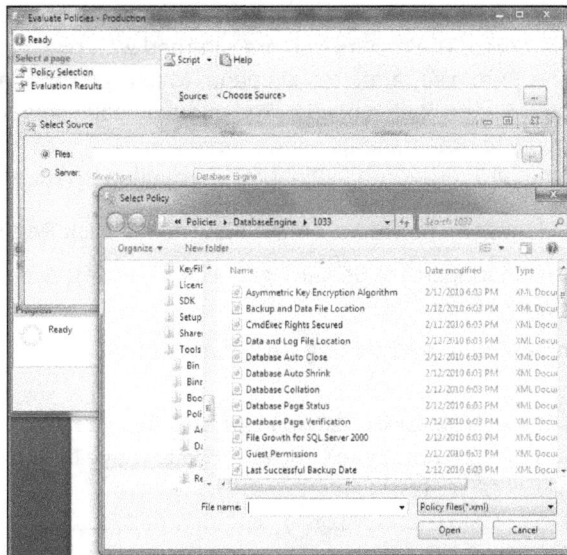

Let us evaluate the policy of Backup and Data File Location against the production instances. This policy will perform the steps to:

▶ Check if the database and the backups are on separate backup devices. If they are on the same backup device, and the device that contains the database fails, your backups will be unavailable.

▶ Putting the data and backups on separate devices optimizes the I/O performance for both the production use of the database and writing the backups, as shown in the following screenshot. (This is one of the Best Practices of Maintenance policies from Microsoft SQL Server 2008 R2 Best Practices Analyzer.)

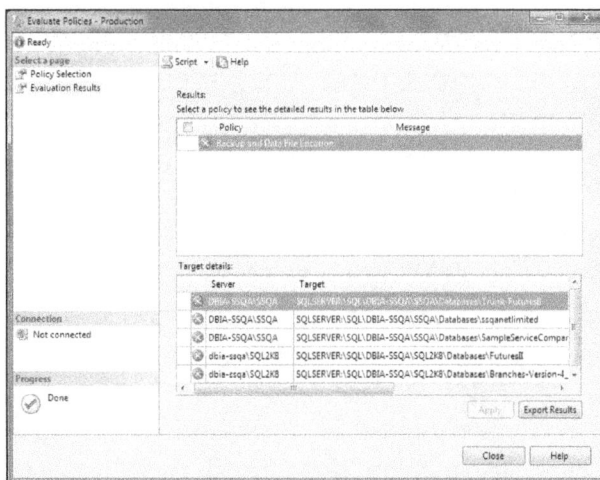

The ease of executing a single query against multiple-servers at the same time is one of my favorite manageability features. The results that are returned with this query can be combined into a single results pane, or in a separate results pane, which can include additional columns for the *server name* and the *login* that is used by the query on each server. To accomplish this task, let us execute a query to obtain the `Product Version`, `Product Level`, `Edition`, and `EngineEdition` that are registered against the Production server group.

1. In SQL Server Management Studio, on the **View** menu, click **Registered Servers**.

2. Expand a Central Management Server, right-click a server group, point to **Connect**, and then click **New Query**.

3. In **Query Editor**, execute the following TSQL statement:

```
SELECT
SERVERPROPERTY('ProductVersion') AS ProductVersion,
SERVERPROPERTY('ProductLevel') AS ProductLevel,
SERVERPROPERTY('Edition') AS Edition,
SERVERPROPERTY('EngineEdition') AS EngineEdition;
GO
```

The results are displayed as follows:

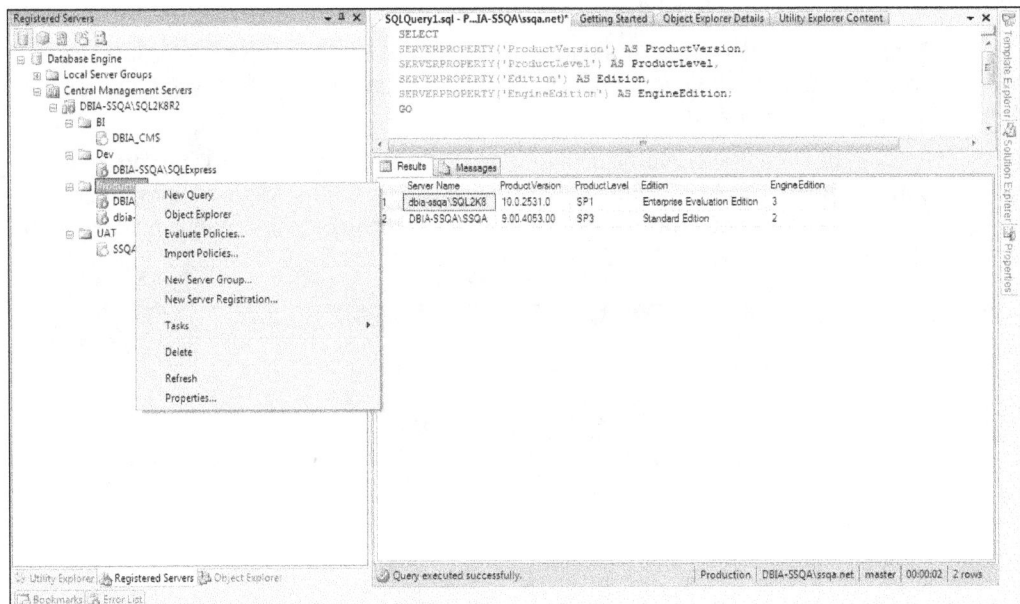

4. From the preceding screenshot, the results with a pink bar at the bottom state that this is a Production group. To change the multi-server results options, in the Management Studio, on the **Tools** menu, click **Options**.

5. Expand the **Query Results**, expand SQL Server, and then click **Multi-server Results**.

6. On the **Multi-server Results** page, specify the **option** settings that you want, and then click **OK**.

We now should have successfully completed the CMS feature implementation into the SQL Server data platform.

How it works...

The SQL Server instance that is designated as a Central Management Server maintains server groups, which maintain the connection information for one or more instances of SQL Server. CMS and all subsidiary servers on the network are registered using Windows Authentication only; in case local server groups are registered using Windows Authentication and SQL Server Authentication.

The storage for centralized management server groups, connection information, and authentication details are available from `themsdb system` database in:

- `dbo.sysmanagement_shared_registered_servers_internal`
- `dbo.sysmanagement_shared_server_groups_internal` system tables
- `dbo.sysmanagement_shared_registered_servers`
- `dbo.sysmanagement_shared_server_groups` system views

The user and permissions information on the registered servers may vary based on the user permission that uses Windows Authentication connection. For instance, in our recipe, on the `dbia-ssqa\SQL2K8` instance, the `login` is a member of the SYSADMIN fixed server role and on the `DBIA-SSQA\SSQA` instance, the `login` is a member of the DBCREATOR fixed server role. In this case, we may not be able to run certain SYSADMIN privileged statements on `DBIA-SSQA\SSQA` instance.

There's more...

Using SQL Server 2008 R2 Management Studio with CMS, we can manage the lower SQL Server version instances, such as 2005 (90), 2000 (80), and 7.0 (70), which is truly a central management of instances.

See Also

The advanced features of the Policy Based Framework are covered in the recipe *Implementing Policy-based management features* in *Chapter 7, Implementing new Manageability features and practices.*

Designing Multi-server management from SQL Server 2008 R2

Taking advantage of the two new manageability features–*Policy Based Management* and *Data Collector of SQL Server 2008* which are independent of each other–the multi-server management addresses problems by providing further solutions to the DBAs. The lack of manageability tools to manage multiple instances by understanding resource utilization and enhancing effective reporting tools is plugged in using multi-server management from SQL Server 2008 R2.

This recipe is intended to design the multi-server management component using SQL Server 2008 R2 for data-tier applications (DAC). By operating the SQL Server Management Studio or Visual Studio with the help of Utility Explorer (UE), we can design the Multi-Server Management (MSM) component. The MSM provides several ways to view summary and detailed data about the health state of managed instances of SQL Server. An additional capability of UE enables the interface to view and manage policy definitions that includes objects, data, and policies managed by the SQL Server utility.

Getting ready

The new feature of SQL Server 2008 R2–Utility Control Point (UCP)—allows DBAs to enroll the SQL Server instances across their Enterprise network into a centralized multi-server management point. Once the instances are enrolled, the default capacity policies of utilization across the instances or applications are set. It is essential to check that you are using an SQL Server 2008 R2 instance to register the UCP to design the multi-server management feature.

The inter-operability with Visual Studio 2010 introduces the facility to create data-tier applications using the project template. The internal components of Visual Studio 2010 distribute several database projects and templates to enable the users to develop the integral part of applications for data-tier applications. These capabilities of Visual Studio 2010 and SQL Server 2008 R2 reduce the trial and error associated with deployments streamlining SQL Server consolidation initiatives; the control point also provides broad control over the hardware utilization of the database environment. Using the most common applications, such as SQL Server Management Studio (SSMS) and Visual Studio, the MSM component can be deployed. SQL Server 2008 R2 SSMS includes a new explorer called Utility Control Point explorer and interoperability with Visual Studio (VS) tool project type, which will help developers to write database applications, capture deployment intent, and produce the data-tier application as a single unit of deployment. In this recipe, we will go through the implementation of the MSM feature with the help of tools, such as VS and SSMS by the developers and DBAs.

How to do it...

To get started, let us go through the steps to implement the MSM feature using Visual Studio tool that will deploy data-tier application components, which are important for database applications deployment:

1. Open the Visual Studio programs from **Start | programs | Visual Studio 2010** program group.

2. Click **File**, click **New**, and then click **Project**. Under **Installed Templates**, expand the Database node, and then click on the SQL Server node.

3. In the template pane, click **SQL Server Data-tier Application**. Then, type the `project name`, `location`, and `solution name` in the appropriate text boxes at the bottom of the form.

4. To use source control for database code, select the **Add source control** check box. After all selections are entered, click **OK** to create the project.

5. The steps are represented in the following screenshot:

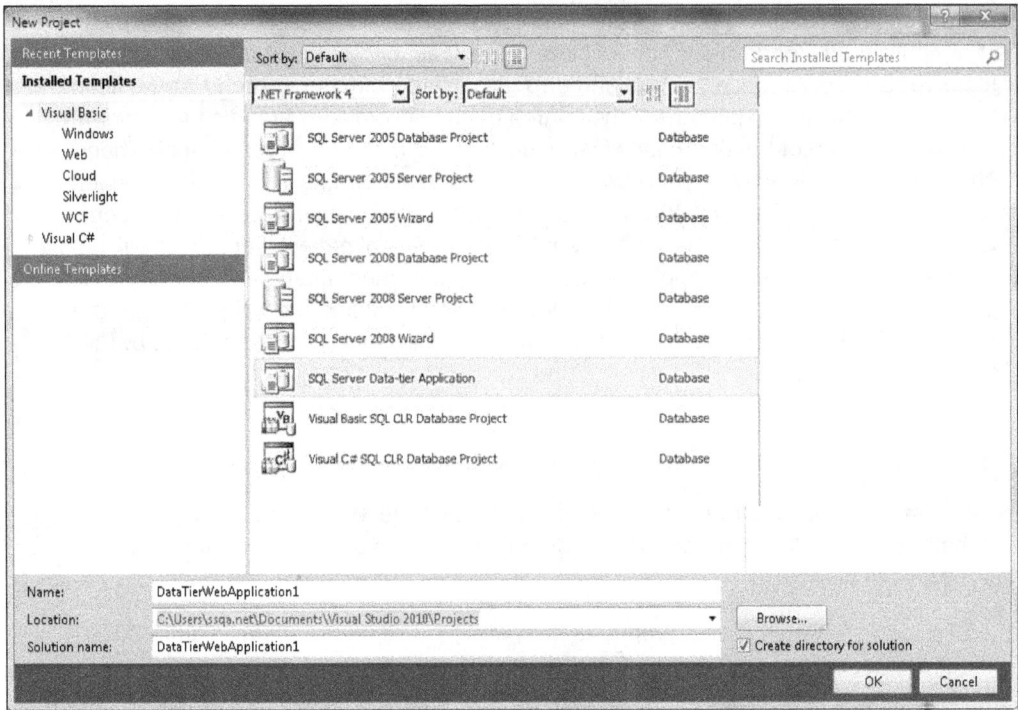

Visual Studio 2010 delivers several database projects and templates that enable users to develop the data portion of their applications in Visual Studio Professional, Visual Studio Premium, and Visual Studio Ultimate editions. To deploy DAC packages, you need to download the templates using online templates.

6. After all selections are entered, click **OK** to create the project.

7. We will use the Scripts pane as shown in the next screenshot from **Solution Explorer** to manage the database or server.

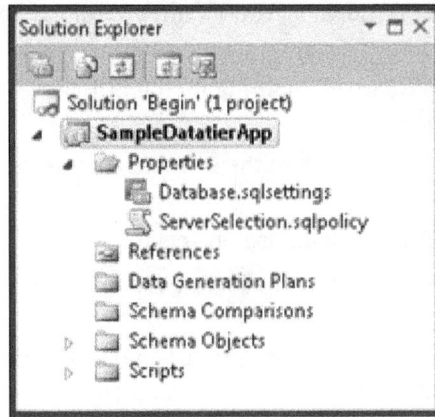

8. Open the Data-tier Application Wizard.

9. Right-click on the **project node**, and then click **Import Data-tier Application** (refer to the next screenshot.)

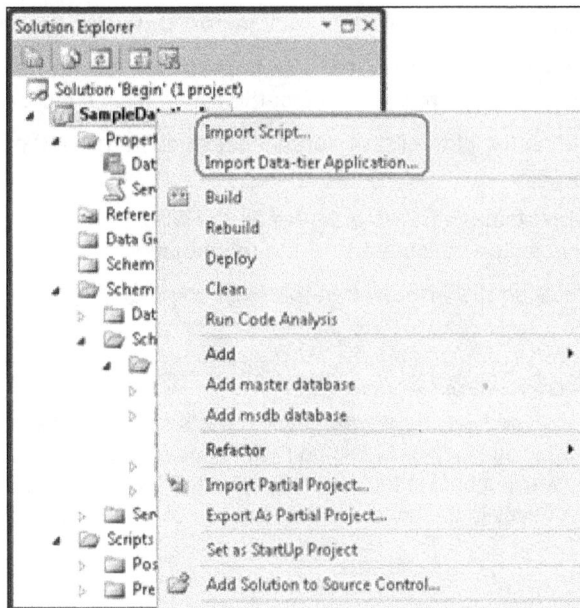

10. In the **Specify Import Options** page, click **Import** from an existing instance of SQL Server.

11. Then, type a value in **Connection string** for the SQL Server instance, or click **Edit** to configure a connection.

12. After that, choose a database from the **Database name list**. When you are done, click **Next**.

13. The **Summary** page lists all database objects that are supported by a DAC.

14. If any objects are not supported, the import cannot be performed successfully. If all objects are supported, click **Next**.

15. The **Import Objects** page tracks progress while the wizard creates the SQL scripts for the database objects and loads them into the project.

16. The final step is to click **Finish** to close the wizard.

We will now go through the deployment using SQL Server Management Studio tool to deploy data-tier application components:

1. Start the Import Data-tier Application Wizard.

2. Right-click the project node and then click **Import Data-tier Application**.

3. In the **Specify Import Options** page, click **Import from a data-tier application package** and then click **Browse** to select the DAC package file; click **Next** to continue.

4. The final confirmation of the list of database objects in the DAC package is shown in the **Summary** page.

5. The **Import Objects** page tracks progress as the wizard creates the SQL scripts for the database objects and loads them into the project.

6. Click **Finish** to close the wizard when the page completes.

> After a data-tier application project has been created, users can add SQL Server database objects as well as instance objects (such as logins) to the project. Objects can be added by using built-in templates or by writing Transact-SQL code directly in the editor, without the use of templates.

The final screenshot of UCP will be as follows:

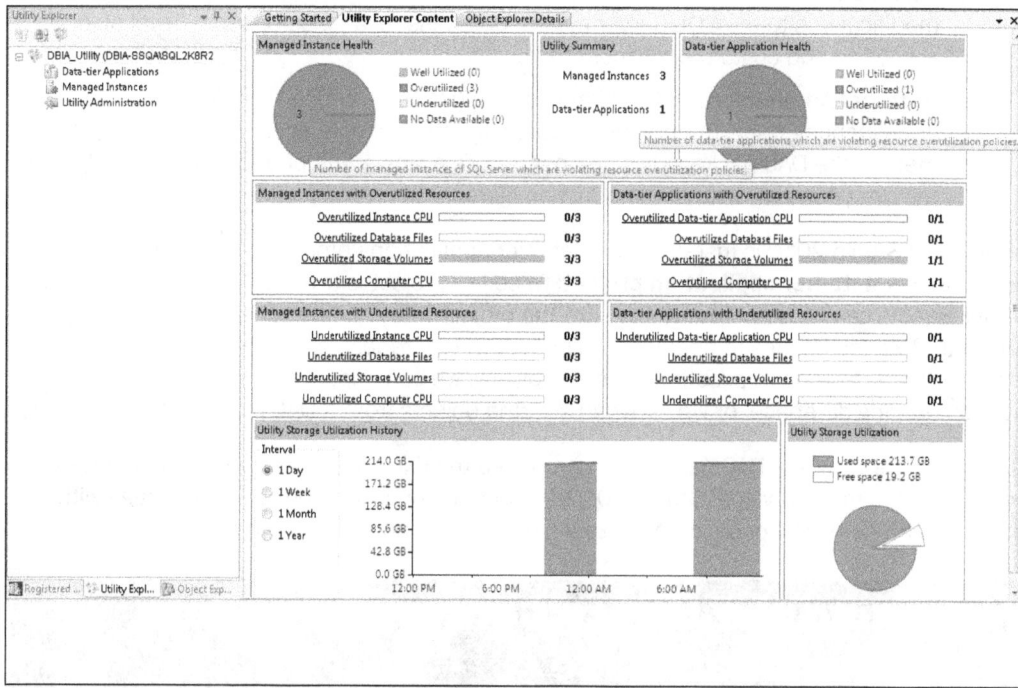

Once the steps are completed, the unified view of MSM is visible on SSMS from the Utility Explorer Content on the right-hand side. The unified view is the representation of a successful implementation of MSM to manage data-tier application deployment.

How it works...

The Data-tier Application (DAC) component helps to adopt a single unit of deployment method to streamline all the consolidation of SQL Server instances into a unified view.

In this recipe, we used the Visual Studio 2010 template to build the data-tier application that will stand as multi-server management. The different types of templates and projects are as follows:

> **Database Project**: Database project templates are available for SQL Server 2005 and SQL Server 2008. You can use these templates to define databases for mission-critical and business-critical applications. All objects implemented by the respective SQL Server version are supported in database projects.

▶ **Server Project**: Server project templates are available for SQL Server 2005 and SQL Server 2008. You can use these templates to define server-level objects as well as modifications to the SQL Server master database. Examples of server-level objects are logins and custom error messages.

▶ **Data-tier Application**: Data-tier application (DAC) projects are useful for implementing departmental applications (or other simple applications). Using this method the DAC package will be operated as a single unit of deployment throughout the development, test, and production lifecycle of an application.

After Visual Studio 2010 is installed, the data-tier applications process can be initiated using **create a new data-tier application project**. Once the project is available, the new database server objects can be authored, to initialize the project with existing schema. We can employ one of the two techniques to populate the project with database and server objects for existing databases and applications. More explicitly, we can import a data-tier application from an existing database, or we can load schema objects from a DAC package file.

Once the extraction of a DAC package is completed the Extract Data-tier Application Wizard can be used. Similar to Visual Studio 2010, restriction importing from a DAC package with SSMS can be done only once, to initialize a new data-tier application project.

Managing the Utility Control Point data warehouse database

Utility Control Point (UCP) is one of the new management features in SQL Server 2008 R2. UCP enables you to manage and monitor multiple instances of SQL Server. Data collected by UCP managed instances of SQL Server are stored in the Utility Management Data Warehouse (UMDW) database called `sysutility_mdw`.

To generate data for UMDW, it is essential to create a UCP on an instance of SQL Server. In this recipe, we will use the SSMS to create the **Utility Management Data Warehouse** (**UMDW**). The steps are wizard-driven to specify a SQL instance–where the UCP is created–and enable the utility collection set to periodically collect and store in UMDW.

How to do it...

The following steps are essential to manage required data for the UMDW database that will be generated by using the Utility Explorer wizard to validate the SQL Server instances:

1. In Management Studio, on the Object Explorer, click **Utility Explorer** to create the Utility Control Point (UCP).

2. The Introductory screen of the UCP wizard is presented as follows:

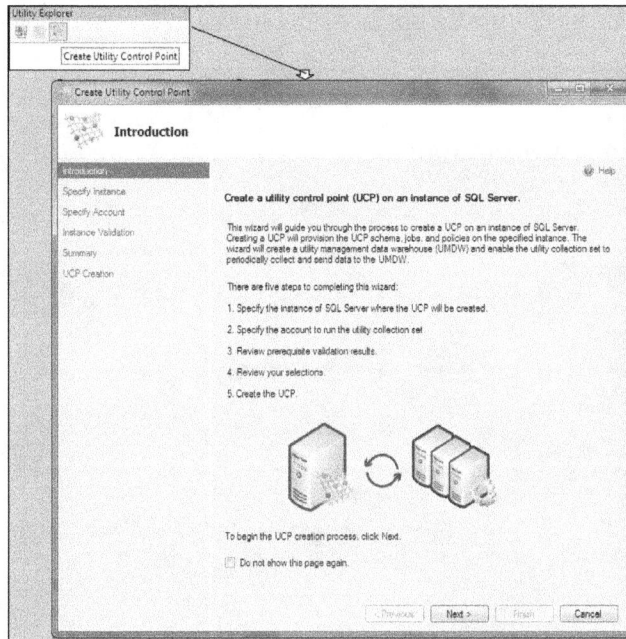

3. The next screen is to specify the instance of SQL Server where the new **Utility Control Point** will be configured.

4. This requires two values to be passed on, **SQL Server Instance Name** and **UCP Name** (circled text in the following screenshot):

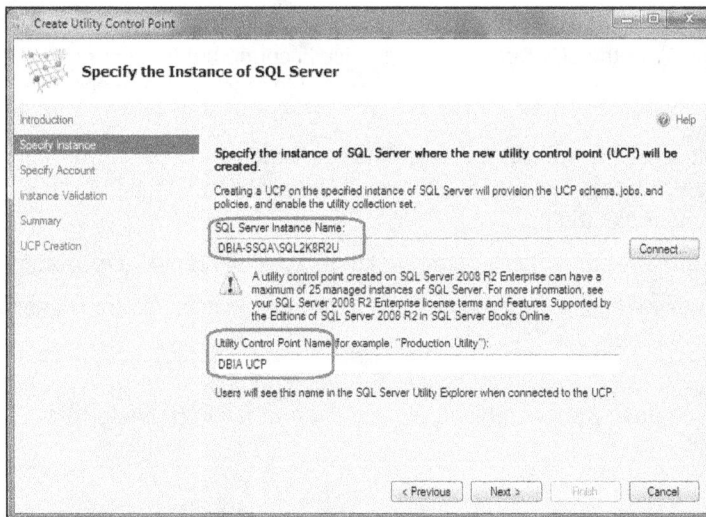

5. The next screen will be the **UCP Collection Set Account** that is essential to ensure that the utility collection has the required privileges to operate within a single Windows domain or across a domain with two-way trust relationships.

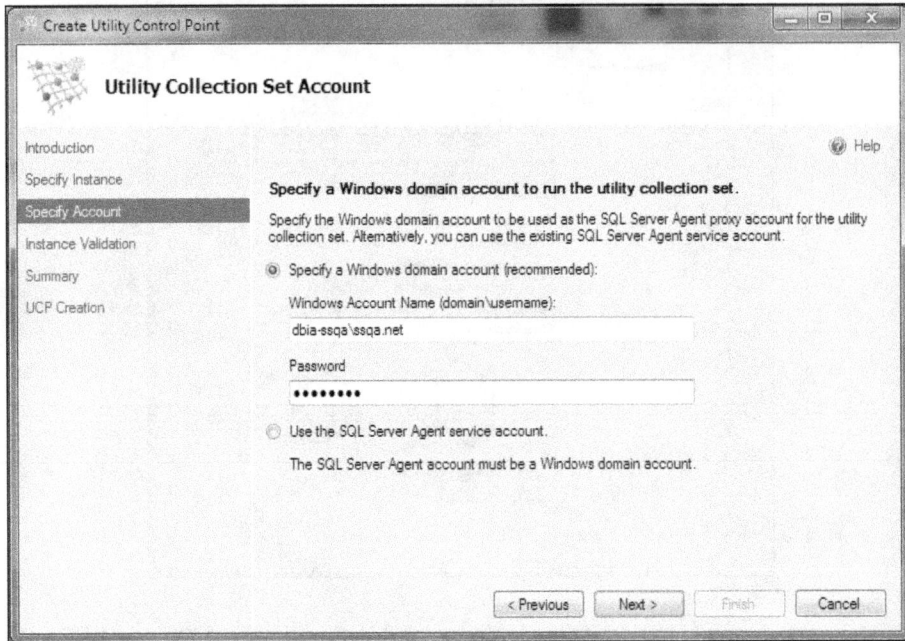

6. Also the SQL Server service account on UCP and all managed instances must have read permission to users in the `Active` Directory.

> To specify the account to collect data, you can choose the SQL Server Agent service account, but for security precautions it is recommended to propose a new account.

7. The next screen is the **SQL Server Instance Validation** screen that will run through 10 rules to validate (as shown in the next screenshot, which is processing these rules).

8. If there are any errors, click on the result that will present the reason for failure.

9. As soon as we fix the error, come back to the instance validation screen to **Rerun validation.**

10. Once the validation rules are successful, you can choose to save the report by clicking on **Save Report**, which will save information in HTML format.

11. Click **Next** to proceed.

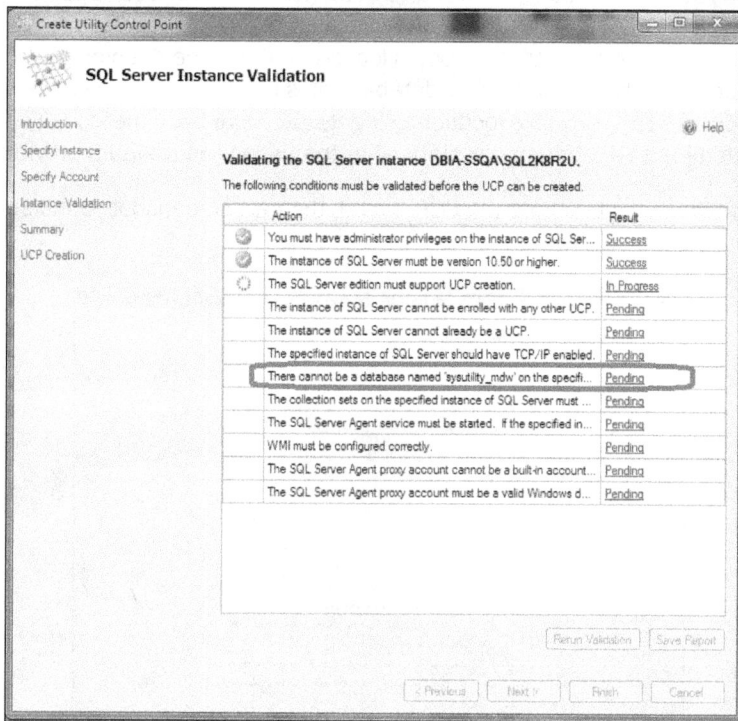

We should now have completed the process to manage a UMDW database that is formed once all the results of SQL Server instance validation process completes as **Success**.

How it works...

From the previous screenshot, if you look at the option, there cannot be a database named sysutility_mdw on the specified instance UMDW (Utility Management Data Warehouse) data file is sysutility_mdw. All the performance data and policies are stored in this database that helps to identify resource use bottlenecks and consolidation opportunities.

The UMDW name will be Sysutility_mdw_<GUID>_Data and SQL Server agent service will handle the data load collection frequency *every 15 minutes*.

> The configuration settings mentioned earlier, such as UMDW name and collection set upload frequency are not configurable in this release of SQL Server 2008 R2.

Whereas, the directory where UMDW files is stored are configurable. The default directory for UMDW is `<System drive>:\Program Files\Microsoft SQL Server\ MSSQL10_50.<UCP_Name>\MSSQL\Data\`, where `<System drive>` is normally the `C:\` drive. The log file, `UMDW_<GUID>_LOG`, is located in the same directory. Based on your environment security policy standards for database files location, you can choose to modify the UMDW (`sysutility_mdw`) file location using `detach/attach` method or `ALTER DATABASE` statement to a different directory other than specified (default) previously.

Continuing from the steps to create the UCP wizard, the next screenshot is the summary of UCP:

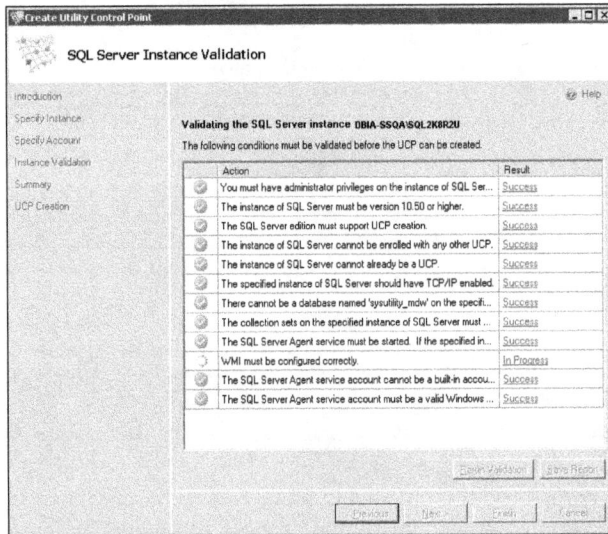

Once the UCP is configured successfully, the Utility Explorer presents the following screenshot.

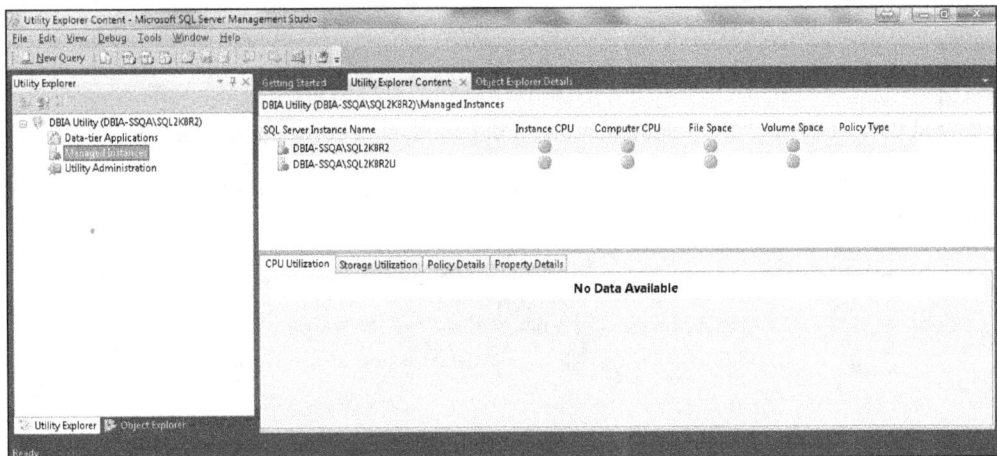

The Managed Instances node is presented as a tree view to access list view data and details tabs at the bottom of the content pane providing data for CPU and storage volume utilization, as well as access to policy definitions and property details for individual managed instances of SQL Server in the SQL Server Utility. Within the Managed Instances the default maximum values for instance processor utilization/computer process utilization/file space utilization is 70 percent that produces a trend of resource usage and the default minimum value for instance processor utilization/computer process utilization/file space is 0 percent.

Implementing Utility & Non-utility collection sets

The Utility information data collection set is installed and automatically started on each instance of SQL Server 2008 R2 when you complete the Utility Control Point (UCP) as we have seen in the previous recipes of this chapter. The data is stored in the UMDW database, which is created during the UCP creation. The SQL Server utility collection set is supported side-by-side with Utility collection sets and non-SQL Server utility collection sets. In this recipe, we will go through the implementation tasks to set up the UCP data collection sets for utility and non-utility categories.

SQL Server 2008 R2 introduces the Utility Control Point (UCP) with a set of pre-defined utility collection sets that are managed by UMDW. Similarly, SQL Server 2008 manages the data collection to monitor CPU, disk, and memory resources of an instance using a Data Collector that is managed by **Management Data Warehouse** (**MDW**). For this recipe, it is necessary to introduce the MDW feature that stands as a non-utility collection set. The Management Data Warehouse is a relational database that contains all the data that is retained. This database can be on the same system as the data collector, or it can be on another computer. The MDW collection set is run in one of the following collection and upload modes:

- ► **Non-cached mode**: Data collection and upload are on the same schedule. The packages start, collect, and upload data at their configured frequency, and run until they are finished. After the packages finish, they are unloaded from memory.

- ► **Cached mode**: Data collection and upload are on different schedules. The packages collect and cache data until they receive a signal to exit from a loop control-flow task. This ensures that the data flow can be executed repeatedly, which enables continuous data collection.

Getting ready

The new feature of SQL Server 2008 R2—Utility Control Point (UCP)—allows DBAs to set up and collect the utility collection sets. Once the instances are enrolled, the default capacity policies of utilization across the instances or applications are set. It is essential to check that you are using a SQL Server 2008 R2 instance to register the UCP to design the multi-server management feature.

How to do it...

Using SQL Server Management Studio, these are the steps to implement the utility and non-utility data collection sets:

1. To implement the utility data collection sets, connect to the **Utility Explorer** where the **UCP** is registered.

2. Right-click on **Managed Instances** and choose **Enroll instance** (refer to the next screenshot).

3. Specify the **instance name** of SQL Server to enroll.

4. Specify the **service account** to run the utility collection set.

> To specify the account to collect data, you can choose **SQL Server Agent** service account, but for security precautions, it is recommended to propose a new account or existing domain user account with the required privileges.

5. Review prerequisite validation results and selections.

6. Enroll the instance.

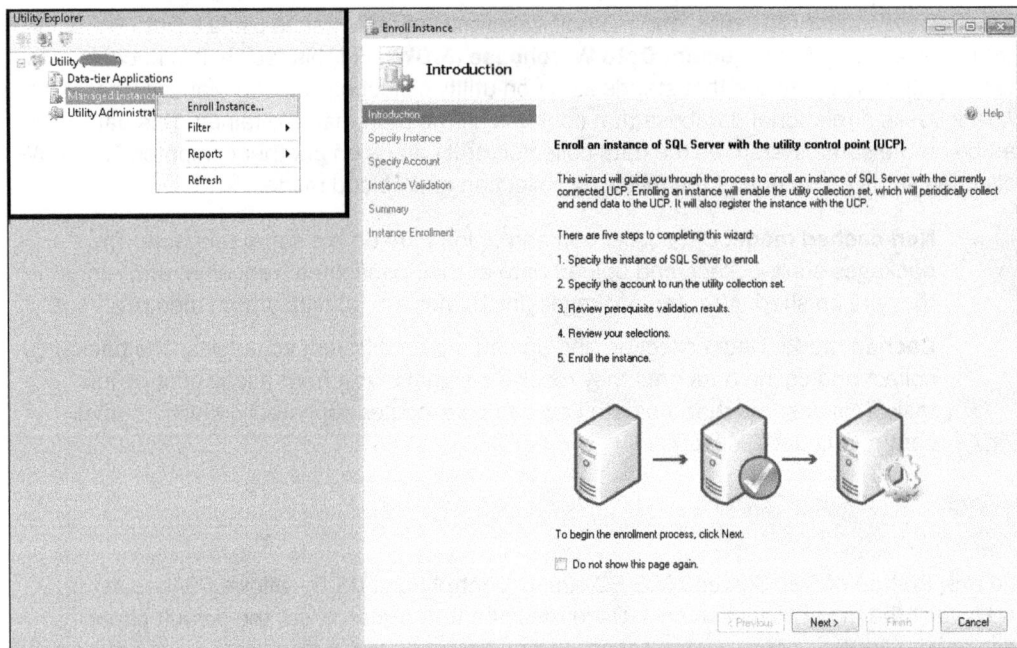

7. After completing the Enroll Instance wizard, click on the **Managed Instances** node in the Utility Explorer navigation pane.

8. On the right-hand side of the **Utility Explorer** content pane, the enrolled SQL Server instances are displayed.

9. Next, to implement the non-utility collection sets, from the **SSMS** tool, use the **Configure Management Data Warehouse** wizard to configure storage for collected data.

10. Create the management data warehouse. You can install the management data warehouse on the same instance of SQL Server that runs the data collector for the utility collection set.

11. Select the configuration task to install the predefined System Data collection sets.

12. Configure the MDW storage by selecting the SQL Server instance to host and collect the non-utility collection sets.

13. Map logins to management data warehouse roles.

14. Once you have completed the MDW wizard, the data collection information for utility and non-utility collection sets are displayed under the `Management` folder, as shown in the next screenshot:

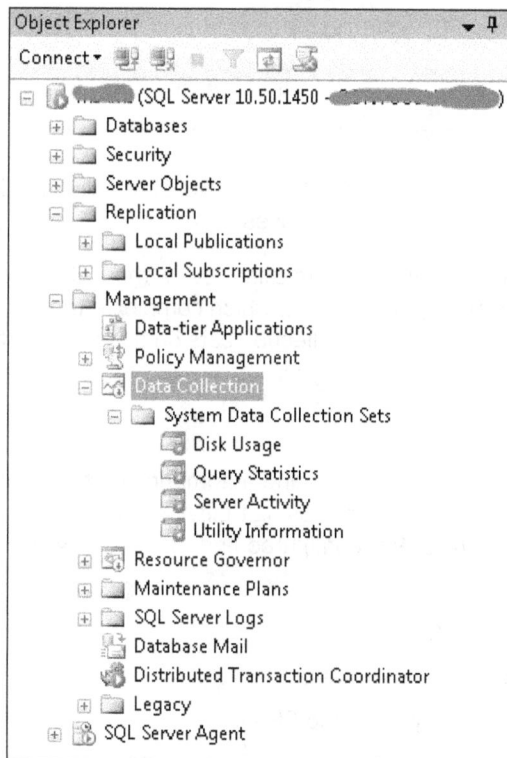

15. Before we proceed to enable the data collection, it is essential to restart and upload the non-utility collection sets to the `Data Collection`.

16. To upload and pass a validation of non-utility collection sets, execute the following TSQL from **Query Editor**:

    ```
    execmsdb.dbo.sp_syscollector_set_warehouse_database_name NULL
    execmsdb.dbo.sp_syscollector_set_warehouse_instance_name NULL
    ```

17. Under the `Management` folder, right-click on **Data Collection** and choose **Enable the data collector** from SSMS, which is shown in the following screenshot:

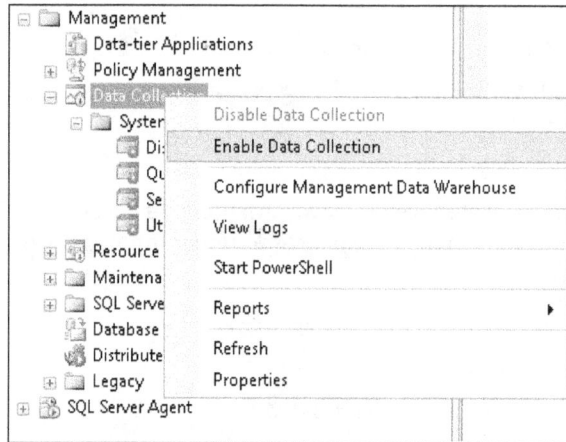

18. Once we have completed the MDW wizard, the data collection information will be stored in the data warehouse databases.

To ensure that both the utility collection sets exist, review the **Data Collection** option from SSMS, as shown in the preceding screenshot, which completes the process as a successful implementation of utility and non-utility collection sets on the same instance.

How it works...

The utility data collection sets are installed and automatically started on each instance of SQL Server 2008 R2 when they are configured using Utility Control Point. The UMDW database is created on the instance where UCP is configured and the following collection set and items are stored:

▶   Utility Information—DAC Information

▶   Utility Information—SMO Information

▶   Utility Information—Utility Allocated CPU Info

▶   Utility Information—Utility CPU-Memory Related Info

- Utility Information—Utility Database FilesInfo
- Utility Information—Utility Performance Counters Items
- Utility Information—Utility Performance Counters Items1
- Utility Information—Utility Volumes Information

The non-utility data collection sets are installed when MDW wizard is completed, but not started until they are enabled. The required schemas and their objects for the pre-defined system collect sets are created when MDW is configured. The various UCP and MDW jobs are created under **SQL Server Agent | Jobs** folder as follows:

- **collection_set_1_noncached_collect_and_upload**
- **collection_set_2_collection**
- **collection_set_2_upload**
- **collection_set_3_collection**
- **collection_set_3_upload**
- **collection_set_4_noncached_collect_and_upload**
- **mdw_purge_data_[MDW]**
- **sysutility_get_cache_tables_data_into_aggregate_tables_daily**
- **sysutility_get_views_data_into_cache_tables**
- **sysutility_mi_collect_performance**
- **sysutility_get_cache_tables_data_into_aggregate_tables_hourly**
- **syspolicy_purge_history**
- **sysutility_mi_collect_and_upload**
- **mdw_purge_data_[sysutility_mdw]**

The core schema is prefixed by 'core', which describes the tables, stored procedures, and views that are used to manage and identify the collected data. These objects are locked and can only be modified by the owner of the MDW database.

The parallel management of SQL Server Utility collection sets (utility and non-utility) requires a preparation on the instance where UCP information is stored and the best practice is to customize the data-collection frequency to avoid any overlap with the MDW data collection schedule. The data collection store contains server activity for all the instances that are configured to manage and host the operating system, such as percent CPU, memory usage, disk I/O usage, network usage, SQL Server waits, and SQL Server activity.

Designing and refreshing a Scalable Shared database

Designing a **Scalable Shared Database** (**SSD**) feature in SQL Server 2008 R2, allows the DBAs to scale out a read-only database (reporting database), which is a copy of a production database, built exclusively for reporting purposes. SSD feature has been part of SQL Server from 2005 Enterprise Edition onwards, that has been enhanced since SQL Server 2008 and this is supported in Enterprise edition and Data Center editions only. To host this reporting database, the disk volumes must be dedicated and read-only, and the scalable shared database feature will permit the smooth update process from production database to the reporting database.

The internals behind such a process of building or refreshing a reporting database are known as the build phase or refresh phase, depending on whether a new reporting database is being built or a stale reporting database is being refreshed. The validity of a scalable shared database begins from building a reporting database on a set of reporting volumes and that reporting data eventually becomes too outdated to be useful, which means that the stale database requires a data-refresh as part of each update cycle. Refreshing a stale reporting database involves either updating its data or building a completely new, fresh version of the database. This scalability feature is supported in Enterprise Edition and Data Center editions only. This recipe will cover how to design and refresh a reporting database that is intended for use as a scalable shared database.

Getting ready

Keeping the reporting database refreshed is a prerequisite as part of each update cycle. The key aspect of having an updated reporting database can be achieved by using the data-copy method, which requires the following:

> ▸ Create or copy a database by designing a `SSIS` package to use. `Execute SQL Task` method or `Transfer Database task` method.

> ▸ From SSMS, use SQL Server Import and Export wizard to copy required objects for the reporting purpose.

> ▸ Restore a backup of the production database into the reporting volume, which will involve a full database backup file to be used.

> ▸ The essential components such as, SAN storage hardware, processing environment, and data access environment must be used. The reporting database must have the same layout as the production database, so we need to use the same drive letter for the reporting volume and the same directory path for the database.

Additionally, verify that the reporting servers and the associated reporting database are running on identical platforms.

How to do it...

To design and refresh a reporting database, you will need to complete the following steps on the production SQL Server instance:

1. Unmask the **Logical Unit Number** (**LUN**) on the disks where the Production database is stored. (Refer to the hardware vendor's manual).

2. Mount each reporting volume and mark it as read-write.

3. Obtain the disk volume information. Logon remotely to the server and open a command prompt window to run the following:

    `DiskPart` **list volumes**

4. Use the `DiskPart` utility to mount the volumes, then on that command prompt window run the following:

    `DISKPART`

5. The `DiskPart` utility will open a prompt for you to enter the following commands:

    `DISKPART> select volume=<drive-number>`

    `DISKPART> assign letter=<drive-letter>`

    `DISKPART> attribute clear readonly`

    `DISKPART> exit`

    > The `<drive-number>` is the volume number assigned by the Windows operating system.
    >
    > The `<drive-letter>` is the letter assigned to the reporting volume.

6. To ensure that data files are accessible and disks are correctly mounted, list the contents of the directory using the following command from the command prompt:

    `DIR <drive-letter>:\<database directory>`

7. As we are refreshing an existing reporting database, attach the database to that server instance using SSMS. On **Query Editor,** enter the following TSQL statements:

    `ALTER DATABASE AdventureWorks2008R2 SET READ_WRITE`

    `GO`

    `ALTER DATABASE AdventureWorks2008R2`

    `SET RECOVERY FULL, PAGE_VERIFY CHECKSUM;`

    `GO`

8. Detach the database from that server instance using the `sp_detach_db` statement from **Query Editor.**

9. Now, we have to mark each reporting volume as read-only and dismount from the server. Go to the command prompt window and enter the following commands:

```
DiskPart
DISKPART> select volume=<drive-number>
DISKPART> attribute set readonly
DISKPART> remove
DISKPART> exit
```

10. To ensure that the reporting volume is read-only, you should attempt to create a file on the volume. This attempt must return an error.

11. Next, go to the command prompt window and enter the following commands:

```
DiskPart
DISKPART> select volume=<drive-number>
DISKPART> assign letter = <drive letter>
DISKPART> exit
```

> The `<drive-letter>` is the letter assigned to the reporting volume.

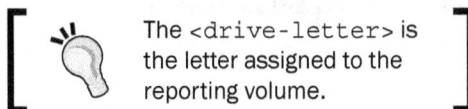

12. Attach the database to one or more server instances on each of the reporting servers using the `sp_attach_db` statement or SSMS tool.

13. Now, the reporting database is made available as a scalable shared database to process the queries from the application.

These steps complete the process of building and refreshing the scalable shared database feature by mounting the reporting database volumes.

How it works...

Using the available hardware vendor-specific servers and disk volumes, the scalable shared database features allow the application to scale out a read-only database built exclusively for reporting purposes.

The 'build' phase is the process of mounting the reporting volume on the production server and building the reporting database. After the reporting database is built on the volume, using the defined `data-copy` methods, the data is updated. Once it is completed, the process of setting each reporting volume to read-only and dismount begins.

The 'attach' phase is the process of making the reporting database available as a scalable shared database. After the reporting database is built on a set of reporting volumes, the volumes are marked as read-only and mounted across multiple reporting servers. The individual reporting server service instance will use the reporting database that is attached.

There's more...

The Scalable Shared Database feature's best practice recommendation:

- ▶ On the basis of hardware, there is no limit on the number of server instances per database; however, for the shared database configuration, ensure that a maximum of eight servers per database are hosted.

- ▶ The SQL Server instance collation and sort order must be similar across all the instances.

- ▶ If the relational or reporting database is spread across the shared servers, then ensure to test and deploy a synchronized update then a rolling update of the scalable shared database.

- ▶ Also, scaling out this solution is possible in SQL Server 2008 Analysis Services with the Read-Only Database capability.

Managing SQL Server Replication processes

Whenever we talk about managing SQL Server replication processes, the best practice is to configure the replication using scripts for better control, using the Replication along with other high-availability features and Dynamic Management Views to obtain a glimpse of system resource usage. In this recipe, we will look at the three processes that are important when managing the SQL Server replication environment effectively.

Scripting the replication process helps to retain the steps to install replication in case you experience a disaster recovery process. The replication script process can be achieved by using replication wizard dialog boxes from SQL Server Management Studio, by using **Replication Management Objects** (**RMO**) concepts or by obtaining information using TSQL statements.

In this recipe, we will work on TSQL methods to manage the SQL Server replication process. Using TSQL methods, gives you more control over the underlying objects generated by the replication services.

How to do it...

To begin the process of managing the SQL Server replication processes, follow these steps:

1. Assuming that you have set up the Distributor and Publisher servers, a script can be executed using **Query Editor** in SSMS.

2. To capture relevant information about the publisher name, which is used in other scripts below, ensure that you use a variable:

```
DECLARE @publisher_namesysname
set @publisher_name = (select name from msdb..MSdistpublishers
where
name=@@servername);
SELECT @publisher_name;
```

3. Drop the publisher, local distributor, and distribution database, by entering the following code:

```
--Are there other Publishers using this Distributor?
execsp_get_distributor;
execsp_dropdistpublisher @publisher=@publisher_name,@no_checks=0;
declare @distributiondb as sysname;
set @distributiondb = (select name from sys.sysdatabases where name
='distribution');

execsp_dropdistributiondb @distributiondb;

execsp_dropdistributor;
go
```

4. Now configure the distributor server and publisher server configuration using the following TSQL script:

```
Use master
go
/* Obtain default instance name as  the Distributor*/
declare @distributor as sysname = convert(sysname,
serverproperty('servername'));
/*Set the @distributorserver_msg variable */
declare @distributorserver_msg as varchar(50)='The name of the
Distributor server.';
SELECT @distributorserver_msg + ' ' +@distributor;
/* Add the Distributor */
execsp_adddistributor @distributor=@distributor;
/* Install the distribution database on the default directory to
use Windows authentication */
declare @distributiondb as sysname ='distribution';
execsp_adddistributiondb@database=@distributiondb,@security_
mode=1;
go
```

5. Let us change the history retention period and maximum retention period:

```
-- Change the history retention period to 24 hours and the
-- maximum retention period to 48 hours.
USE distribution
EXEC sp_changedistributiondb @distributionDB, N'history_
retention', 24
EXEC sp_changedistributiondb @distributionDB, N'max_
distretention', 48
GO
```

6. All the steps are using the script method process, which is similar to how we use a Replication wizard from SSMS. The representation of step 4 is shown in the following screenshot:

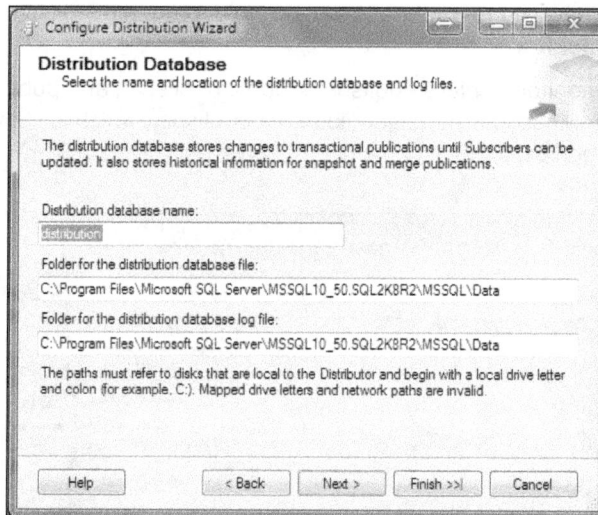

7. Next, we must set the `security_mode` to configure on the publisher server:

```
DECLARE @distributor as sysname= convert (sysname,serverproperty('
servername'));
DECLARE @publisher as sysname;
DECLARE @publisherserver_msg as varchar (50)= 'PublisherServer';
/*Set the Publisher server. Note that both publisher &
distributor will reside on same server */
SET @publisher =@distributor;
SELECT @publisherserver_msg +' '+ @publisher;


USE distributionDB
DECLARE @distributiondb as sysname='distribution';
```

```
EXEC sp_adddistpublisher @publisher, @security_mode=1,
@distribution_db=@distributiondb,
@publisher_type = 'MSSQLSERVER';
```

8. Let us change the history retention period and maximum retention period:

```
-- Change the history retention period to 24 hours and the
-- maximum retention period to 48 hours.
USE distribution
EXEC sp_changedistributiondb @distributionDB, N'history_
retention', 24
EXEC sp_changedistributiondb @distributionDB, N'max_
distretention', 48
GO
```

9. From SSMS, navigate to the `Replication` folder and right-click to choose **Launch replication monitor**.

10. Replication monitor displays Publisher groups, publisher, and publications. In order to view such data, we should add a publisher, which is shown in the following screenshot:

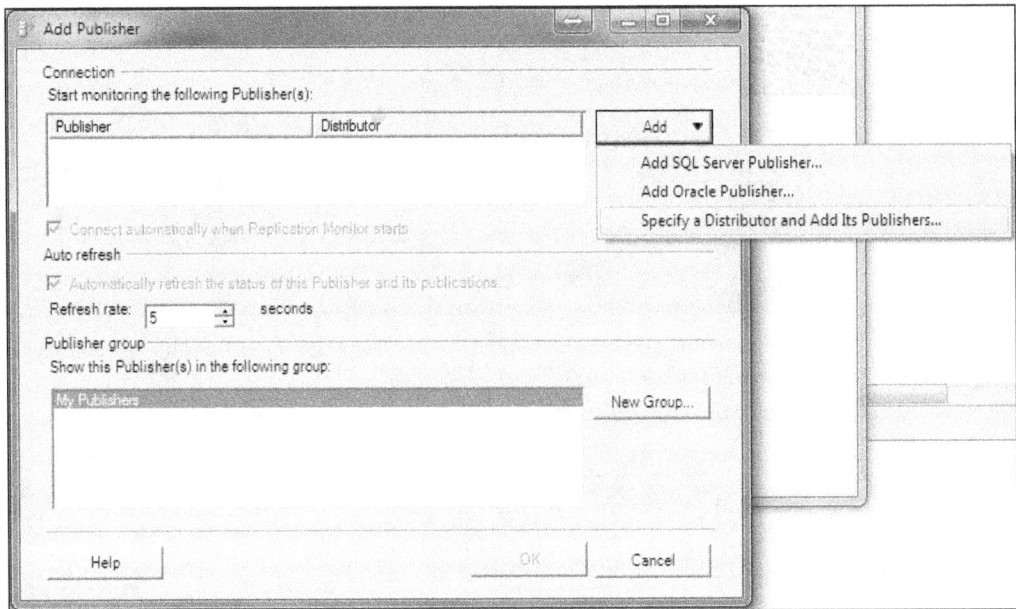

11. The ability to monitor the replication topology is restricted to `SYSADMIN` fixed server role member in addition to the `db_owner` fixed database role.

12. Let us add a user to the `replmonitor` fixed database role on the distributor, from Query Editor by executing the following TSQL statements:

```
CREATEUSER [user_name] FORLOGIN [user_name] WITH
DEFAULT_SCHEMA=[dbo]
GO
EXEC sp_addrolememberN'db_datareader',N'user_name'
GO
EXEC sp_addrolememberN'db_denydatawriter',N'user_name'
GO
USE [distribution]
GO
EXEC sp_addrolememberN'replmonitor',N'user_name'
GO
USE [distribution]
GO
ALTER AUTHORIZATION ON SCHEMA::[db_owner] TO [user_name]
GO
EXEC sp_addrolememberN'db_owner',N'user_name'
GO
```

13. From the previous TSQL statements, the information is now added, which is visible on the left pane of replication monitor (see the next screenshot):

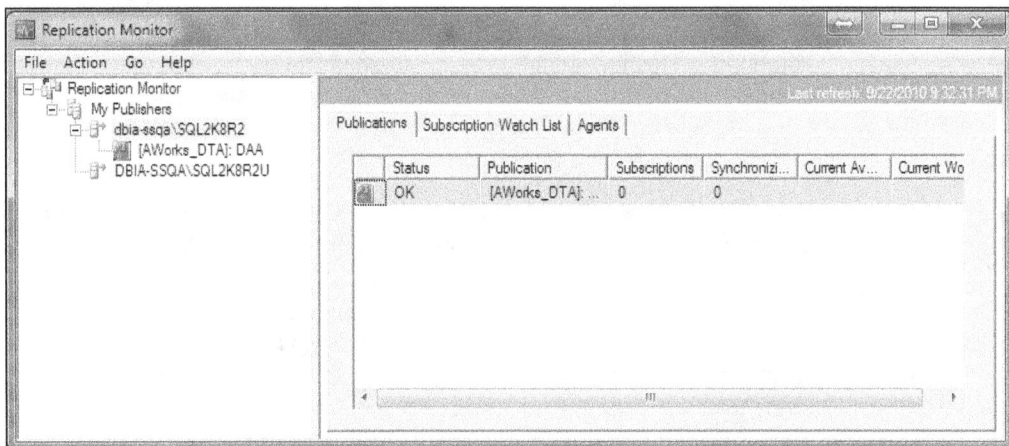

14. The Replication Monitor displays information about the publisher on three tables: **Publications** tab, **Subscription** watch list, and **agents** tab.

15. The **publications** tab provides summary information for all publications at the publisher. The **subscription** watch list is intended to display subscriptions from all publications available at the selected publisher.

16. Further to the replication monitor, the TSQL method also provides the DMVs with the ability to obtain information on the replication process latency. The useful DMVs to manage the replication process information are as follows:

- ❑ `sys.dm_repl_articles`
- ❑ `sys.dm_repl_schemas`
- ❑ `sys.dm_repl_traninfo`
- ❑ `sys.dm_repl_tranhash`

17. Finally, the **agents** tab delivers the status of each replication agent and job that are used by all types of replication, with an additional feature allowance to start and stop each agent and job.

This completes the set of required steps to manage the SQL Server replication process using the scripting feature in SSMS.

How it works...

SQL Server Replication Monitor is designed to monitor the replication processes and the queries that Replication Monitor uses to perform calculations and gather data that is cached and refreshed on a periodic basis. The tool can be invoked from the command line from the folder `\Program Files\Microsoft SQL Server\100\Tools\Binn\sqlmonitor.exe`.

The main **Replication Monitor** window (including all tabs), automatically refreshes by default every five seconds. Automatic refreshes do not force a refresh of the cache. The user interface displays the most recent version of the data from the cache. You can customize the refresh rate used for all windows associated with a Publisher by editing the Publisher settings. You can also disable automatic refreshes for a Publisher.

Cache refresh is handled by an SQL Server Agent job and the Replication monitoring refresher for distribution. The job runs continuously, but the cache refresh schedule is based on waiting for a certain amount of time after the previous refresh. The Replication Monitor detail windows are not automatically refreshed by default, with the exception of windows related to the subscriptions that are synchronizing. By default, all the windows in Replication Monitor can be refreshed by using the *F5* function key, or by right-clicking a node in the **Replication Monitor** tree and clicking **Refresh**. Manual refreshes force a refresh of the cache.

Implementing security for SQL Server Agent jobs management

The integrity of the data is only as good as your ability to secure the data platform. Typically, security doesn't stop in authentication and authorization to access the SQL Server. The additional process of encrypting data and providing a secured backup system is essential. Similarly, scheduling such data management activities is carried over using SQL Server Agent service. An SQL Agent job is a complex database object with many details involved in the definition. There are even more details to consider while a job is actually running, but it's not convenient to examine the details for SQL Agent jobs using SSMS and the filtering is less than ideal.

In this recipe, we will be implementing security for SQL Server Agent Jobs management by using the credentials and proxy methods. A credential is a record that contains the authentication information required to connect to a resource outside of SQL Server. A proxy is really just the mapping of an SQL Server credential to a specific type of SQL Server Agent operation. The SQL Server Agent service manages many different objects on the server, each one responsible for its own function in the larger automation infrastructure. Mastering these objects is critical to effectively implement an automation plan.

The key aspect of securing the SQL Server Agent service is proxies and assigning a login to start the agent service. Although most of the processing that an SQL Server Agent automation structure will perform will be directed to SQL Server objects, a situation might arise in which actions require access to resources that are outside of SQL Server at the operating system level. In this case, authentication and permissions can be a problem. As the agent is an important service that performs the necessary tasks for automated administration, you must also restrict permissions to the minimum to perform the actions.

Getting ready

The SQL Server Agent offers the security context for a job through a proxy without having elevated privileges for the users, not all SQL Server Agent jobs require a proxy. Each proxy corresponds to a security credential that can be associated with a set of subsystems and a set of logins. The proxy can be used only for job steps that use a subsystem associated with the proxy. To create a job step that uses a specific proxy, the job owner must either use a login associated with that proxy or be a member of a role with unrestricted access to proxies.

This process occurs in two steps:

▸ Firstly, you must create the credential at the server level
▸ Secondly, you must map that credential to a proxy, which specifies the contexts and operation types with which you are allowed to use the credential

[For more information on SQL Server agent services refer to the *Designing automated administration practices* recipe mentioned in *Chapter 2, Administration of core database engine*.]

This will provide a trusted authentication identity for the tasks within SQL Server as well as a Windows identity for tasks outside SQL Server. Since this is a security object, you will create the credential from the security section in the Object Explorer of the SSMS.

How to do it...

To begin implementing security for SQL Server Agent Jobs, let us go through the required steps to create a credential as follows:

1. Open the SQL Server Management Studio and connect to the SQL Server instance.

2. Locate the **Security node** in the Object Explorer. Expand the node and locate the **Credentials** node inside.

3. Right-click the **Credentials** node and select **New Credential** from the menu. Provide a name for your credential in the **CredentialName** text box.

4. Enter the name of the Windows account that you wish to map in the **Identity text box**.

5. Enter and confirm the password of the Windows account (as shown in the next screenshot). The system will use this password when it attempts to authenticate under this identity.

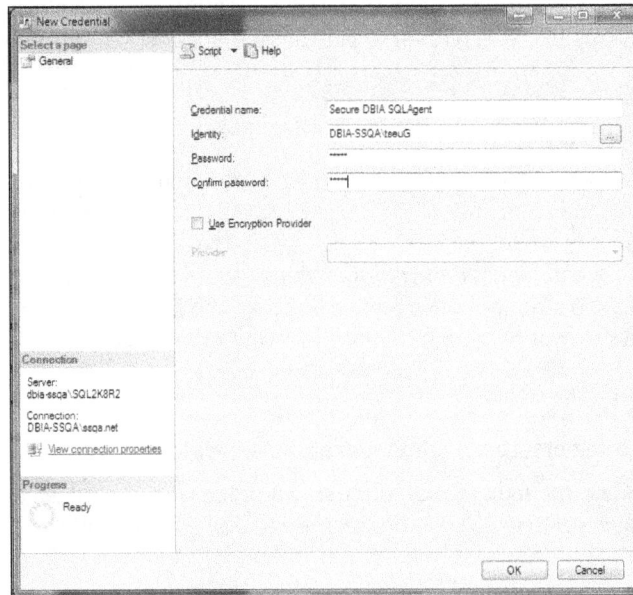

6. Click **OK** to accept the settings.

7. We should see the new credential in the list in the Object Explorer.

8. The steps we followed using GUI tool can be accomplished by using the following TSQL statement:

```
--Implementing SQL Server Agent security
--Creating a SQLAgent credential
USE [master]
GO
CREATECREDENTIAL [Secure DBIA SQL Agent] WITHIDENTITY=N'DBIA-SSQA\
tseuG', SECRET=N'Guest'
GO
```

9. Locate the **SQL Server Agent** node in the Object Explorer. Expand the node and locate the **Proxies** node.

10. If you expand the **Proxies** node, you will see a list of **SQL Server Agent task types**. Any proxy that you have configured for a specific task type will appear in the node list associated with that task.

11. Right-click the **Proxies node** and select **New Proxy** from the menu to open the **New Proxy Account** dialog.

12. Enter a **name** for the proxy in the **Proxy Name** text box.

13. Now enter the name of the previously created credential in the **Credential Name** text box.

14. Select the tasks (refer to the following screenshot) for which you want this proxy to authenticate. If you click the **Subsystem** check box, all tasks will get selected.

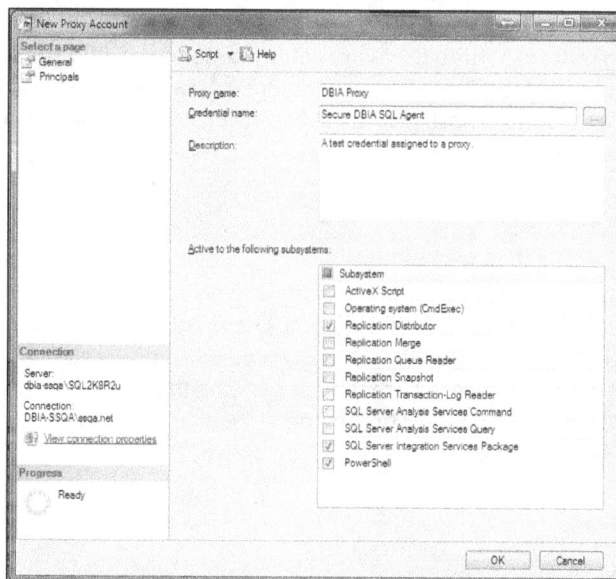

15. Click the **OK** button to accept the settings.

16. For this recipe, we have chosen only 3 task types: **Replication Distributor**, **SQL Server Integration Package**, and **PowerShell**.

We now have successfully created the credential and proxy account to implement security for SQL Server Agent Jobs management using the SSMS tool.

How it works...

Proxy provides the SQL Server Agent service with access to the security credentials for a Windows user without having a need to assign elevated privileges for the users. A job step that uses a proxy can access the specified job subsystems (as we assigned previously) by using the security context.

SQL Server Agent checks the subsystem access for a proxy and gives access to the proxy each time the job step runs. If the proxy no longer has access to the subsystem, the job step fails. The end result of the job can be obtained by referring to the corresponding job details, right-click on **job | view history**. Similarly, we can query `sysJobHistory` table, which contains information about the execution of scheduled jobs by SQL Server Agent. Otherwise, SQL Server Agent impersonates the user that is specified in the proxy and runs the job step. However, when you have a job step that executes TSQL, then it will not use SQL Server Agent proxies, instead TSQL job steps run in the security context of the owner of the job. To avoid any errors or interruption to that job step due to the job owner permissions, you can set the security context for that TSQL job step using `sp_add_jobstep` stored procedure by the passing value to `database_user_name` parameter.

The user specified within the credentials and proxy creation must have permission to connect to that instance of SQL Server. A user must have access to a proxy to use the proxy in a job step. Access can be granted to three types of security principals: **SQL Server logins**, **Server roles**, and **Roles** within the MSDB database. Additionally, if a new job is specified in the credentials, then that user must have `Log on as a batch job` Windows security permission on the computer on which SQL Server is running.

There's more...

In case your SQL Server instance is upgraded from version 2000 to 2008, or 2008 R2, during the upgrade process, all the user proxy accounts that existed on SQL Server 2000 will be changed to the temporary global proxy account `UpgradedProxyAccount`. This temporary global proxy account will have access to those subsystems that were explicitly used, and will not have access to all subsystems after upgrading.

In order to use SQL Server Agent service, the users must be a member of one or more of msdb fixed database roles: `SQLAgentUserRole`, `SQLAgentReaderRole`, or `SQLAgentOperatorRole`. These additional roles are stored in the msdb system database. Users require membership in these roles and it must be granted explicitly. Users who are members of the `sysadmin` fixed server role have full access to SQL Server Agent, and do not need to be a member of these fixed database roles to use SQL Server Agent. If a user is not a member of one of these database roles, or of the `sysadmin` role, the SQL Server Agent node is not available to them when they connect to SQL Server by using SQL Server Management Studio.

See Also

For more information on SQL Server agent service refer to the *Designing automated administration practices* recipe mentioned in *Chapter 2, Administration of Core Database Engine*.

Multiserver Management Using Utility Explorer

SQL Server 2008 R2 improves the ability to manage multiple servers centrally with UCP. The UCP collects configuration and performance information that includes database file space utilization, CPU utilization, and storage volume utilization from each enrolled instance. Using Utility Explorer helps you to troubleshoot the resource health issues identified by SQL Server UCP. The issues might include mitigating over-utilized CPU on a single instance or multiple instances.

UCP also helps in reporting troubleshooting information using SQL Server Utility on issues that might include resolving a failed operation to enroll an instance of SQL Server with a UCP, troubleshooting failed data collection resulting in gray icons in the managed instance list view on a UCP, mitigating performance bottlenecks, or resolving resource health issues.

In order to manage multiple instances efficiently, there are certain settings available within the Utility Explorer tool. In this recipe, we will focus on how to manage multiple instances using Utility Explorer by setting global policies for data-tier applications (DAC), and managed instances.

Getting ready

The UCP and all managed instances of SQL Server must satisfy the following prerequisites:

- UCP SQL Server instance version must be **SQL Server 2008 SP2** [10.00.4000.00] or higher
- The managed instances must be a database engine only and the edition must be Datacenter or Enterprise on a production environment

- ▶ UCP managed account must operate within a single Windows domain or domains with two-way trust relationships

- ▶ The SQL Server service accounts for UCP and managed instances must have read permission to Users in **Active Directory**

To set up the SQL Server Utility you need to:

- ▶ Create a UCP from the SQL Server Utility

- ▶ Enroll data-tier applications

- ▶ Enroll instances of SQL Server with the UCP

- ▶ Define Global and Instance level policies, and manage and monitor the instances.

Since the UCP itself becomes a managed instance automatically, once the UCP wizard is completed, the Utility Explorer content will display a graphical view of various parameters, as follows:

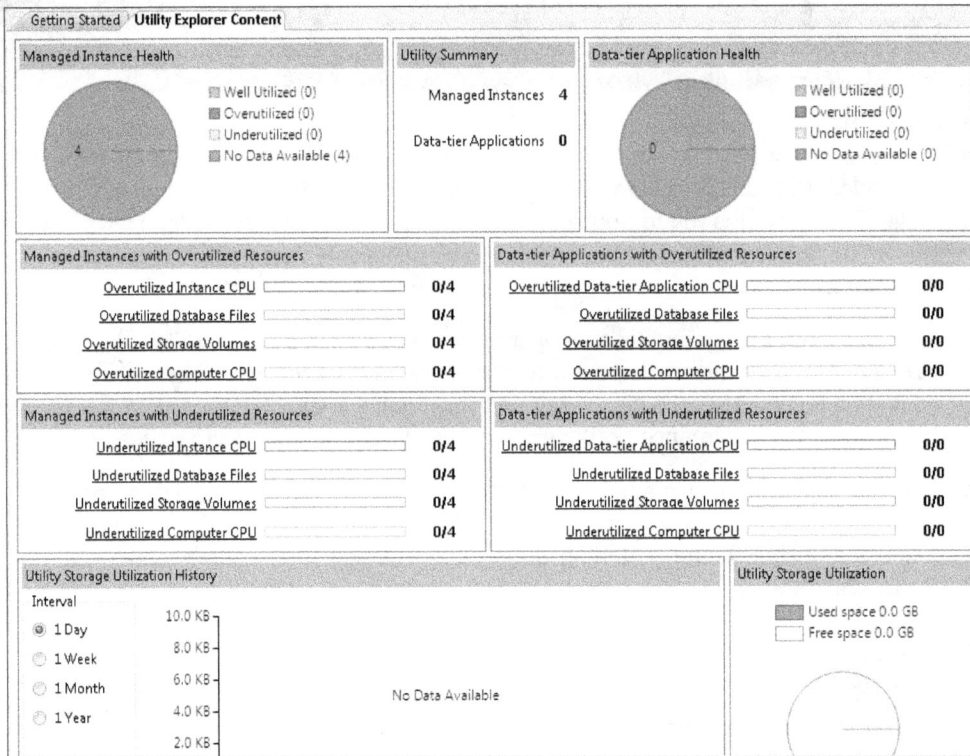

How to do it...

To define the global and instance level policies to monitor the multiple instances, use the **Utility Explorer** from SSMS tool and complete the following steps:

1. Click on **Utility Explorer**; populate the server that is registered as utility control point.

2. On the right-hand screen, click on the **Utility Administration** pane.

3. The evaluable time period and tolerance for percent violations are configurable using **Policy** tab settings.

4. The default upper threshold utilization is 70 percent for CPU, data file space, and storage volume utilization values. To change the policies use the slider-controls (up or down) to the right of each policy description.

5. For this recipe, we have modified the upper thresholds for CPU utilization as 50 percent and data file space utilization as 80 percent. We have also reduced the upper limit for the storage volume utilization parameter.

6. The default lower threshold utilization is 0 percent for CPU, data file space, and storage volume utilization values. To change the policies, use the slider-controls (up only) to the right of each policy description.

> For this recipe, we have modified (increased) the lower threshold for CPU utilization to 5 percent.

7. Once the threshold parameters are changed, click **Apply** to take into effect. For the default system settings, either click on the **Restore Defaults** button or the **Discard** button, as shown in the following screenshot:

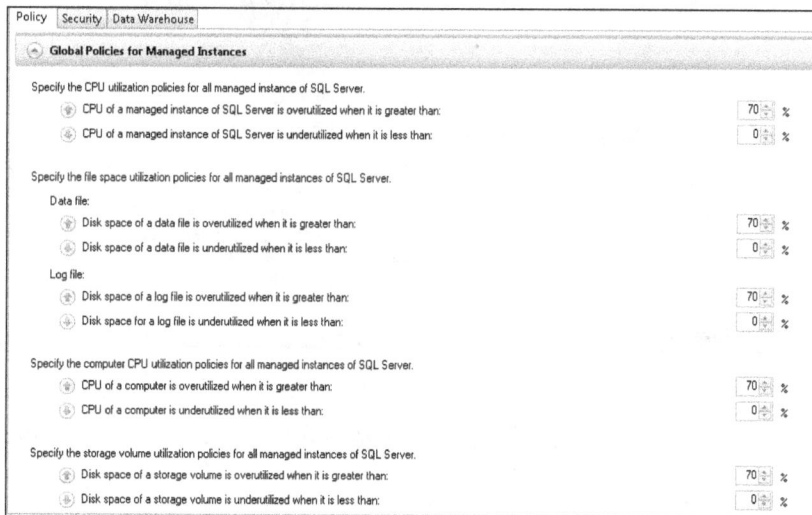

Now, let us test whether the defined global policies are working or not.

1. From the Query Editor, open a new connection against SQL instances, which is registered as **Managed Instance** on UCP, and execute the following time-intensive TSQL statements:

```
create table test (
    x int not null,
    y char(896) not null default (''),
    z char(120) not null default('')
)
go
insert test (x)
select r
  from
(
selectrow_number() over (order by (select 1)) r
  from master..spt_values a, master..spt_values b
) p
where r <= 4000000
go
create clustered index ix_x on test (x, y)
  with fillfactor=51
go
```

2. The script will simulate a data load process that will lead into a slow performance on managed SQL instance. After a few minutes, right-click on the Managed Instances option on Utility Explorer, which will produce the following screenshot of managed instances:

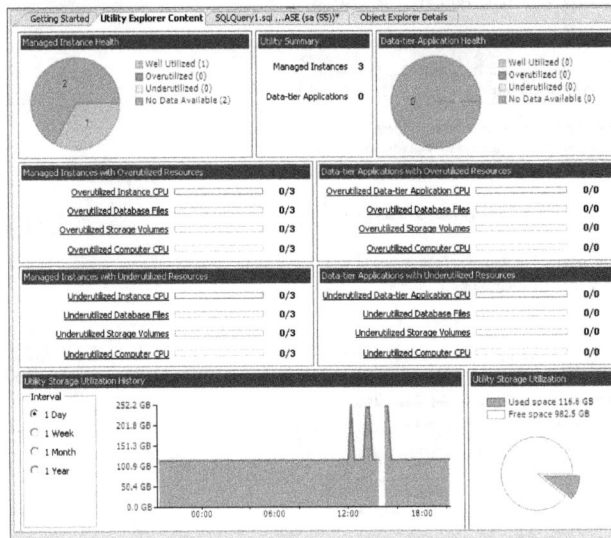

3. In addition to the snapshot of utilization information, click on the **Managed Instances** option on Utility Explorer to obtain information on over-utilized database files on an individual instance (see the next screenshot):

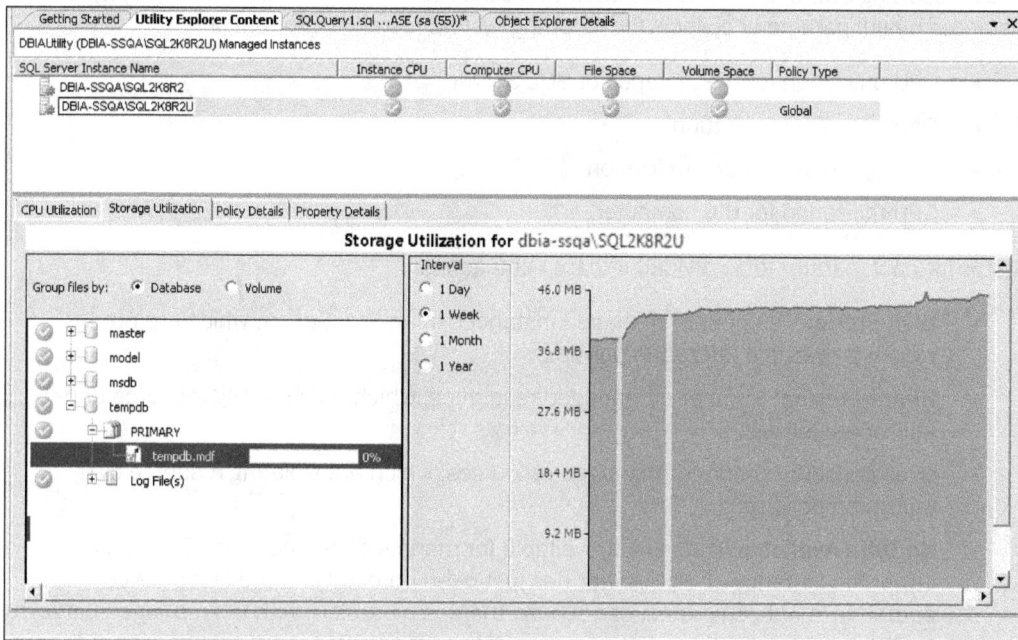

We should now have completed the strategic steps to manage multiple instances using the Utility Explorer tool.

How it works...

The unified view of instances from Utility Explorer is the starting point of application and multi-server management that helps the DBAs to manage the multiple instances efficiently.

Within the UCP, each managed instance of SQL Server is instrumented with a data collection set that queries configuration and performance data and stores it back in UMDW on the UCP every 15 minutes. By default, the data-tier applications automatically become managed by the SQL Server utility. Both of these entities are managed and monitored based on the global policy definitions or individual policy definitions.

Troubleshooting resource health issues identified by an SQL Server UCP might include mitigating over-utilized CPU on a computer on an instance of SQL Server, or mitigating over-utilized CPU for a data-tier application. Other issues might include resolving over-utilized file space for database files or resolving over-utilization of allocated disk space on a storage volume. The managed instances health parameter collects the following system resource information:

- CPU utilization for the instance of SQL Server
- Database files utilization
- Storage volume space utilization
- CPU utilization for the computer

Status for each parameter is divided into four categories:

- **Well-utilized**: Number of managed instances of an SQL Server, which are not violating resource utilization policies.
- **Under-utilized**: Number of managed resources, which are violating resource under-utilization policies.
- **Over-utilized**: Number of managed resources, which are violating resource over-utilization policies.
- **No Data Available**: Data is not available for managed instances of SQL Server as either the instance of SQL Server has just been enrolled and the first data collection operation is not completed, or because there is a problem with the managed instance of SQL Server collecting and uploading data to the UCP.

The data collection process begins immediately, but it can take up to 30 minutes for data to appear in the dashboard and viewpoints in the Utility Explorer content pane. However, the data collection set for each managed instance of an SQL Server will send relevant configuration and performance data to the UCP every 15 minutes.

4
Administering Core Business Intelligence Services

In this chapter, we will cover:

- ▶ Preparing and Installing SQL Server Analysis Services
- ▶ Implementing Scale-Out of SQL Server Analysis Services
- ▶ Administering SQL Server Reporting Services
- ▶ Implementing Scale-Out deployment of SQL Server Reporting Services
- ▶ Preparing and Installing SQL Server Integration Services
- ▶ Managing the ETL process efficiently

Introduction

Business Intelligence (BI) is a method of storing and presenting key enterprise data. Effective BI allows end users to use data to understand and provides the enterprise users with reliable, timely information (reporting), and prediction analysis (trends) for improved decision-making.

Most of the BI related projects are complex, involving business processes and developers to build a solution. These projects usually involve building a huge back-end data store, which is referred to as dimensions, cubes, and data mining models. The other aspect of the BI solution is to use appropriate user interfaces (UI), which must be configured or developed if necessary. To prevent further complexities when implementing solutions using BI concepts, Microsoft has placed new enhancements within the usability of services and tools for developers and administrators in SQL Server 2008 R2.

The success of BI solutions is due to the administration of core services that highlight the concerns on access levels, performance, scalability, and availability; adding further complication to compliance when the financial data is involved. The BI processes include commonly expressed services, such as data mining, ETL and reporting, usability and a sophisticated set of tools to accomplish these three core BI services. This chapter covers the implementation, configuration, and installation of core BI services SSAS, SSRS, and SSIS, which are important steps to build and administer effective BI solutions. The recipes emphasize the scale-out deployment practices on reporting platform and ETL processes.

SQL Server 2008 R2 exhibits new features and enhancements to the existing BI processes and toolset. Before we prepare the recipes to administer core BI services, it is essential to introduce these new features within the data-mining processes and BI toolset.

- ▶ The PowerPivot client add-in and server components provide an end-to-end solution that furthers the BI data analysis for Excel users on desktop and SharePoint sites.

- ▶ PowerPivot for Excel gets a new expression language called data-analysis expressions. This language extends the easy-to-use feature for users to create sophisticated calculations, time intelligence, and perform lookups.

- ▶ All the samples for Analysis Services and PowerPivot are now available externally from the CodePlex site: `http://powerpivotsampledata.codeplex.com/`.

- ▶ Creation of OLAP cubes that are used for data mining make it much easier to design dimensions and related hierarchies and attributes. The new Dimension Designer includes the new Attribute Relationship Designer that helps you to design attribute relationships to follow best practices.

Preparing and installing SQL Server Analysis Services

SQL Server provides a way to install any or all of its components including Analysis Services. The planning and architecture is an important aspect to better understand Analysis Services multi-dimensional database and plan how to implement the multi-dimensional database into your business intelligence solution.

In this recipe, we will evaluate the Analysis Services installation options and SQL Server PowerPivot for SharePoint. These evaluation steps also include the best practice hardware/software requirements, configuration, and security considerations for the installation. The topics highlight the important considerations that you should be aware of before you install Analysis Services. Note that many BI solutions require the installation of additional SQL Server components to enable the development, deployment, administration, and management of Business Intelligence suite.

During the installation of SQL Server 2008 R2 features, windows installer creates temporary files on the system drive. It is essential to ensure that you have at least 4 GB of available disk space on the system drive for these temporary files. Finally, the actual hard disk space requirements depend on your system configuration and the features that you decide to install. For SQL Server Analysis Services and data files, the minimum disk space requirement is 476 MB.

Getting ready

In order to prepare for the installation of SQL Server Analysis Services, you need to ensure that you have the following in place:

- **.NET Framework 3.5 Service Pack 1**: It helps improvements in the area of data platform, such as ADO.NET Entity Framework, ADO.NET data services and support for new features of SQL Server 2008 version onwards.

  You can download .NET Framework 3.5 Service Pack 1 from `http://www.microsoft.com/downloads/en/details.aspx?FamilyID=ab99342f-5d1a-413d-8319-81da479ab0d7&displaylang=en`.

- **Windows Installer 4.5**: It helps the application, installation, and configuration service for Windows. It works as an embedded chainer to add packages to a multiple package transaction. The major advantage of this feature is its ability to enable an update to add or change custom action, so that the custom action is called when an update is uninstalled.

  You can download Windows Installer 4.5 redistributable package from:

  `http://www.microsoft.com/downloads/en/details.aspx?FamilyID=5A58B56F-60B6-4412-95B9-54D056D6F9F4`

The SQL Server setup support files installs SQL Server Native Client and contains SQL OLEDB provider and SQL ODBC driver as a native Dynamic Link Library (DLL). These DLL's support applications using native code APIs to SQL Server.

To install Analysis Services in SharePoint Integrated mode, SQL Server 2008 R2 Setup includes a new Server installation option for installing PowerPivot for SharePoint, so that it is immediately available when the setup is finished. To use this option, you must start with a clean server that has SharePoint 2010 installed but not yet configured.

More importantly, it allows the SQL Server Setup to configure SharePoint by using those settings that are optimal for PowerPivot query processing and server management. In this recipe, we will install PowerPivot for SharePoint prerequisites and run server setup. If you are installing Analysis Services on the existing SharePoint Server, then it is common to configure the server immediately after you install it.

How to do it...

In this recipe, we will follow a two-step approach that will run through the SharePoint 2010 installation steps with a subsequent number of steps to choose relevant SQL Server 2008 R2 Analysis Services installation options and SQL Server PowerPivot for SharePoint. The SharePoint Server 2010 installation offers a choice between a standalone or a server farm installation. The following steps are required to install SharePoint 2010 services:

1. Insert the installation media or open a folder that contains the setup files for SharePoint 2010.

2. Run the `Prerequisite Installer` to add the required operating system roles, features, and other software required for your installation.

3. Run SharePoint Server Setup to install the server software. Accept the Microsoft Software License Terms of agreement, and then click **Continue**.

4. Click **Server Farm**.

> The Standalone installation is intended for single-server deployments. It installs SQL Server 2008 Express Edition and the required SharePoint components on a single host server. The Standalone option precludes the ability to scale out SSAS deployments.
>
> To overcome the limitations, it is essential to choose **Server Farm** to provide a flexible and scaled-out configuration. This option will enable the SQL Server database to be hosted by one server and the SharePoint application and Web front-end roles are consolidated onto another server.

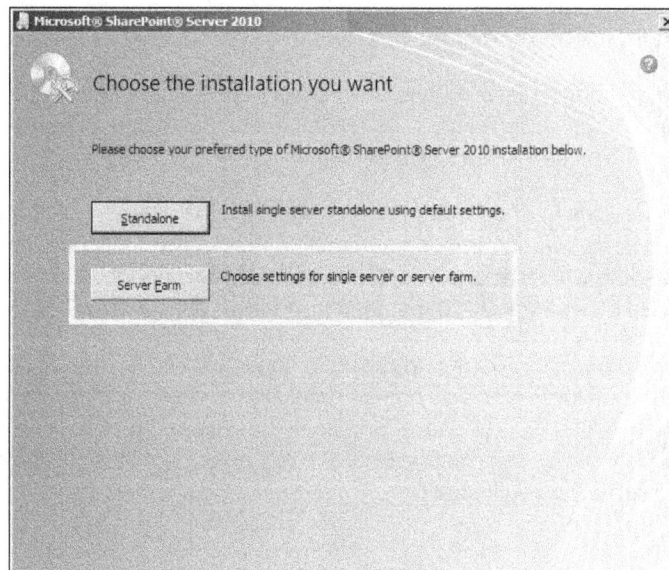

> For the purposes of this recipe, choosing the Standalone deployment is not suitable. Select the **Server Farm** option to enable the infrastructure that supports administrative and data connections.

5. On the **Server Type** page, select **Complete**.

6. By selecting this option, you add all the SharePoint features required for both application server and web front-end roles on the same server.

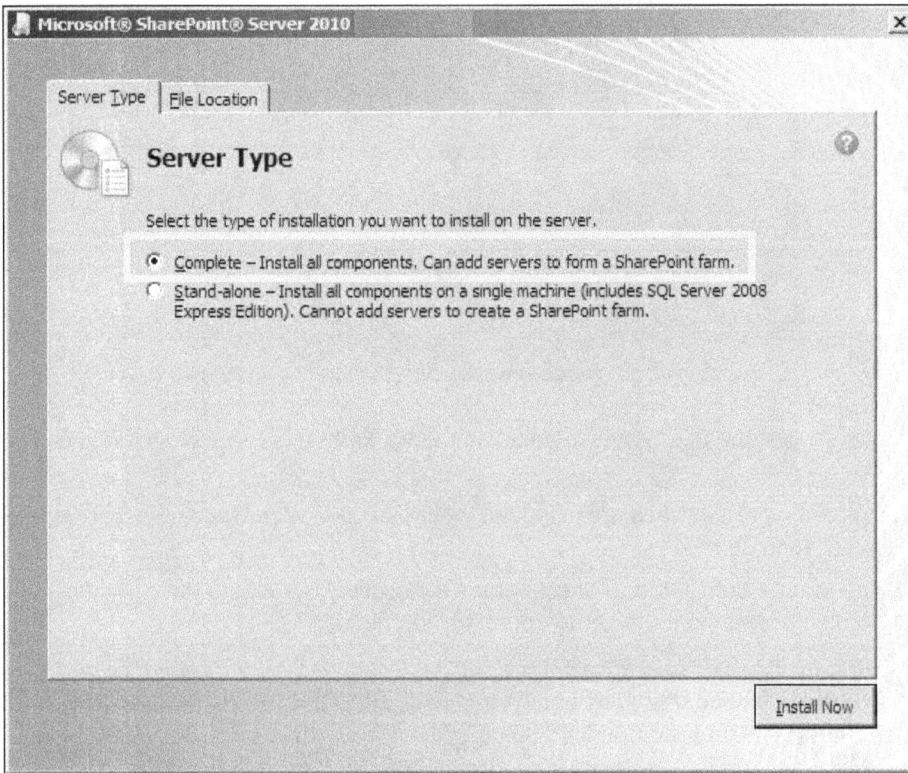

7. Click **Install Now**.

8. Next, you will be prompted to run the SharePoint Products and Technologies Configuration Wizard. Do not proceed to run configuration wizard, as it will result in an error, because the database server is not yet installed.

9. Clear the checkbox next to **Run the SharePoint Products and Technologies Configuration Wizard now**, and click **Close**.

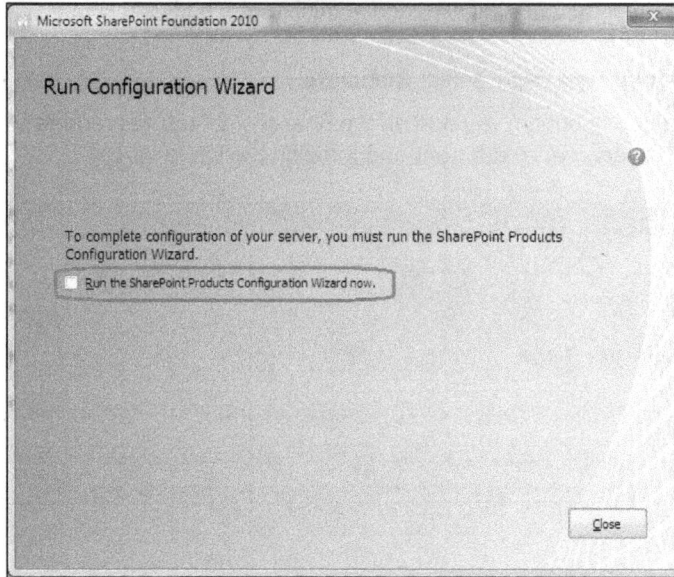

10. Next, insert the SQL Server installation media. From the `root` folder, double-click `Setup.exe`.

11. When the prerequisites are installed, the Installation Wizard runs the SQL Server Installation Center.

12. The System Configuration Checker runs a discovery to validate the computer configuration before the setup operation completes.

13. Now, we are at a stage where the setup installs and configures PowerPivot for SharePoint and a Database Engine instance. This instance will be used as the database server for the SharePoint server.

14. In the Setup Role, select **SQL Server PowerPivot for SharePoint**. In the same page, in **Add PowerPivot for SharePoint to** select **New Server**.

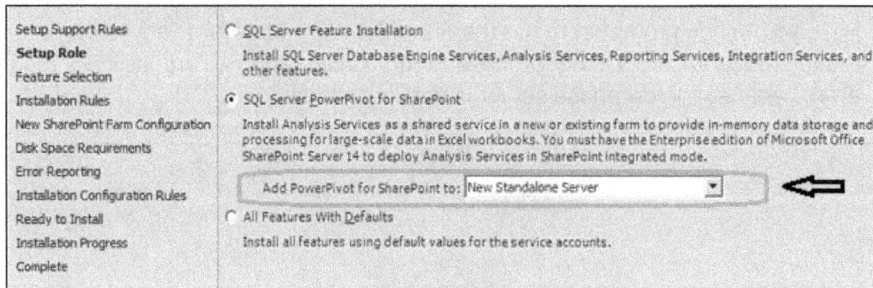

15. On the **Setup Role** page, select **SQL Server Feature Installation**, and then click **Next** to continue to the **Feature Selection** page.

16. On the **Feature Selection** page, select the components **Analysis Services** and **Business Intelligence Development Studio** for your installation.

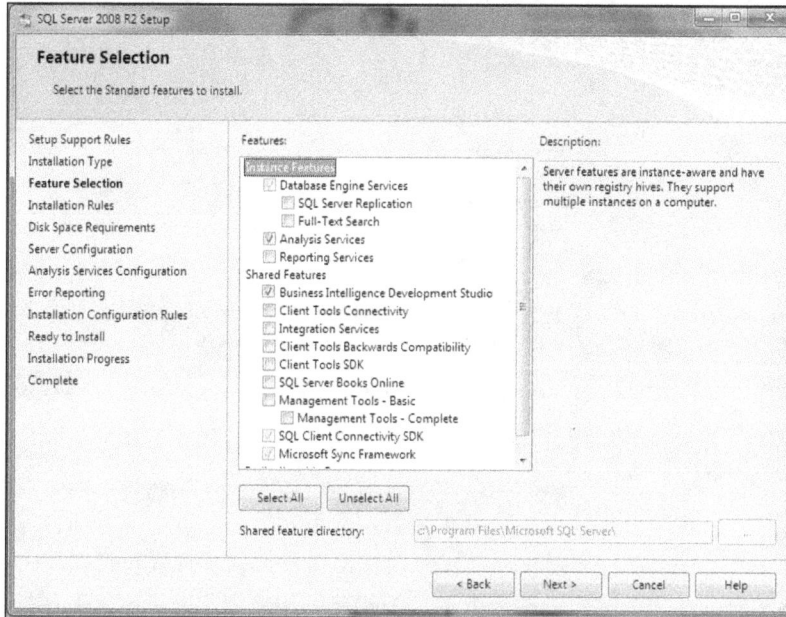

17. In this recipe, we are adding features to the existing services; hence, the instance features for **Database Engine Services** are disabled by default. The **Instance Features** selection will install services and tools that are useful for Analysis Services.

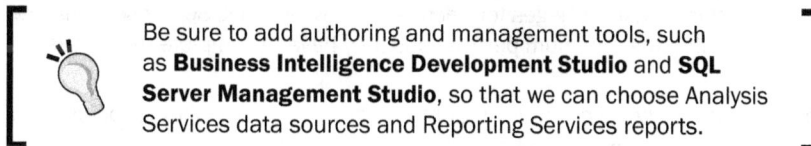

> Be sure to add authoring and management tools, such as **Business Intelligence Development Studio** and **SQL Server Management Studio**, so that we can choose Analysis Services data sources and Reporting Services reports.

18. A description for each component group appears in the right pane after you select the feature name.

19. To change the installation path for shared components, either update the path in the field at the bottom of the dialog box, or click **Browse** to move to an installation directory. The default installation path is `%:\Program Files\Microsoft SQL Server\100\`.

20. Next, the detected instances and features grid shows the instances of SQL Server that are on the computer where the Setup is running. The Disk Space Requirements page calculates the required disk space for the features that you specify.

21. On the **Server Configuration** page under the **Service Accounts** tab, specify the login **account name and password** for SQL Server Analysis services and SQL Server Browser.

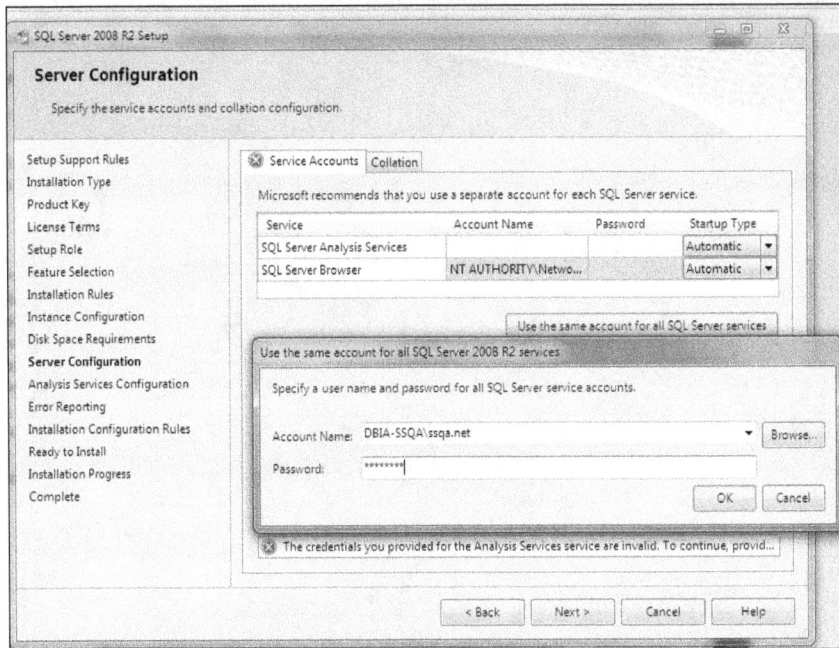

22. You can assign the same login account to all SQL Server services, or you can configure each service account individually.

> It is recommended that you configure the service accounts individually to provide least privileges for each service, where SQL Server services are granted the minimum permissions they have to complete their tasks.

23. This account must be a Windows domain user account. Built-in machine accounts (such as Network Service or Local Service) are prohibited.

24. SQL Server Setup enforces the domain user account requirement by blocking installation whenever a machine account is specified.

25. Next, use the **Server Configuration** page under the **Collation** tab to specify non-default collations for the Database Engine and Analysis Services.

26. At the database **engine configuration | Account provisioning** page, we have the option to set the security mode and assign an account to be a member of SYSADMIN fixed server role.

27. There is no selection to set the Security Mode for SQL Server Analysis Services. The default mode is **Windows Authentication** only.

28. Choose the **SQL Server Administrators** for SSAS service, click **Add Current User** and you can also add any other user to assign SYSADMIN privileges.

29. Make sure you review the summary of the installation log file to ensure no errors are reported.

> For this recipe, we are installing PowerPivot for SharePoint. You should grant administrative permissions to SharePoint farm administrators or service administrators, who are responsible for the deployment of SQL Server PowerPivot for SharePoint in a SharePoint 2010 farm.

30. To specify the installation to default directories, click **Next**. The default directories are `%:\Program Files\Microsoft SQL Server\MSSQL10_50.<InstanceID>\ Data.`

> As per the recipe, when adding features to an existing installation, you cannot change the location of a previously installed feature, nor can you specify the location for a new feature. If you specify non-default installation directories, ensure that the installation folders are unique to this instance of SQL Server.

31. The System Configuration Checker will run one more set of rules to validate the server configuration with the SQL Server features that you have specified.

32. The **Ready to Install** page shows a tree view of installation options that were specified during the Setup. Click **Install** to continue.

33. At this point, the installation should proceed as planned. Unless some unexpected error happens, the process should have a working instance of SSAS deployed on your machine, along with SQL Server.

34. Once the SSAS installation is succeeded, the **Complete page** provides a link to the summary log file for the installation and other important notes.

> If you are instructed to restart the computer, do so immediately. It is important to read the message from the Installation Wizard when you have finished with Setup.

This set of steps will confirm the successful installation of SQL Server 2008 R2 Analysis Services in SharePoint 2010 integrated mode and PowerPivot for SharePoint component.

How it works...

From SQL Server 2008 R2 onwards, the setup program provides the feature to install any or all of its components. Through the setup, you can install Analysis Services with or without other SQL Server components on a single server. The connectivity components are installed that are important for communication between clients and servers that includes the server network libraries. The Analysis Services runs as a Windows service, and appears in the list of installed services in SQL Server Configuration Manager and in Services.

The authoring and development tool such as Business Intelligence Development Studio (BIDS) is installed to provide an integrated development environment for BI projects. The service installation and service account starts and runs as a windows service, each instance of Analysis Services is supported by its own service and each instance can use different settings for collation and server options. The only authentication mode supported by Analysis Services is 'Windows Authentication'.

For the collation of designators and sort order settings, Analysis Services is supported by its own service and each instance can use different settings for collation and other server options. The Analysis Services use similar collation settings that are designated for SQL Server Database Engine service, provided both the services are installed under the same instance name. If required, it is possible to choose different collation settings for each of these services.

Further to these procedures of installing PowerPivot for SharePoint, the SQL Server setup program runs the SharePoint Products and Technologies Configuration program (PSConfig. exe) in the background to create the configuration database and set up PowerPivot features. SharePoint will be initialized with values that you specify in the SQL Server Installation Wizard. When you use the **New Server installation** option, all server products use default values.

There's more...

To achieve a successful installation of PowerPivot for SharePoint feature, there are a few post-installation tasks you should perform:

► Install ADO.NET Data Services 3.5 SP1 to enable data feed export from SharePoint lists. For Windows Server 2003 and 2008 operating systems download from: http://www.microsoft.com/downloads/details. aspx?displaylang=en&FamilyID=21f20103-551e-4501-89b3-e53fcac5cffd.

For Windows 7 and for Windows Server 2008 R2 operating systems download from: http://www.microsoft.com/downloads/details.aspx?displaylang=en&FamilyID=3e102d74-37bf-4c1e-9da6-5175644fe22d.

For a secure deployment:

Grant SharePoint permissions to individuals and groups; this is necessary to enable access to sites and content.

Change the PowerPivot service application's pool identity to run under a different account.

▸ On SharePoint **Service Applications** page in **Excel Services Settings** create additional trusted sites in Excel Services, so that you can vary the permissions and configuration settings that work best for PowerPivot data access.

Implementing Scale-Out of SQL Server Analysis Services

Scalability describes a system's ability to utilize additional resources for an increase in system capacity to perform additional work. The system capacity is important in achieving maximum scalability. There are two types of Scalability: 'scale-up' and 'scale-out'.

▸ **Scale-up**: It enables the data platform to support the increasing numbers of users, or applications, taking SSAS abundance of internal optimization and performance tuning techniques to support the system resource utilization.

▸ **Scale-out**: It provides the path to inherent limitation in a scale-up architecture, increasing server performance by fine-tuning the worker threads, pre-allocation of memory, and disk resource allocation. It purely depends on the technology limits of Symmetric Multi-Processing (SMP) scalability.

While most server applications today can scale up to eight logical processors, it is possible to ramp up Analysis Services with 16, or 32 logical processors. This can be done by adjusting the size of the thread pools for the formula engine and the storage engine. It is vital to optimize the system configuration for the best possible performance, which includes the SAN storage optimization to realize high scalability with SSAS. Once the scale-up is completed up to a satisfactory level, then scale-out can multiply the scale-up gains.

In this recipe, we will look at how to implement the scale out of SQL Server Analysis Services.

Getting ready

The server configuration is an important aspect to design a scale-out implementation and the following list highlights the information that is essential to implement a scale-out process:

▸ Core SQL Server database engine server x 2

▸ Analysis Services processing server x 1

▸ Analysis Services query servers x 3

The following are the recommended server configurations for implementing and demonstrating SSAS scale out:

▶ Four DUAL-core Intel Processor (2.8 GHz), 32 GB RAM

▶ Separate SAN Storage for Analysis Services and core database engine services

▶ 2 GB HBAs connected to fiber-channel

▶ Windows Server 2008 R2 Enterprise X64 Edition and SQL Server 2008 R2 Enterprise X64 Edition

The Analysis Services instance configuration is as follows:

▶ Analysis Services system files are installed in the `C:\Program Files\Microsoft SQL Server\MSSQL.1\OLAP` folder

▶ Analysis Services data folder pointed to drive on SAN; then those data folders will have the same structure

▶ Use the same domain service account for all Analysis Services instances with administrative privileges

The recommended storage server configurations are as follows:

▶ Two nodes

▶ 240 drives—each being a150-GB 10K-RPM (Fiber-channel)

▶ Four 2 gigabit front-end fiber channel ports and 16-GB data cache

▶ Virtual Copy and System Reporter

The client machine configuration is as follows:

▶ Dual-core AMD Opteron 912 processor (2.6 GHz)

▶ 12GB RAM

▶ Windows Server 2003 R2 Enterprise X64 Edition with Service Pack2

▶ ASCMD command prompt utility

How to do it...

The following process enables you to deploy a scale-out methodology for SQL Server Analysis Services. The initial step is to configure the SAN snapshots. We will then complete the following steps:

1. Stop the Analysis Services on the processing server.

2. On the Analysis Services processing server wait for 60 seconds to dismount the LUN on which the Analysis Services data folder resides. It is also ideal to use the hardware vendor's utilities to accomplish the task.

3. To ensure all modified data is stored to disk use SysInternals' Sync Utility tool (You can download it from `http://technet.microsoft.com/en-gb/sysinternals/bb897438.aspx`).

> By using the Sync Utility tool you can quickly flush the LUN from the SAN after Analysis Services is stopped, and before dismounting the LUN.

4. Based on the SAN vendor, using the command-prompt utility, generate a script for a snapshot of Analysis Services data folder.

5. Restart the Analysis Services on the processing server.

> For better results on volume, always mount the disks as the same drive letter.

6. Restart Analysis Services on the query server.

7. As far as the database is concerned, we have used the Analysis Services 2008 R2 DW database. For better results, the database is partitioned as follows:

   - `StoreInventory` measure group
   - `ProductVendor` measure group
   - `RetailInventory` measure group

8. Now, we are at the point where we need to generate a query workload. To generate a large number of query streams that are both CPU and I/O intensive, we have used a sample application tool called `ASQueryGenerator` from the CodePlex site, which can be downloaded from `http://www.codeplex.com/SQLSrvAnalysisSrvcs`.

9. The scale-out approach is increasing the capacity of OLAP applications, such as building the OLAP farm.

10. Choose the server with the higher configuration to be a master server. The master server contains the metadata and manages the whole farm.

11. The processing sever will serve as the front-end server to communicate with clients and execute client requests.

12. The front-end servers (Analysis query servers) are configured to run under a network load-balancing cluster. A front-end server needs a fast CPU for making calculations and a lot of memory to cache the results.

13. You can use a 'synchronization mechanism' to have your data statically replicated across all the front-end servers.

   ❑ **Synchronization mechanism**: Analysis Services includes a Deployment Wizard, which is a step-by-step user interface used to perform deployment tasks. Also, by generating a `script` method, you can deploy your database from a test to a production environment using the `Synchronize` command.

   ❑ **Deployment Wizard**: It is a step-by-step user interface used to deploy the file that results from building an Analysis Services project (`projectname.asdatabase`) to a target server. You start with an Analysis Services project developed in BIDS.

14. Let us create a linked dimension and linked measure groups to load data from the master server, using BIDS.

15. Right-click on the **Dimensions** node in the Solution Explorer and select **New Linked Dimension** to open Linked Object wizard.

16. In the Wizard advance, select **Data Source** page to create a **new data source** that points to the database you want to link your dimension to.

17. Click **Finish** to complete the wizard. Now, each front-end server checks for updates and automatically refreshes the data state, if there is any update on the master server.

18. Now, let us create a process to load and store data on remote servers using the **remote-partitions** feature of Analysis Services to distribute data between multiple back-end servers.

19. On the master server, open the cube's **Partitions** page. Right-click the cube and select **Partitions**.

20. Right-click any partition name and select **Delete**, then add a new partition by clicking the **New Partition link**.

21. Click through the Partition Wizard until you get to the **Processing and Storage Locations** page.

22. Under the **Processing Location**, set **Remote AS** data source to the newly created data source that points to your subordinate database. Complete the wizard by clicking the **Finish** button.

23. Finally, right-click the cube name in **Solution Explorer**, select **Process and fully process** the cube.

The successful completion of the Cube process will complete the process to deploy a scale-out implementation of SQL Server Analysis Services on an existing data platform.

How it works...

The Scalable Shared Database (SSD) is an Enterprise and DataCenter edition feature. All the configuration settings will depend upon the budget within the Enterprise, and at a certain point, scaling up to move your application to more powerful computers gets you into the price range of an enterprise-level hardware. Enterprise-level hardware that enables you to scale to large data volumes is substantially more expensive than lightweight database hardware. To scale your system, you add additional computers to your application. This process works behind the scenes, where Analysis Services takes the query processing techniques; a client application establishes a connection to a virtual IP address. That connection is redirected to one of the front-end servers. The front-end server parses and resolves the queries from the client application, and executes all the calculations defined in your cube.

To execute a query, the front-end server first determines if the answer is already available in its local cache. If not, with the static replication model, it retrieves data from the local storage. Moving data from a staging server to a production server is a simple process. With a scale-up approach, it's relatively easy to backup your database. It's easier to restore the application state from the backup.

For better query optimization techniques, the baselines build the foundation to measure scale-out efficiency. It is possible to recognize that the formula-engine-heavy environment does not support 500 concurrent users very well, while the storage-engine-heavy environment has reached scale-out efficiency. Even though the I/O load is generally low, 100 concurrent users seem to overwhelm the current storage subsystem and thus, query performance suffers. If two query servers can support 200 users with query times of eight seconds, then four servers should be able to support 600 users with about the same performance. Instead, query times exceed 60 seconds and it is predictable that adding further query servers will not bring the query time down to 10 seconds. It is necessary to review the scale-out design and locate the actual bottleneck.

A tabular representation between Scale-out and Scale-up deployment is presented in the following table:

Scale-Out	Scale-Up
Advantages	
More Performance	Less to Manage
More Flexibility	Cheaper per GHz
Disadvantages	
More Expensive	System Design Flaws become Critical
More to Manage	More Single Points of Failure

Administering SQL Server Reporting Services

The BI strategy is centered on two key suites of products—'SQL Server' and 'Office'. SQL Server is used as the data and reporting platform and Office provides popular easy-to-use front-end tools for end users to view and manage the data and analysis. This includes products such as Excel, Word, and SharePoint.

The key point is that SharePoint provides a central way to collaborate online. This is where reports serve the purpose of sharing the data for trends about business processes. SharePoint is a central collaboration tool enabling users to view and manage reports within SharePoint. That is the key motivation behind Reporting Services integration with SharePoint. SQL Server Reporting Services (SSRS) is one of the components in the Business Intelligence platform, which provides the unified, server-based, extensible, and scalable platform to deliver and present data. SSRS is capable of generating reports in various formats (HTML, XLS, PDF, CSV, and more). SQL Server 2008 R2 introduces new features for data visualization, report design, and end-user reporting. The new features are as follows:

- **SharePoint Integration**: SharePoint lists the SharePoint Foundation 2010, SharePoint Server 2010, Windows SharePoint Services 3.0, and Office SharePoint Server 2007.

- **Data Sources and Visualization**: It provides support for three new data source types—SQL Azure, SQL Server Parallel Data Warehouse, and SharePoint list. New Visualization types—maps, spark lines, and data bars with indicators.

- **Report Layout and Processing**: It helps the users to create a report that renders in whatever way you want, such as source of ATOM data renderer feeds being exported to Excel.

- **Report Authoring tools**: It creates queries in query designer to retrieve data from SQL Azure or SQL Server Parallel Data Warehouse; and preview reports in report builder 3.0 with an introduction of edit sessions for better reuse of cached datasets.

- **Report Manager Enhancements**: It helps us to update the color scheme, layout, and is easier to navigate to manage report properties and server items with the new drop-down menu to access various configuration options of each report.

- **Newweb-service endpoint**: It is named as ReportingServices2010, as it merges the functionalities of both Reporting Services 2005 and Reporting Services 2008 with support management operations of report server in native mode and SharePoint integrated mode.

- **New Report definition language schema**: It's a new element `<ReportSections>` that defines map report items.

In this recipe, we will administer by preparing and installing SQL Server Reporting Services. We will also include the best practice requirements for configuration and security considerations for the installation.

Getting ready

Traditionally, by using the `setup.exe`, SQL Server services can be installed. In order to prepare to install SQL Server Reporting Services, you need to ensure that you have .NET framework 3.5 SP1, Windows Install 4.5, and SQL Server setup support files (which are still applicable to Reporting Services installation).

For more information on the pre-requisite files required, refer to the recipe *Adding features of SQL Server 2008 R2 using Slipstream technology* mentioned in *Chapter 1, Getting started with SQL Server 2008 R2*.

Before running the Setup we need to:

- Access an account with administrative privileges to run SQL Server 2008
- Set up several Windows accounts to run SQL Server services, such as Report Server and SQL Server
- Secure a computer on which you are planning to install SQL Server components

> We must avoid hosting a Report Server on a computer that has an underscore in its name, and also on a server that is a domain controller. Computers with underscores in the name break state management capabilities of the Report Server.

How to do it...

The recommended order of the setup and configuration steps is as follows:

- Install Reporting Services
- Install SharePoint and configure Report Server for SharePoint mode
- Install the RS add-in for SharePoint

The following steps are essential to administer SQL Server Reporting Services:

1. To launch the SQL Server 2008 R2 install, run `<setup directory>\x86\setup10.exe` or `<setup directory>\x64\setup10.exe` directly. (The directory name may vary depending on the platform required). It is also possible to install the setup directly from the media.

2. Select **Installation** from the menu of the SQL Server Installation Center.

3. Click **New SQL Server Stand-Alone Installation** or **Add Features** to an Existing Installation.

4. When the prerequisites are installed, the **Installation Wizard** runs the SQL Server Installation Center, click **Next**.

5. The **System Configuration Checker** runs a discovery to validate the computer configuration before the setup operation completes.

6. On the **Feature Role** page, select **SQL Server Feature Installation**, and then click **Next** to continue to the **Feature Selection** page.

7. On the **Feature Selection** page, select the components **Reporting Services** and **Business Intelligence Development Studio** for your installation.

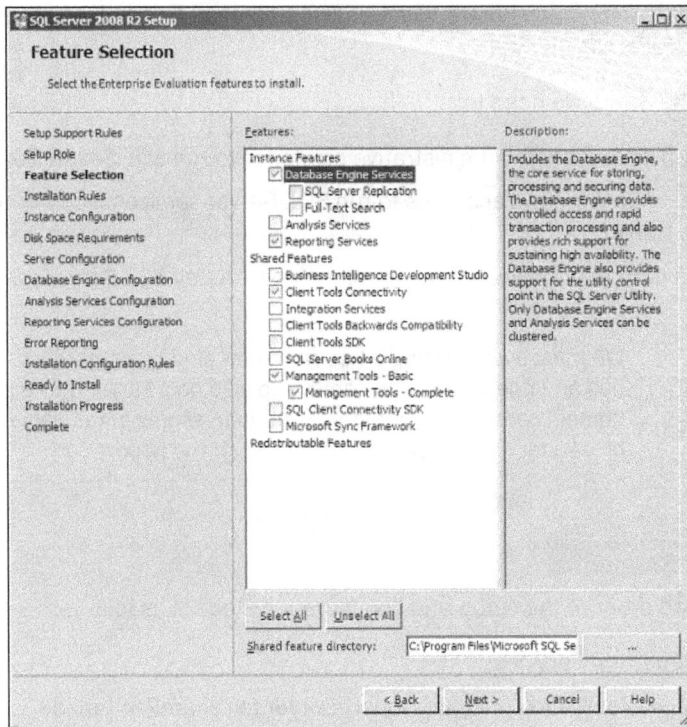

8. For the server-side component installation, check **Database Engine Services**, **Reporting Services**, and **Management Tools**.

9. Select service account information and enter their credentials. It is recommended that you use a different service account for each service.

10. Based on the two selected services, let us now choose the installation mode for SSRS.

11. There are three installation modes: Native mode, SharePoint integrated mode, and Files Only.

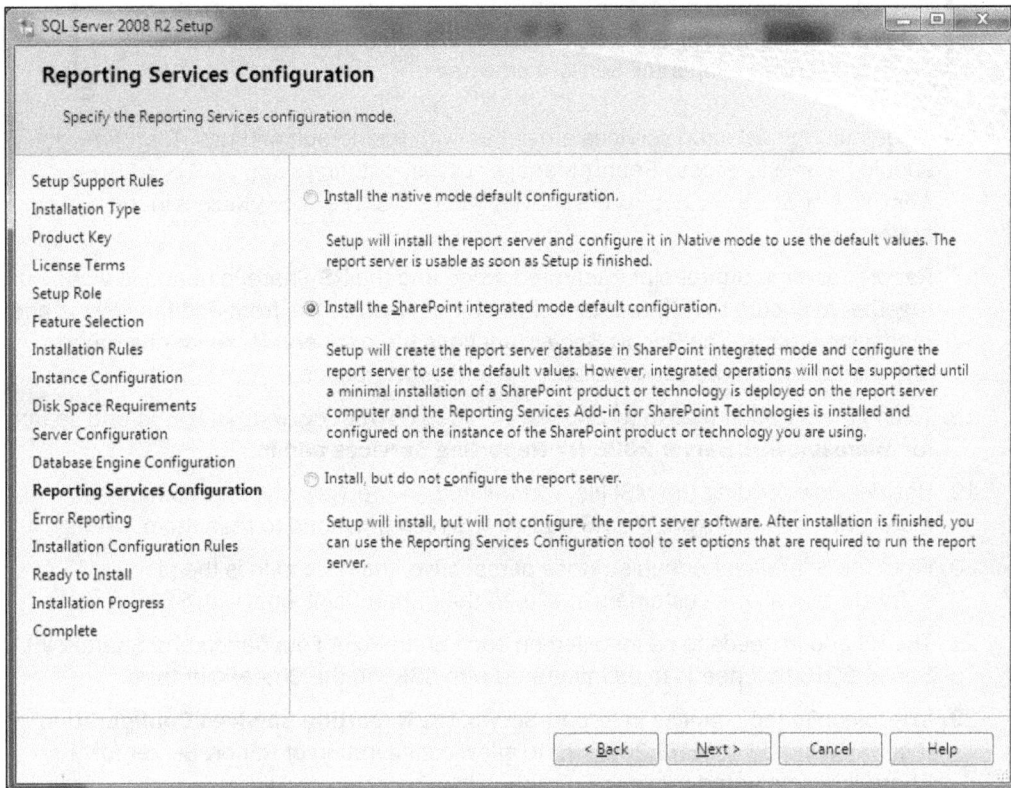

○ **Files Only mode**: It allows you to lay down the Reporting Services files and leave the configuration and activation to later stages

○ **Native mode**: The default configuration will install and pre-configure SSRS with all the default options

12. Select the SharePoint integrated mode button.

13. The next screen is **Installation Rules**, which runs a few final checks before proceeding with the installation. Click **Next** to proceed, if there are no errors present.

14. A summary screen displays the list of actions that will be performed; click **Install** to proceed with the installation.

15. At this point, the installation should proceed as planned. Unless, some unexpected error occurs, the process should have a working instance of SSRS deployed on the machine, along with SQL Server.

> When we deploy the Reporting Services it uses two SQL Server relational databases for internal storage. By default, the databases are named `ReportServer` and `ReportServerTempdb`. Both these system databases are used to maintain, store, cache and process Reporting Services processes.

16. By default, the selected services are set up with the default settings. Therefore, you should be able to access Report Manager by just entering `http://localhost/Reports` or `http://<computername/VirtualDirectoryName>` in the address bar.

17. Report Server in SharePoint integrated mode and the RS SharePoint add-in work together to ensure that SharePoint sites can be used as the front-end for viewing and managing reports. The Report Server functions the back-end for rendering reports and managing features such as caching and subscriptions.

18. To find the RS add-in, go to `http://www.microsoft.com/downloads` and search for **Microsoft SQL Server 2008 R2 Reporting Services add-in**.

19. Besides downloading the MSI file, you will find an overview and instructions on installation and configure the RS add-in. It is recommended to read them.

20. From the SharePoint administrator's perspective, the RS add-in is the piece of software that allows customers to extend their SharePoint sites with SSRS reports.

21. The RS add-in needs to be installed on each SharePoint Foundation and SharePoint Server 2010 that needs to be integrated with SSRS in the SharePoint farm.

22. In addition to the changes in Report Server, the **Reporting Services Configuration** tool was updated in SSRS 2008 R2 to allow configuration of Report Server for SharePoint integrated mode.

> For a best practice implementation, it is ideal to install a new SharePoint Server first. In this way, you can reduce the number of database engines to manage by reusing the SQL Server 2008 and SQL Server 2008 R2 databases, which were installed with SSRS 2008 R2 as your storage location for SharePoint.

23. Here are the basic steps to set up WSS 3.0 for reporting integration.

24. Microsoft Office SharePoint Server with Service Pack 2 is available as a free download setup file called `SharePoint.exe` from `http://www.microsoft.com/downloads/en/details.aspx?FamilyID=EF93E453-75F1-45DF-8C6F-4565E8549C2A`.

25. Click the **Advanced installation** type and select **Web Front End** (WFE). To configure WFE use the SharePoint Configuration wizard.

26. If you are installing just WFE on a machine, choose the **Connect to an Existing Server Farm** option and you are ready. For this recipe, we are configuring a new WFE.

27. Select the Database server where the SharePoint configuration database should be placed.

28. Use the same database that is used by SQL Server Reporting Services 2008 R2. This database is created when the SSRS installation is completed (refer to step 17).

29. Specify the windows account credentials for WSS to connect to the database. In this case, it is recommended that the account be registered as a domain account.

30. Now, create a web application and site collection through the SharePoint Central Administration application. From the **Application Management** table, click to **Create or Extend Web Application link** to create a new web application.

31. Choose the **Use an Existing IIS Web Site** option to use the default website. Now create a New Application pool and select **Network Service** account as the security user for the application.

32. Create a Site Collection link on the **Application create** page and set a name.

33. It is essential to choose a windows domain account as the primary site collection administrator.

34. A new site collection is created with a top-level site—http://DBIASSQA. However, we can create a new subsite under the main site by the name reports as http://dbiassqa/Reports.

    Now, we are at the point where we can configure Reporting Services 2008 R2 in SharePoint 2010 integrated mode and configure the Report Server database.

35. Open Reporting Services Configuration Manager and connect with Reporting Services instance. Make sure that Report Service status is 'Started'. Notice that Report Server Mode is Native.

36. Open the **Report Service Database** section by clicking the **Database navigational** tab button. Click on **Change Database** button to launch Report Server Database Configuration Wizard.

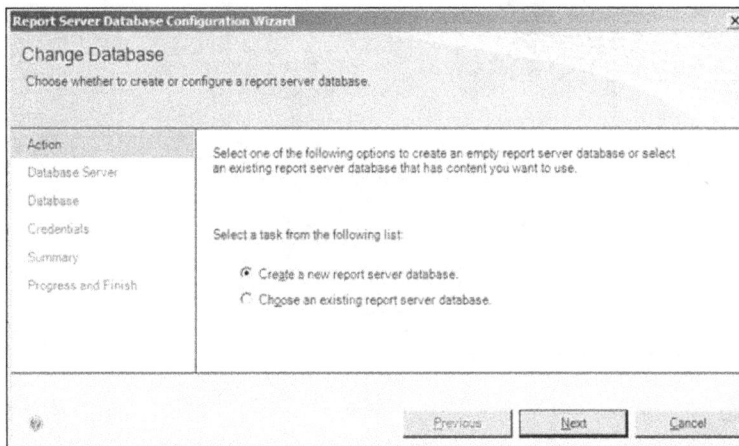

37. Select **Create a new report server database**, which will be the newly installed SSRS instance. Once authenticate is set, click **Test Connection** for a successful establishment.

38. Type the database name `ReportServerSharePointIntegratedTemp` and select the option **Report Server Mode as SharePoint Integrate**. Click **Next** to continue.

39. Set credentials that will be used for connecting to the database. If everything is in one box, **Service Credentials** will be enough. In case you need to change the port of Web Service URL, go to the **Web Service URL** section by clicking **Web Service URL** navigational tab button and set it. The URL will be `http://DBIASSQA:2000/ReportServer` the port number for the web server is 2000.

> The port number can be of any range between 1500 to 3000. If in the case the Web server is behind a firewall, then make sure that you enter the defined port in the Firewall exceptions list.

40. The process to create the database will follow the sequence of Verifying database SKU, Generate database scripts, Execute database scripts, Generate user rights scripts, apply connection rights, and finally setting DSN Connections

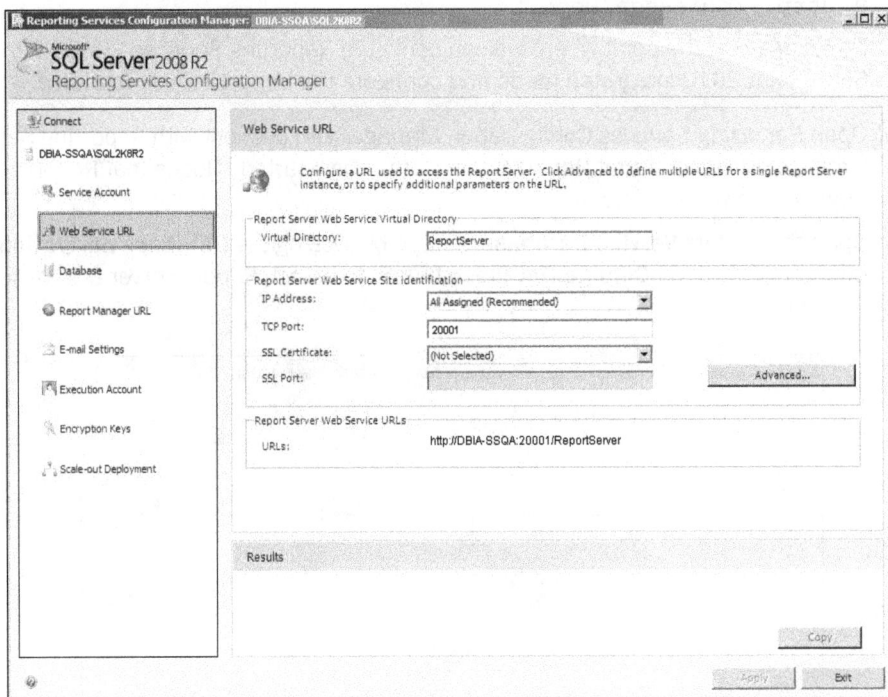

41. Double-click on the file, which is downloaded at step 20, **Microsoft SQL Server 2008 R2 Reporting Services** add-in. Complete the installation.

42. Next, you need to configure SharePoint for Reporting Services. Open SharePoint 2010 Central Administration and click on **General Application Settings** link, as shown in the following screenshot:

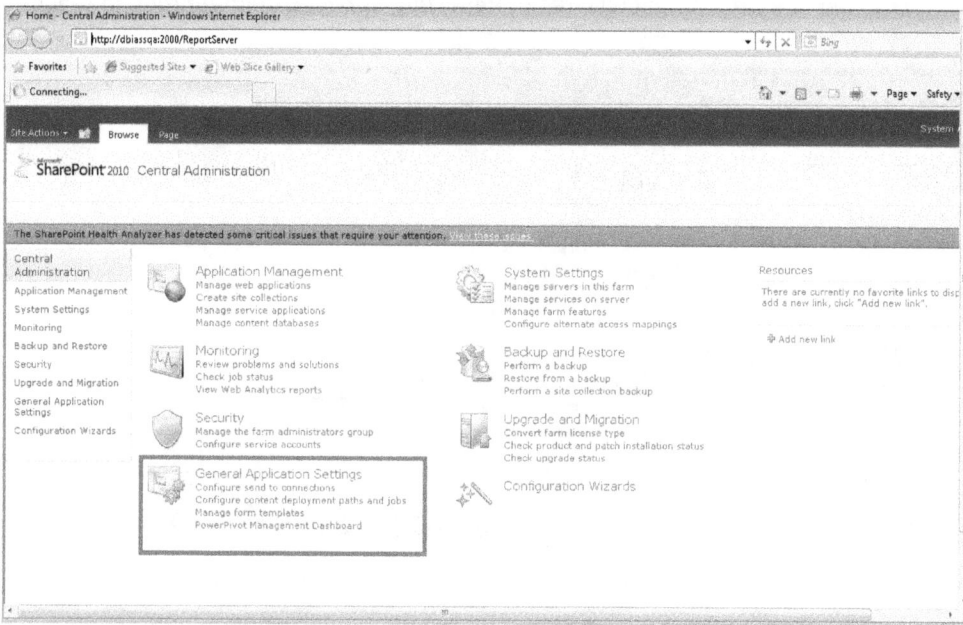

43. Inside the **General Application Settings** link a section called **Reporting Services** can be seen, which manages integration settings.

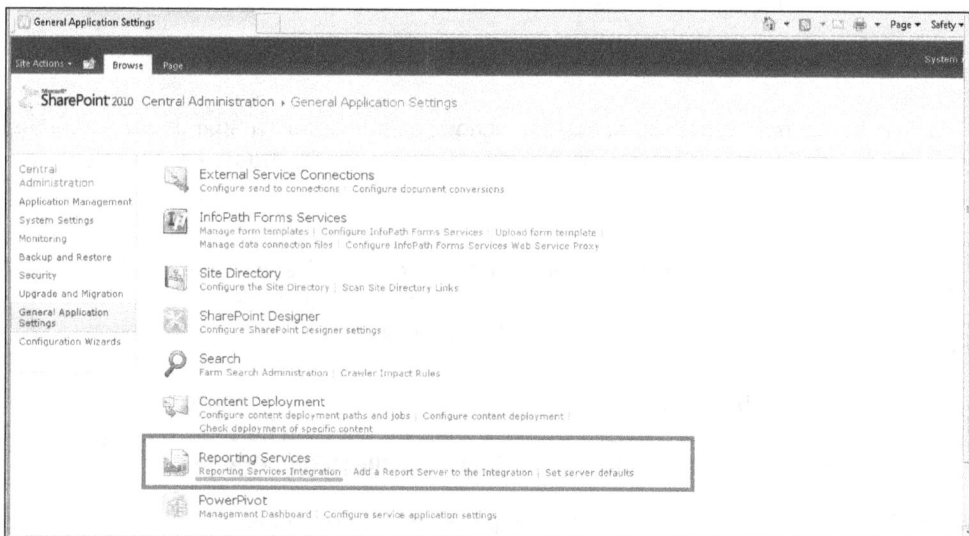

44. The link **Reporting Services Integration** opens a window where Report Server Web Service URL and Authentication Mode can be set.

45. The Report Server Web Service URL should be the URL that has been configured with **Web Service URL** navigational tab of **Reporting Services Configuration Manager**.

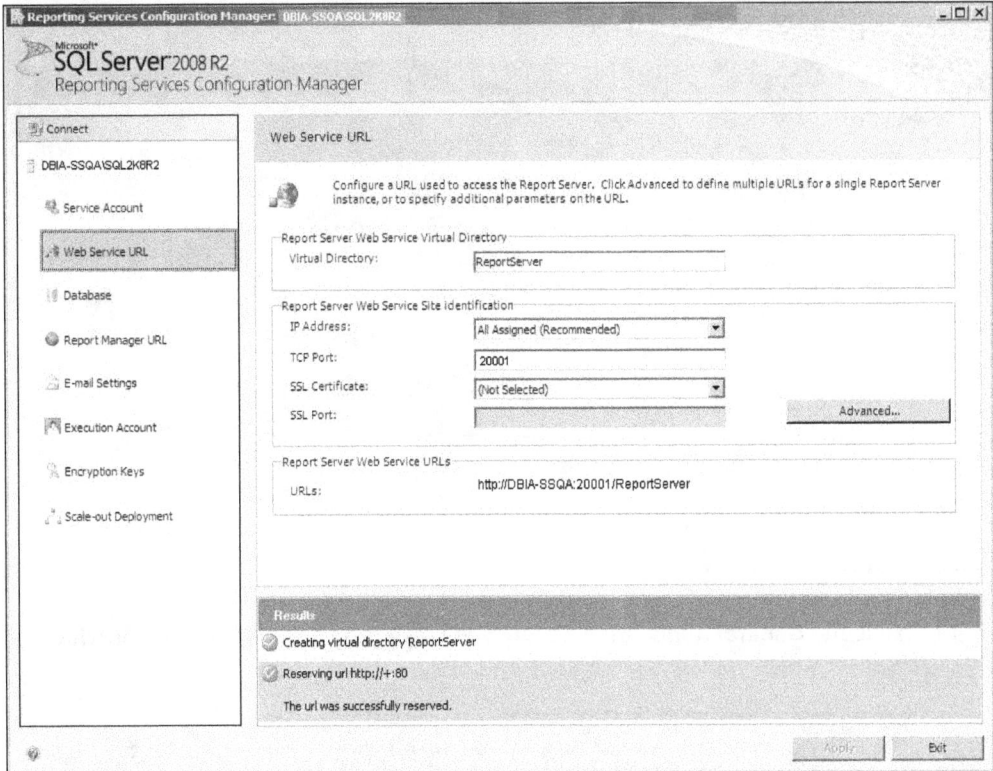

46. The next screen is important for connection security between SharePoint Server and Reporting Services. For best practice implementation, the **Trusted Authentication** must be used.

> The Trusted account impersonates connected SharePoint users and will be used for accessing the Report Server, which is used generally in form authentication without Active Directory or Kerberos authentication.

47. Finally, set the **Server Defaults** under Reporting Services to change default server settings for Reporting Services. Some of the elements can be changed, such as **Number of Snapshots**, **Ad-Hoc Reporting**, and **Client-Side Printing**.

Now, the Reporting Services integration is complete and SharePoint is fully integrated with Reporting Services.

How it works...

Both Reporting Services and SharePoint products use SQL Server relational databases for internal storage. SharePoint installs the Embedded Edition for its database; however, it is best practice to use a different instance. Reporting Services cannot use this edition for its database; it requires that the Evaluation, Developer, Standard, DataCenter or Enterprise edition of SQL Server Database Engine be installed. The earlier versions of SQL Server do not support hosting the SQL Server 2008 R2 Reporting Services Add-in for SharePoint Products, so it is essential to use SQL Server 2008 Reporting Services R2 database only.

On the other hand, SSRS is lenient with prefixed parameters and uses a default value when the value specified in URL access is invalid. For example, `rs:Command= Reindeer` defaults to `rs:Command=Render`. If you want to install Reporting Services and a SharePoint product instance on the same computer, you can run SQL Server Express and another edition of SQL Server side-by-side on the same computer, or you can use the same instance of the Database Engine for the SharePoint configuration and content databases if you choose the **Advanced installation** option when installing a SharePoint product or technology. If you choose the Basic installation option instead, the SharePoint Setup program will install SQL Server Embedded Edition as an internal component and use that instance to host the SharePoint databases.

If you are using a SharePoint farm or a scale-out reporting deployment topology and don't want to repeat these configuration steps manually on each server, you can use SSRS programmability to create configuration scripts. To increase security, an administrator can use **SecureConnectionLevel** to configure SSRS and enforce web service client applications to leverage various levels of SSL communications for Report Server web service method calls. (This configuration also affects **ReportManager**). SSRS uses **SecureConnectionLevel** (located in **RSReportServer.config**) to determine which web service methods require an SSL connection.

There's more...

SQL Server Edition requirements for Reporting Services in SharePoint integrated mode include Developer, Evaluation, Standard, DataCenter, or Enterprise editions. The version of the SharePoint product or technology that you install on the report server computer must be the same version that is used throughout the farm.

If you are adding a report server to a SharePoint Server 2010 server farm, you must have at least a minimal installation of SharePoint Server 2010 on the report server computer. You cannot have a combination of SharePoint Foundation 2010 and SharePoint Server 2010 in the same server farm.

See Also

Adding features of SQL Server 2008 R2 using Slipstream technology mentioned in *Chapter 1, Getting started with SQL Server 2008 R2.*

Implementing Scale-Out deployment of SQL Server Reporting Services

There are various deployment modes available with SQL Server Reporting Services; the recipe *Preparing and Installing Reporting Services* highlights the new deployment mode that is available in SQL Server 2008 R2. Similar to the core database engine and analysis services, the reporting services can also be deployed as a scale-out model by configuring the multiple report servers to use a share report server database.

To provide further high availability to the reporting services platform, you might decide to host the report server database on SQL Server failover cluster nodes. The advantage of this scale-out deployment is a highly available and scalable reporting services platform. In this deployment mode, each report server is referred to as a node. Nodes participate in the scale-out, if the report server is configured to use the same remote report server database. The load balancing of reports is managed by the load balancer component.

In this recipe, we will go through the required steps and tools to configure a scale-out deployment.

Getting ready

There are certain requirements that apply for a reporting services scale-out deployment. They are as follows:

- . NET framework 3.5 SP1, Windows Install 4.5, and SQL Server setup support files that are still applicable to Reporting Services installation
- Run Setup to install an instance of Reporting Services, choose the **Install but do not configure server** option on the **Installation Options** page
- Only Enterprise Edition is supported to deploy the scale-out configuration in a production environment
- All the report servers must have the same version of SQL Server including service pack updates
- The reporting services authentication must be the same across all the report server instances
- Report server nodes can be load-balanced using Network Load Balanced (NLB) cluster software from the operating system

- Reporting Services database size should be as follows:

  - ❑ RSTempDB or ReportServerTempdb: The size of this database varies, depending on the number of concurrent users to access report servers

  - ❑ RSDB or ReportServer: A general rule of thumb is that the report definition will take around 250KB of disk space, which is larger than the actual size of RDL

- The database size is determined by the multiplication result of the size of report and the number of concurrent users; and each live report that is executed will generate a report snapshot that is persisted in ReportServerTempDB database for the duration of the user's session

While going through the requirements of Reporting Services scale-out deployment the users must take the following things into consideration:

- Using the Developer edition or Enterprise Evaluation edition, you can deploy scale-out configuration, but the only limitation is that the Developer edition cannot be used for production purposes and the Enterprise Evaluation will expire after 180 days

- The report servers must be in the same domain or have a trusted-domain relationship enabled in case multiple domains are involved

- Reporting Services do not synchronize custom permission settings between the different authentication types

The required tools to implement reporting services to scale-out deployment are the SQL Server setup media and the Reporting Services Configuration tool (rskeymgmt utility), which is located at <drive>:\Program Files\Microsoft SQL Server\100\Tools\Bin.

How to do it...

The following steps enable you to deploy a scale-out methodology for SQL Server Reporting Services (SSRS). The process is a two-fold method that starts with a deployment model. It is done by configuring multiple report servers to use a shared report server database and manage encryption keys to perform encrypt and decrypt data in a report server database. The initial steps are to configure the report servers explained as follows:

1. Use the SQL Server Setup to install each report server instance, choose a server which is classified as the master server.

2. On each report server, use **Reporting Services Configuration** (RSC) tool to connect to the report shared database.

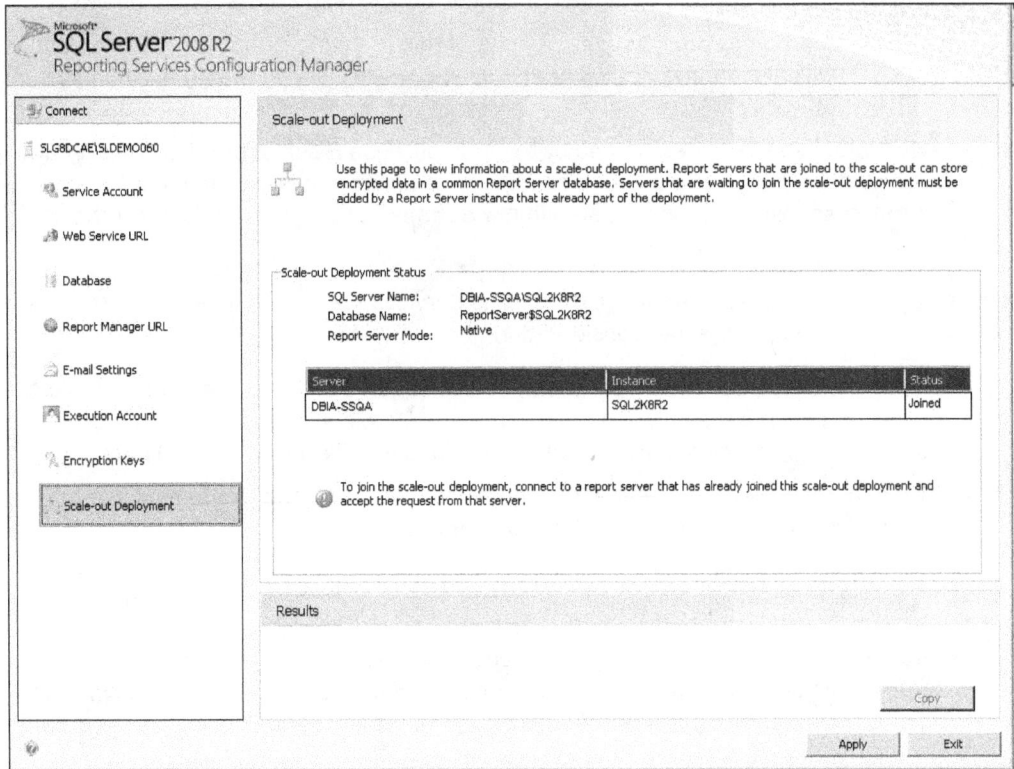

3. Configure the Report Server Web service URL. Do not test the URL yet. It will not resolve until the report server is joined to the scale-out deployment.

4. Configure the Report Manager URL. Do not test the URL yet or try to verify the deployment. The report server will be unavailable until it is joined to the scale-out deployment.

5. Depending on the number of servers you want to join, run the RSC tool to complete the scale-out by joining new report server instances to the first report server instance.

Now, we need to enable the encryption process and join a scale-out deployment. A report server must create and store a copy of the symmetric key in the shared database. The following steps detail the process of enabling the encryption process:

1. Run `rskeymgmt.exe` locally on the computer that hosts a report server that is already a member of the report server scale-out deployment.

2. The utility arguments are:

   - `-j` to join a report server to the report database

- ❏ -i to specify the instance name

- ❏ -m and -n to specify the remote report server instance

- ❏ -u and-v to specify the administrator account on the remote computer

3. The syntax list is as follows:

```
rskeymgmt {-?}
{-eextract}
{-aapply}
{-ddeleteall}
{-srecreatekey}
{-rremoveinstancekey}
{-jjoinfarm}
{-iinstance}
{-ffile}
{-pencryptionpassword}
{-mremotecomputer}
{-ninstancenameofremotecomputer}
{-uadministratoruseraccount}
{-vadministratorpassword}
{-ttrace}
```

4. To join a remote report server named instance to a scale-out deployment run the following statement:

```
rskeymgmt -j -m <remotecomputer> -n <namedreportserverinstance> -u
<administratoraccount> -v <administratorpassword>
```

5. At this point, join the second report server instance to the scale-out deployment.

6. Open **RSC** tool, and reconnect to the first report server instance. By now, the first report server is already initialized for reversible encryption operations. It can be used to join additional report server instances to the scale-out deployment.

7. Click **Scale-out deployment** to open the page that will present two entries, one for each report server instance that is connected to the report server database.

8. The first report server should be joined; the second report server should display the status of **waiting to join**.

9. On the **Scale-out deployment** page, select the report server instance that is waiting to join the deployment and click the **Add Server** button.

10. You should now be able to verify that both report server instances are operational.

11. These steps must be repeated based on the number of report servers that you want to include, which completes steps to perform scale-out deployment.

How it works...

The initialization is a requirement for report server operation; it occurs when SSRS is started for the first time and when you join the report server to the existing deployment. The initialization process creates and stores a symmetric key used for encryption. The symmetric key is created by the Microsoft Windows Cryptographic Services and subsequently used by the Report Server service to encrypt and decrypt data. The following steps describe the initialization process:

> ▸ The Report Server configuration file `RSReportServer.config` plays a key role to get the installation identifier and database connection information.

> ▸ The Report Server service requests a public key from Cryptographic Services. Then, it creates a private and public key and sends the public key to the Report Server service.

> ▸ The Report Server service stores the installation identifier and public key values to the report server database.

> ▸ For symmetric key authorization, the Report Server service calls the Cryptographic Services again to create the symmetric key.

> ▸ The Report Server service connects to the report server database again, and adds the symmetric key to the public key with the installation identifier values that were stored previously.

> ▸ Before storing it, the Report Server service uses its public key to encrypt the symmetric key. Once the symmetric key is stored, the report server is considered initialized and available to use.

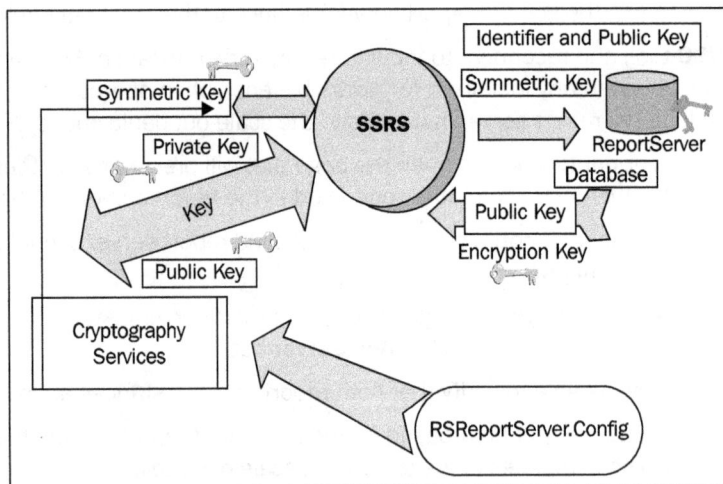

To join a scale-out deployment, a report server must create and store its copy of the symmetric key in the shared database within remote report server. The initialization process for a scale-out deployment differs in how the report server gets the symmetric key.

▶ When the first server is initialized, it gets the symmetric key from Windows

▶ When the second server is initialized during configuration for scale-out deployment, it gets the symmetric key from the Report Server service that is already initialized

▶ The first report server instance uses the public key of the second instance to create an encrypted copy of the symmetric key for the second report server instance; and the symmetric key is never exposed as plain text at any point in this process

We can control scale-out deployment membership by adding and removing encryption keys for specific report server instances using the `rskeymgmt.exe` utility. We need to do this manually from one of the other computers in the scale-out deployment by following these steps:

▶ To list the announced report servers currently in the database: `RSKeyMgmt-l`

▶ This will provide you with a list in the format: `MachineName\Instance—<GUID of the instance>` (Note the GUID of the instance you wish to remove)

▶ To remove the instance of SQL Reporting Services: `RSKeyMgmt -r <GUID of the instance noted previously>`

We will be asked to confirm whether or not we wish to delete the key we have entered. The nodes from the deployment can be removed in any order. If, in case of adding nodes to the deployment, then we must join any new instances from a report server that is already part of the deployment.

There's more...

After all the relevant changes are performed for a scale-out deployment method, when we start up the Reporting Services Configuration tool it might change the `<ReportServerUrl>` settings to the default value.

> It is a best practice to keep a backup copy of the configuration files in case there is a need to replace them with the version that contains the settings that you want to use.

See Also

Preparing and Installing Reporting Services, which highlights the new deployment mode that is available in SQL Server 2008 R2.

Preparing and installing SQL Server Integration Services

The first release of Integration Services in SQL Server 2005 has changed the ETL functionality for SQL Server. It is a successor to SQL Server 2000 version's Data Transformation Services (DTS), and took a significant step forward by providing more intuitive designers, but also a native .NET execution environment. SQL Server 2008 R2 maintains that process with a significant scalability improvement in data pipeline and data warehouse enhancements such as persistent lookups. The SSIS enhancements from SQL Server 2008 R2 are improved scripting experience, data profiling task, an enhanced ADO.NET destination adapter, which also includes an option of **Use bulk insert when available** to improve the performance of bulk insert operations, improved data flow lookup, component with enhanced performance, and caching for Lookup transformation. The development tool for SSIS is Visual Studio 2008 development and in short BIDS too. BI Development Studio is an all-in-one tool, which has a built-in Visual Studio infrastructure that provides a powerful and flexible development environment for SSIS, SSAS, SSRS, and other .NET related programming languages.

In this recipe, we will evaluate the SQL Server Integration Services installation options and best practice hardware/software requirements, configuration, and security considerations for the installation.

Getting ready

In order to prepare for the installation of SQL Server Integration Services, you will need to ensure you have the following in place:

▶ The .NET framework 3.5 SP1, Windows Install 4.5, and SQL Server setup support files are still applicable to Integration Services installation

▶ For more information on the prerequisite files required, refer to the recipe, *Adding features of SQL Server 2008 R2 using Slipstream technology* in *Chapter 1:Getting Started with SQL Server 2008 R2*

How to do it...

By default, all the SQL Server services can be installed using the installation media, best practice is to copy all the files to the local drive of that server for quick and efficient setup completion:

1. From the `root` folder of the installation media, double-click `Setup.exe`.

2. When the prerequisites are installed, the Installation Wizard runs the SQL Server Installation Center.

3. To change the installation path for shared components, either update the path in the field at the bottom of the dialog box, or click **Browse** to move to an installation directory. The default installation path is C:\Program Files\Microsoft SQL Server\100\ folder.

4. On the **Feature Selection** page, select the components from Shared Features **Business Intelligence Development Studio** and **Integration Services** for your installation.

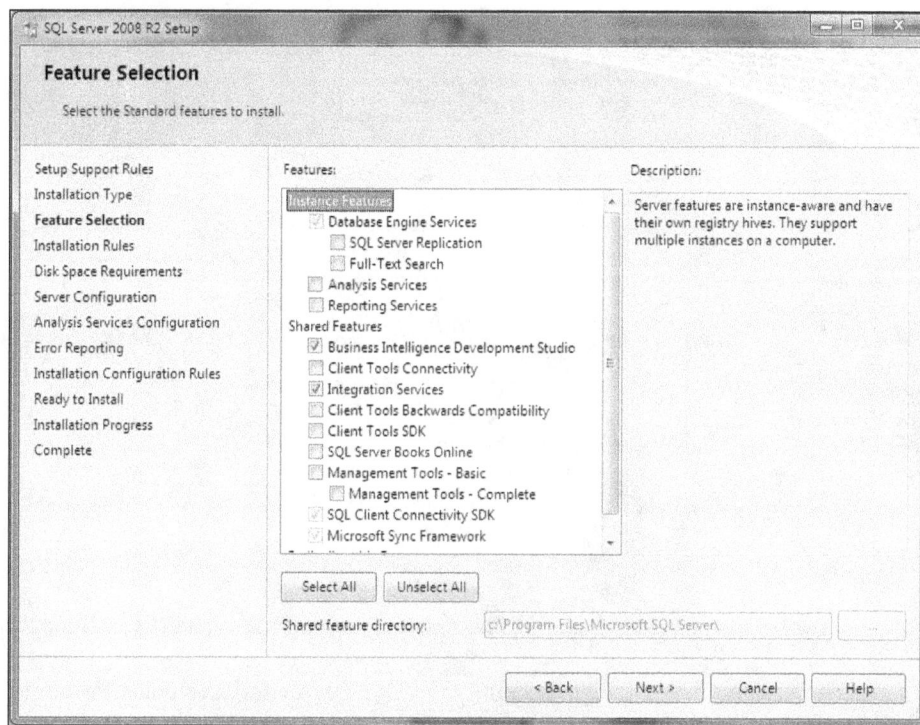

5. In this recipe, we are adding features to existing services, hence, the instance features for Database Engine Services is disabled by default.

6. Be sure to add authoring and management tools, such as Business Intelligence Development Studio and SQL Server Management Studio, so that you can manage Integration Services package and folders in a hierarchal view.

7. These selections will install services and tools that are useful for Integration Services.

8. Next, the detected instances and features grid shows instances of SQL Server that are on the computer where Setup is running. **Disk Space Requirements** page calculates the required disk space for the features that you specify.

9. On the **Server Configuration | Service Accounts** page, specify login accounts for SQL Server Database Engine, SQL Server Agent, Integration services, and SQL Server Browser.

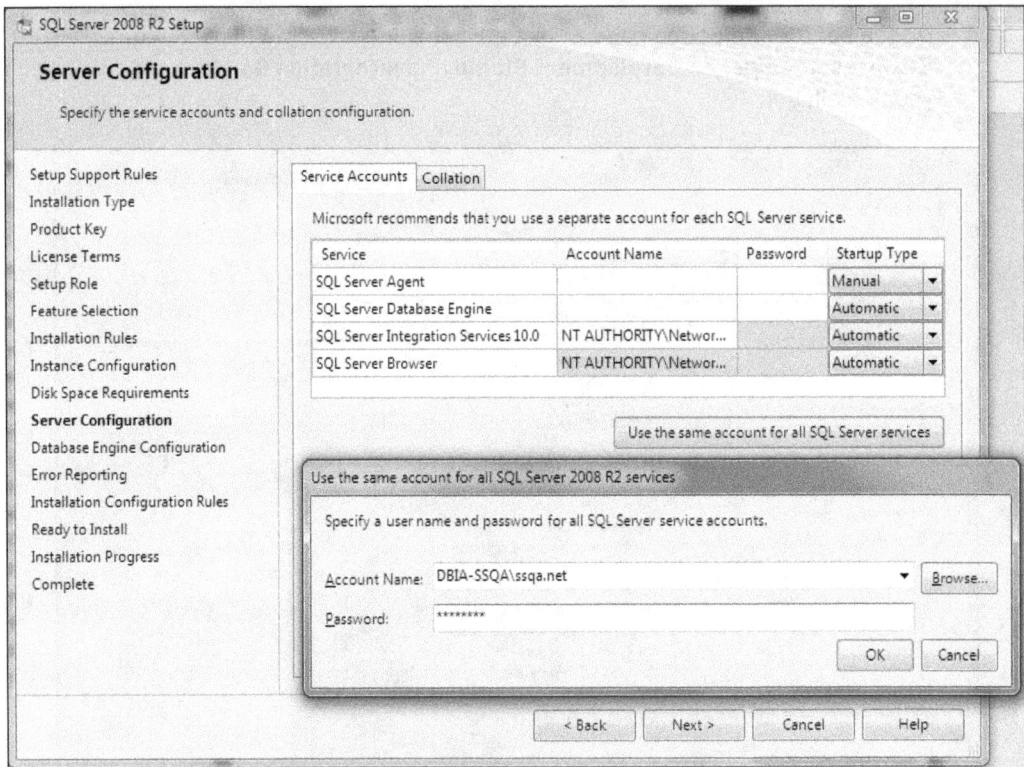

10. You can assign the same login account to all SQL Server services using the same account for all SQL Server services, or you can configure each service account individually. Choose **StartUp** option as **Automatic** for SQL Server Database Engine and SQL Server Integration Services.

> A Best practice is to configure service accounts individually to provide least privileges for each service, where SQL Server services are granted the minimum permissions they have to complete their tasks.

11. SQL Server Setup enforces the domain user-account requirement by blocking the installation whenever a machine account is specified.

12. At the **Database Engine Configuration | Account provisioning** page, we have an option to set the security mode and assign an account to be a member of SYSADMIN fixed server role.

13. You can assign the same login account to all SQL Server services, or you can configure each service account individually.

14. This account must be a Windows Domain User account. Built-in machine accounts (such as Network Service, or Local Service) are prohibited.

15. Choose the **SQL Server Administrators** for SSIS service, click **Add Current User** and you can also add any other user to assign SYSADMIN privileges.

16. You can only install a single instance of Integration Services; the service is not specific to a particular instance of the database engine.

17. You can connect to the service by using the name of the computer.

> By default, the Integration Services is configured to store packages in MSDB system database.

18. On a 64-bit environment, when you install SQL Server and select Integration Services for installation, Setup installs 64-bit Integration Services features and tools.

   ❑ 64-bit features are installed under the Program Files directory, and 32-bit features are installed separately under the Program Files (x86) directory

19. The System Configuration Checker will run an additional set of rules to validate the server configuration with the SQL Server features that you have specified.

20. The **Ready to Install** page shows a tree view of installation options that were specified during Setup. Now, click **Install** to continue.

21. At this point, the installation should proceed as planned. Unless some unexpected error occurs, the process should have a working instance of SSIS deployed on your machine, along with SQL Server.

22. After installation, the **Complete** page provides a link to the summary log file for the installation and other important notes.

23. Make sure you review the summary of installation log file from the %Program Files%\Microsoft SQL Server\110\Setup Bootstrap\Log folder to ensure no errors are reported.

> If you are instructed to restart the computer, do so now. It is important to read and follow the message from the Installation Wizard when you have finished running the Setup.

Now, we have the Integration Services installation complete, and ready to manage the ETL processes using BIDS and SSMS tools.

How it works...

From SQL Server 2008 R2 onwards, the setup program is used to install any or all of its components. Through this setup, you can install Integration Services with or without other SQL Server components on a single server. The connectivity components (which are installed by the setup) are important for communication between clients and servers that includes the server network libraries.

The authoring and management tool such as BIDS and SSMS are essential to design, develop, and manage the packages for ETL purposes. The service installation and service account starts and runs as a Windows service, where each instance of core database engine services and Integration Services is supported by its own service and each instance can use different settings for collation and server options. Integration Services isn't just one application, but a collection of components, utilities, engines, and wizards.

Managing the ETL process efficiently

ETL process efficiency requires a high volume of ETL throughput, where best practices for standard relational databases and high performance techniques for packages are taken into consideration. Similarly, the high volume ETL throughput and management require specific considerations and implementation techniques in a data warehousing environment. The data store that contains trends, patterns, and a history of business is essential to make decisions. Such BI services use facts to record transactions and dimensions that contain information about customer transactions, such as customer name, time, product sales, and sales promotions.

Integration Services from SQL Server 2008 R2 provides a number of specific benefits for meeting the requirements of high-volume ETL processes. High volume ETL is a data warehouse update process that needs the infrastructure support from the technology to attain the throughput. ETL designer from IS design toolbox helps to design the packages as a high throughput ETL system in managing high performance data transfers. Batch windows for ETL data processing are generally time-constrained, particularly when managing large volumes of data. To optimize the data transfer, the **destination adapter** option in Integration Services that enables the setting of **Fast Load** properties on the transfer are used. In order to match up the rows written against a count, it is organized as a part of ETL transfer logic; this requires a syntactical submission where each load should be associated with metadata describing the transfer status, throughput metrics, and downstream reconciliation purpose.

This recipe presents a number of suggestions relating to high volume ETL throughput, laid out specifically using for the use of SQL Server Integration Services. Aspects of both ETL performance and management are described in such a way, that it will help users to manage the overall ETL process efficiently. In this recipe, we will focus on the components that will address the advanced ETL specific processes such as Slowly Changing Dimensions (SCD), and Fuzzy lookup transform. The features within SQL Server 2008 R2 provide the Integration Services beyond simple ETL operations with an advanced and extended set of components that are for enabling various lookup efficiencies, including the Lookup transform and Lookup Cache transform.

How to do it...

Managing the ETL processes efficiently and providing the high volume ETL throughput requires us to consider the best practices and high performance techniques for ETL. The following steps are defined on the aspects of both ETL efficiency and management:

1. Create a new **Integration Services** project. Click the **package** in the new solution.

2. Drop a **Data Flow Task** onto the workflow. Switch to the **Data Flow** tab.

3. Drop an **OLE DB Source Adapter** and double-click it.

4. Click the **New** button to create a **new OLE DB** connection manager. Connect to the Adventure Works database.

5. Select **Table** or **View** for the Data Access mode, which is the default selection.

6. Select **[HumanResources].[Employee]** for the name of the table. Click the **Columns** node. Click the **OK** button to close the OLE DB Source Adapter dialog box.

7. Drop a **Slowly Changing Dimension transform** onto the Data Flow designer.

8. Drag the output from the OLE DB Source Adapter to the **SCD transform**.

9. Double-click the **Slowly Changing Dimension transform** to open the Slowly Changing Dimension Wizard.

10. Within SCD wizard, there are general steps that are involved in SCD for defining additional data flow and runtime behavior of SCD transform.

11. Select a **Dimension Table and Keys** option to choose which dimension table you want to modify and the keys for matching the source records with dimension table records.

12. Select the Slowly Changing Dimension Columns to choose the **dimension** attributes and the change type for each attribute.

13. Select the **Fixed and Changing Attribute** Option to set the SCD transform to **fail** if a fixed attribute has changed, and update all records when a change is detected in a changing attribute.

14. Select the **Historical Attribute** Option to set the SCD Wizard to detect current and expired records.

15. Select the **Inferred Dimension Member** to turn on inferred member support and check how to detect that an incoming record is for a previously inserted inferred dimension record.

16. Click **Finish** to complete the Slowly Changing Dimension Wizard.

17. When you finish the wizard, it takes all input settings and creates data flow that is shown in the following screenshot. Depending on whether or not your dimension table supports historical attribute change types, the output might vary.

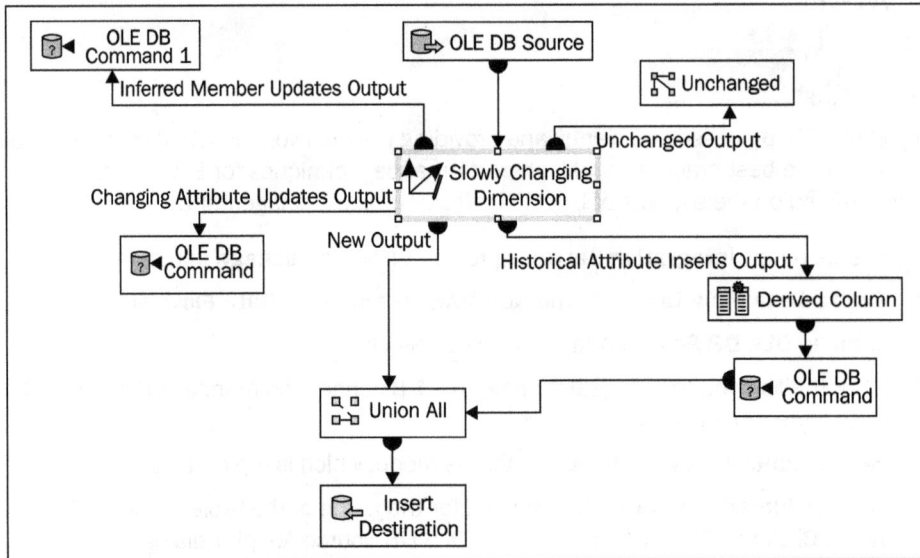

18. Within SSIS, the Fuzzy Lookup and Fuzzy Grouping components use fuzzy matching algorithms to provide fundamental primitives to improve the data quality of existing or new data.

19. To set up and configure, the Fuzzy matching algorithm builds a simple import and export SSIS package using BIDS tool.

20. Depending on the **EventHandler** settings during the `PreExecute` phase of data flow, the fuzzy lookup needs to be set up. The **DataFlow** tab toolbox contains the Fuzzy Lookup and Fuzzy Grouping tasks.

21. Once the reference table is set up, you need to set up the columns. The **Columns** tab allows you to specify the columns you want the fuzzy to match and the columns you want to flow to the outputs.

22. By using the advanced Fuzzy Lookup editor, (right-click on Fuzzy Lookup transformation task and choose **Show Advanced Editor**) you can match contribution values for a higher degree of accuracy that can be considered as a good match.

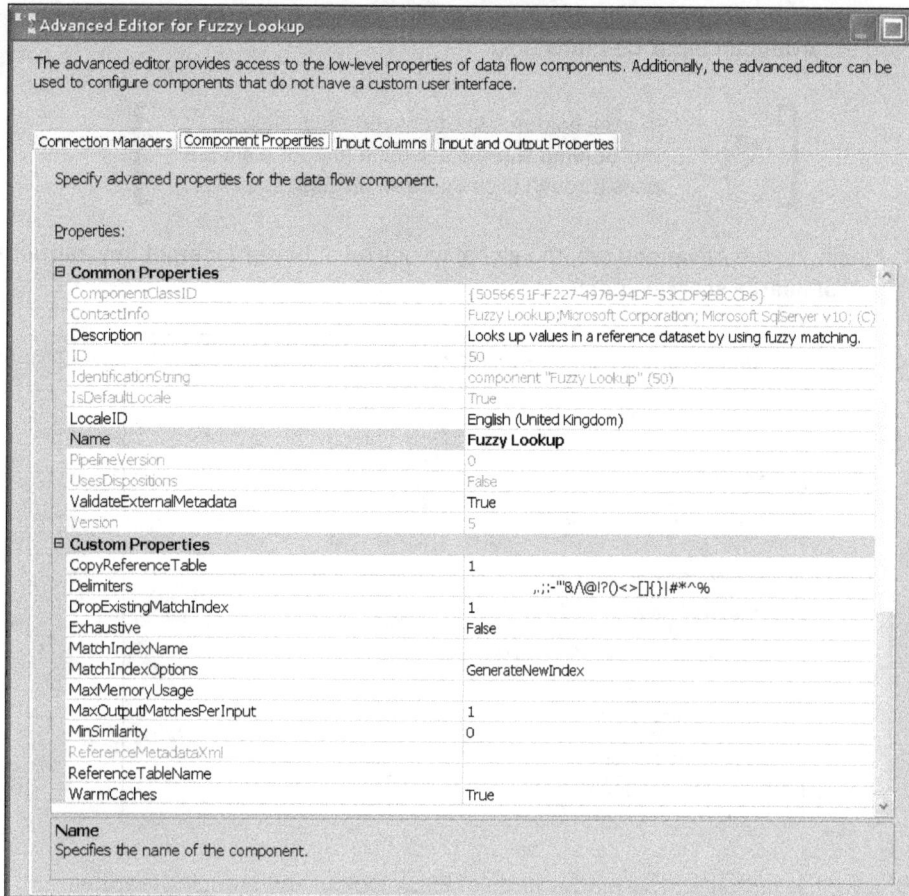

23. To specify the transform, right-click on Fuzzy lookup to open **Fuzzy Grouping Transformation Editor** connection manager.

24. When the component is opened up the **Fuzzy Grouping** transformation is configured over three tabs.

25. Point the OLE DB destination to a connection for which you can write a new table, and then click **New** to create a new connection source.

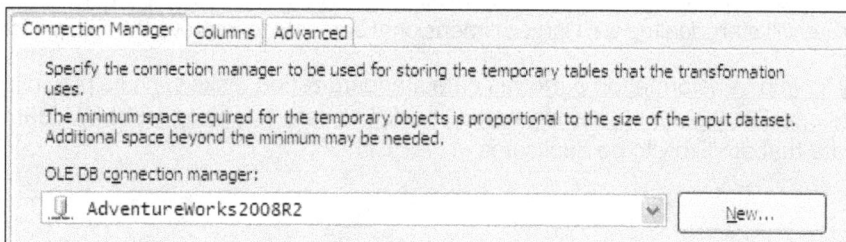

26. Next, on the **Columns** tab, identify the similar rows by using the columns component in the **Available Input Columns** box.

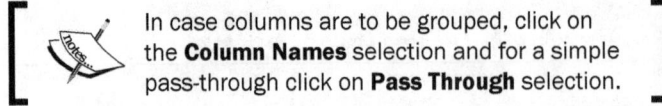

> In case columns are to be grouped, click on the **Column Names** selection and for a simple pass-through click on **Pass Through** selection.

27. Finally, on the **Advanced** tab, the global values must be set for **input key, output key,** and **similarity score** columns.

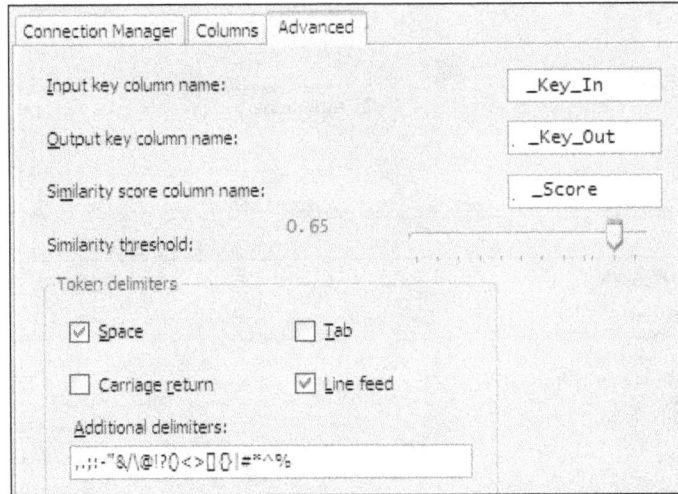

28. Save the package to take advantage of Fuzzy lookup and grouping features.

All the steps mentioned earlier will enable the SSIS package components to provide an advanced functionality of managing ETL activities efficiently beyond typical data transformation.

How it works...

The primary design goal for the SCD wizard and the transform component will enable the process to build a robust SCD data flow. The wizard will quickly build data flow to generate a package that will start dealing with larger dimensional datasets to improve the ETL performance.

The Fuzzy lookup transformation performs data standardization tasks such as providing missing values. Fuzzy grouping transformation performs data cleansing tasks by identifying rows of data that are likely to be duplicates.

The Fuzzy Lookup transformation follows a similar transformation process in a package data flow—it tries to find an exact match. If the search fails, then it provides a close match from the reference table. This search process uses an `equi-join` method to locate matching records. The Fuzzy Grouping transformation requires the connection to the SQL Server for creating temporary tables within `TEMPDB` database–that transforms required algorithm.

The Fuzzy components lookup and grouping will transform the data from the reference table and add an additional column for storing the tokens for each row. Fuzzy Lookup uses an `Error-Tolerant-Index` (`ETI`) to find the matching rows in the reference table. The ETI options will provide a way to store the index table for later updates based on the changes that are made to the reference data. To obtain optimum performance, ETL provides further options such as:

- **Generates New Index**: It is best used when the reference data is small, for quicker data transformation
- **Stores New Index**: It is best used with existing index; and to generate the index, the package must be executed

At runtime, the Fuzzy Grouping transform adds three key fields to the output stream:

- `_key_in`: It is used to uniquely identify each row based on the reference column generated key
- `_key_out`: It is a column that identifies a group of duplicate rows
- `_score`: It is the similarity between the `_key_in` and `_key_out` values where the value between 0 and 1 indicates the similarity of the input row.

The fuzzy lookup transform is useful to find correct values based on similarity and parameters matching during a lookup and the fuzzy grouping is useful to find duplicated values. Both these are very useful to eliminate any administrative/human errors.

5

Managing Core SQL Server 2008 R2 Technologies

In this chapter, we will cover the following topics:

- ▶ Planning and implementing Self-Service Business Intelligence services
- ▶ Implementing Microsoft StreamInsight technologies platform
- ▶ Implementing SQL Azure connectivity features
- ▶ Installing and configuring a Master Data Services solution
- ▶ Designing and deploying a framework to use Master Data Services

Introduction

SQL Server 2008 R2 has a flurry of new enhancements added to the core database engine and business intelligence suite. The new enhancements within the core database engine are: SQL Azure connectivity (SQLAzure), Data-Tier application (DAC PACK), SQL Server Utility (UCP), and network connectivity. In addition to the new features and internal enhancements, SQL Server 2008 R2 includes new developments to the asynchronous messaging subsystem, such as Service Broker (SB) and external components such as Master Data Services (MDS), StreamInsight, Reporting Services with SharePoint Integration, and PowerPivot for Analysis Services.

These recipes involve the planning, design, and implementation of features that are added and they are important to the management of the core technologies of SQL Server 2008 R2.

Planning and implementing Self-Service Business Intelligence services

Self-Service Business Intelligence (BI) is the new buzzword in the data platform, a new paradigm to the existing BI functionalities. Using Microsoft's Self-Service BI, anyone can easily build the BI applications using traditional desktop tools such as Office Excel and specialized services such as SharePoint. The BI application can be built to manage the published applications in a common way and track data usage having the analytical data connected to its source. The data customization can be accomplished easily by sharing data in a controlled way where the customers can access it from a web browser (intranet or extranet) without using Office applications or Server applications. The external tasks such as security administration and deployment of new hardware are accomplished using the features of SQL Server 2008 R2 and Windows Server 2008 operating system.

Self-Service BI can be implemented using PowerPivot, which has two components working together, PowerPivot for Excel and PowerPivot for SharePoint. The PowerPivot for Excel is an add-in that enhances the capabilities of Excel for users and brings the full power of SQL Server Analysis Services right into Excel; whereas, PowerPivot for SharePoint extends the Office SharePoint Services to share and manage the PowerPivot applications that are created with PowerPivot for Excel. In this recipe, we will go through the steps that are required to plan and implement PowerPivot for Excel and PowerPivot for SharePoint.

Getting ready

PowerPivot for Excel is a component of SQL Server 2008 R2 and is an add-in of Excel 2010 from Office 2010 suite, along with the Office Shared Features. To get started you will need to do the following:

- Download the PowerPivot for Excel 2010 add-in from: `http://www.microsoft.com/downloads/en/details.aspx?FamilyID=e081c894-e4ab-42df-8c87-4b99c1f3c49b&displaylang=en`.
  - If you install the 32-bit version of Excel, you must use the 32-bit version of PowerPivot. If you install the 64-bit version of Excel, you must use the 64-bit version of PowerPivot.

- To test PowerPivot features in addition to the Excel add-in you need to download the sample databases for SQL Server 2008 R2. They can be downloaded from: `http://msftdbprodsamples.codeplex.com/wikipage?title=Installing%20SQL%20Server%202008R2%20Databases`.

- In this recipe, the sample database built in SQL Server Analysis Services 2008 R2 based on an imaginary company will be referred to. It is available for download from: `http://www.microsoft.com/downloads/en/details.aspx?displaylang=en&FamilyID=868662dc-187a-4a85-b611-b7df7dc909fc`.

Using the windows installer (`.msi`) package, you can install **SQL Server 2008 R2 sample databases**. However, you must make sure that your SQL Server instance meets the following prerequisites:

▶ Full-Text Search must be installed with SQL `Full-text filter` daemon launcher service running

▶ `FILESTREAM` must be enabled

> To install these prerequisites on existing SQL Server instances, refer to `http://msftdbprodsamples.codeplex.com/wikipage?title=Database%20Prerequisites&referringTitle=Installing%20SQL%20Server%202008R2%20Databases`.

▶ PowerPivot for the SharePoint component can be installed using the SharePoint 2010 setup program

 ❑ SharePoint 2010 is only supported on Windows Server 2008 Service Pack 2 or higher, and Window Server 2008 R2, and only on x64 platform

▶ There are two setup options—a **New Farm install** and an **Existing Farm install**

 ❑ The **New Farm install** is typically expected to be used in a single-machine install where PowerPivot will take care of installing and configuring all the relevant services effectively for you

▶ To view PowerPivot workbooks published to the PowerPivot Gallery, you will need Silverlight

 ❑ Silverlight is not available in a 64-bit version; you must use the 32-bit Web browser to see PowerPivot workbooks using the PowerPivot Gallery's special views

▶ The Self-Service Analytics solution describes the steps required to analyze sales and promotions data and share the analysis to other users

▶ This solution consists of two documents and one sample data file (Access database and Excel workbooks), which can be downloaded from: `http://www.microsoft.com/downloads/en/details.aspx?FamilyID=fa8175d0-157f-4e45-8053-6f5bb7eb6397&displaylang=en`

How to do it...

In this recipe, we will go through the steps required to plan and implement PowerPivot for Excel and PowerPivot for SharePoint:

1. Connect to your SQL Server relational database server using SQL Server Management Studio and restore the Contoso retail sample database on the SQL Server instance.

2. **Office Shared** Features installs `VSTO 4.0`, which is needed as a prerequisite for **PowerPivot for Excel**.

3. To install the client application once the download is completed, run a setup program (`PowerPivot_for_Excel.msi`), which is a self-explanatory wizard installation.

4. The initial PowerPivot installation of `Excel 2010` program requires `COM Add-ins` activation. To do so, on the Excel worksheet click **File | Options** and select the **Add-Ins** page.

5. In the Add-Ins page from the **Manage** drop-down list select **COM Add-ins** and click on the **Go** button.

6. Finally, select the **PowerPivot for Excel** option and click the **OK** button to display the **PowerPivot** tab back in the `Excel 2010` sheet.

7. You can open the PowerPivot window from an Excel file, click on the **PowerPivot** tab on the Excel ribbon.

8. Launch Excel 2010 from **All Programs | Microsoft Office | Microsoft Excel 2010**. On the **PowerPivot** tab, click on the **PowerPivot** Window.

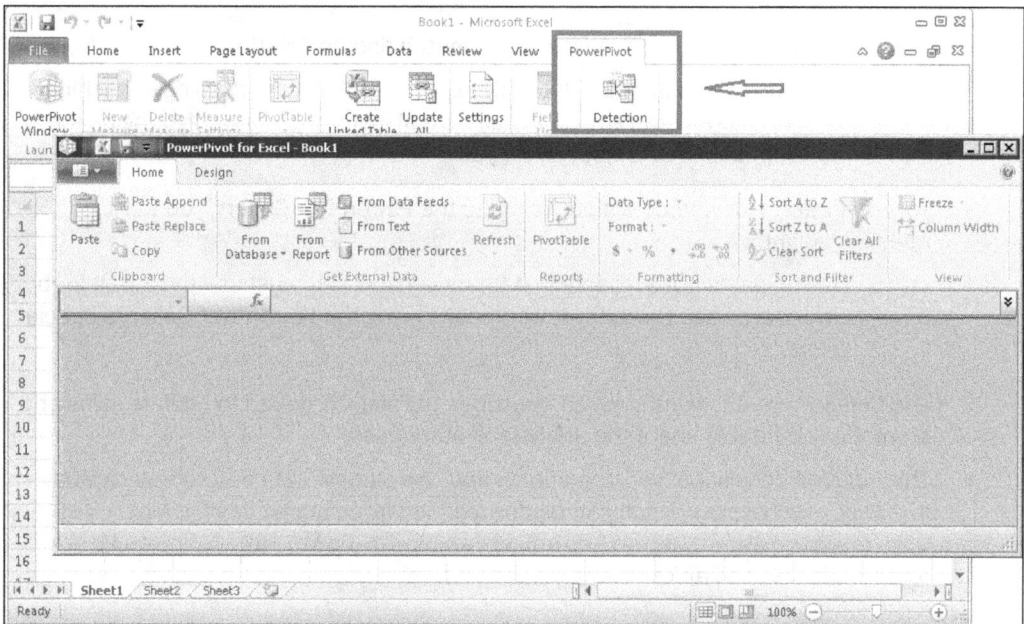

9. Click on the **PowerPivot Window** button that will open a PowerPivot Window, as shown in the preceding screenshot.

10. The **PowerPivot Window** helps you with the key operations of importing data, filtering, and analyzing the data, as well as creating certain Data Analysis Expression (DAX) calculations.

11. Let us see how the PowerPivot provides the several methods to import and enhance data by building a Self-Service BI application.

Task	Description
Add data by selecting **tables to import**	PowerPivot includes a Table Import Wizard that helps you to import data from a large number of sources. You can import several tables into the Excel workbook and filter some of the data. For a list of supported data sources refer to: `http://technet.microsoft.com/en-us/library/ee835543.aspx`.
Add data by using a custom query	You can also import data based on a query that you specify, rather than having PowerPivot generate the query for you.
Add data by using copy and paste	PowerPivot enables you to paste tabular data directly into the PowerPivot window.
Add data by using a linked table	A Linked Table is a table that has been created in a worksheet in the Excel window, but is linked to a table in the PowerPivot window.

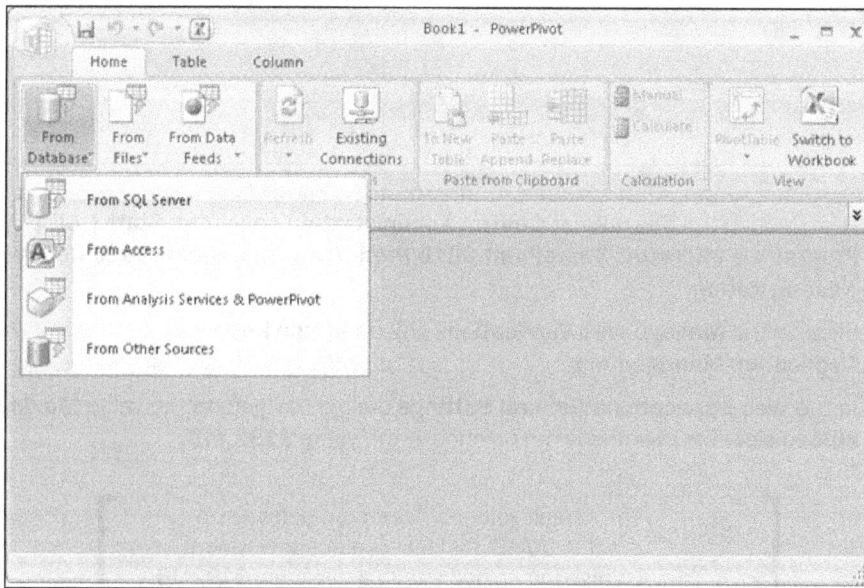

12. PowerPivot for SharePoint configures your SharePoint 2010 as part of the **New Farm install** option.

> For more information on the installation and prerequisite steps to install PowerPivot for SharePoint refer to *Chapter 4: Administration of core Business Intelligence Services*.

13. After successfully installing PowerPivot for SharePoint, you should verify the installation.

14. Open the Web browser in administrator's privilege mode and enter `http://<machinename>` with `<machinename>` being the name of the server machine where you performed the PowerPivot for SharePoint install.

15. You should see a link to the **PowerPivot Gallery** on the left side of the page, as shown in the following screenshot:

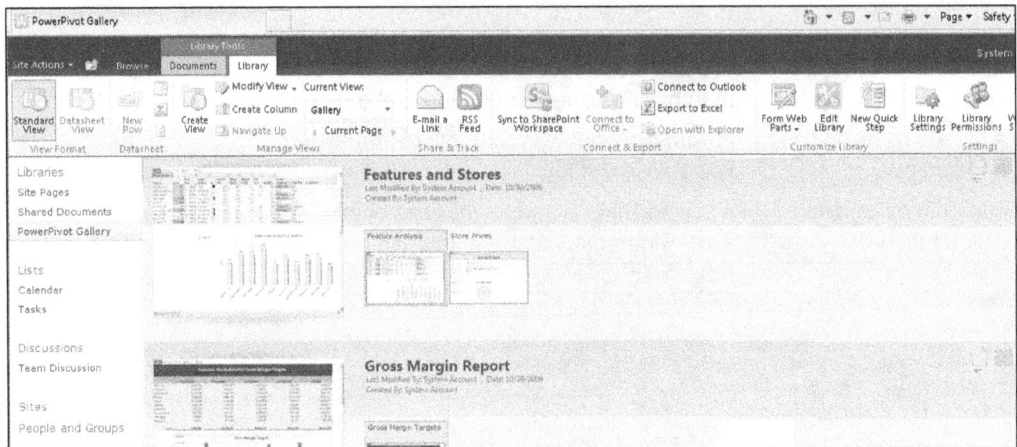

16. Next, launch the **SharePoint Central Administration** page from **Start | All | Programs | Microsoft SharePoint 2010 Products | SharePoint 2010 Central Administration**.

17. Click on the **Manage web applications** link under the heading **Application Management**.

18. In the **Web Applications General Settings** dialog, navigate to the value **Maximum upload size**. For this recipe, let us choose the value **3192 MB**.

> The default value for Maximum Upload size is set to 50MB, for ideal content deployment change the upload size to a minimum 3192MB.

19. Navigate back to **SharePoint Central Administration | Application Management | Manage Service Applications**.

20. Select **ExcelServiceApp1** (Excel Services Application Web Service Application) and click **Manage** to choose **Trusted file locations**.

21. Click on **http://** to change the Excel Services settings. Navigate to the **Workbook Properties** section. For this recipe, choose the value of the **Maximum Workbook Size** as **3192 MB**.

22. The new settings will take effect once the IIS services are restarted.

We have now successfully completed the PowerPivot for SharePoint installation, now the instance is ready to publish and share the PowerPivot workbook.

To ensure the PowerPivot for SharePoint installation is successful and to share a workbook, we can test the process by publishing a PowerPivot workbook instance, as follows:

1. Switch on the machine with Excel and PowerPivot for Excel.

2. Open a workbook.

3. Click on **File | Save** and **Send | Save to SharePoint | Save As**.

4. Enter http://<yourPowerPivotserver>/PowerPivot Gallery in the folder path of the **Save As** dialog, and click **Save**.

How it works...

Microsoft Excel is a popular Business Intelligence tool on the client side, and to present data from multiple sources PowerPivot for Excel is required. The installation process of the PowerPivot add-in on the client side is a straightforward process, though there is no requirement of SQL Server 2008 R2 components on the client side. Behind the scenes, the **Analysis Services VertiPaq** engine from PowerPivot for Excel runs all the 'in-process' for Excel. The connectivity to the Analysis Services data source is managed by MDX, XMLA Source, AMO, and ADOMD.NET libraries, which in turn use the Analysis Services OLE DB provider to connect to the PowerPivot data within the workbook.

On the workstation, the **Analysis Services VertiPaq** engine issues queries and receives data from a variety of data sources, including relational or multidimensional databases, documents, public data stores, or Web services. During data import and client-side data refresh, an ATOM data feed provider is used for importing and refreshing data in the ATOM format.

In case of connectivity to non-Microsoft data sources such as Oracle/Teradata/DB2/SYBASE/SQLAzure/OLEDB/ODBC sources and most commonly used file sources such as Excel or flat files, we must acquire and install these drivers manually.

PowerPivot for SharePoint installs on top of SharePoint 2010, and adds services and functionality to SharePoint. As we have seen, PowerPivot for Excel is an effective tool to create and edit PowerPivot applications, and for data collaboration, sharing, and reporting PowerPivot for SharePoint. Behind the scene, SQL Server 2008 R2 features SharePoint 2010 integrated mode for Analysis Service which includes the VertiPaq engine to provide in-memory data storage. It will also help in processing very large amounts of data, where high performance is accomplished through columnar storage and data compression.

The storage of PowerPivot workbooks is quite large and SharePoint 2010 has a default maximum size limit of 50MB for file size. As per the enterprise storage policies, you need to change the file storage setting in SharePoint to publish and upload PowerPivot workbooks. Internally, PowerPivot for SharePoint components, PowerPivot System Service, and Analysis Services in VertiPaq will provide the hosting capability for PowerPivot applications internally. For client connectivity to publish, it includes a web service component that allows applications to connect to the PowerPivot workbook data from outside the SharePoint farm.

There's more...

Creating an Excel workbook that contains PowerPivot data requires both Excel 2010 and the PowerPivot for Excel add-in. After you create the workbook, you can publish it to a SharePoint Server 2010 farm that has Excel Services, and a deployment of SQL Server PowerPivot for SharePoint. PowerPivot workbooks can be opened in Excel 2007.

However, Excel 2007 cannot be used to create or modify PowerPivot data, or to interact with PivotTables, or PivotCharts that use PowerPivot data. You must use Excel 2010 to get full access to all PowerPivot features.

Implementing Microsoft StreamInsight Technologies Platform

Every Enterprise has always been on a continuous press to reduce the lag between data acquisition and data processing. When talking about moving data from a traditional desktop-based application to an Enterprise data warehouse application, the technology must support complex event processing and provide proactive results from monitoring.

SQL Server 2008 R2 has a new feature, StreamInsight. StreamInsight is a powerful platform that enables the processing of high-speed data streams from multiple data sources. The technology is useful for financial applications such as stock exchanges, banks for fraud detection, retail applications such as ISPs for surveillance of internet traffic, and manufacturing for real-time business intelligence. The StreamInsight Standard edition is available in SQL Server 2008 R2 Standard, or Enterprise, or Web editions, and StreamInsight Premium edition in SQL Server 2008 R2 Datacenter, or Developer, or Evaluation editions. However, the premium version of StreamInsight is recommended only when event rates exceed 5000 events per second or latency requirements are less than 5 seconds. For event rates less than 5000 events per second and/or latency requirements in excess of 5 seconds, the standard version of StreamInsight is recommended.

StreamInsight is built to detect, decide, and respond. Event processing is the main component to monitor a system or process by looking for exceptional behavior and generating alerts when such behavior exceeds the business process levels. The reaction is generated in the form of alerts; for real-time applications it requires a recovery action—automated or manually. The event processing component keeps the logic that processes the events separate from the event producers and consumers. These actions can be divided into:

- **Deterministic**: In this approach, there is an exact mapping between a situation in the real world and its representation in the event processing system

- **Approximate**: Here, the event processing system provides an approximation to real-world events

StreamInsight extends the advantage and effectiveness of event processing, which can reduce the substantial cost of ownership of an event processing application. The cost reduction is visible from the level of abstraction, which is similar to the relational database management system to hold data rather than using a filesystem component. The internals of event processing provide the abstractions for handling events that are higher than conventional programming languages; this is where the reduction in the cost of development and maintenance is visible.

In this recipe, we will look at how to implement StreamInsight onto your existing SQL Server 2008 R2 platform.

Getting ready

Like all other Microsoft products, the StreamInsight client package installs a subset of feature technology, which implements only the client-side functionality. The package installs the components in connecting to an existing StreamInsight server to manage queries and the debugger tool. For the SQL Server 2008 R2 RTM release, StreamInsight client does not require a license, but for server side the license needs to be part of SQL Server license, which is documented in End-User License Agreement (EULA), see `http://www.microsoft.com/downloads/en/details.aspx?FamilyID=9e74964e-afc3-44c2-b05e-1ca87b701c2f&displaylang=en`.

The Microsoft StreamInsight package is available in a 32-bit (X86) and 64-bit (X64) environment.

▶ To download StreamInsight for 64-bit setup, refer to: `http://go.microsoft.com/fwlink/?LinkID=195954&clcid=0x409`

   For 32-bit refer to: `http://go.microsoft.com/fwlink/?LinkID=196065&clcid=0x409`

▶ To download the Microsoft StreamInsight Client package 64-bit, refer to: `http://go.microsoft.com/fwlink/?LinkID=196067&clcid=0x409`

   For 32-bit refer to: `http://go.microsoft.com/fwlink/?LinkID=196068&clcid=0x409`

The prerequisites for the operating system and other components are as follows:

▶ The supported operating systems are Windows Server 2008, Windows 7, Windows Vista, and Windows XP

▶ Windows XP and Windows 2003 will have restrictions on the debugging tool, which has limited functionality; the event tracing functionality of the debugging tool is not designed to work on these operating systems

▶ Microsoft .NET framework 3.5 Service Pack1 is required; to download refer to: `http://go.microsoft.com/fwlink/?LinkId=128220`

▶ If there are any previous versions of Microsoft StreamInsight that exist in the system, uninstall them first to reinstall the latest version of Microsoft StreamInsight

▶ To use the full functionality of Microsoft StreamInsight, you need to install Microsoft SQL Server Compact edition

▶ The StreamInsight instance is limited to 64 characters, it must not contain spaces or special characters and should start with a letter or an underscore

How to do it...

Microsoft StreamInsight has two methods to complete the installation process:

▶ **Attended Installation**: It includes an interactive user interface throughout the setup process

▶ **Unattended Installation**: It includes a command-line setup process that requires parameters during the installation to indicate the acceptance of license terms

It is essential that you ensure the prerequisites are complete before proceeding with the installation. In this recipe, we will look at how to implement StreamInsight onto your existing SQL Server 2008 R2 platform.

1. To install the StreamInsight instance, double-click on the downloaded file and navigate to the Program Maintenance screen.

2. Click **Next** to enter the instance name, proceed to the next screen to enter the license-key or choose **Evaluation edition** that will be activated with a 180-day expiration.

3. Now, specify service and group settings. It is essential to add the current user to the StreamInsight Users group.

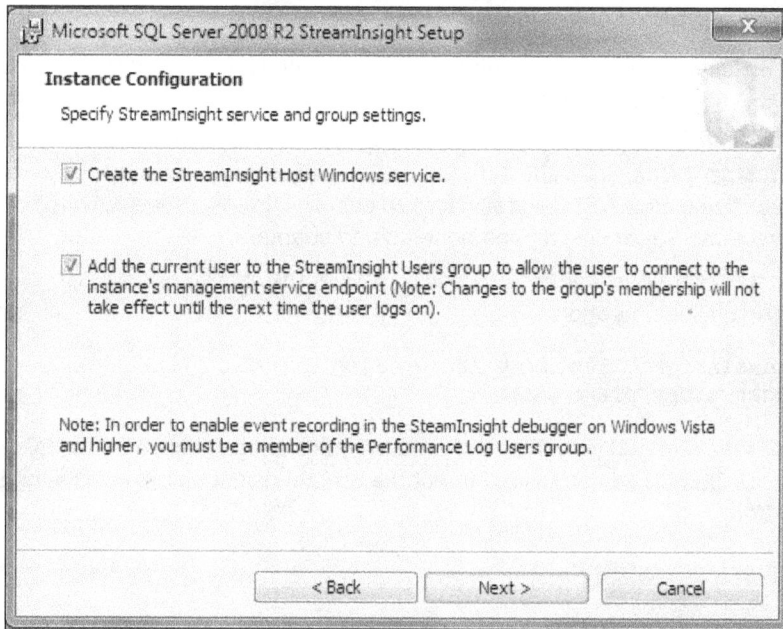

4. Choose **Next** to install the selected services.

5. The client package installs the client-side libraries and it does not require a SQL Server 2008 R2 product key.

6. Run the **command prompt** application as Administrator.

7. For any unattended installation, the properties are defined using the `Property Name=VALUE` method, which are case-sensitive and defined as uppercase.

8. The different Property Names are `INSTANCENAME`, `PRODUCTKEY`, `CREATESERVICE`, `INSTANCENAME`, `IACCEPTLICENSETERMS`, and `ADDUSERSTOGROUP`.

9. We must supply the value for `IACCEPTLICENSETERMS` **Property Name** and all other names can be left as optional.

10. To install a quiet installation, execute the following code from a command prompt window to create StreamInsight as a Windows Service:

```
StreamInsight.msi /quiet /log SI_install_log.
txt INSTANCENAME=DEFAAULT IACCEPTLICENSETERMS=YES
PRODUCTKEY=00000-00000-00000-00000-00000 CREATESERVICE=1
```

11. For the full functionality of StreamInsight, we need to install a new version of SQL Server Compact edition 3.5 Service Pack2.

12. Ensure you remove any previous versions of SQL Server Compact using **Programs | Add/Remove Programs** option.

13. The installation file for Microsoft SQL Server Compact is located in: `C:\Program Files\Microsoft StreamInsight 1.0\Redist\SSCERuntime-ENU-x86. msi`.

14. From **Start | Run**, enter the path to install the file mentioned previously. The SQL Server Compact 3.5 SP2 installation is a self-explanatory process, which will install the required StreamInsight components and adapters.

15. To install client package the process is to enter the following text as a command-line operation:

```
StreamInsightClient.msi /quiet /log log.txt
IACCEPTLICENSETERMS=YES
```

This completes the required installation of the StreamInsight package at server side and SQL Server Compact 3.5 SP2 edition to implement the StreamInsight onto your existing SQL Server 2008 R2 platform.

How it works...

Microsoft StreamInsight supports two deployment scenarios for StreamInsight server:

▶ Full integration into StreamInsight application as a hosted DLL

▶ A standalone server with multiple StreamInsight applications that run as a wrapper or can be packaged as a Windows service

The SQL Server 2008 R2 StreamInsight installation program installs the following on your machine:

- ▸ The SDK to develop StreamInsight applications and adapters
- ▸ The StreamInsight Event Flow Debugger for debugging StreamInsight applications
- ▸ The runtime libraries for StreamInsight
- ▸ The platform libraries in the form of a set of DLLs
- ▸ The documentation and Readme file
- ▸ The StreamInsight host, optionally registered as a Windows Service
- ▸ The StreamInsight Event Flow Debugger tool
- ▸ The SQL CE installation package (required for StreamInsight servers that use the SQL CE-based metadata store)

Implementing SQL Azure connectivity features

SQL Azure is a relational database service in the cloud, which can be used to store business data or system data. It is like database-as-a-service for cloud applications, which is hosted by Microsoft. Its predecessor, SQL Data Services (SDS) built on architecture with full scalability, fault tolerance, and high availability features, has been enhanced to offer the relational database services on top of existing SDS architecture, named SQL Azure.

Like all other Windows Azure services in the cloud, SQL Azure is scalable and Microsoft data centers provide these services with load balancing, failover, and replication capabilities. SQL Azure services comprise three layers: infrastructure, platform, and services that run inside the Microsoft data center and the client layer from the user side. At any point in time, SQL Azure maintains three replicas of user application databases. In case one replica fails, the infrastructure and platform create a new database to maintain the three replicas, making them available at any point in time.

SQL Azure doesn't provide the features such as Service Broker, CLR and so on in SQL Server, but provides the minimum features required to deploy and maintain the database. In this recipe, we will go through the important steps to implement SQL Azure's connectivity features to ensure uninterrupted data access facilities.

Getting ready

SQL Azure is a core component but is not available to download like other Microsoft components.

As it is a service offering from the Microsoft data center, we require a registration that is commercially available on the Microsoft site. To register, visit: `http://www.microsoft.com/en-us/sqlazure/account/default.aspx`.

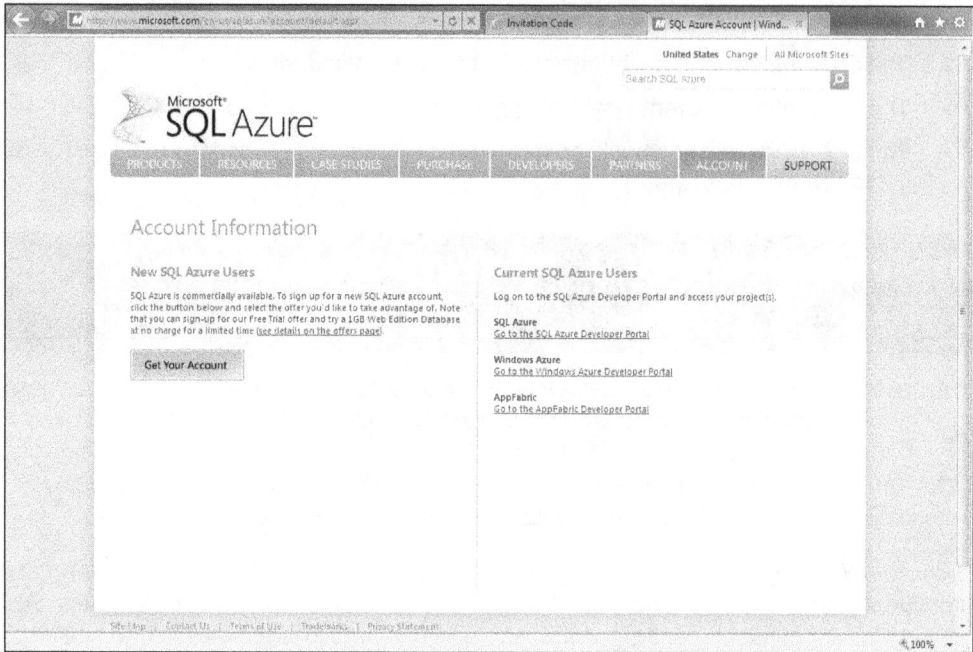

The successful registration is validated with an e-mail that is provided during the registration process, which consists of the relevant login details to create an application to be managed using SQL Azure. To create the relevant user privileges, complete the following steps:

- On the **Create server** page create an Administrator username and password and geo-location
  - The Administrator is the super-user of the database and should be used to execute administrative-related queries on the database
  - The geo-location will represent the data center in which your databases are hosted

- Always configure the **geo-location** so that it is the same as the existing **Windows Azure project**

- To create a database, view the connection strings and the server instance information using the **Server Administration** page

How to do it...

The SQL Azure connectivity features are divided into two pattern methods, they are code-near and code-far.

- The **code-near** connectivity needs data access application deployed on-premises and the same data center as the SQL Azure database. The applications web interface connectivity is exposed through Windows Azure web role that is hosted from an ASP. NET application.

- The **code-far** connectivity needs the application deployed on-premises and in different data centers than SQL Azure. The application executes the SQL queries using the TDS protocol to SQL Azure database.

The required coding techniques for the SQL Azure connectivity feature is used as follows:

Use ADO.NET Connection pooling that will increase code efficiency and remove the need for the re-login process.

```
using (SqlConnection conn = new SqlConnection(
"Integrated Security=SSPI;Initial Catalog=DBIA-Azure"))
{
    connection.Open();
// Pool Connection-A is created.
    using (SqlCommand cmd = conn.CreateCommand())
    {
        cmd.CommandText = ...;
        ...
    }
}
using (SqlConnection conn = new SqlConnection(...))
{
    conn.Open();
    // Process-Application-steps.
}
```

The Parameterization limits the compiles and the two methods are Client-Side and Server-side.

The Client-side parameterization using ADO.NET, ODBC or sp_executesql is a recommended approach for query parameterization to re-use one parameterized query plan.

The following is a parameterized query example that uses sp_executesql:

```
declare @param_value int, @sqlstring nvarchar(500),
@param_definition nvarchar(500), @col2 int;
set @sqlstring = N'select @Sales_person = Person.Name from Person
join Sales on Person.name = Sales.Name where Sales.SaleCount = @
param';
```

```
set @param_definition = N'@param int, @Sales_person int output';

set @param_value = 10;
exec sp_executesql @sqlstring, @param_definition, @param = @param_
value, @Sales_person = @col2 output;
```

Let us execute a similar query using ADO.NET(default client-server application behavior). Here, the data type and length of each parameter must be specified to avoid any slowdown due to cache expansion:

```
cmd.CommandText = "SELECT Person.Name FROM dbo.Person WHERE Person.
Type = @1";
cmd.Parameters.Add("@1", SqlDbType.NVarChar).Value = "16";
cmd.Parameters.Add("@1", SqlDbType.NVarChar).Value = "97";
//this will have the cache expansion causing slowdown of performance.
(@1 nvarchar(1)) SELECT Person.Name FROM dbo.Person WHERE Person.Type
= @1
(@1 nvarchar(2)) SELECT Person.Name FROM dbo.Person WHERE Person.Type
= @1

// if the length is specified, there won't be any cache distend.
cmd.CommandText = " SELECT Person.Name FROM dbo.Person WHERE Person.
Type = @1";
cmd.Parameters.Add("@1", SqlDbType.NVarChar, 128).Value = "16";

(@1 nvarchar(128)) SELECT Person.Name FROM dbo.Person WHERE Person.
Type = @1
```

For frequently executed queries, use stored procedures and batching within the code. Always limit the number of round-trips to the server and the number of columns to be returned.

The default connection timeout is 30 seconds and before reporting a connection failure, it retries connections. If, for any reason, a huge volume of data is transmitted, it is ideal to build the re-try logic in the application. To find out more about SQL Azure connection retry, refer to the following MSDN blog post: http://blogs.msdn.com/b/bartr/archive/2010/06/18/sql-azure-connection-retry.aspx.

If, for any reason, there is a connection failure, reconnect immediately.

If the connection failure persists, wait for 10 seconds and retry. Check the network for any transient errors.

Also check the status of the SQL Azure service as per your geo-location. Refer to http://www.microsoft.com/windowsazure/support/status/servicedashboard.aspx for the current status.

You can also use the SQL Azure web page to report any live-site issue if the connectivity errors are persistent.

Using the trace-connections feature from SQL Azure, you may trace the connectivity problem when necessary. The CONTEXT_INFO value can be used to obtain this value which is set with a unique session GUID value. To obtain more information on the trace-connectivity code example, refer to `http://msdn.microsoft.com/en-us/library/ee730903.aspx`.

Use the `TRY...CATCH` block statements to catch transactions on database operations. SQL Azure rolls back the transaction automatically to free up the resources held by that transaction.

Further, best practices in coding include catching the transient connection termination errors, keeping the connection open and short, and executing the transaction in a continuous loop.

For data transfer methods, always use the Bulk copy utility (bcp.exe) or the SSIS package. For best results on data synchronization, take advantage of the SQL Azure DataSync application from: `http://www.microsoft.com/en-us/SQLAzure/datasync/default.aspx`.

> The recommended pattern is to build your database on-premise in SQL Express and then generate a script and execute the script on the cloud database either using SQL Server Management Studio or SQLCMD.
>
> When creating a logical SQL Azure server, choose the location that is closest to you, to avoid extra bandwidth costs and achieve better performance.

How it works...

The three services of SQL Azure are responsible for all the activities of data access. The services, as mentioned in the previous sections, are Infrastructure, Platform, and Services.

The **infrastructure** layer is responsible for providing the administration of hardware and operating systems required by the services layer. This works similar to a data-center layer, which is shared across multiple services in a data center.

The **platform** layer consists of the SQL Server instances and the SQL Azure fabric components, and required Management services. The instances are represented as the deployed databases and their replicas. The SQL Azure fabric is the internal framework, which automates the deployment, replication, failover, and load balancing of the database servers. This is the most important layer that is responsible for creating three replicas of the database instance to provide automatic failover capabilities to these instances.

The **services** layer, by its name, comprises external (customer) facing machines and performs as a gateway to the platform layer. The TDS protocol (which uses port 1433 over SSL) is responsible for providing the metering and account provisioning services to the customers. In addition to these functions, it maintains the connectivity-routing to the primary database instance and runtime information about your database replicas and routes the TDS coming from client applications to the appropriate primary instance.

The connectivity to the SQL Azure database is managed by Tabular Data Stream (TDS) protocol having limited support. However, the majority of SQL Server client APIs support TDS protocol, so the supported features by SQL Azure work with existing client APIs. The following screenshot is a reference to the SQL Azure network topology. The SQL Azure Network topology diagram (in the next screenshot) is reproduced with permission from the Microsoft Corporation: `http://social.technet.microsoft.com/wiki/contents/articles/sql-azure-connection-management-in-sql-azure.aspx`).

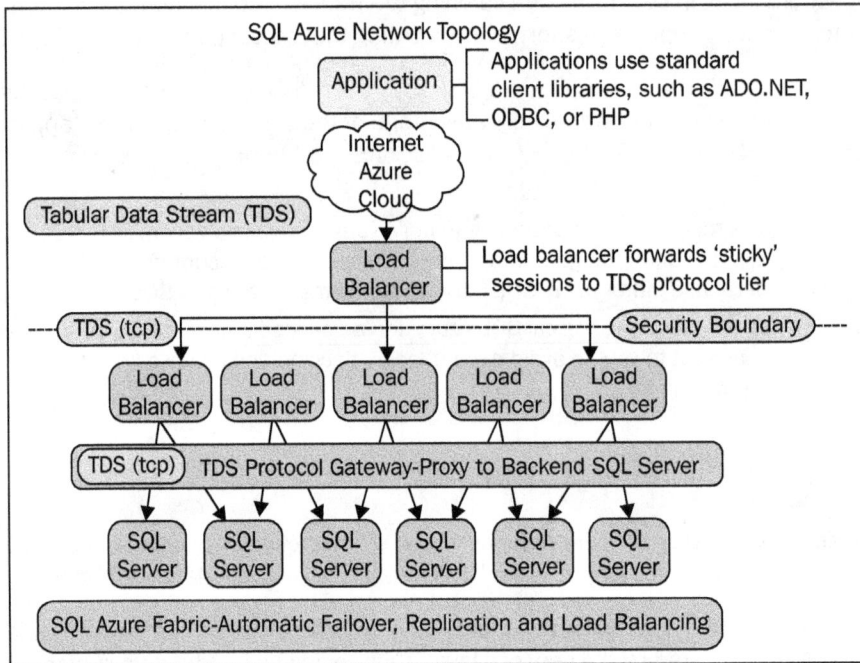

There's more...

For best performance, the code-far connectivity patterns will benefit your application because of direct connectivity to the database in the cloud. The only restriction here is that all the client applications must use the TDS protocol for the data access. Hence, it is essential to develop the client applications using SQL Server client APIs, such as ADO.NET, ODBC, and SQLNCLI.

Installing and configuring a Master Data Services Solution

The administrative control of data is a primary task in any line of business management; as long as the data-flow is intended to meet enterprise level business needs, it serves the purpose. The essence of Master Data Management (MDM) is identified when the data is used for operational and analytical processes; however, those management processes must be able to clearly define the business concepts, identify different ways the data sets represent commonly understood concepts, and integrate the data into a consistent view that is available across the organization.

SQL Server 2008 R2 introduces Master Data Services (MDS), which is designed to provide hierarchies that can be customized to group and summarize the master data. This kind of hierarchical representation helps to change the reporting structures and incorporate new aspects of the business rules by reducing the data-duplication. The best usage of MDS will help us to maintain a central database of master data, which is managed for reporting and analysis. In this recipe, we will go through the important steps to install and configure an MDS solution on an existing data platform. The core components of MDS are MDS configuration manager, MDS manager, and MDS web service.

Getting ready

There are certain pre-installation tasks required to install Master Data Services (MDS) and the setup must meet minimum requirements. The installation requirement is divided into MDS setup, MDM web application services, and MDS database.

The MDS setup prerequisites are as follows:

- The MDS setup is possible only on the 64-bit versions of SQL Server 2008 R2 Datacenter, SQL Server 2008 R2 Enterprise, and SQL Server 2008 R2 Developer editions

- The supported operating systems are Enterprise Editions of Windows Server 2008 R2, Windows Server 2008, and Ultimate editions of Windows 7, and Windows Vista Ultimate. Also, Windows 7 or Vista Professional edition support this feature

- Microsoft .NET framework 3.5 Service Pack1 is required, to download refer to http://go.microsoft.com/fwlink/?LinkId=128220

- The user account used to install MDS must be a member of the Administrators group on the local server

The MDM web application and web services prerequisites are as follows:

- MDM is a web application hosted by IIS
- On a Windows Server 2008 or Windows Server 2008 R2 machine, use Server Manager to install Web Server (IIS) role and refer to `http://msdn.microsoft.com/en-us/library/ee633744.aspx` for the required role services

The MDS database prerequisites are as follows:

- MDS requires a database to support MDM web applications and web services
- In this recipe, the machine that hosts an MDS database is using an instance of SQL Server 2008 R2 database engine

How to do it...

To implement the Master Data Management solution, MDS must be installed, which has two main components, an MDS database component and an MDS web component. Ensure that all of the prerequisites (mentioned in the earlier sections) are in place and by default the MDS is not installed as a part of the regular SQL Server 2008 R2 installation. We need to install the MDS separately as follows:

- On the SQL Server 2008 R2 installation media, navigate to the `\MasterDataServices\X64\1033_ENU` folder and double-click on `masterdataservices.msi` file that will present a welcome screen
- Similar to the SQL Server installation screens, the MDS setup requires default information on the remaining steps that are self-explanatory
- The presented screens are **License Agreement**, **Registration Information**, **Feature selection**, and **Ready to install** to complete the Master Data Services installation

Now that we have installed the Master Data Services components on the server, we need to configure the MDS to make it available for use.

1. The MDM configuration is implemented as a two-fold phase: Databases and Web Configuration.
2. To launch the MDS configuration manager, go to **Start | All Programs | SQL Server 2008 R2 | Master Data Services | Configuration Manager**.

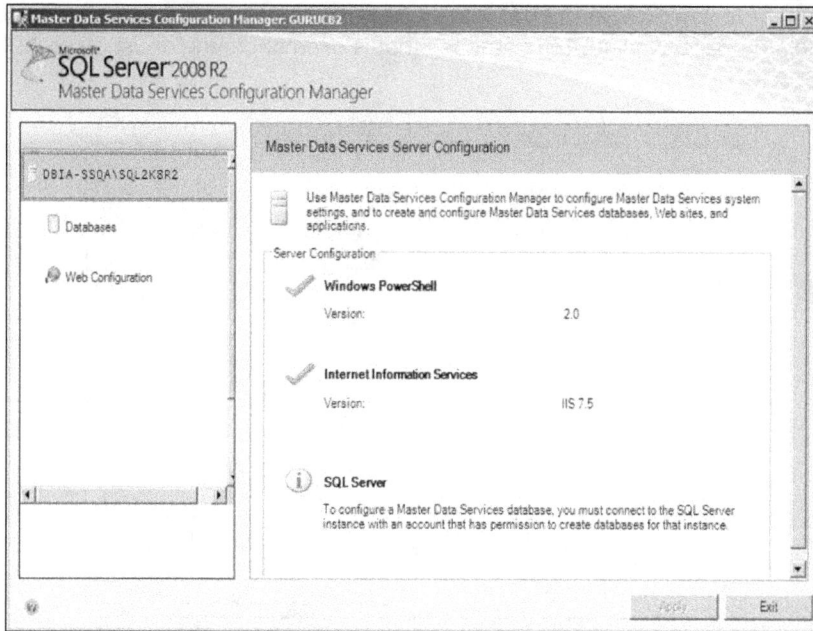

3. The tabs on the left-hand side represent Databases and Web configuration. Databases configure and store MDS configuration, web configuration for MDS, and web service for application integration.

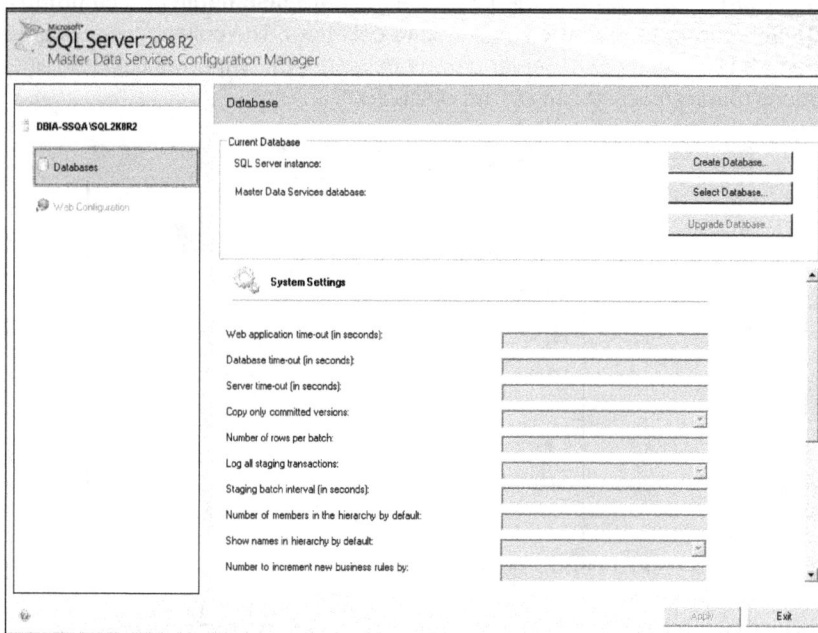

4. Make sure you click on the **Databases** page to create an MDS database to configure and store MDS objects. The database that is used or created must be on SQL Server 2008 R2.

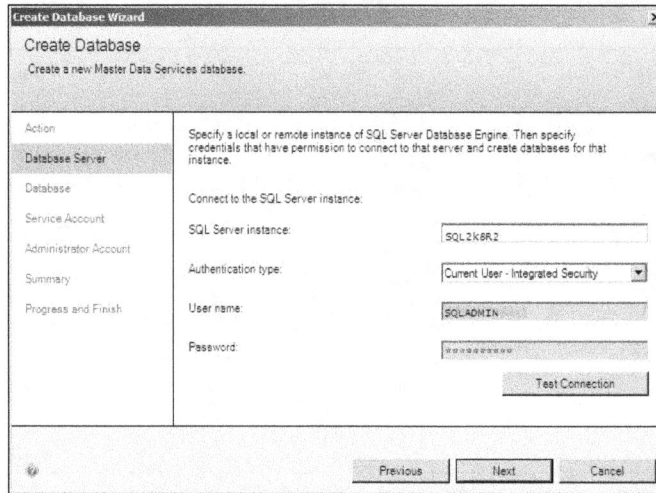

5. To ensure that the supplied configuration is working, click on the **Test Connection** button.

6. Click **Next** to create a new Master Data Services database.

7. On the **Create Database** screen, provide the **database name** and **collation** (choose **SQL Server default collation** or Windows collation). The collation is a single-selection, when we choose the SQL Server default collation, the Windows collation and other options (binary/case-sensitive) are disabled.

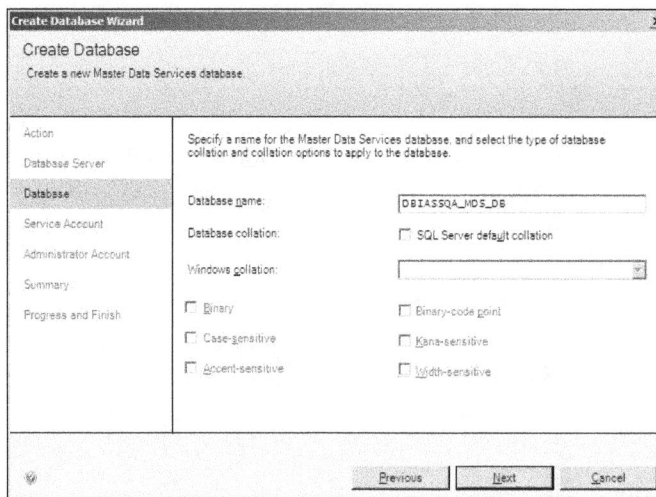

> The Collation is an important step to plan when Unicode data is stored and managed within the database. It is essential to plan proper collation settings during the SQL Server installation.

8. The remaining two options **Service Account** and **Administrator Account** are self-explanatory.

9. The username specified in the **Service Account** screen is added as member of dbo role for DBIASSQA_MDS_DB database. The user name specified in the **Administrator Account** screen will be the site administrator (super user) and will also have permissions to log on and add users to MDM applications.

10. The account must be a domain account that is required to use application pools to connect to a database. Access the database using **MDS manager site** and web services based on the permissions.

11. The **Summary** screen is an informative window that will help to review the details, click **Next** to start the configuration.

12. The status for the MDS database creation and configuration will be shown as a **Success**.

13. Click **Finish** to complete the **Create Database** wizard. To hold the metadata for the MDS repository, proceed to **Metadata Services configuration manager**.

14. It is ideal to leave all the **System Settings** to default except **Master Data Manager URL for notifications** value.

15. The MDS configuration manager for Databases is complete, so we will now proceed to the **Web Configuration** tab.

16. Click on the **Web Configuration** option, which will present the following screenshot.

17. The configuration will provide you with various options such as:

    ❑ Select the required website (from **Web site** drop-down) and web applications that hold MDS and can be configured

    ❑ Select required websites that do not have MDS and click on **Create Application**

    ❑ Create a new website by clicking on **Create Site**–that is specific to MDS only–that automatically creates a web application

18. To choose an existing SQL server instance and database for MDS web application to access, click on the **Select** button.

19. For this recipe, we will use an existing website: DBIASSQA-MDS, so select an existing SQL Server instance: DBIA-SSQA\SQL2K8R2 and database: DBIASSQA_MDS_DB.

20. To configure the web services to enable programmatic access to MDS, click on the **Enable Web services for this Web application** option.

21. Click on **Apply** to complete the MDS configuration. This completes the configuration and presents a popup indicating that the MDS configuration is complete.

22. On the **Configuration Complete** screen, choose the **Launch Web application in browser** option and click **OK** to open the MDS Getting Started page in the browser.

This completes the configuration of the Master Data Services databases and web configuration that will enable you to feature the MDS solution on an existing data platform.

How it works...

The Master Data Services setup will host the MDS web application and installs relevant MDS folders and files at the location and assigns permission to the objects. The setup will register MDS assemblies in the Global Assembly Cache (GAC). The MDS snap-in for Windows PowerShell is registered and installs the MDS configuration manager. A new windows group called MDS_ServiceAccount is created to contain the MDS service accounts for application pools. The MDS installation path creates a folder MDSTempDir where temporary compilation files are compiled for the MDM web application, and permissions are assigned for the MDS_ServiceAccount group.

The **web application configuration** section follows a different workflow method, by including an option to **Create Site** followed by specifying settings for the new site and the MDS web application configured as the root web application in the site. This process will not allow you to configure the MDS web application under any virtual paths or specify an alias for the application. The **Create New Application** process enables you to select a website to create an MDS application in and the **Create Application** screen allows you to specify settings for the new application. The MDS application will be configured as an application in the selected site at the virtual path and at a specified alias.

Designing and deploying framework to use Master Data Services

The Master Data Services (MDS) helps to solve the problem of storing, integrating, and enforcing processes. This helps to decide which data we want to manage, build a model and rules for, load data and establish workflows and notifications. In this recipe, we will go through the process of designing and deploying a framework to use MDS effectively, that includes deploying a package of a model to a target MDS environment.

Getting ready

The prerequisites for this recipe are as follows:

► Ensure that the account used to perform the procedure has permission to access the **System Administration** functional area in the target MDS environment

> ► Ensure that a model deployment package exists. We can create a package of a model from the source system and deploy it directly to another MDS environment; use the package to create a new model or update an existing model

For this recipe, we will use the sample package files that are included when installing MDS. These package files are located by default under `\%Program Files%\Microsoft SQL Server\Master Data Services\Samples\Packages` directory or the installation path that is chosen when installing MDS. When we deploy these packages, sample models are created and populated with data.

How to do it...

The following steps are essential for package deployment and building a model to design and deploy a framework to use MDS. As per the sample package files installation directory, the three packages are installed: `ChartofAccounts`, `Customer`, and `Product`.

1. Open the **Admin** page of MDS from the Browser.

2. The MDS web page can be opened using **IIS**. Navigate to **Start | Run | Inetmgr** and go to the website that is hosting the MDS application. In this case, go to `DBIASSQA_MDS`.

3. Navigate to **Master Data Services Application** and right-click to choose the **Manage Web Site** option to click on **Browse**.

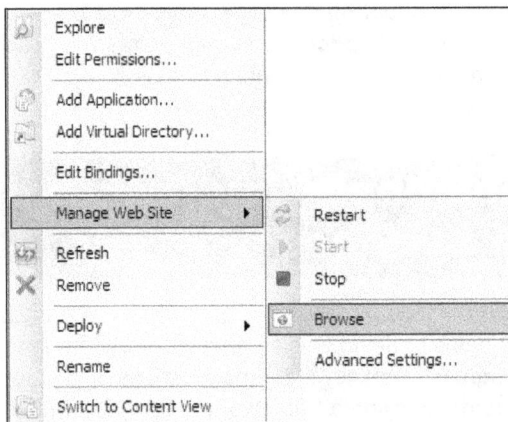

4. The MDS homepage will present you with the options **Explorer, Version Management, Integration Management, System Administration, User,** and **Group Permissions**.

5. Click on the **System Administration** option to open the Model deployment wizard that will deploy an existing package.

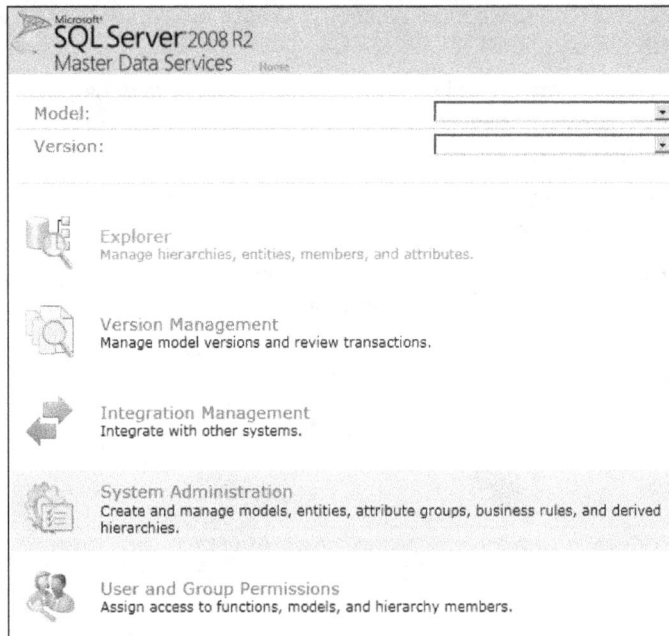

6. This will redirect you to a new page by presenting a drop down selection **deployment** option. Click on the **Deployment** option.

7. The **Deploy Package** will appear, click on the **Browse** button to point to the package file (`.pkg` extension) located under `\%Program Files%\Microsoft SQL Server\Master Data Services\Samples\Packages` directory.

8. Click **Next** and **Next** again to begin the deployment process.

9. If the model already exists, we can update it by selecting the **Update the existing model** option and selecting a version to update.

10. To create a new model, we must select the **Create new model** option and enter the name for that new model.

11. For this recipe, we are choosing the `Product.pkg` file to deploy. Similarly, the previous steps can be followed to deploy `ChartOfAccounts` and `Customer` packages.

12. The successful deployment will present a message: **The Package for the model was deployed successfully**.

13. Click **Refresh** on the browser and select the drop-down list from **Model** to see the successful deployment of the `Product` package.

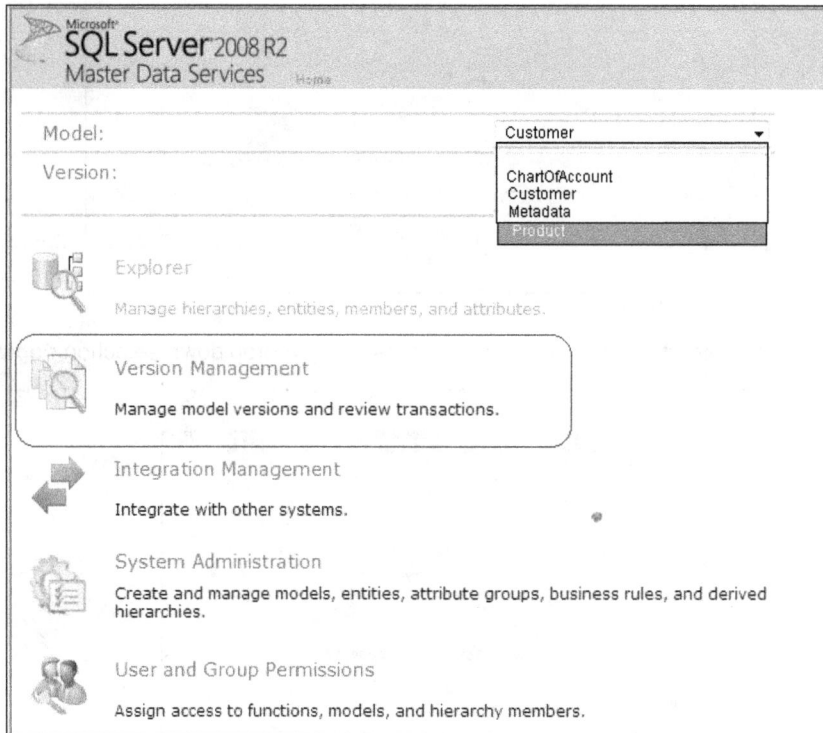

14. Select the `Product` package from **Model** drop-down and click on **Explore** to view the information about entities and attributes of a selected model.

15. The different entities of the Product model are presented as a drop-down list along with the highlighted **Attributes** and **Derived Hierarchies**.

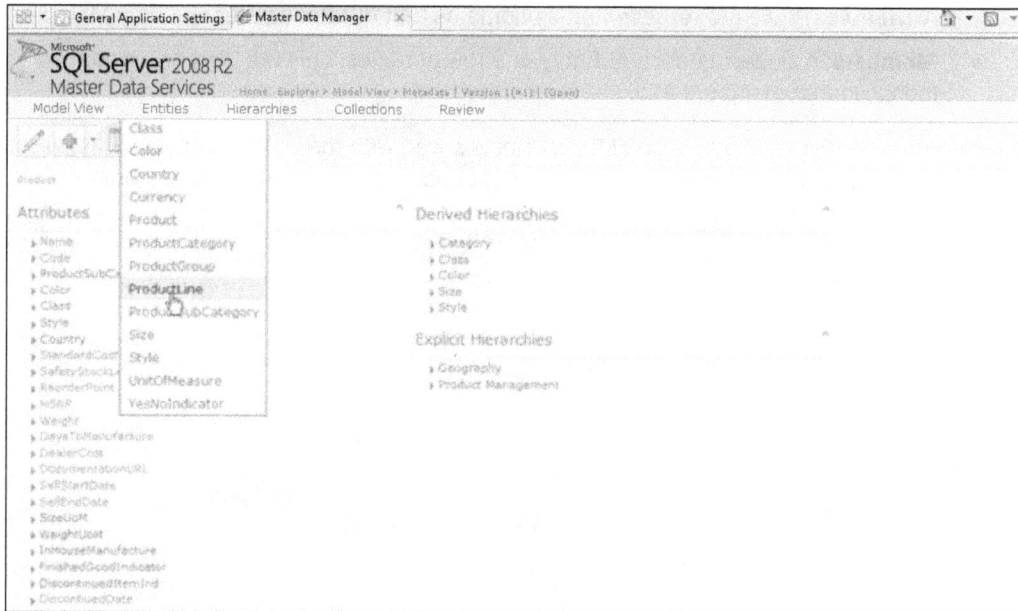

You should now have successfully designed and deployed a framework to use MDS effectively.

How it works...

The package deployment process is a pre-defined process within MDS that follows the steps to create a package of a model from the source system (file based), and deploy it to a defined MDS environment. The Model deployment wizard can be used to create a new model or update an existing model. When creating a deployment package, we can decide whether or not to include data. If data is included, then we must select a version of data that will compile the data by using the MDS staging process.

It is essential to know about the model view presentation that represents various components for each model object, such as:

- **Model**: Highest level of data abstraction layer, which contains multiple entities and other related objects
- **Entities**: These are objects in the MDS model and a container of members, which are defined by various attributes

- ▶ **Attributes**: These are represented as domains that differentiate each Entity Member
- ▶ **Members**: A single instance of Entity or a row of tables. This will have two types (consolidated members and leaf level members)

Furthermore, a model package is an XML file that is saved with the `.pkg` extension. It is ideal to refer to the steps for the Model Deployment package using XML schema from `http://msdn.microsoft.com/en-us/library/ff486971.aspx`.

6
Improving Availability and enhancing Programmability

In this chapter, we will cover:

- ▶ Preparing new Failover Cluster features
- ▶ Installing and configuring Failover Cluster Services
- ▶ Recovering and troubleshooting Failover Cluster Failure
- ▶ Implementing Database Mirroring features and performance enhancements
- ▶ Managing Database Mirroring in a Failover Cluster environment
- ▶ Managing log shipping scenarios in a Database Mirroring environment
- ▶ Improving Replication scalability at multiple sites
- ▶ Implementing compressed storage features for tables and indexes
- ▶ Designing a storage solution for unstructured data and new collations
- ▶ Designing data partitioning solutions for tables and indexes
- ▶ Implementing sparse columns and wide table features
- ▶ Designing spatial data storage methods
- ▶ Designing and managing data-tier applications

Introduction

This chapter highlights the new enhancements to availability and programmability features in SQL Server 2008 R2.

The new features for availability in the database engine are specific to improvements in database mirroring. They include the creation of hot standby for the databases to provide rapid failover support with no data loss on committed transactions. By default, the stream of transaction log records compression occurs in all mirroring sessions, and the ratio is around 12.5 percent. The availability enhancements also include an automated process to resolve certain types of errors on data pages to avoid any failure on the principal database.

SQL Server 2008 R2 programmability enhancements and improvements include compressed storage of tables and indexes, new collations, sparse columns, and spatial data storage methods. The data partitioning feature helps to manage and access subsets of data quickly, while maintaining the integrity of the entire data collection. In addition to this, the sparse column feature is useful for the data storage that results in 40 percent of space savings. Also, the spatial feature helps to store data related to physical location and share of geometric objects in a database.

Preparing new Failover Cluster features

Failover Clustering is a high-availability feature, which requires the certified hardware (referred to as **Hardware Compatibility List** or **HCL**) or Window Server catalog for the Windows Server 2003 or earlier operating systems. To prepare and install the Windows operating system cluster, from Windows Server 2008 onwards, it is no longer a requirement to follow an HCL test process as it is replaced by a new process called **Cluster validation**. SQL Server 2008 R2 Failover Clustering is built on top of the Windows operating system failover clustering to provide availability for the entire SQL Server instance. The downtime for an application is minimized and 99.99 percent uptime is guaranteed. The Failover Clustering functionality represents an SQL Server instance with a Virtual SQL network name or Virtual SQL IP address and performs failover from one node to another, which is handled by Windows Server cluster service. Failover Clustering is only a feature of DataCenter and Enterprise editions of Windows Server 2008, 2008 R2 operating systems, and SQL Server 2008 R2 version. However, the Standard Edition also allows hosting a two-node cluster to provide the equivalent availability for a mission-critical application.

In this recipe, we will go through the steps to prepare a new failover cluster, which is the new feature of setup operations for failover clustering SQL Server 2008 R2 version.

Getting ready

Although there is no pre-configured hardware requirement defined to install failover clustering, it is essential to go through the following pre-installation check list of components for the hardware, operating system, and environment versions that are being deployed. Ensure that the following prerequisites are completed:

- The preliminary prerequisite for SQL Server Failover Cluster is having identical hardware:
  - The system components such as CPU and Memory must be identical for all the nodes within the failover cluster
  - **SAN configuration**: A combination of one or more disks as a resource group in Microsoft Cluster Services (MSCS) group
  - A network name for failover cluster instances with relevant IP Address
- Ensure that the operating system is installed properly and designed to support failover clustering. It is essential that the operating system is equipped with the latest service pack on which SQL Server will run.
- Ensure that you configure MSCS on one node which is supported, if it is installed on a hardware configuration that has been tested for compatibility with the MSCS software.
- Ensure the hardware drivers for x64-bit such as network interface cards (NIC) and host bus adapters (HBA) are available from the vendor and installed.
- Ensure that you deploy the Windows servers and clusters on SAN shared storage devices.
- Ensure that you design the cluster disk for use as the quorum disk as a separate physical or virtual disk on the shared cluster disk array.
- Ensure that there is 5 GB free disk space available on the server.
- Ensure that you install Microsoft Distribution Coordinator for distributed transactions and also when installing Database Engine, SSIS service, and Workstation components for SQL Server 2008 R2.
- Verify that NETBIOS is disabled for all private network cards and the network name (virtual server name) and IP address of the SQL Server instance is not being used by any other machine on the network.
- Ensure that the Remote Registry service is up and running. To access, click **Start | All Programs | Administrative Tools** and navigate to **Services**.
- Identify and remove the disabled network adapters by opening **Device Manager** from **Control Panel | System** right-click for properties and navigate to **Network Adapters**.
- When the source installation files are on a different domain, ensure that you copy the installation files to the current domain available to the SQL Server failover cluster.

- ▶ To install and configure the MSCS on a Windows Server 2003 operating system refer to `http://go.microsoft.com/fwlink/?LinkId=30741`.

- ▶ For geographically-dispersed cluster nodes, additional items like network latency and shared disk support must be verified. The entire solution must be on the Geographic Cluster Hardware Compatibility List. Refer to the Microsoft knowledge base article `http://go.microsoft.com/fwlink/?LinkId=116970` for more information.

How to do it...

SQL Server 2008 R2 offers a new method to install a clustered instance of SQL Server, which is classified as cluster preparation. The following are the steps to perform the failover cluster preparation:

Run the SQL Server Setup program to open up SQL Server Installation center.

1. Click on **Advanced** link to open the advanced installation options.

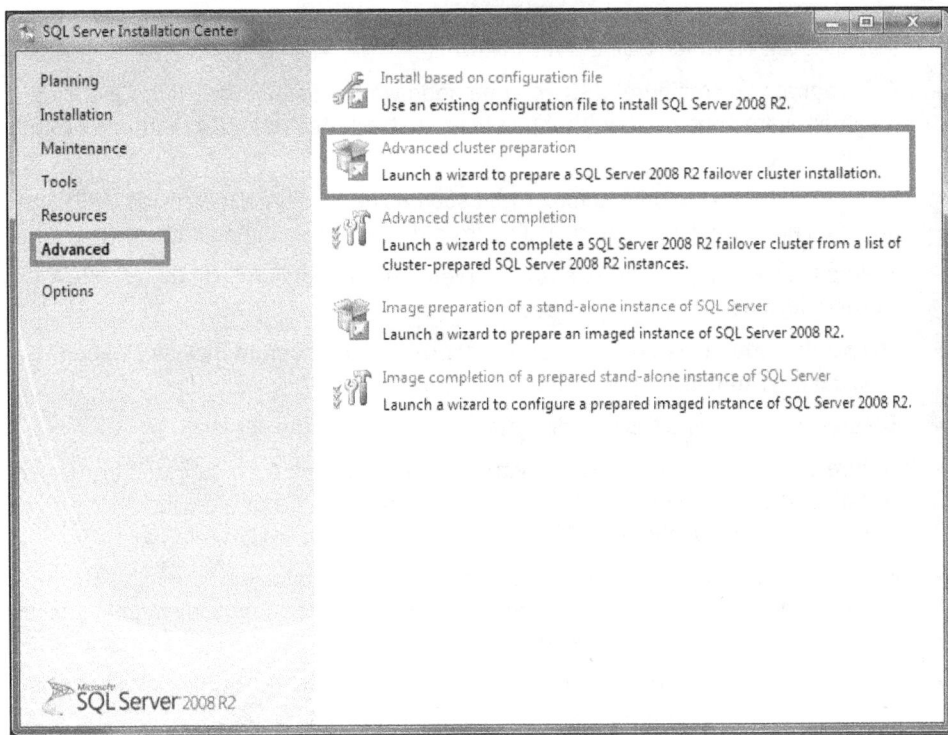

2. Click on **Advanced cluster preparation** to launch a wizard to prepare an SQL Server 2008 R2 failover cluster installation.

3. The System Configuration Checker (SCC) runs a set of setup support rules to identify problems that might occur when installing SQL Server support files. Any failures that are reported under the **Status** column must be corrected to proceed further. Click **OK** to process the SQL Server 2008 R2 setup operation.

4. Click **Next** after entering the product key to validate the instance of SQL Server 2008 R2 and accept the license terms. Click **Install** to continue to setup support files.

5. On the **Feature Selection** page, select the relevant components to install. For Failover Clustering, only the **Database Engine** and **Analysis Services** components can be selected.

6. Define the custom directory for shared components or click **Next** to accept the default to install under C:\Program Files\Microsoft SQL Server\ MSSQL10_50.xx\ folder.

7. On the **Instance Configuration** page, specify whether to install a default or a named instance.

8. As a best practice, always use the same **InstanceID** for all the nodes that are prepared for the failover cluster. Click **Next** to continue.

9. The information screen is presented for the Disk Space Requirements of the features that are selected in step 6. Click **Next** to continue.

10. The **Cluster Security** policy page is essential to configure the security policy and specify the global or local domain groups for clustered services. For the Windows Server 2008 operating system, specify the Service SIDs (security ID) and choose the default setting.

11. For this recipe, as the Windows Server 2008 operating system is used, we will choose the default setting as referred to in the previous steps. Click **Next** to continue.

12. On the **Service Accounts** page, specify the login accounts for SQL Server services, and make sure to choose a domain account only. Click **Next** to continue.

13. On the **Server Configuration | Collation** tab, choose any collation for Database Engine and Analysis Services components. The **Server Configuration | FileStream** enables the FILESTREAM feature on SQL Server services. Click **Next** to continue.

14. The **Error and Usage Reporting** page is presented for error reporting, which is enabled by default. Click **Next** to continue.

15. The **Prepare Failover Cluster Rules** screen is important to determine if the failover cluster process is blocked. Click **Next** to continue.

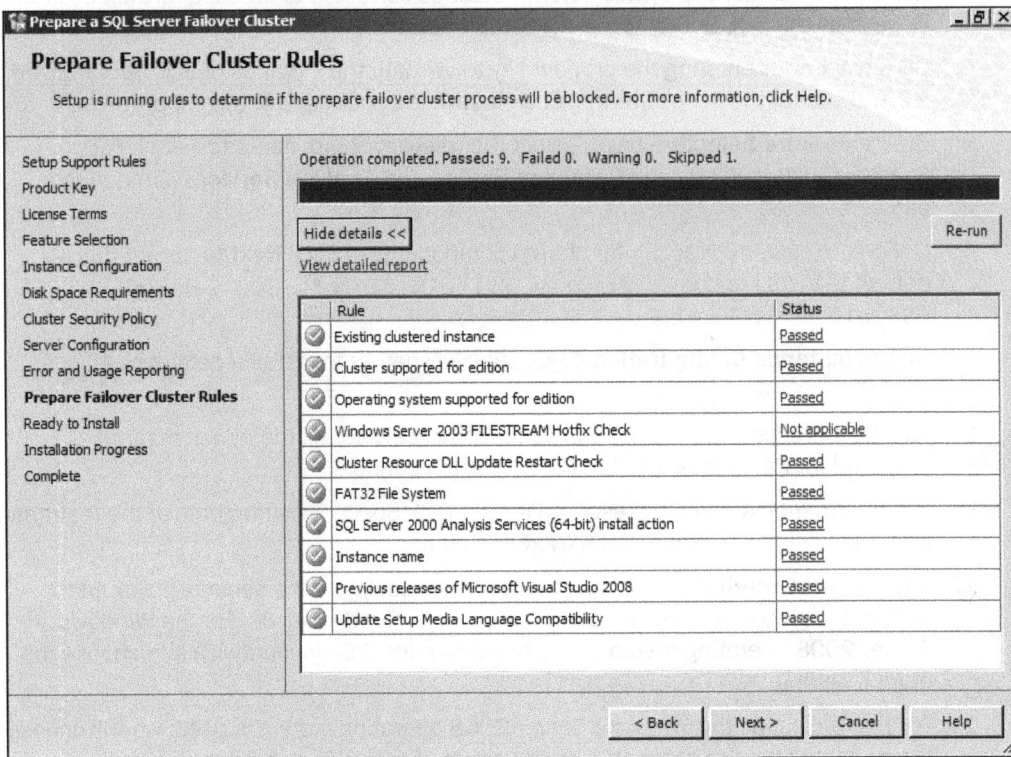

16. Again, the SCC runs a set of rules to validate the configuration with the selected SQL Server features.

17. The **Ready to Install** page is presented as a tree-view of the installation options as per the selection made in the previous steps. The **Installation Progress** page provides the status to monitor the installation progress as the setup continues.

18. You should now have successfully completed the preparation to install the database engine and analysis services on a single node of the failover cluster. If required, a popup box will be presented to restart the computer to complete the SQL Server setup, click OK to reboot.

19. Repeat all these steps for every node that will be a part of the failover cluster environment.

> The maximum number of failover clustering nodes for both DataCenter and Enterprise editions are limited by the operating system maximum. But Standard edition can only support up to two nodes. The Windows Server 2008 and higher supports a maximum of 16 failover cluster nodes.

This completes the process for preparing new failover cluster features by creating a `Configuration.ini` file. These steps will prepare the nodes to be clustered but there will be no operational instance of SQL Server when the setup is completed.

How it works...

The Advanced installation phase for SQL Server 2008 R2 presents two methods, integrated installation and advanced installation:

▶ **Integrated Installation**: The integrated installation is useful to create and configure a fully-functional single-node SQL Server failover cluster instance. We need to run and use the **Add Node** setup functionality process from SQL Server installation.

▶ **Advanced Installation**: The advanced installation allows the users to simulate the steps of failover cluster setup to avoid any unforeseen issues during the installation. This method is further divided into two steps: Prepare and Complete.

  ❑ The **Prepare** step is useful to perform the prepare failover cluster setup on one node with a `Configuration.ini` file that consists of all of the settings that were selected. Once the prepare-nodes step is completed for failover clustering, run Setup on the node that owns the shared disk resource to configure the failover cluster instance and finish the installation that will present the operational SQL Server failover clustered instance. The prepare step does not require any underlying Windows Server cluster (MSCS) to be installed.

  ❑ Once the nodes are prepared for clustering, run the setup on nodes, which are referred as **Complete**. However, the complete step does require the specified hardware and software services to complete the successful installation of failover clustering.

Installing and configuring Failover Cluster Services

SQL Server Failover Clustering is created within the Microsoft Cluster Services (MSCS), which is capable of detecting the hardware and software failures to switch the managed resources for the instance automatically. Clustering provides availability for the most critical applications and flexibility in managing the workload within the cluster.

The setup change for SQL Server 2008 needs to run the setup program on each node that is involved as part of the failover cluster and also offers an option to create an enterprise push node from the active node with a configuration file. Many of the SQL Server services are cluster-aware, such as Analysis Services, Full-Text search, Integration Services, and FILESTREAM. In this recipe, we will go through the important steps required to install and configure the SQL Server 2008 R2 failover cluster services within the data platform.

Getting ready

Although there are no pre-configured hardware requirements defined to install the failover clustering, it is essential to go through the following pre-installation list of components for the hardware, operating system, and environment versions that are being deployed.

While the identical hardware is not essential for failover clustering, it is best practice to obtain the following configuration to host the failover cluster services:

- The system components such as CPU and Memory must be identical for all the nodes within the failover cluster.
- SAN configuration is a combination of one or more disks as a resource group in Microsoft Cluster Services (MCSS) group.
- A network name for failover cluster instances with the relevant IP Address.
- Ensure that the operating system is installed properly and designed to support failover clustering. It is essential that the operating system is equipped with latest service pack on which SQL Server will run.
- Ensure the following components for the SQL Server failover clustering are configured:
  - IP Addresses on Windows Cluster machines
  - Network names
  - Disk drives on the shared drive array
  - SQL Server service accounts
  - Configure a unique IP address on the public network segment in the cluster with a unique network name that is registered into DNS to resolve by name
- Configure Microsoft Cluster Services (MSCS) on one node, which is supported if it is installed on a hardware configuration that has been tested for compatibility with the MSCS software.

> Ensure all the hardware drivers for X64-bit such as Network Interface Cards (NIC) and Host Bus Adapters (HBA) are available from the vendor and installed.

- Deploy the Windows servers and clusters on SAN shared storage devices.

- Design the cluster disk for use as the quorum disk and as a separate physical or virtual disk on the shared cluster disk array.

- Ensure that at least 5 GB of free space is available on the server.

- Create necessary cluster service accounts on the domain.

- Install Microsoft Distribution Coordinator for distributed transactions and also when installing Database Engine, SSIS service, and Workstation components for SQL Server 2008 R2.

> Verify that NETBIOS is disabled for all private network cards and ensure that the network name (virtual server name) and IP address of the SQL Server instance is not being used by any other machine on the network.

- Ensure that the Remote Registry service is up and running.

- Identify and remove the disabled network adapters by opening **Device Manager** from **Control Panel | System** (right-click for properties and navigate to) **Network Adapters**.

- When the source installation files are on a different domain, ensure you copy the installation files to the current domain available to the SQL Server failover cluster.

- Install and configure the MSCS on a Windows Server 2003 operating system by referring to: `http://technet.microsoft.com/en-us/library/cc783714(WS.10).aspx`.

In order to begin the preparation for SQL Server Failover Clustering, we need to ensure that we have the following in place:

- .NET Framework 3.5 Service Pack1, which helps improvements in the area of data platform, such as ADO.NET Entity Framework, ADO.NET data services, and support for new features of SQL Server 2008 and 2008 R2.

  - Download .NET Framework 3.5 Service Pack 1 from `http://www.microsoft.com/downloads/en/details.aspx?FamilyID=ab99342f-5d1a-413d-8319-81da479ab0d7&displaylang=en`

- Windows Installer 4.5 helps the application installation and configuration service for Windows, which works as an embedded chainer to add packages to multiple package transactions.

  - Download Windows Installer 4.5 redistributable package from `http://www.microsoft.com/downloads/en/details.aspx?FamilyID=5a58b56f-60b6-4412-95b9-54d056d6f9f4&displaylang=en`

▶ When the prerequisites are installed, the installation wizard opens up the **SQL Server Installation Center** window.

▶ The next step of the installation is to run **Setup Support rules** to identify any issues that may occur during the installation, click on **Show Details** to display a window.

▶ On the **Show Details** screen, if no errors are reported, then we can proceed further by clicking **OK**.

▶ Click **Install** to initiate the installation of the Setup Support Files.

▶ The SQL Server 2008 R2 setup implements failover clustering based on the clustering features of MSCS.

▶ For SQL Clustering, install a new SQL Server instance within a minimum two-node cluster.

How to do it...

The SQL Server 2008 R2 installation process for a failover clustering is different compared to the previous versions, as there are three different methods. The three methods are as follows:

▶ A setup interface

▶ A command line or INI file

▶ A new cluster preparation feature

In this recipe, we will go through the steps to install and configure an SQL Server 2008 R2 failover cluster using the setup interface.

1. From the SQL Server media (or in case if the setup files are stored in the local server) double-click on `setup.exe` to invoke SQL Server setup installation center.

2. On the Installation Center click on **New SQL Server failover cluster installation**.

3. Once the System Configuration Checker runs the discovery operation, click **OK** to continue. For more information on the discovery operation, we can click on **Show Details** or **HTML report** for a detailed report.

4. If there are specific requirements for a localized operating system, then on the **Language Selection** page choose the relevant option. Otherwise, click **Next** to continue.

5. On the **Setup Support Files** page, choose **Install** to install the setup support files. Again, the System Configuration Checker verifies the system state to continue the setup. On successful completion, click **Next** to continue.

6. On the **Product Key** page, enter the relevant PID key to validate the edition installation.

7. On the **License Terms** page, read the license agreement, and then select the checkbox to accept the license terms and conditions. Click **Next** to continue.

8. On the **Feature Selection** page, select **Database Engine Services** and leave the default path for Shared Feature to install under %\Program Files\Microsoft SQL Server\% directory. Click **Next** to continue.

9. On the **Instance Configuration** screen, it is essential to enter an applicable SQL Server Network Name. For this recipe, let us apply the DBIACluster name that will be used to identify the failover cluster on the network.

10. Once the Network name is defined, choose whether to install a default instance or specify a name to install a named instance.

11. Next, in the **InstanceID** box, do not accept the default value of MSSQLSERVER. For this recipe, we need to choose **DBIACI01** as InstanceID, and then click **Next** to continue.

> For the default instances, the **InstanceID** needs to be the same as the SQL Server Network name or a combination of the network name and the instance name for a better administrative perspective.

12. The **Disk Space Requirements** page calculates the required disk space for the selected features, click **Next** to continue.

13. On the **Cluster Resource Group** screen, specify the cluster resource group name where the SQL Server Virtual server resources are located. We have two options, either use the drop-down box to specify an existing group or create a new group name.

14. The SQL Server cluster resource group name is selected by default for Cluster Group, Available Storage, and MSDTC. Click **Next** to continue.

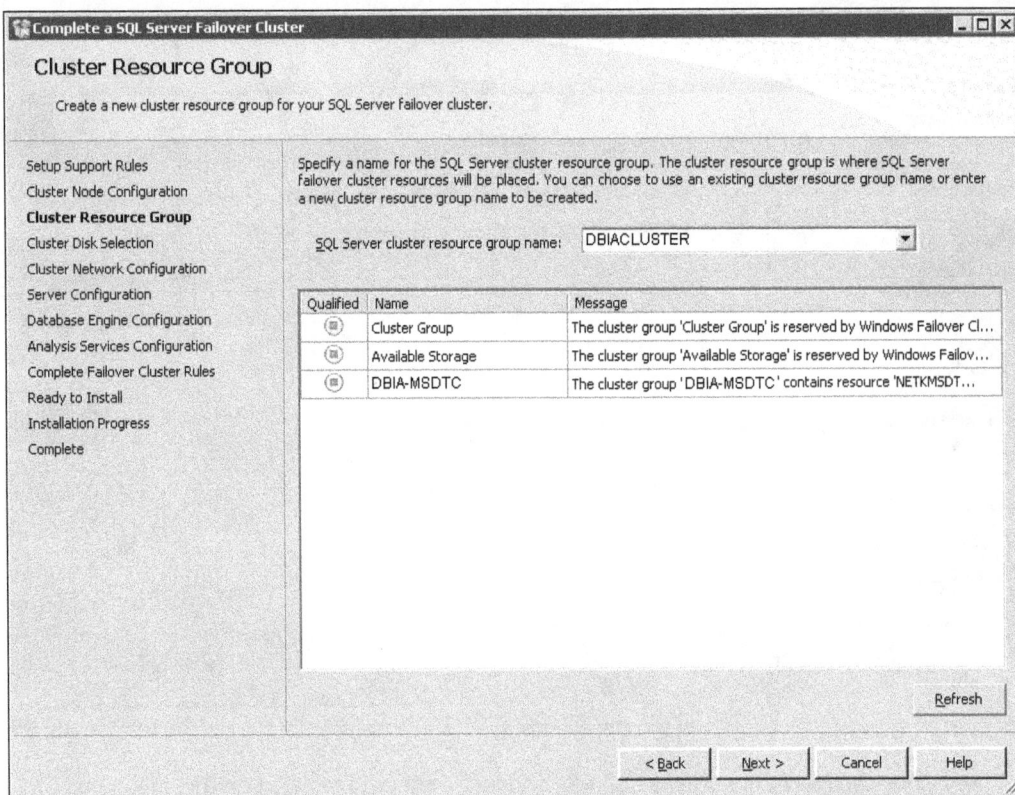

Complete a SQL Server Failover Cluster		_ □ X

Cluster Resource Group

Create a new cluster resource group for your SQL Server failover cluster.

Setup Support Rules
Cluster Node Configuration
Cluster Resource Group
Cluster Disk Selection
Cluster Network Configuration
Server Configuration
Database Engine Configuration
Analysis Services Configuration
Complete Failover Cluster Rules
Ready to Install
Installation Progress
Complete

Specify a name for the SQL Server cluster resource group. The cluster resource group is where SQL Server failover cluster resources will be placed. You can choose to use an existing cluster resource group name or enter a new cluster resource group name to be created.

SQL Server cluster resource group name: `DBIACLUSTER` ▼

Qualified	Name	Message
⊚	Cluster Group	The cluster group 'Cluster Group' is reserved by Windows Failover Cl...
⊛	Available Storage	The cluster group 'Available Storage' is reserved by Windows Failov...
⊚	DBIA-MSDTC	The cluster group 'DBIA-MSDTC' contains resource 'NETKMSDT...

Refresh

< Back | Next > | Cancel | Help

15. Next, the **Cluster Disk Selection** screen will be presented, which is essential to select the shared cluster disk resource for the failover clustering installation.

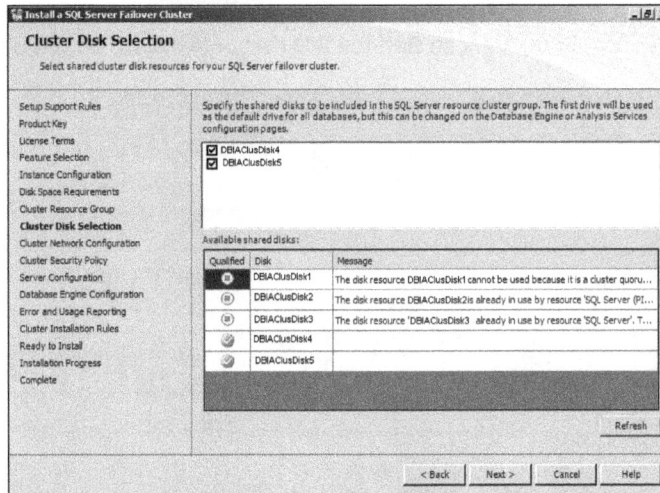

16. The available disks are presented with a green tick mark and unavailable disks are presented with a red square inside a circle under the **Available shared disks** tab. Specify the shared disks to be included in the SQL Server resource cluster group, click **Next** to continue.

17. The **Cluster Network Configuration** screen is presented to enter a static IP Address, which is a recommended best practice. Click **Next** to continue.

> When the underlying Windows operating system is configured with Internet Protocol version 6 (IPv6), SQL Server Native Client recognizes the existence of IPv6 without any special configuration setup.

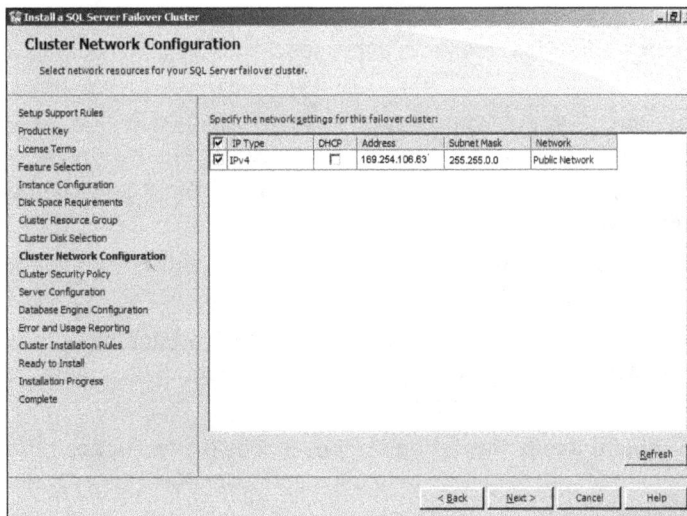

18. At the **Cluster Security Policy** screen, two options are presented. For Windows Server 2008 versions or later, choose **Service SID** (Security ID), which is a default setting.

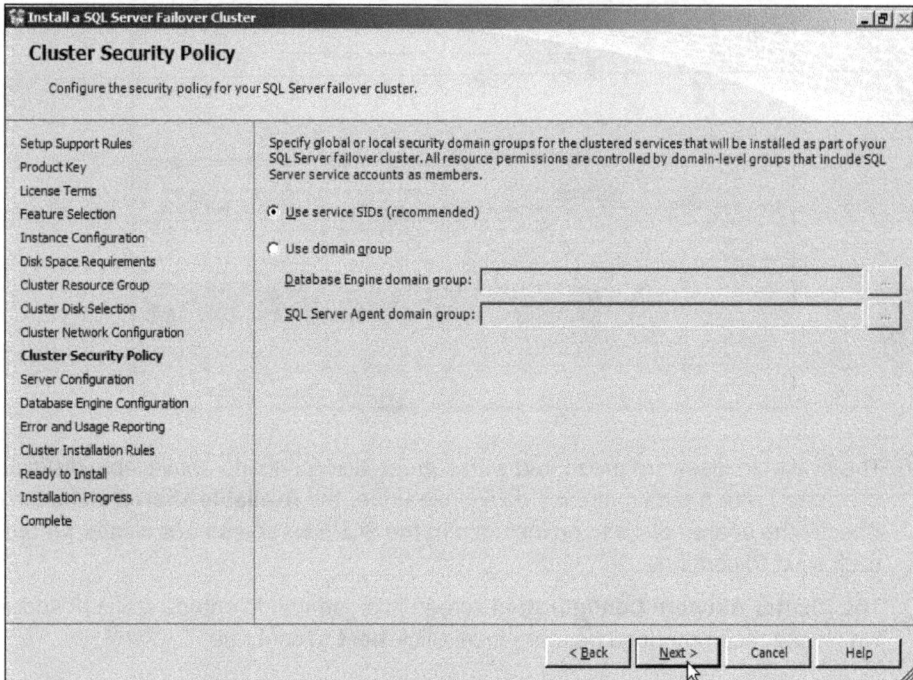

19. As we are using Windows Sever 2008, we should use the recommended option as referred to in the previous steps. Click **Next** to continue and the remaining screens are similar to the standard SQL Server installation.

20. Click on **Advanced** to open the advanced installation options. On the **Server Configuration | Service Accounts** page, specify the login account name and password for SQL Server Database Engine Services.

21. You can assign the same login account to all SQL Server services, or you can configure each service account individually. This account must be a Windows domain user account. Built-in machine accounts (such as Network Service or Local Service) are not recommended.

22. Next, use the **Server Configuration | Collation** tab to specify non-default collations for the Database Engine services.

23. At the **Database Engine Configuration | Account provisioning** page, we have the option to set the security mode and assign an account to be a member of SYSADMIN fixed server role. Click **Next** to continue.

24. On the **Error and Usage Reporting** screen, choose the two option boxes if there is a requirement to automatically send to Microsoft. Click **Next** to continue to the **Cluster Installation rules** screen.

25. During the Cluster Installation rules process, a warning may be presented (as shown in the next screenshot) on a multi-site SQL Server cluster installation. Make sure you review the summary of the installation log file to ensure no errors are reported. Click **Next** to continue.

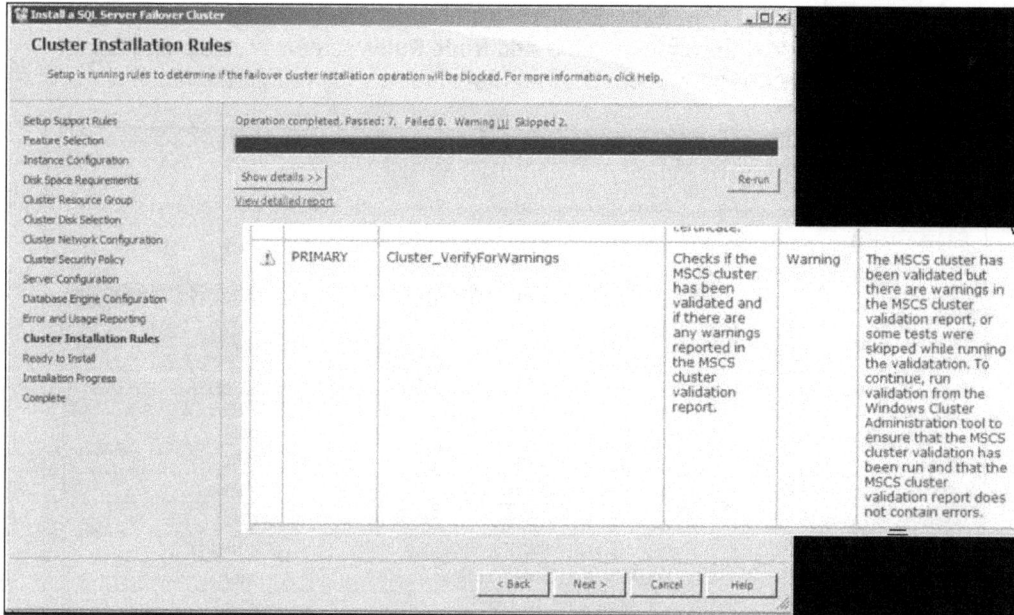

26. The **Ready to Install** page shows a tree-view of the installation options that were specified during the setup, then click **Install** to continue. Once the installation process is complete, a message box will appear: **You must restart the computer to complete SQL Server setup**. Click **OK** to continue the reboot of the server.

27. At this point, the installation should proceed as planned. Unless some unexpected error occurs, the process will get us a working SQL Server instance of a single-node failover cluster.

Now, let us continue to add the other nodes to the existing clustered instance. You need to follow the SQL Server setup again depending upon the number of nodes that will be added to failover cluster.

1. The installation process and approach is similar to installation and configuration of an SQL Server 2008 R2 failover cluster from steps 1 to 12.

2. On the **Cluster Node Configuration** screen, from the drop-down box, select the instance of SQL Server where this node will join. For this recipe, the instance name will be DBIACluster.

> The screens **SQL Server cluster resource group name**,
> **Cluster Disk Selection,** and **Cluster Network Configuration**
> are not presented when the add-node process is followed.

3. Again, follow steps from 20 to 24 of the installation and configuration of the failover cluster, click **Next** to continue to the **Add Node Rules** screen. At this point, a final validation check will run to ensure that there are no reported problems.

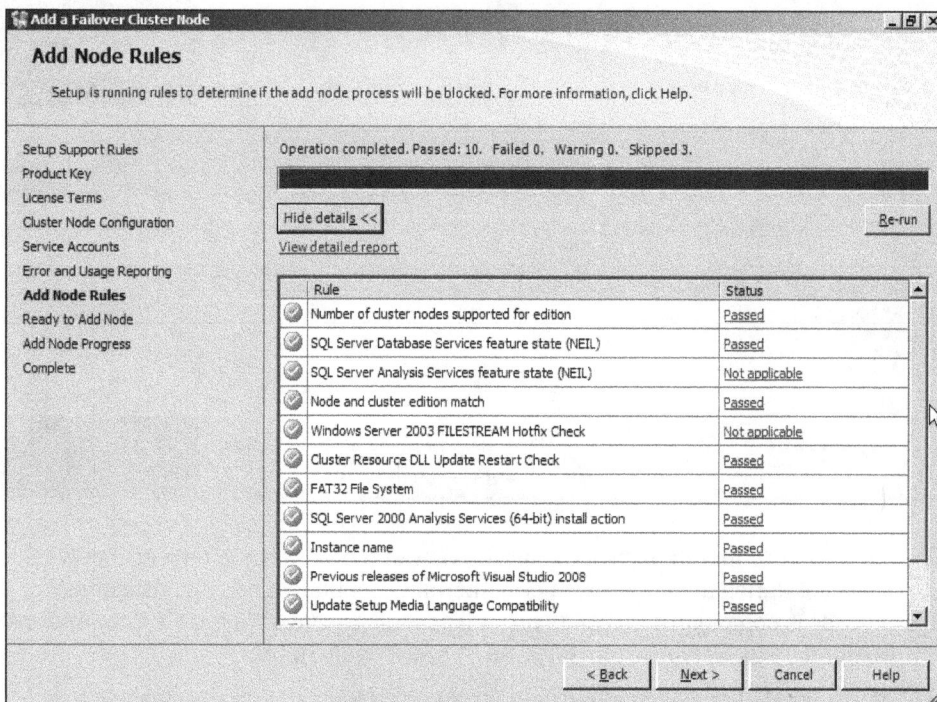

```
Add a Failover Cluster Node                                                    _ | B | X

  Add Node Rules

    Setup is running rules to determine if the add node process will be blocked. For more information, click Help.

  Setup Support Rules          Operation completed. Passed: 10.  Failed 0.  Warning 0.  Skipped 3.
  Product Key
  License Terms
  Cluster Node Configuration     Hide details <<                                       Re-run
  Service Accounts               View detailed report
  Error and Usage Reporting
  Add Node Rules                   Rule                                          Status
  Ready to Add Node                Number of cluster nodes supported for edition     Passed
  Add Node Progress                SQL Server Database Services feature state (NEIL)  Passed
  Complete                         SQL Server Analysis Services feature state (NEIL)  Not applicable
                                   Node and cluster edition match                    Passed
                                   Windows Server 2003 FILESTREAM Hotfix Check       Not applicable
                                   Cluster Resource DLL Update Restart Check          Passed
                                   FAT32 File System                                  Passed
                                   SQL Server 2000 Analysis Services (64-bit) install action   Passed
                                   Instance name                                      Passed
                                   Previous releases of Microsoft Visual Studio 2008  Passed
                                   Update Setup Media Language Compatibility          Passed

                                           < Back      Next >      Cancel      Help
```

4. Click **Next** to continue the **Ready to Add** Node process.

> At this point, the installation should proceed as planned. Unless
> some unexpected error happens, the process will continue to
> add a node to the existing SQL Server failover cluster.

5. The installation progress is presented under the **Add Node Progress** screen and the successful installation will be shown at the **Complete** screen.

6. Once the installation process is complete, a message box will appear: **You must restart the computer to complete SQL Server setup**. Click **OK** to continue the reboot of the server.

This completes the required steps to install and configure an SQL Server 2008 R2 failover cluster using the setup interface. For this recipe, we installed a three-node cluster having two active nodes at any time to enable a mission-critical high-availability provision.

How it works...

The SQL Server failover cluster installation involves steps to create and configure a single-node SQL Server instance. When the node is configured, we have a fully functional failover cluster instance without a high-availability feature, because the installation is configured on only one node in the failover cluster environment.

Additional nodes can be added to the existing SQL Server failover cluster using the Setup feature that uses the **Add Node** functionality. The setup will prepare a node, preferably on the node that owns the shared disk, which has the failover cluster using the defined feature.

Recovering and troubleshooting Failover Cluster Failure

The installation of failover clustering is not an error-resistant process. Maintaining the cluster instances is another important task to keep up. The failure may occur during the failover process, when adding a node to an existing cluster farm, or due to a hardware failure. Viewing the cluster-wide events requires supportive tools and methods to recover a failover clustering instance failure and troubleshoot any problems that are repetitive in the clustering nodes. A cluster on an expensive hardware system is of no value, if the support infrastructure is not fault tolerant, such as power redundancy or network redundancy.

Once the failover cluster nodes are installed, the first step is to test the failover and failback methods to ensure that the nodes are configured properly to provide the high-availability solution. In this recipe, we will go through the process of recovering and troubleshooting a failover clustering failure with a scenario, which is classified as administering an SQL Server Failover Cluster.

Getting ready

To test the failover clustering, ensure that the cluster services are up and running by referring to the SQL Server Configuration Manager program.

Next, perform health checks against the SQL Server failover cluster instance; the default tests are `LooksAlive` test and `IsAlive` test.

To simulate the continuity of SQL server services, perform the following two actions:

1. Register the new Virtual SQL Server within SQL Server Management Studio (SSMS) to manage the instance as similar to other SQL Server instances.

2. Execute the following TSQL by opening a **New Query** window within SSMS:

```
declare @loop1 int
declare @loop2 int,@j int
print 'enter number'+ Cast(@loop2 as varchar)
set @loop1=1
while (@loop1<=100)
begin
print @loop1
set @j=@loop1*@loop2
print @loop2
set @loop1=@loop1+1
end
go
```

The common cause for a failover cluster may be due to hardware failure or an operating system failure. To perform the recovery steps, let us assume the following two scenarios as an example:

▶ Scenario one is a failure caused by corruption of the Windows operating system. This is a serious problem to resolve.

▶ Scenario two is a failure of the disk controller due to a mismatch of firmware drivers. This is a less serious problem where the node is offline but not irretrievably broken.

How to do it...

In the event of a failover cluster failure, it is essential to recover from the failure as quickly as possible. Let us have a look at the required steps in recovering and troubleshooting a failover cluster failure.

1. The most efficient way to monitor the failover cluster nodes is to monitor the log files. Open the utility named **Failover Cluster Management** (**FCM**) snap-in from **Start | Programs | Administrative tools**.

2. In case the operating system is Windows Server 2003, then use **Cluster Administrator** (or cluadmin.exe) **MMC** (**Microsoft Management Console**) snap-in by navigating to **Start | Programs | Administrative tools**. Using the Cluster Administrator snap-in displays the properties of each new node by right-clicking on a resource.

3. The FCM displays the status of the Windows failover cluster in the middle pane. This console can also be used to configure nodes and services in addition to the information status displayed.

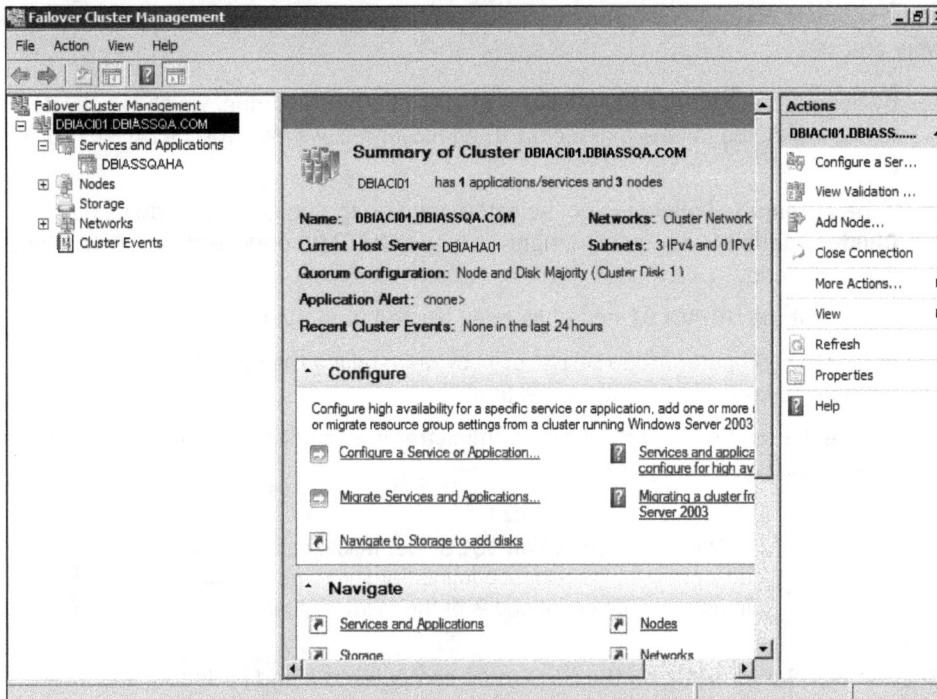

4. The **FCM** snap-in displays all cluster-related events when we click on **Cluster Events** on the left-hand pane.

5. Using the **Cluster Events** option from the right-hand pane, we can build a user-defined query to extract failed events that are specific to a time and node.

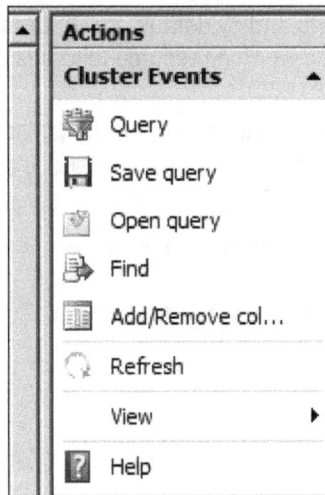

As per the scenario on the specifications discussed previously, let's move on to the Recovery process.

1. By default, the **Automatic Failover** is enabled in the clustering, which is activated when a resource failure is detected. The failover follows from the DBIACL01 to DBIACL02.

2. If the **Automatic Failover** is not selected, then on the DBIACL02 node using the **Cluster Administrator** snap-in, right-click on **DBIACL01** node and click **Evict Node** to evict the node.

3. Verify that the **DBIACL01** node has been evicted from the cluster definition.

4. Repair the computer (node DBIACL01) by re-installing the operating system to replace the corrupted operating system.

5. Ensure the existing failover cluster administrator account has the required permission on the DBIACLO1 computer.

> To update or remove an SQL Server failover cluster, the account must be a local administrator with permission to log in as a service on all nodes of the failover cluster.

6. Run SQL Server setup on the DBIACL01 computer to a add node to the failover cluster. (Refer to *Installing and configuring failover clustering services* recipe for the relevant steps).

7. Using the Cluster Administrator snap-in, ensure that node **DBIACL01** is added by checking the properties of the added node.

8. As per the scenario, and the two specifications discussed previously, let's move on to the Recovery process. In continuation to scenario one, the active node is DBIACL02.

9. As per the current scenario and by default, the **Automatic Failover** is enabled in the clustering, this is activated when a resource failure is detected. The failover follows from the DBIACL02 to DBIACL01.

10. If automatic failover is not selected, then on the DBIACLO1 node use Cluster Administrator snap-in, right-click the DBIACLO2 node and click Move Group to move the resources from the current failed node.

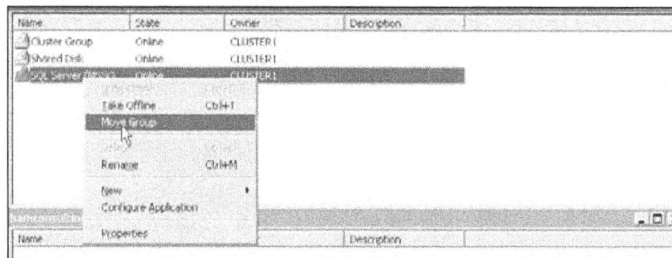

11. Resolve the disk controller problems on the `DBIACL02` node by installing the required firmware drivers.

12. Ensure that MSCS cluster service is working on `DBIACL02` node.

13. On the `DBIACL01` node, attempt to failover to the recovered node `DBIACL02`.

14. If the failover process succeeds, then no further action is required.

15. However, if the SQL Server services fail to come online on the `DBIACL02` node, open the **FCM** snap-in on the `DBIACL01` node to review the cluster log to obtain the relevant information of the failure.

This completes the steps to recover and troubleshoot the failover cluster failure. For further information on failover cluster troubleshooting scenario examples, refer to: `http://msdn.microsoft.com/en-us/library/ms189117.aspx`.

How it works...

The utility named Failover Cluster Management (FCM) snap-in uses the MSCS on the Windows operating system. The important FCM tool features are: validate configuration, create cluster or add node, and migrate settings from a cluster running Windows Server 2003. The tool highlights the required features, which are useful to monitor and administer the failover cluster management. Using the FCM utility, both Windows and SQL Server events such as health and performance can be monitored. In addition to FCM, we can make the best of use of SQL Server tools and services with failover clustering, refer to `http://msdn.microsoft.com/en-us/library/ms175549.aspx` for more information.

See also

Refer to the recipe *Installing and configuring failover clustering services* for the relevant steps.

Implementing Database Mirroring features and performance enhancements

Database mirroring involves re-applying every modification operation that occurs in the primary database onto the mirror database. The physical log record is applied to the mirror database and keeps an exact copy of the primary database.

SQL Server 2008 provides many enhancements that are related to the performance of database mirroring. In this recipe, we will go through the important steps required to implement database mirroring features and performance enhancements using SQL Server 2008 R2.

Getting ready

To setup and configure the database mirroring environment, ensure the following requirements are met:

- All the server instances are on the same level of service packs and hotfix packages for the Windows operating system and SQL Server services.

- Ensure that the SQL Server edition is DataCenter, Enterprise, or Standard.

- When any of the database mirroring partners is using Standard Edition (SE), then the other partner must be same version; the SE supports the full safety mode only, which is a single-threaded operation.

- Ensure the network connectivity is consistent with no latency. Establish the endpoint configuration for each server that is part of the database mirroring pair. The endpoint uses the TCP/IP addressing and listening ports for all the communications between the servers.

- Use the **SSMS** tool to register both PRINCINPAL and MIRROR instances that will be part of the database mirroring pair including the WITNESS server.

- Ensure the service account (domain account), which is used for database mirroring has GRANT access on the endpoint for access to be allowed for each server to the other.

- Ensure that the database that is to be mirrored is using the FULL database recovery model, as database mirroring is performed based on the transaction log sequence.

- Ensure that the SQL Server service account is a part of sysadmin group on the SQL Server instances that are part of database mirroring.

- Perform a full database backup and an immediate transaction log backup from the source (PRIMARY) server, copy both the backup files to the (MIRROR) server.

- Restore the database and restore the transaction log with the **NORECOVERY** option only, which is until the tail of transactions and to the point of being able to mirror.

- As a named mirroring instance pair references, let us choose the names as follows, principal: DBIAPR, mirror: DBIAMR, and witness: DBIAWT

> Ensure that all the mirroring partners consist of identical folder names and paths to avoid any mismatch during the RESTORE operation.

How to do it...

The following steps are required to implement the database mirroring features and performance enhancements using SQL Server 2008 R2.

1. The Configure Database Mirroring Security Wizard automatically creates the database mirroring endpoint (if none exists) on each server instance, and enters the server network addresses in the field corresponding to the role of the server instance (Principal, Mirror, or Witness).

2. To configure Database Mirroring, in **Object Explorer** click the server name to expand the server tree and expand Databases to select the databases to be mirrored.

3. Right-click the database, select **Tasks** and then click **Mirror** to open up the Mirroring page of the **Database Properties** screen.

4. To begin configuring the mirroring process, click the **Configure Security** to launch the Configure Database Mirroring Security Wizard.

5. The wizard automatically creates the database mirroring endpoint (in our case, `tcp://DBIASSQA:5022`) on each server instance and enters server network addresses in the field corresponding to the role of the server instance as Principal, Mirror, or Witness.

6. In continuation to the Implementing Availability feature enhancements recipe steps, the last step in the Configure Database Mirroring wizard is the Security. Click **Next** to see a summary of choices made in the wizard, then choose Finish to configure the mirroring session.

7. The next screen provides you with the command buttons **Start Mirroring** or **Do Not Start Mirroring**. Select **Start Mirroring** immediately.

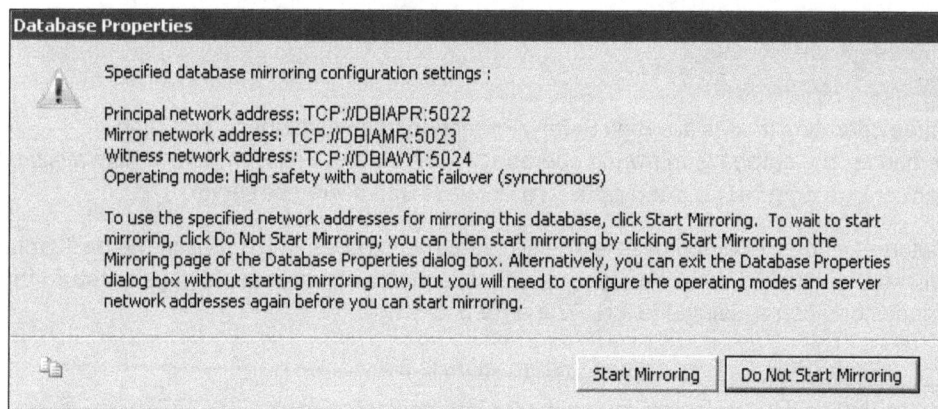

Database Properties

⚠ Specified database mirroring configuration settings :

Principal network address: TCP://DBIAPR:5022
Mirror network address: TCP://DBIAMR:5023
Witness network address: TCP://DBIAWT:5024
Operating mode: High safety with automatic failover (synchronous)

To use the specified network addresses for mirroring this database, click Start Mirroring. To wait to start mirroring, click Do Not Start Mirroring; you can then start mirroring by clicking Start Mirroring on the Mirroring page of the Database Properties dialog box. Alternatively, you can exit the Database Properties dialog box without starting mirroring now, but you will need to configure the operating modes and server network addresses again before you can start mirroring.

[Start Mirroring] [Do Not Start Mirroring]

---

8. Next, the active mirroring session will start and to verify look at the SQL Server error log for the entries indicating the database mirroring is active. The entries will be similar to the following:

```
11/21/2010 22:33:33,spid231s,Unknown,Database mirroring is active
with database 'AdventureWorks2008R2' as the principal copy. This
is an informational message only. No user action is required.

11/21/2010 22:33:33,spid231s,Unknown,Starting up database
'AdventureWorks2008R2'.


11/21/2010 22:34:13,Server,Unknown,SQL Server is now ready for
client connections. This is an informational message; no user
action is required.

11/21/2010 22:34:13,spid232s,Unknown,The Database Mirroring
protocol transport is now listening for connections.

11/21/2010 22:34:39,spid232s,Unknown,Server is listening on [
'any' <ipv4> 5022].
```

9. Now we have active mirroring, the next step is to monitor the mirroring topology using the **Database Mirroring Monitor** tool from **SSMS**.

10. From SSMS, on the PRINCIPAL database, select **Tasks | Launch Database Mirroring Monitor** (DMM).

11. The DMM tool includes the two server instances' status and specifies the log after being moved from the PRINCIPAL to the MIRROR instance. This helps us to determine if the MIRROR database is keeping up with the PRINICPAL database.

This completes the process of setting up the database mirroring and performance enhancements using SQL Server 2008 R2.

How it works...

The three operating modes are High Safety/Protection, High Availability, and High Performance. The database mirroring operating mode that was chosen here is high-availability (synchronous mode with automatic failover) with a witness server.

The automatic page repair process is an asynchronous process which runs in the background, and allows the mirrored database operation that requests an unreadable page to return the error code condition causing a failure. The error codes are:

  ▶ 823: ERROR_CRC, operating system value is 23

  ▶ 824: Logical data errors, torn write, or bad page checksum

  ▶ 829: indicates a page has been marked as restore pending

The automatic page repair process on the principal database is attempted when the node is in a SYNCHRONIZED state.

Automatic page repair is the enhancement to the database mirroring feature from SQL Server 2008 onwards that will perform a repair process and replace it with the corresponding copy of its partner. The sequence to attempt automatic page repair is, when a data page error occurs, the principal server inserts a row in the suspect_pages table in the msdb system database. Briefly, the page is marked as restore pending, which will be inaccessible for normal transactions and the same page will be replaced from the mirror database.

> The page types such as File header, Database boot, and Allocation pages cannot be automatically repaired.

The log stream compression is applied automatically irrespective of operative mode that is chosen during database mirroring setup. Before sending the log records to the MIRROR database, the stream is compressed to reduce the network latency, which improves the performance of a synchronous mirroring topology.

The log performance improvements result in a write-ahead on the incoming log stream on the mirror server that writes the incoming log records to the disk asynchronously. This improvement uses log-send buffers that are used at the undo-phase, after a failover to improve the speed of the undo phase.

See also

To configure the database mirroring using wizard, refer to the *Implementing Availability feature enhancements* recipe mentioned in *Chapter 2*.

Managing Database Mirroring in a Failover Cluster environment

The two important high-availability features from SQL Server 2008 R2 are failover clustering and database mirroring. Both of these features are fundamentally different in terms of implementation, having instance level availability for failover clustering and database level availability for database mirroring.

In terms of architecture, both have the same concept of quorum, heartbeat, and witness server to support automatic (for database mirroring it depends on the implementation mode) and manual failover. In terms of connectivity, during a failure, failover clustering does not require any changes in the application connection string. However, for database mirroring, the application may require changes to the connection string, to force a reconnection after a failover. In such cases, ensure to cache the partner information to update the connection string, or retry connectivity when the first connection attempt fails.

However, as a best practice many installations out there may not use 1433 as a default port for SQL Server instance, in addition to using Microsoft SQL Server JDBC driver (see `http://msdn.microsoft.com/en-us/library/ms378749.aspx`). So when a named port is defined with a firewall exception and a JDBC is used, then the automatic failover is not supported. To provide extra availability support and standby for the application, database mirroring can be used on a failover clustering instance. In such cases, the principal server and mirror server both reside on clusters between the data centers. The principal database will be hosted on an active node of one cluster and the mirror database will be hosted on an active node of another cluster. It is also possible to establish a mirroring session between the clustered and un-clustered instances. However, the availability for applications is dependent on the database mirroring operating mode. In this recipe, we will go through the process of managing database mirroring in a failover clustering environment.

Getting ready

All the prerequisites to install failover clustering can be referred to in the *Installing and configuring failover cluster services* recipe and for database mirroring, refer to the *Implementing database mirroring features and performance enhancements* recipe.

To manage database mirroring in a clustered environment, the selected operating mode for mirroring is significant. SQL Server 2008 R2 has changed the operating modes for database mirroring, and they are:

- High Performance
- High Safety with automatic failover
- High Safety without automatic failover

How to do it...

The following steps are required to set up the database mirroring partners and failover cluster nodes in a clustered environment, which is an essential task in managing database mirroring in a failover cluster environment.

1. On the database mirroring pair, when the high-safety mode with automatic failover is used, it is ideal to set up the mirroring between two cluster environments (in different data centers) for maximum availability. The witness instance can reside on the active node or on an un-clustered machine within the same network.

2. On the database mirroring pair, when the high-performance mode is used, it is ideal to host the principal server on the failover clustered instance of a cluster and place the mirror server on an un-clustered server outside of the cluster environment.

3. It is highly recommended that you change the default value 10 for database mirroring PARTNER TIMEOUT to a higher number as follows:

```
ALTER DATABASE AdventureWorks2008R2 SET PARTNER TIMEOUT 300
```

The PARTNER TIMEOUT value is referred to as guidance. As a best practice, you must test partner timeout with different values that are suitable for your network.

4. In a failover cluster environment, it is essential to configure the ENDPOINT, to use clustered IP addresses and not the IP address on the cluster nodes.

How it works...

In case of system failure, the default action on the failover cluster initiates the failover action to another node. In such cases, where the high-safety mode with automatic failover is used, the node that is running the current principal will start the automatic failover within a few seconds or based on the set up of the PARTNER TIMEOUT value. The DBM fails to mirror the server, which becomes the principal server for the DBM pair; whereas the WITNESS is critical to invoke automatic failure mode, which acts on quorum to meet the failover needs. Immediately, the new principal server rolls forward its copy of the database as quickly as possible and brings it online as the principal database. In parallel to the database mirroring action, the cluster failover completes the failover clustered instance that was a principal server previously, which then becomes the mirror server instance.

In case of the high-performance mode without automatic failure (asynchronous), the failover cluster will continue functioning as the principal server in the database mirroring session and in case of an entire cluster problem, we must force the service to the mirror server instance.

Managing Log Shipping scenarios in a Database Mirroring environment

Log shipping has been part of SQL Server as a core standby feature (backup and restore), but it is also considered a high-availability feature. However, it cannot be matched to failover clustering or database mirroring feature.

Like database mirroring, the log shipping feature includes database level protection with no automatic failover option. It is also possible to implement log shipping in a database mirroring environment, as both features complement the log sequence number to function.

The SQL Server 2008 R2 high-availability feature enables the database to perform mirroring and log shipping simultaneously. In this recipe, we will go through the required steps to manage log shipping in a database mirroring environment.

Getting ready

For the prerequisites to install database mirroring, please refer to the *Implementing database mirroring features and performance enhancements* recipe. In order to configure the log shipping feature, the following prerequisites must be completed:

▸ For database mirroring, register both `PRINCINPAL` and `MIRROR` instances that will be part of the database mirroring pair including the `WITNESS` server.

▸ For database mirroring or log shipping, the collation and sort order should match between the server instances.

▸ Choose servers for the primary instance, secondary instance, and an optional monitor server instance; no specific or special hardware configuration is required for log shipping.

▸ SQL Server 2008 introduced backup compression, which is an Enterprise edition feature, and beginning in SQL Server 2008 R2 Standard edition supports the backup compression. When creating the log shipping configuration, we can choose the backup compression for transaction log backups.

▸ Create a file share for the transaction log backups on a separate server, which is not a part of the log shipping configuration for maximum availability of database backups.

▸ Ensure that the primary database recovery model is set to `FULL` and perform a full database backup; set the backup schedule for the primary database and create a folder on a secondary server into which the log backup files will be copied by the log shipping process.

You should set up a single share as the backup directory (a backup share). This ensures that after role switching between the principal and mirror servers, backup jobs continue to write to the same directory as before. A best practice is to ensure that this share is located on a different physical server from the servers hosting the databases involved in mirroring and log shipping.

How to do it...

The following steps are required in order to manage log shipping in a database mirroring environment.

1. The database mirroring session must be established between the partners before the log shipping process begins.

2. The principal database is configured as the log shipping primary database.

3. Additionally, the mirror database must be configured as the log shipping primary database. The log shipping secondary database is set on a different server instance, which is not a part of database mirroring partners.

4. By design of the database mirroring, the mirror database will be in a restoring state, which prevents the log shipping backup jobs from backing up the transaction log on the mirror database. This is to ensure that the mirroring database does not interfere with log shipping backup patterns and when an automatic failover occurs the log shipping can continue.

5. The interoperability between log shipping and database mirroring is supported and provides an additional standby to the existing data platform.

6. The database mirroring session can run in any operating mode, synchronous (transaction safety set to FULL) or asynchronous (transaction safety set to OFF).

7. Restore the backup of the Principal/Primary database with NORECOVERY onto the mirror server instance, then configure and set up the database mirroring.

8. Set up the log shipping configuration on the principal database as the primary database.

9. Create a file share on the entire server instance, which is part of the database mirroring partner in addition to the log shipping secondary server.

10. Manually perform a database mirroring failover from the principal to the mirror instance.

11. Now, set up the log shipping configuration on the new principal (previously mirror) as the primary database by using the same database backup that was performed earlier.

12. Perform a database mirroring failback from the existing principal database to the original principal server instance.

13. Configure the log shipping monitor server to monitor the log shipping pair.

This completes the steps to manage the log shipping in a database mirroring environment, which runs in high-safety mode with automatic failover mode. This setup will enable extra standby for an existing high-availability environment.

How it works...

The log shipping process is dependent on SQL Server Agent service. The primary server instance executes the backup job to back up the transaction log on a primary database, and then sends the same file to a backup folder-share, which is created as part of the prerequisite steps. The principal database in a mirroring session can also act as the primary database in a log shipping configuration or vice-versa.

Internally, for the log shipping process to prevent the spurious alerts, whenever a backup job is executed on the mirror/primary database, the backup job logs a message to the log_shipping_monitor_history_detail table in the msdb system database, which enables the agent job to return a status of success.

Furthermore, the database mirroring session–which is running in synchronous mode–will guarantee that the transaction log chain is unaffected by the mirroring failover and only the valid log is restored all the time by managing the Log Sequence Number (LSN). Next, the secondary server will continue to copy the log backups without the knowledge of any changes that occurred due to the failover of a different server instance, which has become the new primary server. So, if the principal server is lost for any reason after the database is synchronized and the mirror server and witness servers continue to communicate, then automatic failover occurs. This automatic failover causes the mirror server to assume the principal role and brings the database online as the principal database to continue the log shipping job schedules.

Improving Replication scalability at multiple sites

In a distributed environment, whether it is intranet or internet based, it is crucial to keep the data flow autonomous and available online when needed. The transaction is atomic and a certain level of scalability is needed as the load against the database increases. In any case, the application is dependent on more reads than writes, for such scenarios it is a compulsory requirement to scale out the 'read' processes of the workload by caching read-only data across the multiple database and instances where the web server connectivity is directed. If the databases are geographically dispersed, then it is highly essential to scale out the data flow between the sites to support read and write requests for scalability and improve availability.

In this recipe, we will go through the common requirements for replication, scalability, and provide appropriate solutions with the type of replication to use.

Getting ready

The prerequisite for this process is to ensure the appropriate SQL Server version is used and replication is deployed.

 ▶ Further, the system should allow changes to be made at any server and have the ability to perform changes replicated to all other servers

 ▶ The replication model must consist of a minimum of one publisher and more than two subscribers and distributors (locally or remotely)

 ▶ The types of replication suited for this recipe are: snapshot, transactional, and merge replication;

 ▶ The source must be a publisher having the required data at the source that is included in the publication

 ▶ Each cache is a subscriber to the publication where the schema and data is received as subscription

▸ The transactional consistency must be maintained with a low latency such as updates at one server must reach the other server

▸ The **filtering** option must be enabled, so that the tables at Subscribers contain only the data required by the application

▸ The network throughput should be high to handle the replication of a large number of transactions

▸ The database recovery model must be `FULL` at all the times

▸ Ensure to create a publication and subscriptions, and then initialize each subscription

▸ Ensure that adequate disk space and system resources are available across all the servers involved in this setup

▸ Ensure that SQL Server agent service is up and running with no errors

> The best advantage of SQL Server 2008 version onwards is the Peer-To-Peer topology wizard that helps the users to alter the configuration online using the SSMS tool.

How to do it...

Once the prerequisite options are met as per the recipe requirement, follow the steps mentioned next to improve the replication scalability at multiple sites in the environment.

1. The first option is to configure the distribution that stores the metadata and data history for replication.

2. Create a `snapshot` folder, which is used by **Publishers** and has appropriate permissions set.

3. All the publishers are authorized to use the **Distributor**. Size the distribution database to accommodate the data load having **auto-grow** enabled.

4. Set the **sync with backup** option on the distribution database.

5. If the distributor is remotely located, then use the **SSMS** tool to configure a publisher to use that remote distributor server instance.

6. The next step is to configure the data publication and database objects.

7. To create a publication, ensure it contains the information about distributor, location of snapshot files, publication database, and the type of publication to create (snapshot/transactional/transaction with updatable subscriptions).

8. Using the **SSMS** tool, create the publication by choosing the data and the relevant articles (database objects) to include in the publication.

9. Set up the static row and column filters. If it is a merge replication, then set the parameterized row filters along with join filters.

10. Now, we are at a point where we can create a subscription that defines which publication will be received. The type of subscriptions can be **push** or **pull**.

11. The `merge` agent or `distrbution` agent on the distributor is responsible for the **push** subscription and the agent run at the subscribers is responsible for the **pull** subscription.

12. Again using the **SSMS** tool, create the subscription with information such as name of publication, name of subscriber and subscription database, service accounts for distributor agent or agents, and choose the schedule method as **continuous**, **scheduled basis,** or **on-demand** only.

13. To create a push subscription from the publisher, on SSMS connect to the **Publisher** and expand the **replication** folder | **Local Publications** folder. Right-click on publication to create one or more subscriptions and click **New Subcription** to complete the wizard.

14. To create the **pull** subscription from the **Subscriber**, connect to the subscriber from the **SSMS** tool and expand the **Replication** folder. Right-click on **Local Subscription | New Subscriptions | Publication** page. Select <**Find SQL Server Publisher**> or <**Find relevant Publisher**> from the publisher drop-down list. Connect to the Publisher in the **Connect to Server** dialog box to select the Publication and then complete the pages in the **New Subscription** wizard.

15. Now, we need to initialize the created subscriptions, so that the copy of schema from each article is replicated in addition to the initial dataset.

16. On the publisher, using SSMS, expand the **Replication** folder | **Local Publications** folder. Right-click the publication to create a **snapshot | View Snapshot Agent Status | <Publication>**, then click **Start**.

17. Repeat these steps on multiple subscribers to ensure the process is scaled out.

How it works...

By default the replication uses the internal process in publishing the data as per the components that include publisher, subscribers, publications, articles, and subscriptions.

The default initialization method uses a full snapshot, which includes the schema along with replication objects when the SQL Agent service is up and running. During the snapshot initialization, we can choose the data to publish without a full snapshot.

Implementing compressed storage features for tables and indexes

Whenever data is inserted into a table or an index is rebuilt, the database engine requires more space in the database, which is usually the underlying storage where the data file is located. The database engine needs the process to determine where space is available within the pages to be allocated. Therefore, the insert process must find a mixed extent with one or more pages available that can be allocated, if the index or data is more than eight pages or larger than what a free uniform extent needs to be allocated.

SQL Server 2008 has introduced the data compression feature as a part of the programmability enhancements. The main benefit of compression is that it can be enabled or disabled at object level, which means at database-wide, page-level, or row-level. In this recipe, we will go through the important steps in implementing compressed storage features for tables and indexes. When the compression option is configured on a partitioned table and index, then all the partitions of an object do not have the same compression setting. However, when partitions are split then both partitions will inherit the same data compression attribute from the original partition.

Getting ready

The following points must be considered in order to implement the compressed storage features;

- ▶ The SQL Server edition must be Data Center, Enterprise, or Developer (for Development purposes only)
- ▶ The application database chosen for this implementation must represent the OLTP environment, which means both read-only and read/write transactions are implemented ranging from simple to fairly complex
- ▶ The database consists of medium and large tables with primary keys, foreign keys, clustered/non-clustered indexes, composite indexes, and reference integrity checks
- ▶ The database that will be involved and underlying columns in the tables must span a wide variety of data types with rows populated on Unicode data (multi-lingual); by default SQL Server 2008 R2 enables compression for Unicode UCS-2 data
- ▶ Ensure that the data in the table holds numeric, varchar, datetime, and fixed-length character data types to take advantage of data compression significantly
- ▶ Ensure that data holds NULLABLE columns where the number of rows has a NULL value for the column
- ▶ Ensure that the tables store scores of repeating data values or repeating prefix values in the data

> ► The following points are considered for PAGE and ROW compression:

  □ If vardecimal storage is used, then row-size-check is performed; when the object is initially in compression and always checked as each row is inserted or modified

  □ The compression type can be set to ROW, PAGE, or NONE when a list of partitions are specified. By default, a new table or index is created and the data compression is always set to NONE unless otherwise specified

  □ Non-clustered indexes do not inherit the compression property of the table

  □ When a clustered index is created on a heap, it will inherit the compression state of the heap unless the compression state is specified

  □ When new pages are allocated in a heap, the DML operations will not use PAGE compression until the heap is rebuilt (create and drop a clustered index)

  □ The disk space requirements must be calculated for row or page compression, such as when creating or rebuilding an index

How to do it...

In this recipe, we will look at how to implement compressed storage features for tables and indexes using simple TSQL statements such as CREATE TABLE and ALTER TABLE. The procedure is as follows:

1. Create a new table and enable the row compression. To do so, we need to designate the DATA_COMPRESSION table option using the value of either **ROW** or **PAGE** and disable the compression by using **NONE**.

2. Open a new query window on SSMS and execute the following TSQL:

```
CREATE TABLE dbo.ArchiveSalesData
(SalesID INT not NULL IDENTITY(1,1) PRIMARY KEY CLUSTERED,
ProductID int NOT NULL,
ProductName Char(60),
SalesQty int NOT NULL,
SaleDescription char(3000) NULL)
```

3. Let us input our data into 100,000 rows in the newly created object dbo. ArchiveSalesData table. You can use the following TSQL to do so:

```
INSERT dbo.ArchiveSalesData (ProductID,ProductName,Sale
sQty) VALUES (CAST(RAND()*5 as INT), REPLICATE('Product
X',2),(CAST(RAND()*10 as INT)))
GO 100000
```

4. The INSERT script mentioned earlier will execute 100,000 times that will populate 100,000 rows into the dbo.ArchiveSalesData table.

5. To enable the ROW compression on this newly created object, we can execute:

```
ALTER TABLE dbo.ArchiveSalesData REBUILD WITH (DATA_
COMPRESSION=ROW)
```

6. As the data is populated, let us execute the `dbo.sp_estimate_data_compression_savings` system stored procedure to get an estimated value on storage savings.

7. Execute the following TSQL with `data_compression='ROW'`:

```
EXEC sys.sp_estimate_data_compression_savings
@schema_name = 'dbo',
@object_name = 'ArchiveSalesData',
@index_id = NULL,
@partition_number = NULL,
@data_compression = 'ROW'
```

8. The result will be as follows:

```
object_name                                           ArchiveSalesData
schema_name                                                        dbo
index_id                                                             1
partition_number                                                     1
size_with_current_compression_setting(KB)                         3368
size_with_requested_compression_setting(KB)                       3400
sample_size_with_current_compression_setting(KB)                  3368
sample_size_with_requested_compression_setting(KB)                3400
```

9. Execute the following TSQL with `data_compression='PAGE'`:

```
EXEC sys.sp_estimate_data_compression_savings
    @schema_name = 'dbo',
    @object_name = 'ArchiveSalesData',
    @index_id = NULL,
    @partition_number = NULL,
    @data_compression = 'PAGE'
```

10. The result will be as follows:

```
object_name                                        ArchiveSalesData
schema_name                                                     dbo
index_id                                                          1
partition_number                                                  1
size_with_current_compression_setting(KB)                      3368
size_with_requested_compression_setting(KB)                    1056
sample_size_with_current_compression_setting(KB)               3400
sample_size_with_requested_compression_setting(KB)             1072
```

11. From the previous scenario, the **PAGE** level compression is a definite savior that shows additional benefits on the storage level.

12. At any time, the compression type can be configured on the table using the following TSQL statement:

```
ALTER TABLE dbo.ArchiveSalesData REBUILD WITH (DATA_
COMPRESSION=PAGE)
```

13. The value used in the `DATA_COMPRESSION` will take care of the compression of clustered indexes and heaps.

14. Now, let us enable the compression on non-clustered indexes using the `CREATE INDEX` and `ALTER INDEX` statement.

15. Using the following TSQL statement, let us compress non-clustered indexes with a **PAGE** level compression:

```
CREATE NONCLUSTERED INDEX NCI_ArcSalesData_ProdIDSalesQty
ON dbo.ArchiveSalesData (ProductID, SalesQty)
WITH (DATA_COMPRESSION = PAGE)
```

16. As we have created the index, let us see how far we are saving the storage with this new object. Execute the following TSQL with `data_compression='PAGE'`:

```
EXEC sys.sp_estimate_data_compression_savings
  @schema_name = 'dbo',
  @object_name = 'ArchiveSalesData',
  @index_id = NULL,
  @partition_number = NULL,
  @data_compression = 'PAGE'
```

17. The results are as follows (observe the results of two objects):

object_ name	schema_ name	index_ id	Partition _number	size_with_ current_ compression_ setting(KB)	size_with_ requested_ compression_ setting(KB)	sample_size_ with_current_ compression_ setting(KB)	sample_ size_with_ requested_ compression_ setting(KB)
ArchiveSalesData	dbo	1	1	3368	1056	3400	1072
ArchiveSalesData	dbo	2	1	992	848	952	816

18. At any time, the compression type can be configured on the table using the **PAGE** or **ROW** value at the **DATA_COMPRESSION** option.

This completes the steps to implement compressed storage features for tables and indexes.

How it works...

SQL Server 2008 R2 provides great flexibility in how data compression is used. Row and page compression can be configured at the table, index, indexed view, or partition level. The TSQL statements that are demonstrated in this recipe use PAGE-level and ROW-level compression to a table. Clustered indexes use the CREATE TABLE statement and to modify the compression settings use the ALTER TABLE statement.

To obtain the savings on the storage space, the stored procedure sp_estimate_data_compression_savings statement will perform an estimation of the amount of space saved by compressing a table and its indexes. The main function of this system stored procedure is to take a sample of the database and then compress the data in the TEMPDB database. It is a resource-intensive operation and in order to obtain the prior information on how best we can benefit out of this feature, always execute it on the production server while there is less traffic on the server.

The SQL Server 2008 R2 compression feature has the added advantage of enhancing I/O performance and extended compression capability for UCS-2 Unicode data, in addition to non-Unicode data, which is useful to store data in a language that uses large character sets. There is a suggestive CPU cost to reading and decompressing the compressed data, hence, it is recommended to test the procedures before deploying the feature in a production environment.

There's more...

However, once the data compression procedures are complete, the space saved is released to the respective database data files, without releasing the same to the file system because the file size does not reduce automatically as part of data compression. In order to release the unused space on the data file or file group, perform the DBCC SHRINKFILE or SHRINK DATABASE operation on the database, unless it is compulsory as it will negate the database performance.

Designing a storage solution for unstructured data and new collations

The data stored in the database is structured to maintain transactional consistency and concurrency. Data that is stored outside the database such as text files, images, documents, and videos is unstructured data.

SQL Server 2008 integrates the new data type called `FILESTREAM`, which integrates the database engine with the `NTFS` file system by storing in the format of `VARBINARY(MAX)`. The storage limit on such data can exceed the 2GB limit on the stored values to take advantage of the relational capabilities of the core database engine, by handling the files on SQL Server. Similarly, the collations affect how characters (data) for a specific language or accent are recognized and sorted; by default SQL Server installation uses the default collation. Furthermore, the `FILESTREAM` takes the operating system cache for caching file data to avoid the usage of memory that is available for query processing which helps the performance. In this recipe, we look at how to design a storage solution for unstructured data and new collations.

Getting ready

To take advantage of unstructured data storage, we need to ensure that `FILESTREAM` is enabled on the operating system level and the SQL Server instance level.

1. Enable the `FILESTREAM` storage on the operating system level during the SQL Server installation.

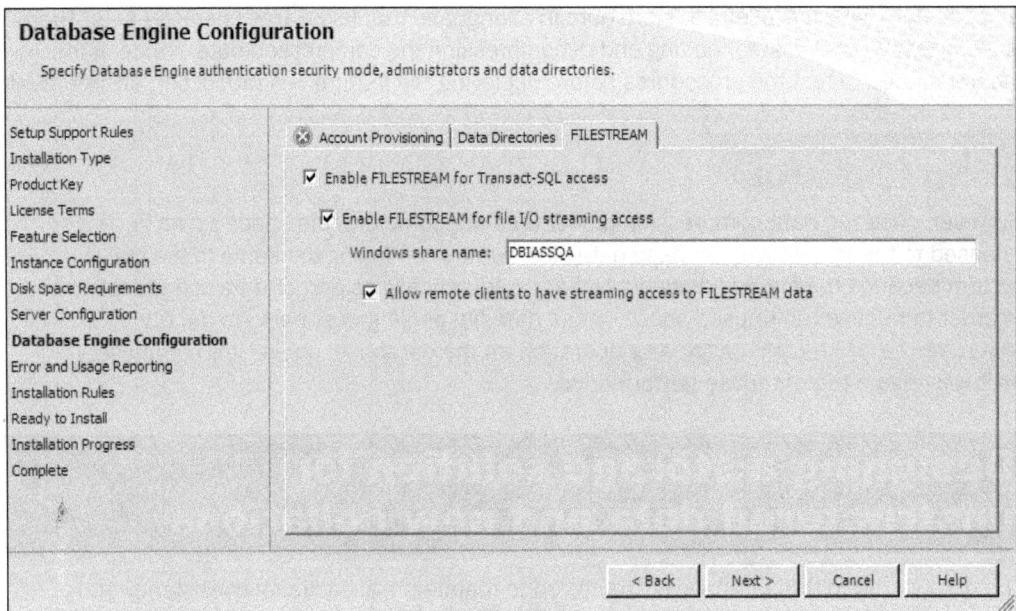

2. At the **Database Engine Configuration** screen:

   ❑ To select `Win32 API` streaming access, click on **Enable FILESTREAM** for Transact-SQL access

   ❑ Click on **Enable FILESTREAM** for I/O streaming access and provide the windows share name in which the `FILESTREAM` data will be stored

> When a 32-bit SQL Server instance is running on a 64-bit operating system, we cannot enable `FILESTREAM` due to environment limitations.

   ❑ As per the business rules, if there is a plan to allow remote clients to access this `FILESTREAM` data, click **Allow remote clients** to have streaming access to the **FILESTREAM data** option

   ❑ The previous operation can be achieved using the TSQL: `EXEC sp_configure_filestream_access_level, 2`

   ❑ Once the SQL Server installation has finished, enter the following TSQL to validate the FILESTREAM configuration for the SQL Server instance:

```
SELECT SERVERPROPERTY('FilestreamShareName') ShareName,
SERVERPROPERTY('FilestreamEffectiveLevel') EffectiveLevel,
SERVERPROPERTY('FilestreamConfiguredLevel') ConfiguredLevel,
```

3. The result will be 0, 1, or 2 and they will be represented as follows:

   ❑ `Disabled (0)`: FILESTREAM access is not permitted

   ❑ `Transact SQL Access Enabled (1)`: FILESTREAM data can be accessed only by TSQL commands

   ❑ `Full Access Enabled (2)`: Both TSQL and Win32 access to FILESTREAM data are permitted

Now, let us work on new collation settings. SQL Server 2008 is fully aligned with Windows Server 2008 on codepage, where every collation in SQL Server maps to a specific language locale and ANSI code page for case-sensitive and accent-sensitive data sorts. There are 80 new collations, denoted by `*_100` version references to provide up-to-date and accurate sorting conventions. There may also be some situations where a different collation is required at the **Database Engine Configuration** screen:

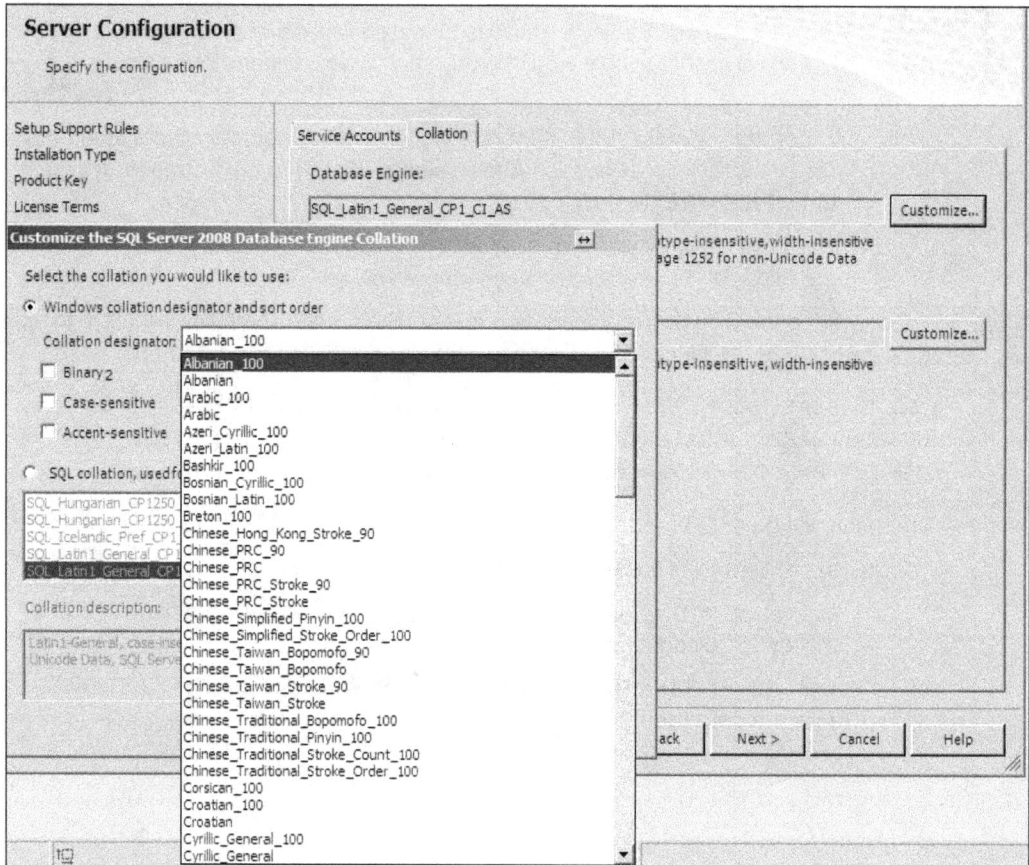

- ▸ Select the **BINARY2 collation** option if the binary code point based sorting is required

- ▸ Select **Windows Collation designator** and sort order for a consistent comparison across the data types

- ▸ In addition to instance level and database level collation settings, we can also configure the individual column level using the `COLLATE` command within the column definition

- ▸ The specific collations for Windows or SQL use the `CREATE TABLE` or `ALTER TABLE` statements

How to do it...

Once the prerequisites for FILESTREAM and Collation are completed, complete the following steps to design a storage solution for unstructured data and new collations. Initially, we will create a solution for unstructured data:

1. Let us create a new database by associating a file group with a specific path and also designate the name of the folder that was created during the SQL Server installation on the file system.

```
USE master
GO
CREATE DATABASE EntzStreaming ON PRIMARY
( NAME = N'EntzStreaming',
FILENAME = N'd:\entz\FS\data\EntzStreaming.mdf',
SIZE = 4048KB , FILEGROWTH = 1024KB ),
FILEGROUP FS_EStreaming CONTAINS FILESTREAM
(NAME = 'FG_EntzStreaming',
FILENAME = N'd:\entz\FS\DBIASSQA')
LOG ON
( NAME = N'PhotoRepository_log',
FILENAME = N'd:\entz\FS\log\EntzStreaming_log.ldf',
SIZE = 1024KB , FILEGROWTH = 10%)
GO
```

2. The database is created along with the FILESTREAM folder to share the name as DBIASSQA.

3. We will use the dbo.MuzikStore table to store a music file, which is classified as unstructured data.

```
USE EntzStreaming
GO
CREATE TABLE dbo.MuzikStore
(MuzikID uniqueidentifier ROWGUIDCOL NOT NULL PRIMARY KEY,
MuzikName varchar(50) NOT NULL,
MuzikFile varbinary(max) FILESTREAM)
GO
```

4. Now that we have created a database and table to store the data, let us insert the data using the regular INSERT statement and import file using the OPENROWSET command.

```
INSERT dbo.MuzikStore
(MuzikID, MuzikName, MuzikFile) SELECT NEWID(),
'The Last Waltz - Dreaming and Relaxing', BulkColumn FROM
OPENROWSET(BULK
'D:\ENTZ\FS\DBIASSQA\The Last Waltz.mp3', SINGLE_BLOB) AS Muzik
```

5. The successful execution of the `INSERT` process will create a new subdirectory and file, the sample filename will be `00000023-00000082-0007` under the folder `D:\ENTZ\FS\DBIASSQA\091665b3-a692-4e74-8ae0-42d7f7cb2737\d9da9467-541b-4a4c-94e2-f7876f1647de`.

6. As we can see, files created using FILESTREAM are accessed within the context of TSQL and associated with Win32 APIs. Using the TSQL context, let us view the contents of the `dbo.MuzikStore` table:

    ```
    SELECT * from dbo.MuzikStore
    ```

7. Let us assume that our application uses OLEDB to query the SQL Server data and collect the appropriate information about the file system file in order to stream using the application. To obtain the default collation of the server instance, execute the following TSQL statement:

    ```
    SELECT SERVERPROPERTY('Collation')
    ```

8. In addition to the instance level collation, we also need to obtain information on the database collation using the following TSQL statement:

    ```
    SELECT DATABASEPROPERTYEX ( 'AdventureWorks 2008R2' , 'Collation' )
    ```

9. Unless otherwise selected, the SQL Server setup offers the `SQL_Latin1_General_CP1_CI_AS` collation as the default collation for server installations. To obtain the actual settings that a collation is applied to, run the following TSQL statement:

    ```
    SELECT description FROM sys.fn_helpcollations() WHERE name = 'SQL_Latin1_General_CP1_CI_AS'
    ```

10. Now, there is a requirement to add extra information on the `dbo.MuzikStore` table to store the filename in internationalization text. Use the following TSQL statement to add a new column with matching collation:

    ```
    ALTER TABLE dbo.MuzikStore
    ADD ItalianFileName nvarchar(50) COLLATE Latin1_General_100_,
    IndianFileName nvarchar(50) COLLATE Indic_General_100_
    ```

This completes the required steps to design a storage solution for unstructured data and new collations recipe.

How it works...

The FILESTREAM feature and new collations setup can be managed during the SQL Server setup or using SQL Server configuration manager or TSQL statements.

After we enable FILESTREAM during the setup or using SQL Server Configuration Manager, a new share is created on the host server with the specified name. This share name is intended only to allow or use a low-level streaming interaction between the SQL Server and authorized application clients.

Within the TSQL statements, we have used the FILESTREAM attribute, which is used to handle the data. By default, Win32 streaming APIs is preferred to perform actual read and write operations using the `OpenSqlFileStream` API process. The FILESYSTEM attribute of the `VARBINARY(MAX)` data type is used to store unstructured data on the file system, which is not readable from the operating system.

On the new collations, the Windows or SQL collation can be explicitly defined during the `CREATE TABLE` or `ALTER TABLE` operation for columns that use `VARCHAR`, `CHAR`, `NCHAR`, and `NVARCHAR` data types. The collations handle three settings on SQL Server, which are:

- ▶ Code-page used to store non-Unicode character data types
- ▶ Sort order for non-Unicode character data types
- ▶ Sort order for Unicode data types

The default collation for the SQL Server instance is determined during the installation process where we can choose the default or select the appropriate settings for the data storage. In a multi-instance and multi-database environment, when we define different collations within the same database or across the databases, we may encounter data compatibility issues and the cross-collation join statement may not always work. If a data transfer process is used, then it may result in corrupted data.

There's more...

The SQL Server service account must have access to the FILESTREAM share in order to handle unstructured data storage. If, in case, the share is created after the installation of SQL Server, then the change can only take place on operating system level and SQL Server level; we need to restart the SQL Server services.

Designing data partitioning solutions for tables and indexes

As part of performance improvement techniques, partitioning the table or index may improve the query performance depending upon the query types and hardware configuration. SQL Server 2005 introduced the data partitioning solutions and from the beginning of SQL Server 2008, this feature has been enhanced with native table and index partitioning, which provides better scalability to the data platform.

As the data grows, tables grow larger and similarly, the data access time also tends to increase. By designing the data partitioning solutions with appropriate hardware, we will be able to build a scalable and high performance platform. In this recipe, we will look at designing data partitioning solutions for tables and indexes using SQL Server 2008 R2. This solution will essentially allow us to manage large tables and indexes at a lower level of granularity. The partitioning solution is differentiated as horizontal and vertical.

Getting ready

In order to begin the planning and design of the data partitioning solution, make sure the SQL Server instance is a Datacenter or Enterprise edition for the production environment. For testing purposes, we can use the Developer edition, which is equivalent to the Enterprise edition and cannot be used as a production platform. There are three types of partitioning: hardware, horizontal, and vertical.

- Hardware partitioning designs the solution by taking advantage of available hardware architecture.

- Horizontal partitioning designs the solution dividing a table into multiple partitioned tables, horizontally, depending upon how data is analyzed, which is ideal for queries that require data for a specific value (date) to reference the appropriate table.

- Vertical partitioning designs the solution dividing a table into multiple tables that contain fewer columns. This feature is helpful for queries to scan less data with increased performance, provided the partitions are not larger.

To start with the data partitioning solution, we need to create a partitioned table, which is listed as follows:

- Create additional `filegroups` if the partition needs to spread over multiple file groups

- Place the newly created `filegroups` across different physical disk partitions. In theory the maximum number of partitions allowed is 1000

- Create a `partition` function that will determine how the data is partitioned

- Create a partition scheme that will assign partitions to `filegroups`

- Create a table with a non-clustered primary key using the partition scheme

> For more information and detailed steps, refer to the recipe *Designing Scalable Shared database features and enhancements* mentioned in *Chapter 3, Managing the Core Database Engine.*

- Create a clustered index for the table using the partition scheme and the partition function

- Create the indexes and by default these objects will also use the same partitioning scheme and partitioning column

- For better manageability, indexes can be created using different partitioning functions or on non-partitioned filegroups

How to do it...

The following process is essential to implement the horizontal process that will enable you to design a data partitioning solution for tables and indexes.

Initially, let us plan for the horizontal data partitioning:

1. Split the table into multiple tables (partitions) with the same table structure storing different data sets.

2. All the constraints and triggers to manage the business rules must be maintained across the partitions.

3. To split the table horizontally, the analysis on data is essential which is an optimal way to split the table. For instance, the sales history data can be partitioned based on the sale date, customer type, or product attribute.

4. The syntax for designating a table's filegroup is as follows:

```
CREATE TABLE ...[ ON {filegroup | "default" }]
[ { TEXTIMAGE_ON { filegroup | "default" } ]
```

5. Let us demonstrate the table on a non-default newly created filegroup:

```
ALTER DATABASE AdventureWorks2008R2
ADD FILEGROUP ADW_FG2
GO
ALTER DATABASE AdventureWorks2008R2
ADD FILE ( NAME = ADW_F2,
FILENAME = 'F:\Data\ADW_F2.ndf',
SIZE = 1024MB
) TO FILEGROUP ADW_FG2
GO
ALTER DATABASE AdventureWorks2008R2
ADD FILE ( NAME = ADW_IDX,
FILENAME = 'F:\Data\ADW_IDX.ndf',
SIZE = 1024MB
) TO FILEGROUP ADW_INDX
GO
```

6. Let us create a new table on this new filegroup as follows:

```
CREATE TABLE Sales.ADWCompany(
ADWCompanyID int IDENTITY(1,1) NOT NULL PRIMARY KEY,
ParentCompanyID int NULL,
ParentCompanyName varchar(25) NOT NULL,
CreateDate datetime NOT NULL DEFAULT (getdate())
) ON ADW_FG2
```

7. Create a clustered index as follows:

```
CREATE CLUSTERED INDEX  IX_PARTN_ADWCompany ON Sales.ADWCompany
(ParentCompanyID, CreateDate) ON ADW_IDX
```

Now let us plan for the vertical data partitioning:

1. Divide the tables based on the number of rows on a page, which depends on the width of the table.

2. Vertical splitting is a method of reducing the width of the table by splitting the column of the table into multiple tables.

3. It is ideal to keep frequently used columns in one table and other columns in other tables.

4. In order to help the performance, it is ideal to involve equi-join between two or more partitioned tables by ensuring the partitioning column is the same on which the tables are joined.

5. The tables and indexes should be collocated, which means they should use the same named partition function and mapping should be based on the Partition Scheme for an aligned index.

Now, let us plan for the hardware configuration and filegroup placement:

1. To achieve performance and better I/O operations for data, always place each partition filegroup on a different physical disk drive.

2. Hardware-based solutions can be implemented by using RAID (Redundant Array of Independent Disks) levels such as 0, 1, 5, and 1+0.

3. The RAID levels are as follows:

   ❑ RAID 0 is data striping with no redundancy or fault tolerance

   ❑ RAID 1 is mirroring, where every disk is managed as a copy

   ❑ RAID 5 is stripping with parity, disk contents can be recreated from the parity stored on the other disks in the array

   ❑ RAID 10, or 1+0, is a combination of RAID 1 and RAID 0. This is the best configuration for write performance as each disk has a mirrored duplicate, offering the fault tolerance of RAID 1 with the performance advantages of RAID 0

4. The hardware-based RAID uses intelligent drive controller and a redundant array of disk drives to help protect against data loss in case of media failure and performance improvement on read and write operations.

5. Using RAID level 1 through 5 will automate redundancy and fault-tolerance at the hardware level with no overhead on the system processor.

6. Place the filegroups on the single RAID 5 array, this is not optimal for TEMPDB database or transaction logs.

How it works...

The options on the partitions may look familiar as they correspond directly to the options on the page in the index. SQL Server optimizer can process the join faster because the partitions can be joined themselves based on the filegroup placement on each physical drive. The best solution in terms of performance is to strip the data files of the partitions across more than one disk by setting up an appropriate RAID. The data is sorted by the partition and can access each partition at the same time, irrespective of single or multiple filegroups.

Depending on the configuration, hardware-based RAID generally provides good performance. Hardware-based RAID also makes it much easier to manage multiple disks. This lets you treat an array of disks as one disk. You might even be able to replace a failed drive without shutting down the system. A disadvantage of a hardware-based solution is cost. You might also be dependent upon one vendor.

Implementing sparse columns and wide table features

Using SQL Server 2008, a new space saving storage option is available–which is referred to as sparse columns–that can provide optimized and efficient storage for columns that contain predominant NULL values. Querying and manipulation of sparse columns is similar to regular columns by using standard INSERT/UPDATE/DELETE statements. The sparse columns are normal columns in a table that have an optimized storage format by reducing the space requirements.

In this recipe, we will look at how to implement sparse columns and wide table features. The sparse columns are useful for the applications such as Windows SharePoint Services that will help to manage the efficient way to store and access a large number of user-defined properties.

Getting ready

The database compatibility must be 100 or 105 to implement sparse column features. The table columns can be any structured data type and the following restrictions are applicable to implement sparse column features:

► A sparse column must be nullable and the data types such as text, ntext, geometry, image, or user-defined data type

► The column data cannot have ROWGUIDCOL or IDENTITY properties

► The column cannot have a default value or be bound to a rule or a computed column

▶ A sparse column cannot be a part of a user-defined table such as `Table Variables` and `Table-Valued Parameters` (TVP)

▶ The sparse columns cannot be added to compressed tables or allowed to be compressed

How to do it...

The following steps need to be completed in order to implement sparse columns and wide table features;

1. To define a sparse column, we need to add a sparse storage attribute using `CREATE TABLE` or `ALTER TABLE` statements.

2. Let us create a new table with sparse columns by using the following TSQL statement:

```
CREATE TABLE dbo.SparseDemo
(ProductID INT NOT NULL PRIMARY KEY,
ProductName NVARCHAR(50) NOT NULL,
ProductColor NVARCHAR(18) SPARSE NULL,
ProductWeight DECIMAL(12,2) SPARSE NULL,
SellDate DATETIME SPARSE NULL,
ProductDesc XML COLUMN_SET FOR ALL_SPARSE_COLUMNS)
```

3. Next, insert the data from the `AdventureWorks2008R2 database Production. Product` table:

```
INSERT INTO [dbo].[SparseDemo]
            ([ProductID]
            ,[ProductName]
            ,[ProductColor]
            ,[ProductWeight]
            ,[SellDate]
            )
SELECT ProductID, Name, Color, Weight, SellEndDate
FROM Production.Product
```

4. The data that is inserted into the table can be queried by using the specified sparse columns as follows:

```
SELECT ProductID, ProductName, ProductColor,ProductWeight,SellDate
from dbo.SparseDemo
```

5. If we use `SELECT * FROM` in a query, then only the column set is returned as an XML column instead of each column. This is advantageous to reduce rendering time and obtain populated data only; however, it may miss out the column name specifically.

6. In order to return the result as relational column, the sparse columns must be explicitly listed in the query.

7. Now, let us update the ProductDesc column with an XML value using the following statement:

    ```
    UPDATE dbo.SparseDemo SET ProductDesc='<Color>Blue</Color>
    <SellDate>2010/12/01</SellDate> WHERE ProductID=201
    ```

8. From the previous statement, we have specified the ProductColor and SellDate, but not ProductWeight. In this case, the value will be NULL.

9. When the sparse columns are explicitly referred to in the UPDATE statement, the other column values will not be changed:

    ```
    UPDATE dbo.SparseDemo SET ProductColor='Black' WHERE ProductID=201
    GO
    SELECT ProductID, ProductName, ProductColor,ProductWeight,SellDate
    from dbo.SparseDemo
    ```

10. When the table has many sparse columns, then using the XML string to populate data will be more useful than having a statement for an individual column.

This represents the wide-tables concept where the sparse columns allow a large number of columns to be defined for a table (by default 30,000 sparse columns are allowed in a table).

How it works...

Defining a column as SPARSE is as easy as adding a relational column using a default DML statement. Most of data types are allowed, except the image, ntext, text, timestamp, geometry, or user-defined data types.

Any sparse columns that are not referenced in a DML operation will be set to a NULL value. Once a column set is defined for a table, performing the SELECT * query will no longer return each individual sparse column. When updating a column set using an XML value, you must include values for all the columns in the column set you want to set, including any existing values. Any values that are not specified in the XML string should be set to NULL.

Designing spatial data storage methods

The support of SQL CLR allows applications to manage rich user-defined data such as mathematical or geographical based data. SQL Server 2008 enables the native support of .NET CLR data types by providing two data types: GEOMETRY and GEOGRAPHY.

Managing a spatial type of data will require high-performance and high-end hardware with a massive data storage solution. However, SQL Server features on these two new data types have enabled the applications to support various methods that will allow for creation, comparison, analysis, and spatial data retrieval. In this recipe, we will go through the process of designing spatial data storage methods using SQL Server 2008 R2.

> For more on OGC and the WKT/WKB/GML XML transport formats, review `http://www.opengeospatial.org/standards/sfa`.

Getting ready

Every edition of SQL Server 2008 R2 supports the spatial data services, and the only exception for SQL Express edition is, there is no graphical interface to view the results. Ensure that the database used in this recipe has a compatibility level of 100 or 105 to support the SPATIAL features.

The process is simple where we create a new table, insert the geo-data and select the inserted data using the relational TSQL process.

How to do it...

The recipe steps are performed in a two-fold method, where both of the geography and geometry data types are used. The following steps are required to design spatial data storage methods using SQL Server 2008 R2.

1. Let us start with GEOGRAPHY, by using the following TSQL statement to create a table:

    ```
    USE AdventureWorks2008R2
    GO
    CREATE TABLE dbo.NewSalesRegion_Europe
    (SalesRegionID int NOT NULL IDENTITY(1,1) PRIMARY KEY,
    SalesRegionName varchar(50) NOT NULL,
    SalesRegionGeoLocation Geography NOT NULL,
    RegionalLocationWKTxt AS SalesRegionGeoLocation.STAsText())
    GO
    ```

2. The data for `RegionalLocationWKTxt` (Well-known text) is a calculated column based on the `SalesRegionGeoLocation` column. Insert a row based on the Europe Sales geographical area:

    ```
    INSERT into dbo.NewSalesRegion_Europe (SalesRegionName,
    SalesRegionGeoLocation)  VALUES ('SalesEuorpe', geography::Regio
    nalLocationWKTxt('POINT(-3.147583007812494 55.86298231197633)',
    4326))
    ```

3. Insert a row based on the Scotland Sales geographical area:

    ```
    INSERT into dbo.NewSalesRegion_Europe (SalesRegionName,
    SalesRegionGeoLocation)  VALUES('SalesScotland',  geography::Regi
    onalLocationWKTxt('POINT(-2.98212330008122324 51.8233578776760)',
    3903))
    ```

4. Next, let's have a look at how to query the stored data:

```
SELECT SalesRegionID,SalesRegionName, SalesRegionGeoLocation,Regio
nalLocationWKTxt from dbo.NewSalesRegion_Europe
```

5. By default, the native geographical data for Sales Europe and Sales Scotland is not in a readable format and the same can be represented by using the `RegionalLocationWKTxt` column to show well-known text (WKT) as a readable text.

Next, let's look at GEOMETRY, we will assign a value to a column or variable using static methods to parse the representation of data into spatial data type.

1. Use the following TSQL statement to use local variables in a batch:

```
Declare @geom-ex1 GEOMETRY
Declare @geom-ex2 GEOMETRY
PRINT @geomex1.ToString()
SET @geom-ex1 = geometry::STGeomFromText('LINESTRING (130 90, 30
160, 180 140)', 1)
SET @geom-ex2 = geometry::STGeomFromText
('POLYGON ((0 10, 120 0, 150 120, 0 120, 0 1))', 0)
```

2. Now, let's us create a demo table by inserting data and selecting inserted values as follows:

```
USE AdventureWorks2011
GO;
CREATE TABLE geo_demo
(GeoID INT IDENTITY NOT NULL,
GeoName GEOMETRY)
GO;

--Insert data in GEO demo table
INSERT INTO #geom_demo (GeomCol)
VALUES ('LINESTRING (130 90, 30 160, 180 140)', 1),
('POLYGON ((0 10, 120 0, 150 120, 0 120, 0 1))', 0),
('POINT(10 10)')

--Select the inserted data
SELECT
GeoID,
GeoName.ToString() AS WKT,
GeoName.STLength() AS LENGTH,
GeoName.STArea() as Area
FROM geo_demo
GO
```

```
SELECT
GeoID,
GeoName.ToString() AS WKT,
GeoName.STLength() AS LENGTH,
GeoName.STArea() as Area
FROM geo_demo
```

	GeoID	WKT	LENGTH	Area
1	3	LINESTRING (130 90, 30 160, 180 140)	273.393015661553	0
2	4	POINT (10 10)	0	0

3.   The GEOMETRY type supports the implicit conversion to and from a string. The string format supported by the GEOMETRY type for implicit conversion is WKT.

This completes the process of designing spatial data storage methods using SQL Server 2008 R2.

How it works...

The SQL Server Management Studio tool has a built-in capability to query spatial data and plot to display basic maps, which is an integral feature of SQL Server 2008 R2.

Both the SQL CLR data types GEOMETRY and GEOGRAPHY use latitude and longitude angles to identify points on the earth. Latitude measures how far north (or south) of the equator a point is, while longitude measures how far a prime meridian point is. The feature also supports the relational data to represent the inventory or stock, area-wise in a map format.

Both data types are implemented as a **Common Language Runtime (CLR)** data type that is used to represent data in a flat co-ordinate system.

Deploying and managing data-tier applications

Data-tier application (DACPAC) enables developers to develop, deploy, and manage their applications using traditional development methodologies. SQL Server 2008 R2 added several new features and enhancements with a new unit of deployment to make the deployment and upgrade processes of data-tier applications from Visual Studio 2010 and SSMS tool easier. The management aspect of DACPAC trend analysis is handled by the SSMS tool using SQL Server Utility Control Point (UCP), which enrolls them to monitor the performance and configuration of instance and application level.

In this recipe, we will go through the required steps in order to design and manage data-tier applications in the data platform.

Getting ready

There are no specific hardware or software requirements for data-tier applications except that the SQL Server version must be 2008 R2. Additionally, the data-tier applications can be used to work with existing databases using SSMS or used to implement new projects and releases using Visual Studio 2010.

- A DAC-in-place application can be created by registering the database as a data-tier application, by using the Register Data-tier Application Wizard in SSMS or through PowerShell snippets

- Users can then extract each database to produce a DAC package for further development where developers can use Visual Studio to author data-tier changes to package them accordingly

- The authorized packages can be re-deployed in the production by the DBAs using the upgrade method from SSMS using automatic methods and tools that are available for the data-tier application framework

- In the case of new projects, the developers can create a new data-tier application project in Visual Studio and build the DAC package for each application, then these packages are forwarded to DBAs for deployment

- For more information on new projects and deployment processes refer to the *Working with data-tier applications* recipe, mentioned in *Chapter 1*.

- In this recipe, we will use the SSMS tool to invoke the Deploy Data-tier Application Wizard for the applications that are installed for the first time

> DACPAC is suitable for smaller databases having frequent release changes with limited structures and few features, such as SQLCLR, Service Broker, and security.

How to do it...

In order to design and manage the upgrade of data-tier applications using the SSMS tool, you will need to complete the following steps:

1. Locate the DAC package file that needs to be deployed.

2. In **SSMS** under the **Object Explorer** pane, select the node of the target instance of SQL Server on which the new DAC package will be deployed and create a new database.

3. After the instance is selected, expand the **Management** node, right-click the Data-tier Applications node, and then click **Deploy Data-tier Application** to launch the wizard.

4. The initial screen of the wizard is an introduction that presents a description about the deployment process, click **Next** to continue.

5. On the **Select Package** page, click **Browse** and navigate to the file that was specified in step 1. Examine and review the package details, such as **Application Name** and **Version** and then click **Next**.

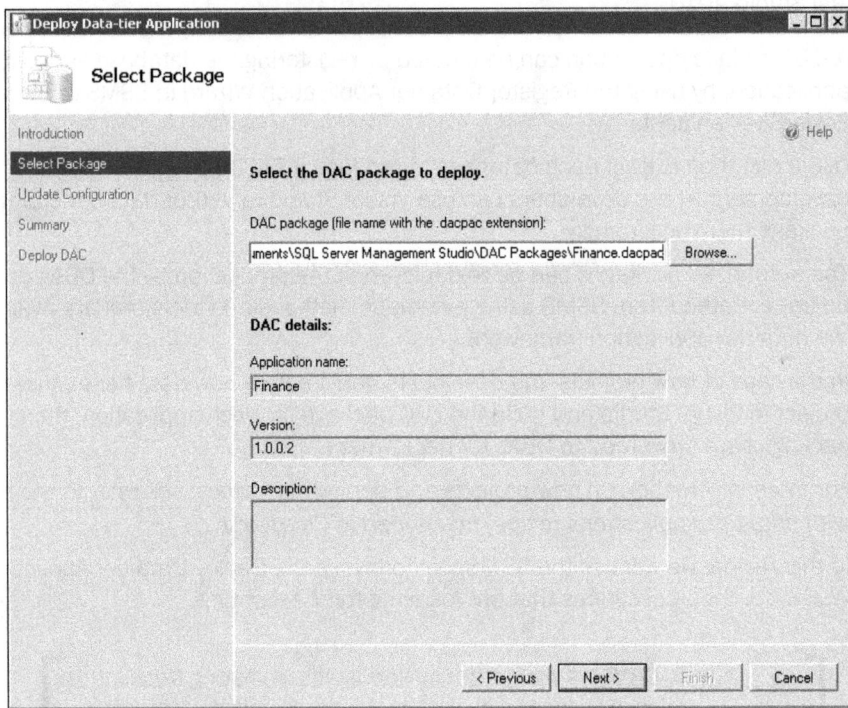

6. As per the DAC package configuration, the **Review Policy** page appears, if it contains the server selection policy. For instance, a new application can only be deployed on SQL Server 2008 instances.

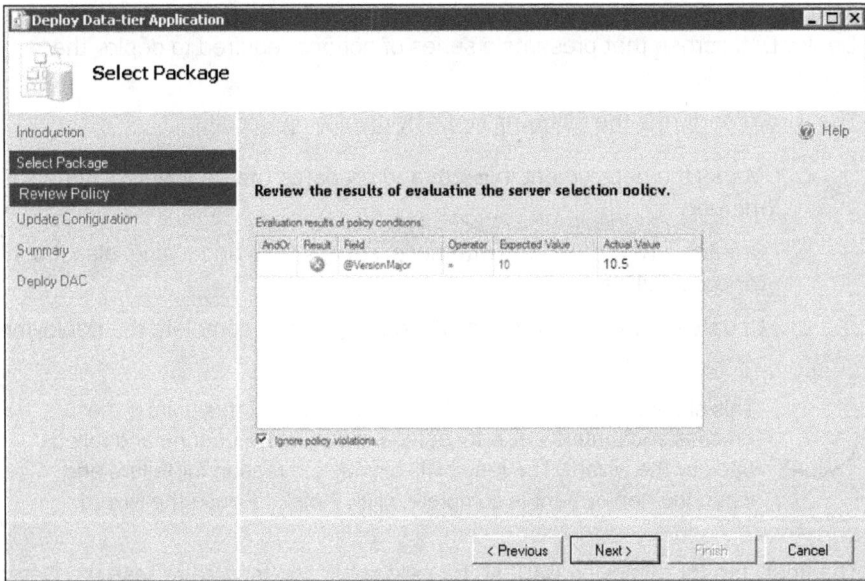

7. If the policy conditions are met, the **Next** button will be visible, otherwise the policy evaluation results can be overridden by clicking on **Ignore policy violations** and then **Next**.

8. The deployment will create a new database and then populate the database with the necessary objects. On the **Update Configuration** page, the database details will be displayed. Review the information and update if necessary, then click **Next**.

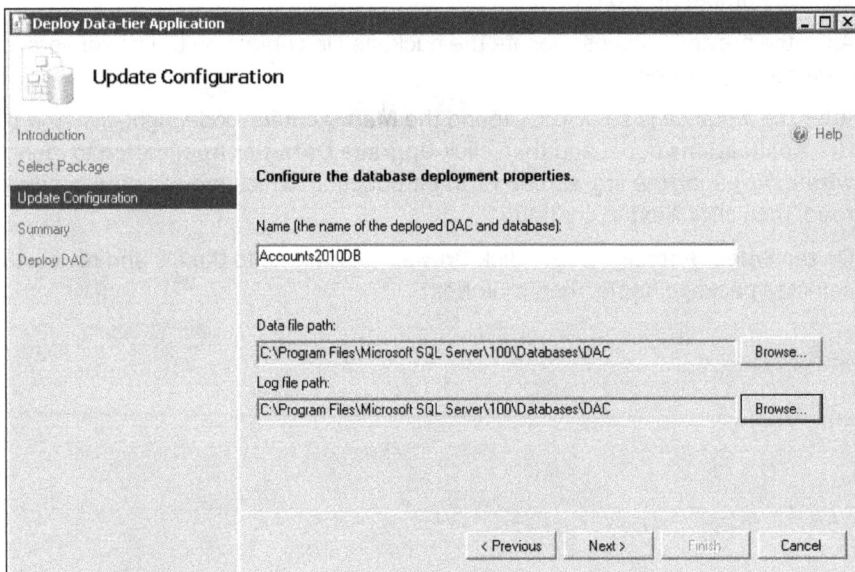

9. Next, the **Summary** page will be displayed, click **Next** to continue towards the Deploy DAC screen that presents a series of actions required to deploy the data-tier application.

10. The wizard performs the following steps by displaying Results:

   ❑ Marks the deployment in msdb and prepares the deployment scripts in memory

   ❑ Creates a new database with necessary objects and logins, also it contains a random GUID string

   ❑ Updates msdb to record the DAC definition and complete the deployment

> This should complete the deployment process. At this point if the process encounters any error, all the changes are undone and rolled back by the wizard. The result will display the reason for failure and when the deployment is complete, click **Finish** to close the wizard.

11. The final step for deploying DACPAC for new applications, is to refresh the Databases node under SSMS, select and refresh the Data-tier applications node and then expand to view the entry for the new DAC package.

12. Now we have reached the point where we should follow the instructions to upgrade a data-tier application to a newer version using the Upgrade data-tier application wizard.

13. For this recipe, the scenario is that after few weeks of Finance application deployment, there are a few new changes and bugfixes by the Developers bearing the version number as 2.0.0.0.

14. As in the previous process, locate the package file containing the newer version of the data-tier application.

15. After the instance is selected, expand the **Management** node, right-click the **Data-tier Applications** node, and then click **Upgrade Data-tier Application** to launch the wizard. As usual, the first screen is an introduction, which provides the description to read, then click **Next** to continue.

16. On the **Select Package** page, click **Browse** to navigate to the file and review the selected package name, then click **Next**.

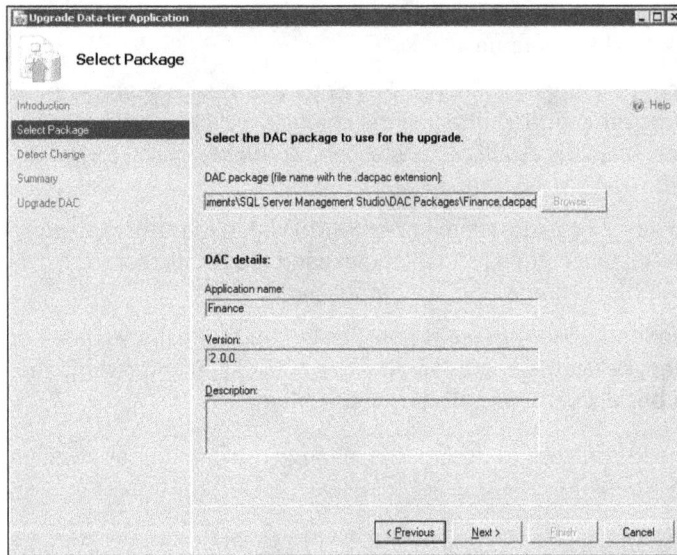

17. To upgrade, the DAC package must match the name of the data-tier application.

18. As in step 6, the **Review Policy** page will be presented again, so you need to follow the same process to proceed further to the **Detect Change** screen.

19. The **Detect Change** page compares the DAC 1.0 definition in msdb to the database used by DAC 1.0. All the changes are prompted to acknowledge the change of objects in the data-tier application.

20. Click on **Save Report** to store the list of modified objects in an HTML report. Click **Next** to continue.

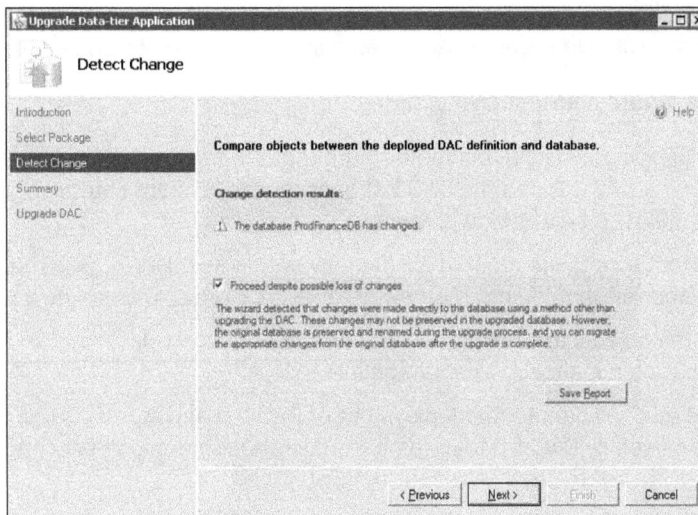

21. The **Summary** page lists the action steps that are to be taken to upgrade the DAC, then click **Next** to continue.

22. At this point, the Upgrade DAC package process must be completed successfully. If any errors are reported, then all the changes will be undone and rolled back by the wizard. Once the result pane is shown as **Success** click **Finish** to complete the wizard.

23. As a final step of confirmation, under **SSMS** within the **Object Explorer** pane, expand the server instance, then refresh and expand the Databases node. Navigate and browse the DAC2.0 and DAC.10 databases.

24. Finally, under the **Management** node, select and refresh the Data-tier Applications node. Then, select the upgraded data-tier application and refer to the **Object Explorer Details** pane to verify the new version.

This completes the list of steps to design and manage the data-tier application using the SSMS tool.

How it works...

The design and upgrade procedures for data-tier applications are managed using the **SSMS** tool. During the DACPAC deployment for new applications, the database is created along with the required objects to store the relevant information on the DAC package. The name of the new database contains a random string.

During the DACPAC upgrade process, the source database (DAC1.0) is set to read-only mode and all the relevant data is copied to a newly created database.

Finally, the source database is renamed, then the new database takes the name of the original DAC1.0 database, and the DAC definition data is updated in msdb. The upgrade process is called a **side-by-side upgrade** as it creates a new database to hold the newer version of DAC objects and coexists with older DAC objects on the same instance of SQL Server.

The DAC upgrade wizard performs the following steps:

▶ Checks user permissions and makes sure that the application name matches between the DAC 1.0 and the DAC 2.0 package file. System database msdb marks the beginning of the upgrade process.

▶ Deployment scripts are created for the new database together with the database objects and relevant logins. The new database for DAC 2.0 contains a random string.

▶ Installs the objects from the DAC 2.0 package in the new database and creates all logins that do not already exist on the instance.

▶ Updates msdb to denote the deployment of DAC 2.0 and stores its definition. Sets the database used by DAC 1.0 to read-only mode and terminates user connections to it.

- Further, query `dbo.sysdac_instances` to display information about DAC deployed to an instance of the database engine. This system catalog queries information from `msdb` system database.

- Generates a script to copy data to the new database by performing a comparison for each table and column that exists in all three sources.

- Generates an `INSERT` statement to populate tables and columns in the DAC 2.0 database from the corresponding tables and columns in the original DAC 1.0 database.

- Disables table constraints in the DAC 2.0 database, by executing the `INSERT` statements script and enables constraints that were disabled before.

- Sets the original DAC 1.0 database to read/write mode. Then, renames the original DAC 1.0 database, where the new name contains the DAC version and a random string.

- Renames the new DAC 2.0 database to the original database name used by DAC 1.0 and updates `msdb` to record the upgrade completion.

There's more...

The Management of DACPAC is essential once it has been deployed to an instance of the database engine, using the **SSMS** tool. It is also essential to perform regular backups for the system database to maintain the relationship with DAC.

See also

For more information on new projects and deployment processes refer to the *Working with data-tier applications* recipe mentioned in *Chapter 1*.

7
Implementing New Manageability Features and Practices

In this chapter, we will cover:

- ▶ Implementing auditing and service level security features
- ▶ Managing server-level securable and database-level permissions
- ▶ Implementing backup compression for a VLDB environment
- ▶ Designing change tracking methodology
- ▶ Implementing Policy-Based Management features
- ▶ Implementing and running PowerShell for SQL Server features
- ▶ Implementing SQL Server Best Practices Analyzer
- ▶ Designing Transparent Data Encryption features

Introduction

Manageability is highly essential to optimize database management. Since SQL Server 2005, manageability has been integrated as a management tool suite with support for the automation of day-to-day tasks. There are multiple features within the core database engine, and the SQL Server Management Studio tool provides integrated management, proactive health monitoring, and improved performance techniques.

SQL Server 2008 and SQL Server 2008 R2 have a flurry of manageability features in the database administration arena. In this chapter, we will go through the important features such as auditing, security, compression, change tracking, policy-based management, data-tier applications, and SQL Server PowerShell Provider `Cmdlets`.

Implementing auditing and service level security features

SQL Server provides various tools and methods to maintain a secure environment and several methods to involve tracking and logging of events that occur in the system. It is essential for DBAs and System Administrators to implement a defensive strategy to avoid any breach of security and meet the necessary compliance to audit the data platform.

The security is an integral part of SQL Server 2005 and 2008. SQL Server 2008 introduces the native capability of auditing from instance level to database-scoped activity in addition to C2 audit mode. In this recipe, we will go through the essential steps to implement auditing and service level security features using SQL Server 2008 R2.

Getting ready

The most common Security features within an Enterprise are classified into the following methods:

- C2 compliant audit mode
- SQL Server audit mode (fine-grained auditing)

However, the additional security features that are important in implementing auditing are SSL for login, Transparent Data Encryption (TDE), Certificate-Based Login, and Policy-Based Management Framework.

In this recipe, we will go through the C2 compliant audit mode that is available in all editions of SQL Server 2008 R2 including the Express edition.

The fine-grained auditing mode is only available in the Datacenter or Enterprise edition, for production purposes and in the Evaluation Enterprise or Developer edition, for testing purposes.

The traditional auditing technique is where an auditing table is created for each base table that needs to be audited. The underlying mechanism for this method is using a trigger-based process, which might be cumbersome when the application is mission-critical and highly transactional. Auditing can also be accomplished whereby a generic table stores the data needed in conjunction with a lookup table to identify the original column for the audited data. The following steps are different than the previously mentioned traditional approach, which is driven on the native capability of SQL Server 2008 R2 features to audit the SQL Server instance and data-scoped activity.

How to do it...

The following steps are essential to implement auditing and service level security features on an existing SQL Server instance. The initial phase of the implementation is concentrated on the auditing features:

1. The first step in configuring the auditing for the SQL Server instance is to create a Server Audit object with a file target or Security log from Windows event viewer log target.

2. To create a server audit object of a file target, we will use the CREATE SERVER AUDIT command and the steps are as follows:

```
USE master
GO
CREATE SERVER AUDIT DBIASSQA_Marketing_Server_Audit
TO FILE
( FILEPATH = 'd:\Entz\FS\',
MAXSIZE = 500 MB,
MAX_ROLLOVER_FILES = 15,
RESERVE_DISK_SPACE = OFF)
WITH ( QUEUE_DELAY = 1500,
ON_FAILURE = CONTINUE)
```

> The default option for the **ON_FAILURE** option is **CONTINUE**. This argument is essential and the login issuing this statement must have the SHUTDOWN permission. If the login does not have such permission, then the function will fail with an error: **MSG_NO_SHUTDOWN_PERMISSION** message.

3. To create a server audit object to the Windows application log, use the following statement:

```
USE master;
go
CREATE SERVER AUDIT DBIASSQA_Marketing_Server_Audit
TO APPLICATION_LOG
WITH ( QUEUE_DELAY = 1000, ON_FAILURE = CONTINUE);
GO
```

> The QUEUE_DELAY is determined in milliseconds, and the minimum delay value that can be set to process an audit is 1000, which is one second and the maximum value is 2,147,483,647, which is 24 days, 20 hours, 31 minutes, and 24 seconds.

4. To check and validate the configuration, check the `sys.server_audits` catalog view:

```
SELECT audit_id,
type_desc, on_failure_desc,
queue_delay, is_state_enabled
FROM sys.server_audits
The result should be as follows:
audit_id     type_desc        on_failure_desc     queue_delay    is_
state_enabled
----------   -------------------------------------------------------
------    -------------------------------------------------
65537        FILE                                 CONTINUE
1500                          0
```

5. The columns from `sys.server_audits` represent the value for `audit_it`, `type_desc`, `on_failure_desc`, and `queue_delay`, which were supplied during the `CREATE SERVER AUDIT` command. The two values are zero (disabled) or one (enabled). The `is_state_enabled` column's default value shows **0**, which means the object is created in a disabled state.

> The reason for leaving the Server Audit object in a disabled state is to create an associated Server and Database audit specification in the audit process.
>
> The audit destination is important and the disabled state of audit does not automatically audit any actions. It is essential for us to enable where the audit destination captures the required data from the audit.

6. The next step is to create the server audit specification using the `CREATE SERVER AUDIT SPECIFICATION` command.

7. Next, it is essential to obtain audit action groups on the server scope using the `sys.dm_audit_actions` system catalog, which returns an abridged result related to server-scoped actions. Let us query the information using the following TSQL:

```
SELECT name
FROM sys.dm_audit_actions
WHERE class_desc = 'SERVER' AND
configuration_level = 'Group'
ORDER BY name
```

> The several levels of auditing involve server audit action groups per instance and either database audit action groups or database audit actions per database. The `class_desc` value can be any one of the `SERVER`, `DATABASE`, or `SCHEMA` scope objects, but does not include Schema objects.

8. For this recipe, we will track the server-scoped actions such as backup, restore, failed logins, database object access, and server state groups by using the following TSQL to audit the audit groups mentioned earlier:

```
CREATE SERVER AUDIT SPECIFICATION DBIASSQA_Marketing_Server_Audit_
Spec
FOR SERVER AUDIT DBIASSQA_Marketing_Server_Audit
ADD (BACKUP_RESTORE_GROUP),
ADD (FAILED_LOGIN_GROUP),
ADD (DATABASE_OBJECT_ACCESS_GROUP)
ADD (SERVER_STATE_CHANGE_GROUP)
WITH (STATE = ON)
```

9. Again, let us run the TSQL to obtain the configuration and validation of the newly created server audit specifications using the system catalog `sys.server_audit_specifications` as follows:

```
SELECT sas.server_specification_id,
sas.name, sas.is_state_enabled,sasd.audit_action_name from
sys.server_audit_specifications as sas inner join sys.server_
audit_specification_details as sasd
on sas.server_specification_id=sasd.server_specification_id
```

The results are as follows:

```
server_specification_id       name                          is_state_enabled
audit_action_name

65536  DBIASSQA_Marketing_Server_Audit_Spec       1       DATABASE_
OBJECT_ACCESS_GROUP

65536  DBIASSQA_Marketing_Server_Audit_Spec       1       BACKUP_
RESTORE_GROUP

65536  DBIASSQA_Marketing_Server_Audit_Spec       1       FAILED_LOGIN_
GROUP

65536  DBIASSQA_Marketing_Server_Audit_Spec       1       SERVER_STATE_
CHANGE_GROUP
```

10. The result set returns the individual audit action names that are enabled for the `DBIASSQA_Market_Server_Audit_Spec` specification.

11. To track the server scope and database level usage, before we enable the server audit object, add the database level audit specification object.

12. Now, you are required to obtain the audit action groups on the database level using the `sys.dm_audit_actions` system catalog, which returns abridged results related to database level actions. Let us query the information by using the following TSQL:

```
SELECT name
FROM sys.dm_audit_actions
WHERE configuration_level = 'Action' AND
class_desc = 'OBJECT'
ORDER BY name
```

13. The query mentioned earlier returns the atomic events on the object securable scope such as DELETE, EXECUTE, INSERT, RECEIVE, REFERENCES, SELECT, and UPDATE.

> For mission-critical financial applications the audit of events is important and of all the atomic events mentioned, SELECT is highly advantageous as it offers a granular level of audit without any performance hindrance.

14. Use the following statement to create the database audit specification:

```
CREATE DATABASE AUDIT SPECIFICATION AdventureWorks2008R2_DB_
AuditSpec
FOR SERVER AUDIT DBIASSQA_Marketing_Server_Audit
ADD (DATABASE_OBJECT_ACCESS_GROUP),
ADD (INSERT, UPDATE, DELETE
ON Sales.Customer
BY public)
WITH (STATE = ON)
GO
```

15. Now, the setup of the database level audit specification is complete, it will capture both the audit action groups and audit events. The final step is to enable the server audit using the following TSQL:

```
ALTER SERVER AUDIT DBIASSQA_Marketing_Server_Audit WITH (STATE=ON)
```

This completes the steps to implement auditing and service-level security features on an existing SQL Server instance.

How it works...

The native capability to audit the SQL Server instance level and database-scoped activity is captured to a target data destination. The Server Audit object defines a target destination of collected audit events, which is the first step in setting up an audit. The `ON_FAILURE` option is important, which indicates the process of writing to the target should continue or stop if the target is unable to complete the action due to a permission issue. Using a Server Audit Specification object, the SQL Server instance-scoped events will be captured and forwarded to a specific server audit object target such as to the file path `d:\Entz\FS\` as per the code or written to the Windows Application event log. We can use the system catalog function `fn_get_audit_file`, which returns the information from an audit file created by a server audit.

A Server Audit object creation allows the audit process to designate whether or not the SQL Server instance should be shut down, if it is unable to write to the target. Once a Server Audit object is created, we can bind a Server Audit Specification or Database Audit Specification object to it.

A Server Audit Specification is used to define which events to capture at the SQL Server instance scope. A Database Audit Specification object allows us to define which events we wish to capture at the database scope. Only one Server Audit Specification can be bound to a Server Audit object, whereas one or more Database Audit Specifications can be bound to a Server Audit object. A single Server Audit object can be collocated with a Server Audit Specification and one or more Database Audit Specifications. Once the server or database level audit is enabled, then all the corresponding actions such as any update on a table– for instance, DML statements–is captured to the audit destination. In our recipe, the audit action is logged to the Windows event viewer application log and to a log file, for instance: `DBIASSQA_Marketing_Server_Audit_xxxx.SQLAUDIT` filename.

Managing server-level securable and database-level permissions

The security for an SQL Server instance and database is mainly about managing permissions. These are tied to principals and are securable at a granular level that provides a greater flexibility and control.

To manage the server-level securable and database-level permissions, it is essential to know how the SQL Server control access is managed. The top level of the hierarchy is server scope, which contains logins, the database, and endpoints. The next level is managed on the database scope, which is contained within the server scope that controls securables such as database users, schemas, and roles. The bottom level for permissions is the schema scope that controls the schema itself and objects within the schema such as tables, views, and stored procedures. The permissions are applied to SQL Server objects on three securable scopes: server, database, and schema. On the database level, it will enable a principal to perform actions on securables.

In this recipe, we will go through the process of managing server-level securable and database-level permissions.

Getting ready

There are no specific prerequisites for this recipe. However, the target instance must be an SQL Server instance with a user database to manage server-level securable and assign database-level permissions.

The various levels of permissions and securable information can be returned using system catalog functions, Dynamic Management Functions (DMF), and Dynamic Management Views (DMV). The permissions revolve around three statements: GRANT, REVOKE, and DENY.

How to do it...

The following steps are required to manage the server-level securable and database-level permissions on an SQL Server instance.

1. The implementation is a two-fold procedure. Initially, we will manage a securable with the help of GRANT/REVOKE/DENY statements and then set relevant server-scope or database-level permissions.

2. You will need to obtain available permissions on an SQL Server instance and view a specific permission hierarchy using the system catalog function as follows:

   ```
   SELECT class_desc, permission_name, covering_permission_name,
   parent_class_desc, parent_covering_permission_name
   FROM sys.fn_builtin_permissions(DEFAULT)
   ORDER BY class_desc, permission_name
   ```

3. The previous statement will return complete information of assignable permissions with complete securables scope. The abridged result set is presented (for screen purposes) as follows:

class_desc	APPLICATION ROLE	DATABASE	OBJECT
permission_name	ALTER	ALTER	VIEW DEFINITION
covering_permission_ name	CONTROL	CONTROL	CONTROL
parent_class_desc	DATABASE	SERVER	SCHEMA
parent_covering_ permission_name	ALTER ANY APPLICATION ROLE	ALTER ANY DATABASE	VIEW DEFINITION

4. The value (DEFAULT) will return all the parent class permissions regardless of securable scope. The various parent classes (essential audit perspective) are SERVER, DATABASE, and SCHEMA. Also, the server objects such as Endpoints, Event Notifications, or Linked Servers are represented with a NULL value.

5. To manage the securable, we need to use Data Control Language (DCL) to create permissions used to control access to the database by securing it. The syntax is as follows:

```
GRANT { ALL [ PRIVILEGES ] }
      | permission [ (column [ ,...n ] ) ] [ ,...n ]
      [ ON [ class:: ] securable ] TO principal [ ,...n ]
      [ WITH GRANT OPTION ] [ AS principal ]
```

6. The following TSQL can be used to manage server-scoped securables and set database-level permissions to a principal on a securable:

```
-- Create recipe new login
IF NOT EXISTS
(SELECT name
FROM sys.server_principals WHERE name = 'DBIAUser')
BEGIN
        CREATE LOGIN [DBIAUser]
        WITH PASSWORD=N'$ql3rver',
        DEFAULT_DATABASE=[master],
        CHECK_EXPIRATION=OFF,
        CHECK_POLICY=ON
END
--User will have permission to GRANT permission to other grantees
GRANT VIEW ANY DATABASE TO [DBIAUser] WITH GRANT OPTION

--GRANT additonal securable
GRANT CREATE ANY DATABASE TO [DBIAUser]

--DENY permission to a securable
DENY SHUTDOWN TO [DBIAUser]

--REVOKE permission on a server securabe
REVOKE ALTER TRACE FROM [DBIAUser] CASCADE
```

7. Obtain information on the server-scoped permission for the new login created earlier:

```
--Query server-level permissions
SELECT p.class_desc, p.permission_name, p.state_desc
FROM sys.server_permissions p
INNER JOIN sys.server_principals s ON p.grantee_principal_id =
s.principal_id
WHERE s.name = 'DBIAUser'
```

The result will be as follows:

Class_desc	Permission_name	State_desc
SERVER	CONNECT SQL	GRANT
SERVER	CREATE ANY DATABASE	GRANT
SERVER	SHUTDOWN	DENY
SERVER	VIEW ANY DATABASE	GRANT_WITH_GRANT_OPTION

8. From the previous step, we have accomplished the steps to manage a securable. To report on permissions for that securable use the `Has_perms_by_name` function as follows:

```
USE AdventureWorks2008R2
GO
SELECT Has_perms_by_name ('AdventureWorks2008R2', 'DATABASE',
'ALTER')
```

9. The returned value will be either `0` or `1`. `0` meaning the current connection does not have permission to `ALTER` and `1` means the current connection has permission to `ALTER` the specified database.

10. Similarly, the `Has_perms_by_name` function can also be used to identify the permissions on a database object for the current connection.

11. Finally, let us work on reporting the permissions for a principal by securable scope. Execute the following TSQL statement to check the server-scoped permissions:

```
SELECT permission_name
FROM fn_my_permissions(NULL, N'SERVER')
ORDER BY permission_name
```

> The `securable_class` will result in various levels of permissions such as APPLICATION ROLE, ASSEMBLY, ASYMMETRIC KEY, CERTIFICATE, CONTRACT, DATABASE, ENDPOINT, FULLTEXT CATALOG, LOGIN, MESSAGE TYPE, OBJECT, REMOTE SERVICE BINDING, ROLE, ROUTE, SCHEMA, SERVER, SERVICE, SYMMETRIC KEY, TYPE, USER, XML SCHEMA COLLECTION and so on.

12. The result set returns almost all the permissions names being the example executed under context of the `sysadmin` privileges.

This completes the required steps to manage the server-level securable and database-level permissions on a SQL Server instance.

How it works...

The security context is managed by precedence (nested hierarchy of securable permissions)—permissions denied at a higher scope in the security model override grants on that permission at a lower scope. GRANT permission removes DENY or REVOKE of that permission on the specified securable. If the same permission is denied at a higher scope that contains the securable, the DENY takes precedence. But revoking the granted permission at a higher scope does not take precedence.

Database-level permissions are granted within the scope of the specified database. If a user needs permissions to objects in another database, then they will need to create the user account in the other database, or grant the user account access to the other database, as well as the current database. When allocating permissions on a securable to a principal, the person doing the allocation is the Grantor, and the principal receiving the permission is the Grantee.

To explicitly deny permissions on a securable to a server-level principal, use the DENY command. To revoke permissions on a securable to a principal, use the REVOKE command. Revoking a permission means you are neither granting nor denying permission. Revoking removes the specified permission(s) that had previously been either granted or denied.

The Has_perms_by_name system function evaluates whether or not the current connection has granted permissions to access a specific securable (granted permissions either explicitly or inherently through a higher scoped securable).

Implementing backup compression for a VLDB environment

VLDB (Very Large Databases) have a specific requirement in terms of storage. The time required to backup increases, the method of backup is changed compared to normal databases and the recovery process is only a partial recovery process. Since SQL Server 2008, native backup compression was introduced for the Enterprise edition and SQL Server 2008 R2 has extended the feature to the Standard and Datacenter editions, for production purposes. The functionality allows the backup process to consume less disk space. The amount of compression gained depends on the data within the database. From the SQL Server 2008 Service Pack 2 onwards, every edition of SQL Server 2008 version and higher versions can restore a compressed backup.

Filegroups are often used for very large databases for the ease of backup administration and to improve performance by distributing data files over disk LUNs. In order to provide a quicker recovery process for a VLDB environment, backup compression must be considered. In this recipe, we will go through the important steps in implementing backup compression for the VLDB environment.

Getting ready

For backup compression, the SQL Server instance must be the Standard, Enterprise, or Datacenter edition for production purposes. In case of development or testing purposes, the Developer or Evaluation Enterprise edition will suffice.

The following are specific metrics that will help you to classify a database as VLDB:

- ▸ The Database table storage with billions and billions of rows
- ▸ The Database storage with multiple Gigabytes (GB) or higher (a Terabyte (TB))
- ▸ Longer recovery time for database
- ▸ Slower network and storage mechanism
- ▸ Intermittent corruption of data and backup storage systems

The process of the backup compression feature can be implemented using the TSQL statement options, such as WITH COMPRESSION or WITH NO_COMPRESSION. The default backup compression feature for a SQL Server instance is off.

How to do it...

The following steps can be used to implement backup compression for a VLDB environment. First, we will see how to enable compression for an SQL Server instance and manage the efficiency of the backup compression regardless of the server-level option.

1. To check and change the default backup compression method, execute the following TSQL statement:

    ```
    --Check and enable backup compression default setup
    USE master
    GO
    EXEC sp_configure 'backup compression default'
    GO
    EXEC sp_configure 'backup compression default', '1'
    RECONFIGURE WITH OVERRIDE
    GO
    EXEC sp_configure 'backup compression default'
    GO
    ```

2. The previous statement's result set will show the default value for backup compression before and after the configuration of backup compression:

Name	Minimum	Maximum	config_value	run_value
–Before backup compression configuration				
backup compression default	0	1	0	0
–After backup compression configuration				
backup compression default	0	1	1	1

3. Now, let us run the backup statement using both the WITH COMPRESSION and WITH NO_COMPRESSION options.

4. Let's backup the database using the WITH COMPRESSION option first:

```
--BACKUP database compressed way
BACKUP DATABASE AdventureWorks2008R2
TO DISK = 'D:\SampleDBz\AdventureWorks2008R2_compressed.bak'WITH
COMPRESSION
```

The result set is as follows:

Processed 1232 pages for database 'AdventureWorks2008R2', file 'AdventureWorks2008R2_Data' on file 2.

Processed 1 pages for database 'AdventureWorks2008R2', file 'Adventureworks2008R2_log' on file 2.

BACKUP DATABASE successfully processed 1233 pages in 0.774 seconds (12.445 MB/sec).

5. Now let's backup the database using the WITH NO_COMPRESSION option:

```
--BACKUP database uncompressed way
BACKUP DATABASE AdventureWorks2008R2
TO DISK = 'D:\SampleDBz\AdventureWorks2008R2_uncompressed.bak'
WITH NO_COMPRESSION
```

The result set is as follows:

Processed 1232 pages for database 'AdventureWorks2008R2', file 'AdventureWorks2008R2_Data' on file 1.

Processed 1 pages for database 'AdventureWorks2008R2', file 'Adventureworks2008R2_log' on file 1.

BACKUP DATABASE successfully processed 1233 pages in 0.698 seconds (13.800 MB/sec).

6. Let us query the statistics of both the backup execution processes using the `backupset` system table:

```
SELECT database_name, backup_size, compressed_backup_size
FROM msdb..backupset where database_name='AdventureWorks2008R2'
ORDER BY backup_finish_date DESC
```

The results are as follows:

database_name	backup_size	compressed_backup_size
AdventureWorks2008R2	10568704	10568704
AdventureWorks2008R2	10569728	1455709
AdventureWorks2008R2	10569728	10569728

You should now have implemented backup compression for a VLDB environment.

How it works...

The backup compression feature allows you to create database backups that run faster and occupy less disk space. In addition to the space savings, the compression of the backup increases the backup speed due to less I/O requirement on disks. However, the I/O cost savings will always come at the expense of increased CPU usage caused by the compression process.

> As a best practice, it is recommended that the VLDB backup jobs or job steps are scheduled during the usage hours on the SQL Server instance.

The backup compression feature can be enabled server wide using the `SP_CONFIGURE` statement or the `WITH COMPRESSION` option within a `BACKUP` statement. However, if there is a need to not use the backup compression for a particular database, then this can be achieved by using the `WITH NO_COMPRESSION` statement as demonstrated in the previous sections. The status of the backup set can be obtained by querying the `backupfile` and `backupset` system tables in the `msdb` database. If the database backup was not compressed, this value would be the same size as the `backup_size` column.

Designing change tracking methodology

Change Data Capture (CDC) and Change Tracking (CT) can be classified as the same names but both have different purposes, which are introduced in the SQL Server 2008 version.

CDC is an asynchronous process mechanism that captures all changes of a data row from the transaction flow and stores them in change tables. CDC is useful in avoiding the expensive query methods such as triggers or multiple-join to capture the changes made to the data.

CT is a light-weight synchronous mechanism that tracks data modifications but records only the fact that the row has been changed, like writing leaf level information of modified data. CT is very useful to represent a consistent view of modified data and detect data conflicts quickly.

In this recipe, we will look at how to design a change tracking methodology that uses CT functionality to detect DML operations.

Getting ready

The underlying SQL Server instance level must be SQL Server 2008 R2 and the database compatibility level must be 100 to design the change tracking feature.

To show the CT functionality, let us create a new database called PWD_WEF with default values using the TSQL statement or the SSMS tool. This will create a new table that will be used to demonstrate the CT functionality:

```
USE [PWD_WEF]
GO

CREATE TABLE [dbo].[WEF_Passwords](
    [per_id] [numeric](8, 0) NOT NULL IDENTITY(1,1) PRIMARY KEY
CLUSTERED,
    [fullname] [varchar](71) NULL,
    [per_web_login] [varchar](50) NULL,
    [per_web_password] [varchar](10) NULL
) ON [PRIMARY]

GO
```

In order to enable the change tracking on a table, the underlying table requires a primary key on the table.

How to do it...

The following steps are required to design the CT functionality on an existing SQL Server instance and database.

1. To use Change Tracking, we must first enable it for the database and then enable it at the table level.
2. CT can be enabled through TSQL statements or through the **SSMS** tool.

3. To enable Change Tracking for the database in SSMS, right-click on the database in **Object Explorer** to open the **Properties** dialog and navigate to the **Change Tracking** page.

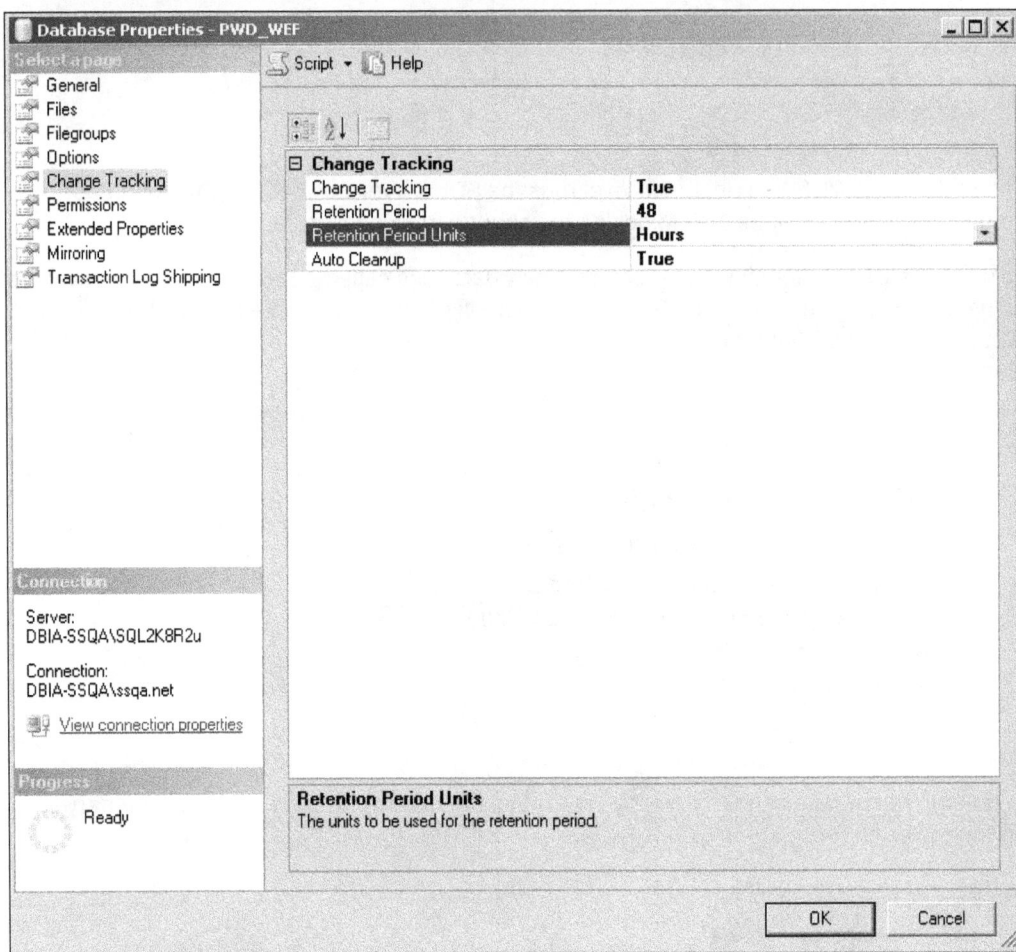

4. On the **Database Properties** page, we can configure the Retention Period based on the Retention Period units (days/hours/minutes) for how long SQL Server retains the change tracking information for each data row. Also, the Auto Cleanup process can be triggered automatically when the retention period has been exceeded. Click **OK** to enable this setting. Once CT has been enabled on the database level, we can then enable CT for the tables. To enable Change Tracking for the table in SSMS, right-click on **Table** in the **Object Explorer** pane to open the **Properties** dialog to select the **Change Tracking** page.

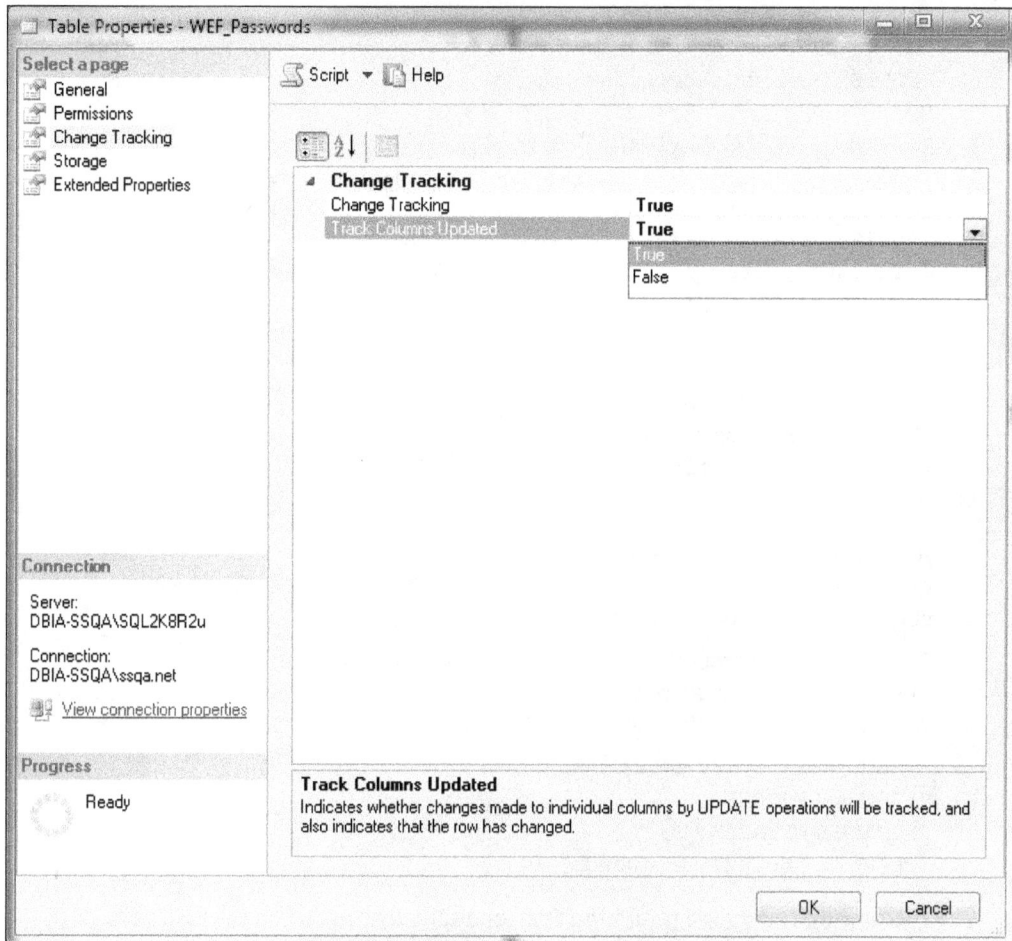

5. Select **True** for Change Tracking and the **Track Columns Updated** option to specify that SQL Server should store the internal change tracking table.

6. Now the change tracking functionality is applied on the PWD_WEF database, let us populate the data and perform the DML operations in the dbo.WEF_Passwords table using the following statements:

```
INSERT        TOP (200)
INTO              WEF_Passwords(fullname, per_web_loginy, per_web_
password)
VALUES        ('Marketing User', 'MarketUser', 'M@rket1'),
('Inventory User','InventryUser','In&vent9'),
('Business User','BizUser','B7$user'),
('SysAdmin','SA','$ySadm1n')
GO
```

```
SELECT * FROM dbo.WEF_Passwords
GO
DELETE FROM dbo.WEF_Passwords
GO
INSERT          TOP (200)
INTO            WEF_Passwords(fullname, per_web_login, per_web_
password)
VALUES          ('Marketing User', 'MarketUser', 'M@rket1'),
('Inventory User','InventryUser','In&vent9'),
('Business User','BizUser','B7$user'),
('SysAdmin','SA','$ySadm1n')
GO
UPDATE dbo.WEF_Passwords
SET per_web_password='Inv3n&'
WHERE per_web_login='InventryUser'
GO
```

7. To obtain the current data version, we can use the `SELECT CHANGE_TRACKING_CURRENT_VERSION()` function, where the returned value can be deemed as a current version to determine the changes at a later stage.

8. Furthermore, to detect the changes on the data, we can use the `CHANGETABLE` function that returns a specific synchronized version and the latest change tracking version for the rows. The two keywords `CHANGE` and `VERSION` are used as follows:

```
SELECT Per_id,SYS_CHANGE_OPERATION,
SYS_CHANGE_VERSION
FROM CHANGETABLE
(CHANGES dbo.WEF_Passwords, 0) AS CT
```

9. The previous query will return the DML operations occurred on the `dbo.WEF_Passwords` table based on the `Per_id` primary key value:

Per_id	SYS_CHANGE_OPERATION	SYS_CHANGE_VERSION	SYS_CHANGE_COLUMNS
1	I	1	NULL
2	I	1	NULL
3	I	1	NULL
4	I	1	NULL
13	D	3	NULL
14	D	3	NULL
15	D	3	NULL
16	D	3	NULL
20	I	6	NULL

Per_id	SYS_CHANGE_OPERATION	SYS_CHANGE_VERSION	SYS_CHANGE_COLUMNS
21	U	8	0x00000000021000
22	I	6	NULL
23	I	6	NULL

This completes the process to design the CT functionality on an existing SQL Server instance and database.

How it works...

The Change Data Capture (CDC) and Change Tracking (CT) functionality is used to detect the net row changes having a minimum storage of data with less overhead. CDC works with all three types of database recovery models and all CDC operations for simple or bulk-logged recovery-modeled databases are fully logged. The key ingredient for CDC is the transaction log I/O, as it will significantly grow when CDC is enabled in a database. Furthermore, log records will stay active until CDC has processed them as per the feature. So, in an environment such as a highly-transactional database or a very large database environment, the log file can be exponential and the log space cannot be reused as long as CDC scan job completes the processing of log records.

In this recipe, we have demonstrated the change data retention period as 48 hours with an AUTO clean-up process. Once the data is populated and a few DML operations are performed, the change tracking system tables will have data to show the results.

The designated column level changes are tracked by using the TRACK_COLUMNS_UPDATE option on dbo.WEF_Passwords table. To obtain the changes and operation of the change-tracked status, the sys.CHANGE_TRACKING_TABLES system catalog view is used. In addition to the previous system catalog view, a system function is used to retrieve change tracking data; the system function is the CHANGE_TRACKING_CURRENT_VERSION, which returns the version number from the last committed transaction for the table.

Implementing Policy-Based Management features

One of the best administrative features for DBAs is Policy-Based Management (PBM) that is introduced in SQL Server 2008. PBM has three components such as policy management, explicit administration, and evaluation modes that contain the concepts of targets, facets, and conditions.

The best practices are implemented as policies that are based on a predefined list of SQL Server recommendations as policy files. The evaluation of policies against a target set includes instances, databases, or database objects. The policies are used to determine whether there are potential issues in the database environment or instance meets best practices guidelines and recommendations.

Once a policy or multiple policies are implemented, they can be evaluated on the target system. The evaluation mode can be automated or performed manually by the DBA to reduce any manual intervention in administering and increase the ease of deployment.

In this recipe, we will go through the process of implementing policy-based management features on an existing SQL Server 2008 R2 instance.

Getting ready

SQL Server 2008 R2 fully supports the policy-based management and the database engine is shipped with several predefined policies that are stored under `%:\Program Files\ Microsoft SQL Server\100\Tools\Policies\DatabaseEngine\1033\%`.

Furthermore, the policies for Reporting Services and Analysis Services are also stored under the subdirectory of the `Policies` directory, but the PBM is unavailable for SSRS and SSAS services. Only SQL Express and SQL Express with Advanced Services do not have the capability of policy automation, as there is no SQL Server Agent service available for these editions.

The generic terms and concepts used in Policy-Based management are facets, conditions, policies, categories, targets, and execution mode. Let us look at how to implement policy-based management. In this recipe, we will implement a Database Security facet to expose properties of the database object that encapsulate security aspects of a database. Before implementing this facet, let's create a user and set a database owner on the `AdventureWorks2008R2` database:

```
USE [master]
GO
CREATE LOGIN [DBIA-SSQA\tseuG] FROM WINDOWS WITH DEFAULT_
DATABASE=[master]
GO
USE [Adventureworks2008R2]
GO
CREATE USER [DBIA-SSQA\tseuG] FOR LOGIN [DBIA-SSQA\tseuG]
GO
USE [Adventureworks2008R2]
GO
EXEC sp_addrolemember N'db_owner', N'DBIA-SSQA\tseuG'
GO
```

How to do it...

The following steps are to be followed in order to implement and administer policy-based management:

1. To create a Condition, connect to an SQL Server 2008 R2 instance using SSMS, on which a policy is created.

2. In **Object Explorer**, expand the **Management** folder and the **Policy Management** folder, and then navigate to the **Facets** folder.

3. Within the **Facets** folder, right-click on the **Database Security** facet and click on **New Condition**. Enter the name for the condition and select the property on which the condition needs to be created.

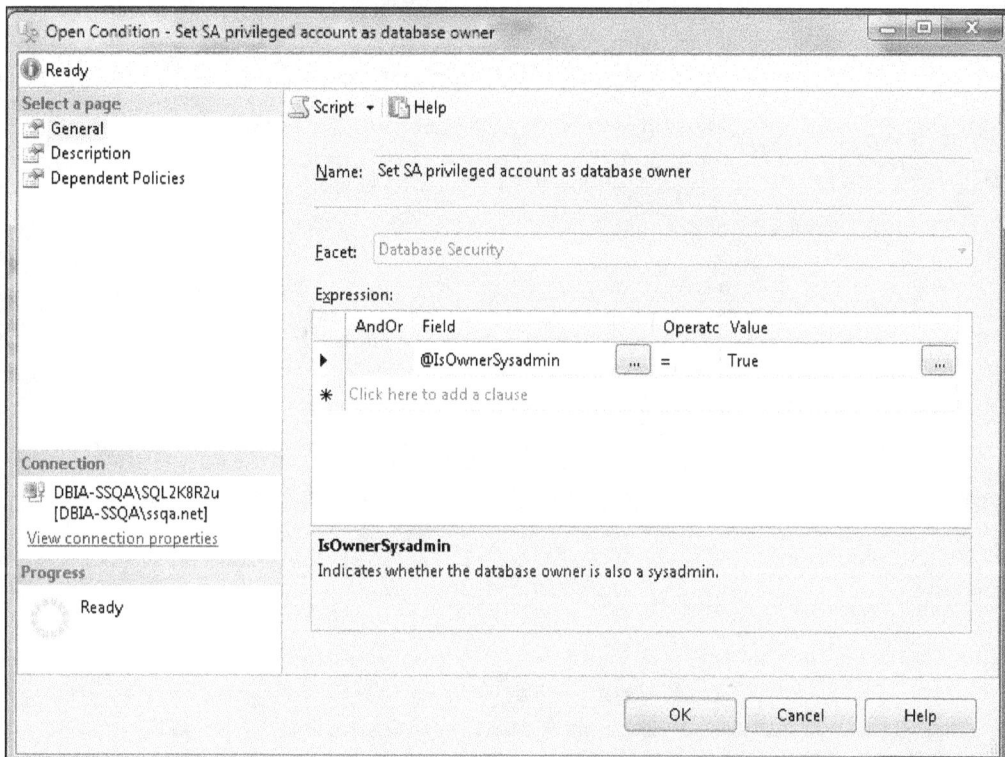

4. Click **OK** to finalize the creation of the condition.

5. Now that the condition is created, we need to create a policy that can be enforced on one or more SQL Server instances to support.

6. Within **Object Explorer**, navigate to the **Policy** folder by expanding the **Management** folder. Right-click on the **Policies** folder and select **New policy**.

7. On the **General** tab of the **Create New policy** dialog, enter the name for the new policy and in the **Check condition** drop-down box, select the condition that was created in step 3.

8. Under the **Against targets** window, click on **Every database** to set the condition. Set the Evaluation mode as **On Schedule** and click on the **Pick** command button to set `CollectorSchedule_Every_60min`. Click **OK** to finalize the creation of the new policy.

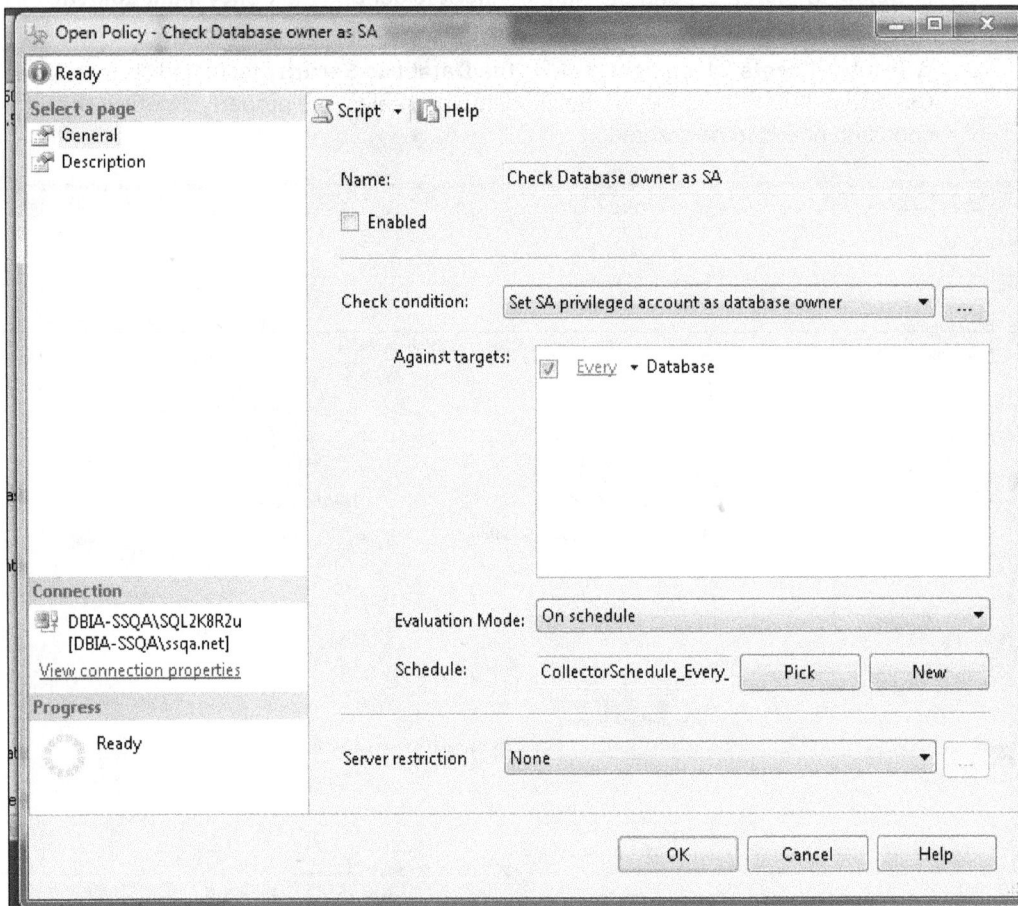

9. Now that we have created a policy, it should be categorized to allow us to group the policies into administrative units and allow relevant objects to subscribe to specific categories.

10. To create a category, expand the **Management** node, right-click on **Policy Management** and choose **Manage Categories** to define the policy categories.

11. To create a Category, click on the **Description** pane in the **Create Policy** dialog box.

12. To create a new category, click in the **Name** field on the last row and type in the name for the category. Enter a name as **Administer Database** the category and under Text to display as **This category must be used on all the databases of SQL Server**.

As the condition and policy is created, it is essential to evaluate the newly created policy to determine which of your servers and databases are out of compliance. The policy evaluation can be leveraged using the following methods:

1. Right-click on a server instance, server object, database, or database object in SQL Server Management Studio and select **Policies** and then **Evaluate**.

2. Expand the **Management** folder, then expand the **Policy Management** folder, and right-click on **Policies** and select **Evaluate**.

3. On the **Evaluate policies** page, check the policy and click the **Evaluate** button.

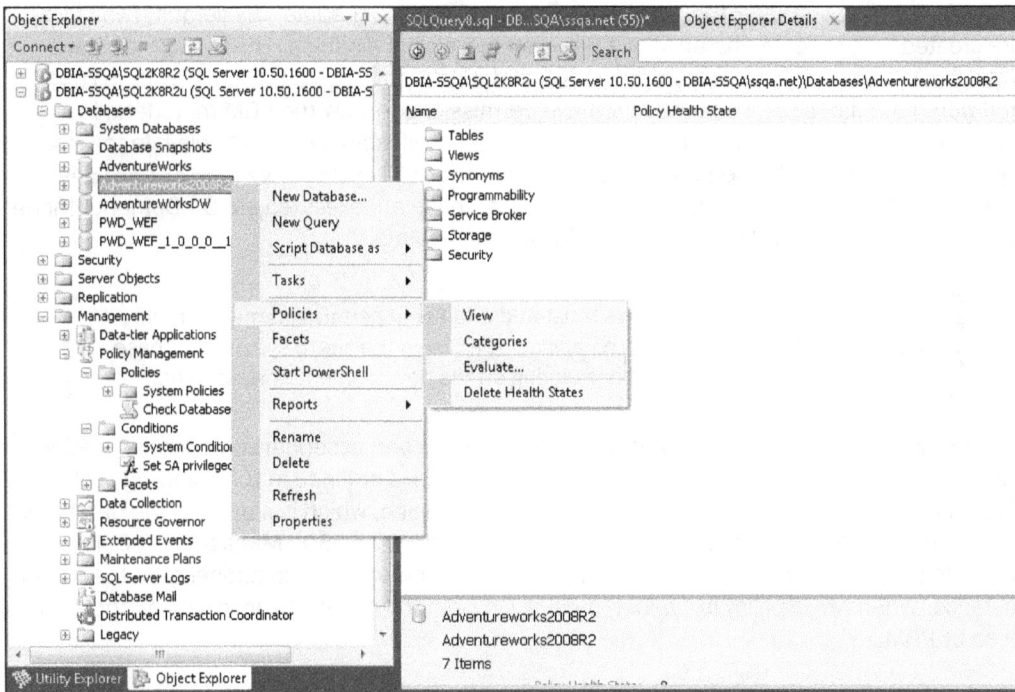

4. The **Evaluation results** pane will display the servers where the policy has failed under target details. Click the **View hyperlink**, which will allow us to browse and get more details on why that individual target server and policy target failed.

This completes the steps to implementing and administering policy-based management.

How it works...

The Policy-Based Management component uses the SQL Server Agent service to evaluate the created policies against a target. So the SQL Server Agent service must be up and running to implement the PBM policies. The target can be an SQL Server instance or a database to deploy. The policies can be used to enforce the compliance to best practices or to report an out-of-compliance object.

The managed targets are entities that are managed by Policy-Based Management, such as an instance of the SQL Server Database Engine, a database, a table, or an index. All targets in a server instance form a target hierarchy.

All the PBM metadata management is stored in `msdb` system database with a prefix of `syspolicy`. Also, the PBM will stick to two execution modes in evaluating the defined policies on an SQL Server instance; they are "On Demand" and "On Schedule". By default, two logins are created on the server instance by PBM system which is disabled. These two logins are `##MS_PolicyEventProcessingLogin##` and `##MS_PolicyTsqlExectionLogin##` and within the database, users need to have permissions to view the PBM metadata. In a nutshell, the `MS_PolicyEventProcessingLogin` will help the PBM to elevate to `sysadmin` to capture the required metadata. The `MS_PolicyTsqlExecutionLogin` is used for TSQL processes and to construct policies; these are executed as "On Demand" model and opened up as to run "On Schedule" with limited privileges.

> As a best practice, we must add additional permission membership in the `PolicyAdministratorRole` in the `msdb` system database to this login with a prior testing on the development environment.

Besides, it is essential to understand the inner-workings and essential components of PBM that are beneficial to follow the execution process, which is outlined in the following sections. The On Demand execution mode consists of a policy engine, which is similar to the database engine that contains system catalog views with policy store and SQL Management Objects (SMO) to process the hierarchical object model that represents the components of the server instance. Whenever a policy is evaluated using On Demand mode, the following methods are used by PBM:

1. The policy evaluation will load the policy from the storage format into memory, which is stored as an XML file, or from `syspolicy` tables in the `msdb` system database.

2. Once the policy is loaded into the database engine, the evaluation will begin by retrieving the set of required target objects. Then, SMO retrieves the required information by constructing a query against PBM catalog views.

> It is worth pointing out that this is an optimization that PBM has for limiting the number of stored procedures that are retrieved (the database returns the requested data to SMO and the SMO constructs the collection).

3. The policy engine will then iterate through each stored procedure evaluable and the check condition, here the PBM will record each object's evaluation as passed or failed to report at the end of evaluation.

4. Finally, the result of evaluation is committed/reported back into the policy store's execution history tables to store the record of the evaluation.

The On Schedule execution mode components are similar to On Demand mode. However, the On Schedule workflow is dependent on SQL Server Agent service that is essential to schedule and execute a policy evaluation process. Whenever a policy is under evaluation using On Schedule model, the following methods are used by PBM:

1. The agent mechanizes the evaluation to trigger the loading of policy.

2. The SQL Server engine employs the PowerShell provider based on the schedule, such as every day at a certain time.

3. The SQL Server Agent uses the PowerShell script to accomplish the steps for policy evaluation, the step retrieves all the policies from the policy store to choose relevant policies that were set to the scheduled agent job.

4. Finally, the job is selected to execute the PowerShell command: `Invoke-PolicyEvaluation.cmdlet`. This will load the policy into the database engine to complete the entire process that is executed by the On Demand policy.

There's more...

▶ When SQL Server policy administrators use PBM, SSMS tool will showcase the policy creation methods and other essential execution modes of PBM depending upon the settings.

▶ The On Demand execution mode will evaluate the policy when directly specified by the user.

▶ The policies that have On Schedule evaluation mode will use SQL Server agent jobs that are owned by the `sa` login or logins, which are part of `sysadmin` server role.

Implementing and running PowerShell for SQL Server features

Windows PowerShell is a powerful scripting tool that can help System Administrators to manage the servers in an automated way using scripts. A .NET assembly contains Windows PowerShell providers and `CmdLets` that extends the functionality of the shell. Similarly, PowerShell for SQL Server is available from SQL Server 2008 version onwards. During the SQL Server installation process, PowerShell and PowerShell snap-ins are installed to expose the SQL Server functionality from PowerShell.

In this recipe, we will go through the steps to implement and run PowerShell for SQL Server in an existing data platform.

Getting ready

In order to implement PowerShell for SQL Server, the operating system must have the PowerShell feature installed. In Windows Server 2008 onwards, PowerShell is a separate install, which requires you to download and install an external package.

- To ensure PowerShell is installed on the operating system, open **Server Manager** from **Administrative Tools** program group and go to the **Features** node to see if the **Windows PowerShell** checkbox is ticked

- If the Windows PowerShell is not ticked, then click **Add Features** and check the box for Windows PowerShell to install

- Once PowerShell is installed on Windows Server, then PowerShell for SQL Server can be installed using the SQL Server installation setup utility

- The PowerShell for SQL Server feature can be installed during the initial installation of SQL Server 2008 R2 or later by accessing the installed features from the SQL Server setup utility

- The Management Studio add-in is required to install specific PowerShell features:

    - The add-in installs a PowerShell graphical interface to SSMS

    - The graphical interface is presented as the `SQLCMD` utility to manage scripting

    - The SQL Server PowerShell provider will add specific functionality in PowerShell for SQL Server

    - The SQL Server PowerShell provider can be downloaded from the SQL Server feature pack: `http://www.microsoft.com/downloads/en/details.aspx?FamilyID=228de03f-3b5a-428a-923f-58a033d316e1&displaylang=en`

How to do it...

Once the previously mentioned prerequisites are met and installed, let us work on the following steps to implement and run PowerShell for SQL Server provider features.

1. PowerShell for SQL Server can be accessed by two methods.

    - Open SQL Server PowerShell through **SSMS** by right-clicking on any object in the **Object Explorer** and select **Start PowerShell**

    - Access the **PowerShell** (**SQLPS**) console by opening a `command prompt window`; type `sqlps.exe` and press *Enter*

2. Launch Windows PowerShell and then manually add the SQL Server PowerShell provider functionality. Execute the following commands:

```
Get-PSSnapin -registered
Add-PSSnapin SqlServerProviderSnapin100
Add-PSSnapin SqlServerCmdletSnapin100
```

3. For this recipe, let us right-click on SQL Server instance to the Start PowerShell console:

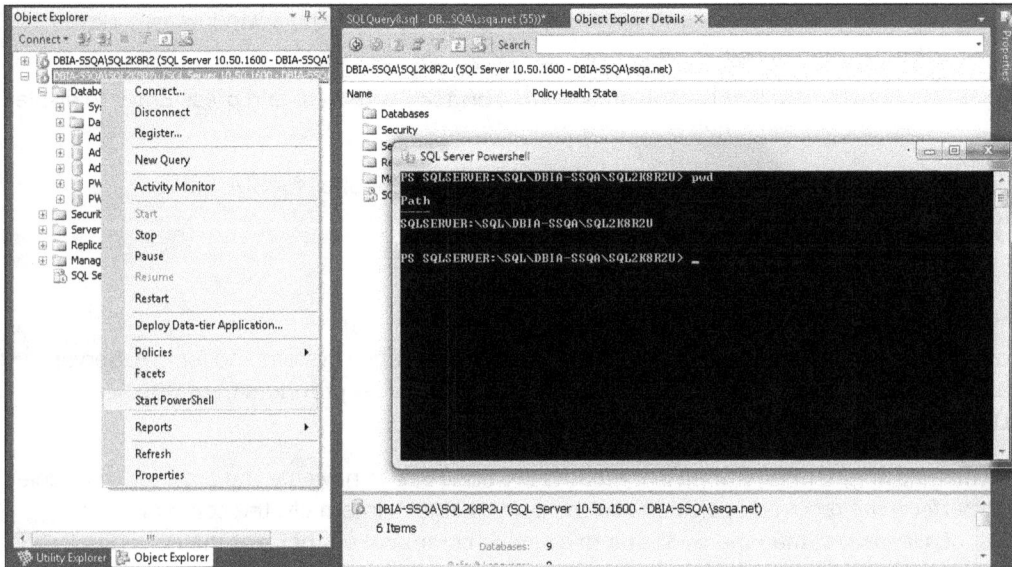

4. When we invoke SQL Server PowerShell using SQL provider from SSMS, depending on what object we right-click to access SQL Server PowerShell, the prompt opens in the context of that particular object.

> The four hierarchies are SQL, SQLPolicy, SQLRegistration, and DataCollection. In this recipe, we are discussing about SQL hierarchy, which involves database engine objects.

5. The previous image shows the path within the console, PS SQLSERVER:\SQL\ DBIA-SSQA\SQL2K8R2U> whereas, when we start the SQL Server PowerShell console from the command prompt using sqlps.exe, the prompt opens at the root of the SQL Server provider.

6. Using SQL Server PowerShell console, many administrative tasks can be performed such as general tasks to send out e-mails containing a particular report or a result from a TSQL statement.

7. Using the SQL Server Agent service, all the PowerShell scripts can be scheduled to run automatically based on the schedule. To obtain more information on the method to call scripts, run the `powershell.exe /?` from the PowerShell console or `sqlps.exe /?` from the Windows command prompt. he default install location of scripts are at:

   ❑ T 64-bit: `%:\Program Files (x86)\Microsoft SQL Server\100\Tools\Binn\`

   ❑ 32-bit: `%:\Program Files\Microsoft SQL Server\100\Tools\Binn\`

8. To obtain a status about a Windows service within the SQLPS window, type `Get-Service` and press *Enter*.

9. To obtain more information on a specific `cmdlet` type **help** and press *Enter* to display help about PowerShell `cmdlets` and concepts.

This completes the steps to implementing and running PowerShell for SQL Server provider features.

How it works...

PowerShell is an internal component of the Windows operating system and for SQL Server based providers. SQL Server service provides an additional six providers from SQL Server 2008 R2.

The methodology for PowerShell implements the `cmdlets` to navigate the provider hierarchies and perform the required operations on the current object. Internally, the commands are a set of aliases that map the `cmdlets` to a similar command prompt. For the PowerShell, the hierarchy of objects are classified as server-level on top, then on the list is databases, and finally, database objects. By default, when a reference of an instance of the database engine is specific in the `PowerShell cmdlet`, SQL Server Provider uses SMO to open a windows authentication connection to the instance. In supplement to this, the `SQLSERVER:\` SQL hierarchy uses these SMO namespaces: `Microsoft.SqlServer.Management.Smo`, `Microsoft.SqlServer.Management.Smo.Agent`, `Microsoft.SqlServer.Management.Smo.Broker` and `Microsoft.SqlServer.Management.Smo.Mail`. Then the connection is made using the credentials of the Windows account running the Windows PowerShell session. The SQL Server authentication will not be used by SQL Server provider in any case.

> The SQL Server PowerShell provider includes the `cmdlet`, `Invoke-SqlCmd`, which is a useful method for executing adhoc queries and stored procedures from PowerShell.

There's more...

In order to consider the PowerShell for SQL Server as a main scripting tool, there is a lot more to be included by Microsoft. As of now, PowerShell support in SQL Server 2008 R2 is a good starting point to manage administrative tasks in your platform and a number of `cmdlets` are available in SQL Server PowerShell that are part of the basic PowerShell functionality. The additional `cmdlets` for SQL Server PowerShell are as follows:

- ▸ `Invoke-PolicyEvaluation` for SQL Server Policy-Based Management.
- ▸ `Invoke-SqlCmd` to run regular TSQL statements that are supported by `SQLCMD` utility.
- ▸ `Encode-SqlName` encodes SQL Server identifiers into a format that PowerShell can use.
- ▸ `Decode-SqlName` helps to return the original SQL Server identifiers from a value previously obtained by `Encode-SqlName` cmdlet.
- ▸ `Convert-UrnToPath` converts the SMO Uniform Resource Name to the SQL Server provider path.

Implementing the SQL Server Best Practices Analyzer

A best practice is a task or set of steps that best meet particular needs within the day-to-day administrative tasks. As a DBA, you must evaluate the commonly accepted practices, best practices and determine the best ones to apply to the environment.

To implement best practices, we should first evaluate and analyze if the existing environment is managed efficiently according to the practices accepted in the industry. There are plenty of tools available that enable the user to analyze the system on a particular set of best practices.

For SQL Server environments, Microsoft is offering two sets of tools that will help DBAs to analyze the set of SQL Server instances and recommend best practices to implement. The tools are Microsoft Codename Atlanta and SQL Server 2008 R2 Best Practices Analyzer. Microsoft Codename Atlanta (still in beta testing at the time of writing) is a secure cloud service that proactively monitors the SQL Server deployment.

In this recipe , we will go through the process of implementing the SQL Server Best Practices Analyzer diagnostic tool (SQL Server 2008 R2 Best Practices Analyzer (BPA)) to evaluate the existing SQL Server data platform.

Getting ready

The SQL Server Best Practices Analyzer tool can be installed on a desktop machine or a central windows server to analyze and evaluate the SQL Server platform. The following list contains the software and system prerequisites for installing the Best Practices Analyzer tool:

- ▶ Any one of the following operating systems can be used:
  - ❑ Windows Server 2003/Windows Server 2008/Windows Server 2008 R2/ Windows Vista/Windows 7

- ▶ PowerShell V2.0 will be installed by default on Windows Server 2008 R2 and Windows 7. Otherwise, the package can be downloaded from: `http://support.microsoft.com/kb/968929` and installed by expanding the downloaded `.msi` package file.

- ▶ Microsoft Baseline Configuration Analyzer (MBCA) V2.0 can be downloaded from `http://www.microsoft.com/downloads/details.aspx?displaylang=en&FamilyID=1b6e9026-f505-403e-84c3-a5dea704ec67` and installed by expanding the downloaded `MBCA_Setup32.msi` package file.

- ▶ SQL Server 2008 R2 BPA is freely available for download from: `http://www.microsoft.com/downloads/en/details.aspx?displaylang=en&FamilyID=0fd439d7-4bff-4df7-a52f-9a1be8725591`.

- ▶ The BPA tool can be downloaded and installed for a 64 bit or 32 bit environment.

- ▶ If SQL Server 2008 R2 BPA is installed on a standalone machine then open a PowerShell 2.0 command prompt, using an administrative account and enable Powershell Remoting using the command `Enable-PSRemoting`.

How to do it...

Once the earlier mentioned prerequisite software is installed and BPA is downloaded, you will need to complete the following steps to implement SQL Server Best Practices Analyzer in an existing environment:

1. Open the **MBCA** tool, which is installed as a standalone program from **Start | Programs**.

2. At the **Select a product** option, click on the drop-down box to select **SQL Server 2008 R2 BPA** and click on **Start Scan** to run.

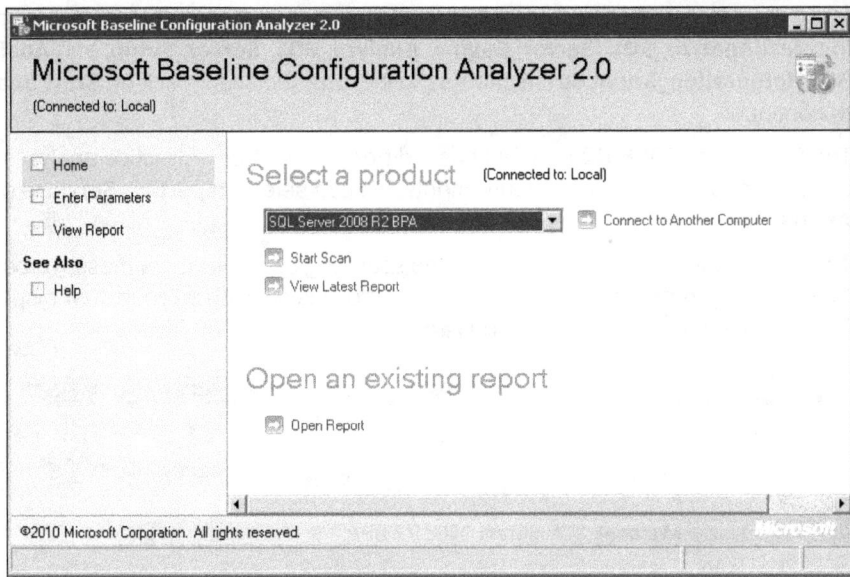

3. For the recipe, we need to install MBCA on the server where the SQL2K8R2U instance is installed. The following screen is presented to enter the SQL Server instance name:

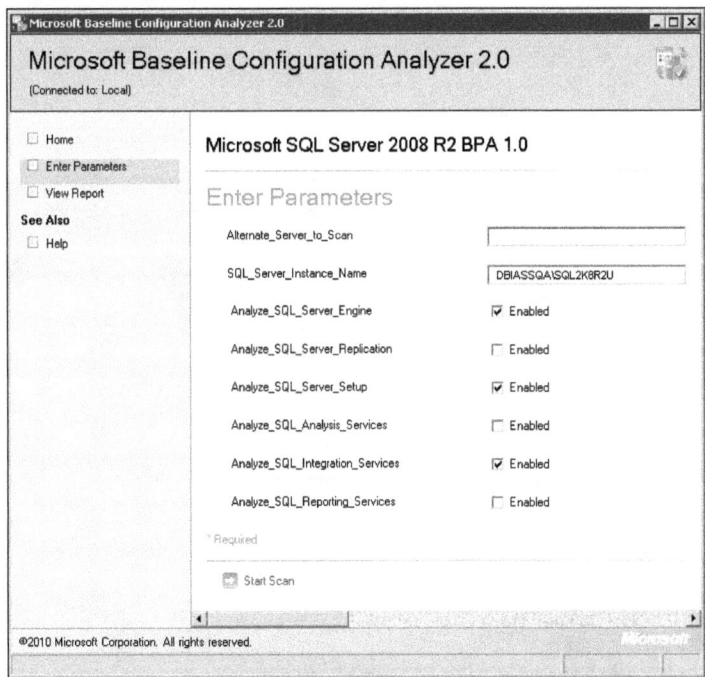

4. Enter the desired SQL Server instance and for the purposes of this recipe, we have to select **Analyze_SQL_Server_Engine**, **Analyze_SQL_Server_Setup**, and **Analyze_ SQL_Integration_Services** checkboxes to perform the scan. Click on **Start Scan** to continue.

5. The SQL Server 2008 R2 BPA tool has a different set of best practice analyses to perform. Based on these requirements, we can select **Reporting Services** or **Analysis Services**.

6. The **Start Scan** process will continue the scanning by displaying a message box **Scanning in Progress** and the results will be displayed with a report that displays Noncompliant issues as **Error** and **Warning**.

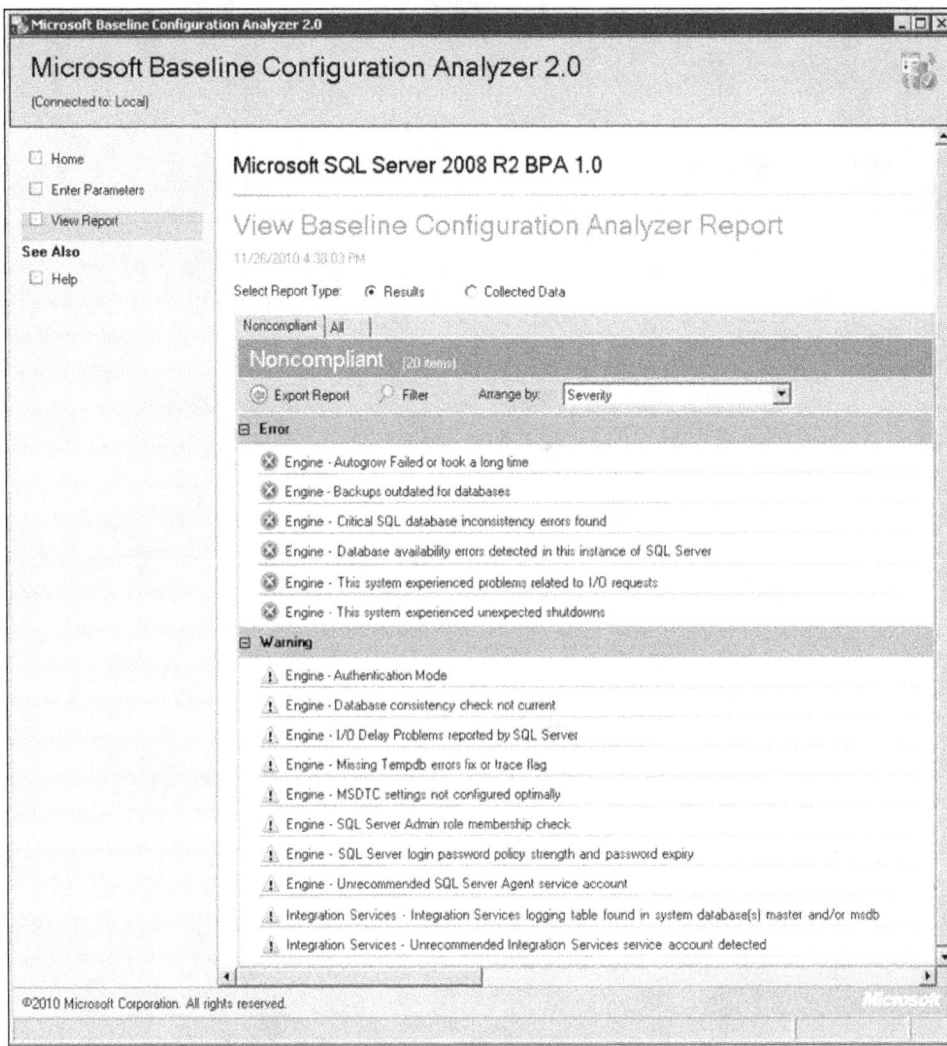

7. The second tab **All** will display all the best practices that were analyzed in addition to the noncompliant best practices list.

8. As we can see six errors and ten warnings, when we click on the listed error or warning, a brief explanation of the issue will be displayed, which shows the noncompliance reason.

9. Furthermore, a **More** information link will be presented that opens a web page with an explanation of the issue. The web page that opens is originated from the Microsoft Support knowledge base articles site.

10. This is the starting point to evaluate the existing environment and analyze the required instances to see whether best practices implementation is followed or not. All the errors that are displayed from the BPA report must be addressed without any further delay.

This completes the process to implement SQL Server Best Practices Analyzer in an existing environment.

How it works...

The SQL Server 2008 R2 BPA tool scans both local computer and remote computers including the specified SQL Server instance. The underlying scan is performed by the PowerShell service that requires support for PowerShell remoting features and increases the maximum number of concurrent shells for a user.

The process is straightforward as BPA tool will start the `WinRM` service by setting the service to Automatic. It creates a listener component to accept requests on any IP address and also enables a firewall exception for WS-Management communication that will allow all registered Windows PowerShell session configurations to receive instructions from a remote computer. A session configuration named `Microsoft.PowerShell` is registered to enable the `WinRM` service to make all preceding changes effective.

Finally, the tool gathers all the information about a server (operating system) and instance (SQL Server) to determine if the configurations are set according to the recommended best practices. All the information and noncompliance are reported, indicating settings that differ from recommendations. The report is highly essential to indicate all the potential problems in the installed instance of the SQL Server, and the detailed explanation of the error or warning recommends the solution to the user by referring to those Microsoft knowledge base articles.

For more information on the BPA tool that needs to be installed on a standalone machine, refer to the following blog post: `http://blogs.msdn.com/b/psssql/archive/2010/06/21/known-issues-installing-sql-2008-r2-bpa-relating-to-remoting.aspx`.

Designing Transparent Data Encryption features

Security and User administration always highlights the importance of methods to secure and control the access to the SQL Server platform from instance level to database scope. To implement the SQL Server security feature, data encryption at the column level is the unsurpassed choice to provide security to the data platform. This will enable the first level of granularity for a specific data, whereas Transparent Data Encryption (TDE) is applicable for the entire database, most importantly for database and data encryption.

SQL Server 2008 opens up a new dimension in encryption methods by introducing Transparent Data Encryption (TDE), which allows entire database encryption without affecting client applications or code changes. This will also encrypt the corresponding database backup without having any additional step to encrypt such a backup.

In this recipe, let us go through the important aspects of designing transparent data encryption features using SQL Server 2008 R2. TDE supports several encryption options, such as AES with 128-bit, 192-bit, 2560-bit, or 3 key triple DES, which are industry standard methods.

TDE is purely dependent on an encryption key, which is a server asymmetric key that secures the encrypted database. The Database Encryption Key (DEK) is protected using certificate storage in a master database of the SQL Server instance where the encrypted user database is installed.

Getting ready

TDE is an enterprise-wide solution, which requires the Enterprise or Datacenter edition of SQL Server 2008 R2. For testing purposes, we can use the Developer Evaluation Enterprise edition.

To design the TDE feature, you are required to complete the following steps:

- ▶ Create a master key
- ▶ Create or obtain a certificate protected by a master key
- ▶ Create a DEK and protect it by the certification
- ▶ Set the database to use encryption

How to do it...

The following steps must be followed to design and implement transparent data encryption on an existing database without making any changes to client applications.

1. TDE can be managed by using TSQL statements or by using the SSMS tool. For this recipe, let us use TSQL statement methods.

2. To implement the transparent data encryption, enter the following TSQL statements from the SSMS tool query window:

```
--Encrypting AdventureWorks database
USE master;
GO


--First create the master key which is stored in the master
database
CREATE MASTER KEY ENCRYPTION BY PASSWORD =
'EncR^pt$erverDAta8ase';
GO


-- Then create a certificate to encrypt user database that is also
stored in the master
-- database.
CREATE CERTIFICATE DBIA_DBEncryptCertificate
with SUBJECT = 'Adventure Works 2008 R2 certificate store'
GO
```

3. As soon as we execute the TSQL statement, a warning message will be displayed as follows:

Warning:

The certificate used for encrypting the database encryption key has not been backed up. You should immediately back up the certificate and the private key associated with the certificate. If the certificate ever becomes unavailable, or if you must restore or attach the database on another server, you must have backups of both the certificate and the private key or you will not be able to open the database.

4. Now, let us continue to create a DEK based on a previously created certificate by using the following TSQL statement:

```
USE AdventureWorks2008R2
GO
CREATE DATABASE ENCRYPTION KEY
WITH ALGORITHM = AES_256
ENCRYPTION BY SERVER CERTIFICATE DBIA_DBEncryptCertificate
GO
```

```
-- Finally let us turn ON the encryption for the
AdventureWorks2008R2 database
ALTER DATABASE AdventureWorks2008R2
SET ENCRYPTION ON
GO
```

5. To obtain basic information on the database encryption information, run the following query:

```
--Obtain the encryption status for databases
SELECT * FROM sys.dm_database_encryption_keys ;
GO
```

6. The previous mentioned query returns the database encryption state value; 2 means the encryption has begun and 3 indicates that the encryption has been completed. In addition to the encryption state, the value key algorithm and key length information is also displayed.

7. The different values for `encryption_state` are as follows:

   - 0= No database encryption key present, no encryption
   - 1= Unencrypted
   - 2= Encryption in progress
   - 3= Encrypted
   - 4= Key change in progress
   - 5= Decryption in progress
   - 6= Protection change in progress (The certificate or asymmetric key that is encrypting the database encryption key is being changed)

8. As we have completed the database encryption tasks, it is essential to perform the backup of the certificate, private key, and master key for the server using the following TSQL statements:

```
--Steps to Backup certificate, Private key and master key

--Master key
BACKUP MASTER KEY TO FILE = 'D:\SampleDBz\ServerMasterKey'
ENCRYPTION BY PASSWORD = 'Op3n$esame'

--Certificate and private key
BACKUP CERTIFICATE DBIA_DBEncryptCertificate TO FILE = 'D:\
SampleDbz\DBEncryptCertPrivateKey'
WITH PRIVATE KEY ( FILE = 'D:\SampleDBz\DBEncryptCertPrivateKey',
ENCRYPTION BY PASSWORD = 'Op3n$esame')
```

This completes the process of designing and implementing transparent data encryption on an existing database without making any changes to client applications.

How it works...

As you can see, designing and implementing TDE is a simple and effective way to encrypt the database without making any changes to the client application code. TDE uses DEK for encrypting entire databases. The DEK is stored in the database boot record, which is secured by a certificate stored in the master database.

The database master key is protected by the service master key, which in turn is protected by the Data Protection API, which disallows any action of restore or attach process of the database file to another server until the certificate that was used to secure the DEK is available on the same server.

The encryption and decryption operations are scheduled on the background threads by the SQL Server memory pool. Furthermore, the tempdb system database will also be encrypted as soon as the user database on the instance of SQL Server is encrypted using TDE methods.

> As a best practice, it is highly recommended that you backup the certificate and private key associated with the certificate. Even though the database is not encrypted, the database encryption key is retained in the database, which is required for some operations within the SQL Server process.

Furthermore, TDE compresses significantly less than equivalent unencrypted data. So if TDE is used to encrypt a database, then backup compression will not be able to progress to a significant compression on the backup storage. Therefore, when using TDE, using the backup compression feature is not recommended.

There's more...

Though TDE is highly essential to implement a securable data platform, it is worthwhile to mention a few points about the interoperability with tempdb system database and replication.

- When the TDE is applied on a user database, then the tempdb system database on that SQL Server instance will be encrypted. This may lead to problems for the databases that do not have TDE feature enabled; so it is essential to separate these databases on separate instances.

- Similarly, the replication feature does not automatically replicate data from a TDE-enabled database, so it is required to encrypt both the distribution and subscriber databases.

- By default, the FILESTREAM data is not encrypted even when the database is enabled with TDE.

8
Maintenance and Monitoring

In this chapter, we will cover:

- ► Implementing performance baseline practices
- ► Monitoring resource usage with Extended Events
- ► Implementing Management Data Warehouse features
- ► Designing maintenance tasks on a mission-critical environment
- ► Implementing Piecemeal restore strategies
- ► Planning and designing of a Disaster Recovery environment
- ► Implementing sustainable index maintenance practices for a VLDB and 24/7 environment
- ► Configuring a manageable database consistency and integrity process for multiple databases and a VLDB environment
- ► Configuring a server storage system for scalability
- ► Configuring SQL server storage architecture for quick recovery
- ► Managing a storage system for analyzing bottlenecks

Introduction

Maintenance and Monitoring are essential parts of database administration and any relational database has no exclusion from these tasks. There are various tools available from the SQL Server product in addition to the tools from the Windows operating system. The key aspects of SQL Server maintenance is to keep up the availability and achieve optimal performance, thereby minimizing the time for users to obtain the results of queries and provide out of the box scalability. In order to reduce manual intervention, monitoring will help us to track the resource usage, network traffic, and transactions usage on the data platform. For a DBA to improve the system performance, it is essential to line-up baseline and benchmarking of the data platform.

> **Baseline**: It is a series of measurements taken when a system is newly configured or an existing system has been extensively reconfigured.
>
> **Benchmarking**: It is an inclusive report of system performance that is captured at multiple times and loads.

Monitoring involves taking periodic snapshots of the system state to isolate processes that are causing problems and to gather information continuously over time to track a performance trend. In practical terms, it is essential to record system performance against predefined metrics, when the server becomes operational with a measurable load. This information is beneficial to establish the baseline of the database server, which can indicate the areas in need of tuning or reconfiguration. In addition to baseline setup, the information can supply the benchmarking of the platform that will clarify how the system resources are used under heavy load. Maintenance tasks help the system to keep up performance and scalability over a period of time, and the tasks must be continued irrespective of database sizes due to the changes in data. In turn, this is effective to define capacity planning and to identify the system statistics at peak hour traffic and lean periods. By monitoring and maintaining the response times for frequently used queries, we can determine whether the changes to the query or indexes on the tables are required. It also helps us to determine whether security is set up adequately and test the applications. Database Maintenance and Performance Monitoring are two sides of the same coin that must flip on a regular basis. Both of these practices can keep up with the baseline and benchmarking of the platform. This chapter covers all of the aspects of maintaining and monitoring best practices with real world examples. The recipes will help the DBAs to adopt best methods with available technologies to the database functionality at peak performance.

Implementing performance baseline practices

Let's see what practices we need to measure a performance baseline and how best we can implement them. These measurements must be taken during on-peak and off-peak hours on the data platform from a typical resource-intensive operation. All the subsequent measurements are compared with relevant baselines, and to determine the course of action we need to establish performance thresholds. These thresholds will help the DBAs to trigger fine tuning methods before a performance downtrend approaches. In this recipe, we will implement the performance baseline practices on the data platform that will help us to keep up the scalability and availability.

Getting ready

The essential tools to implement performance baseline practices are:

▶ Using the SQL Server 2008 R2 instance with a database that will perform unit testing for a baseline.

▶ **Dynamic Management View** (**DMVs**): These are pre-installed within the core database engine.

▶ **Data collector**: It is an automated way to collect data and obtain summary reports about disk usage, query statistics, and server activity.

▶ **Windows Performance Monitor—PERFMON** (**SYSMON**): This tool is used to collect a range of counters.

▶ SQL Server tracing tool—**SQL PROFILER**.

▶ Preparing the SQL Server instance for peak workloads. Use a load testing tool such as **Visual Studio Team System** (**VSTS**) 2008 Database Edition or 2010 Development Edition.

  ❏ Download VSTS 2008 from `http://www.microsoft.com/downloads/en/details.aspx?FamilyID=bb3ad767-5f69-4db9-b1c9-8f55759846ed&displaylang=en`.

  ❏ To use the generated code (own scripts) in a load test scenario, we need to have the VSTS2008 Test Edition and VSTS2008 Team Suite installed on the same machine where the SQL Server instance exists.

  ❏ Refer to `http://www.microsoft.com/downloads/en/details.aspx?FamilyID=bb3ad767-5f69-4db9-b1c9-8f55759846ed&displaylang=en#Instructions` for instructions on VSTS2008 tool installation.

How to do it

Once the essential tools are installed, go through the following steps to implement performance baseline practices to complete the task:

1. Open the **Activity Monitor**.

2. Obtain a list of all tables on the user database to review the permissions. Let us call it as a **schema reconciliation report** to verify the information about integrity constraints, indexes, and columns.

3. Review all the database maintenance scheduled jobs history to determine success or failure.

4. Open the **SSMS** tool, right-click on server instance, and open, **Activity Monitor** to obtain an instantaneous window view of **Processes**, **Resource waits**, **Data File I/O**, and **Recent Expensive Queries**.

> As best practice it is ideal to close down the **Activity Monitor** window within the **SSMS** tool when it is not required.

5. Within the **Activity Monitor** window look at the **Overview** window that displays the graphs on **% Processor Time (%)**, **Waiting Tasks**, **Database I/O (MB/sec)**, and **Batch Requests/Sec** information that will have a default value of ten seconds Refresh Interval.

6. To obtain a trend of resource usage, it is ideal to increase the refresh interval to 30 seconds or higher by right-clicking on any of the graphs in the **Overview** tab.

> Using the Performance Monitor (**Perfmon**) tool, we will create a custom Data Collector set containing performance counters based on selective counters activity.

7. Download the SQL Server PERFMON Counters poster document from `http://www. quest.com/backstage/images/promotions/SQLServer-Perfmonance-Poster.pdf` from Quest Software, which shows the essential list of counters for baseline.

8. To open the **Performance Monitor MMC** tool, either choose to **Start | Run** and type **perfmon** and press **OK**, or **Start | Administrative Tools | Performance Monitor**.

9. Within the **Performance Monitor** tool, expand the **Data Collector Sets** folder, and right-click on **User Defined** to choose **New | Data Collector Set**.

10. Set the new Data Collector Set with an appropriate name and choose the **Create manually (Advanced)** radio button, and click **Next** to continue.

11. On the **What type of data do you want to include?** screen, select **Create data logs** to set Performance Counter and System configuration information options. Click **Next** to continue.

12. On the **Which performance counters would you like to log?** screen, click the **Add** button to add all the counters that are specified in the **SQL Server PERFMON** Counters poster document.

13. Once the counters are added, click **OK** and **Next** to choose the directory to save data on the **Where would you like the data to be saved?** screen.

14. On the **Create the data collector set** screen, enter and choose the appropriate user login that has local administrator group privilege on the specified SQL Server. Leave the default selection of the **Save and close** radio button and click **Finish** to complete the data collector.

15. Under the **User Defined** folder, right-click on the newly created data collector set to Start the collection of specified counters.

16. By default, the performance counter data will be saved on the `%systemdrive%\PerfLogs\Admin\` folder with the specified name as per step 11.

> Let us generate a report detailing the status of local hardware resources and system response times on the server.

17. Expand the **Data Collector Sets** folder to choose System node, right-click on **System Diagnostics**, and click **Start** to run the diagnostic process.

18. The process will execute for few minutes depending upon the server activity. To obtain the report of system diagnostics, expand the **Reports** folder and **System | System Diagnostics**, as shown in the following screenshot:

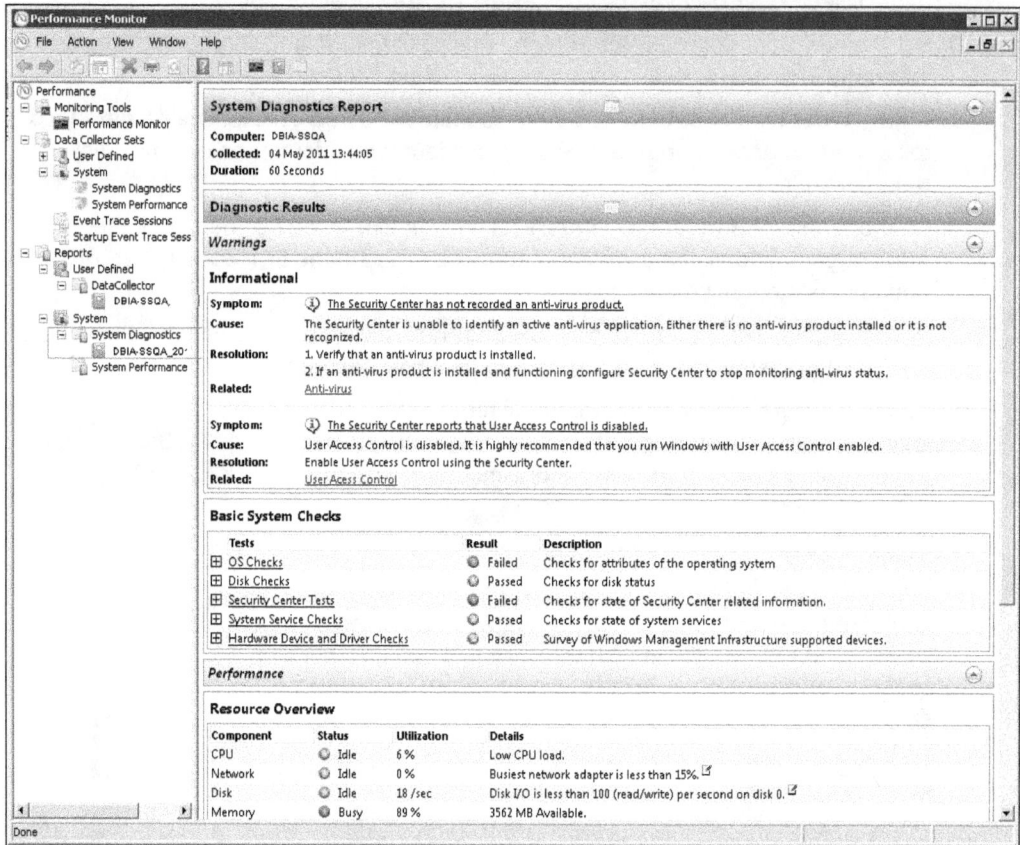

19. Similarly, for system performance information, right-click on **System Performance** and click **Start** to run the performance collection process.

20. The process will execute for few minutes depending upon the server activity. To obtain the system performance report, expand the **Reports** folder and **System | System Performance**(refer to the following screenshot):

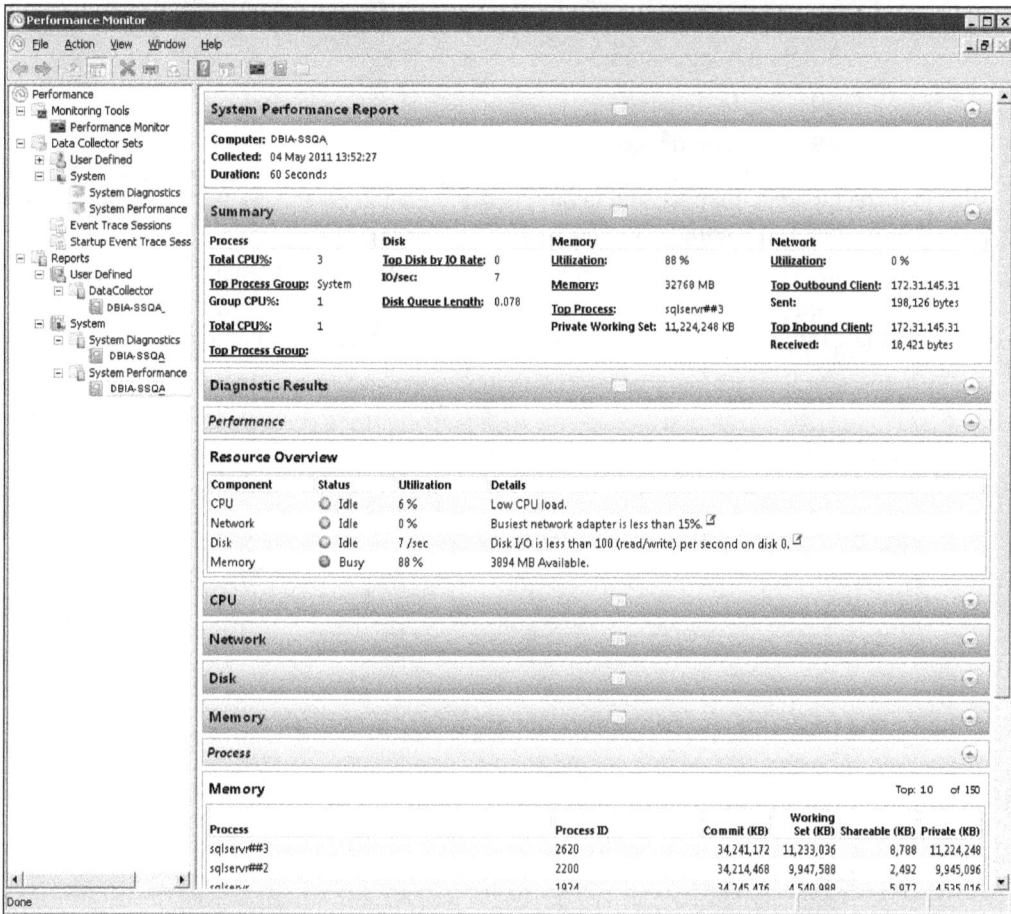

21. Open the **SQL Profiler** tool.

22. To collect SQL Profiler data, on the **SSMS** window click on **Tools** and select **SQL Profiler**.

23. On the **File** menu, point to **New** and then click **Trace**.

24. Make sure that the **All Event Classes** and the **All Data Columns** options are selected. Click **OK** to create a new trace.

25. On the **General** tab, specify a trace name and select **Table** to capture the data. On the **Events** tab, add the following event types to your trace:

   ❑ Exec Prepared SQL

   ❑ Execution Plan

   ❑ Missing Column Statistics

   ❑ SP: Recompile

- ❏ SP: StmtCompleted
- ❏ SQL:BatchCompleted
- ❏ SQL:StmtCompleted
- ❏ RPC:Completed

26. It is ideal to limit the data to a minimum and monitor the events such as Stored procedures: **RPC Completed** and TSQL: **BatchCompleted**.

27. Further, to perform a collective collection of PERFMON and PROFILER data, use the `SQLNexus` tool from the `http://sqlnexus.codeplex.com/` site. Before installing the SQLNexus tool, go through the **Getting Started** link of the URL.

> To monitor and manage the data platform using PowerShell, we can obtain related cmdlets from `http://psx.codeplex.com/`.

28. Open Dynamic Management Views (DMV).

29. Finally, the following list of DMVs are useful to obtain the snapshot of system resources usage:

- ❏ `sys.dm_os_sys_info`
- ❏ `sys.dm_os_wait_stats`
- ❏ `sys.dm_os_performance_counters`
- ❏ `sys.dm_os_memory_clerks`
- ❏ `sys.dm_exec_procedure_stats`
- ❏ `sys.dm_os_waiting_tasks`
- ❏ `sys.dm_exec_sql_text`
- ❏ `sys.dm_exec_requests`

30. Once these tools are used to set up, perform the application activities that are considered as day-to-day and important for business as usual tasks.

This completes the steps to implement a performance baseline on an existing SQL Server instance.

How it works...

When troubleshooting a slow performance task and setting up a performance baseline for tasks, Performance Monitor and SQL Server native tools come in handy. The **Integrated Resource View** screen from **Activity Monitor** gives the required snapshot of system resources usage. Further, using **PERFMON** tool shows the condition of the CPU, disk, network, and memory of the local server in real time. Also, for each of the resource types, the detail section also shows a list of processes running. This can help you identify the process causing the bottleneck.

To view the collected **Data Collector Sets** from **PERFMON**, stop the collection and right-click on collector set to choose **Load Report** to display the collected information for that instance:

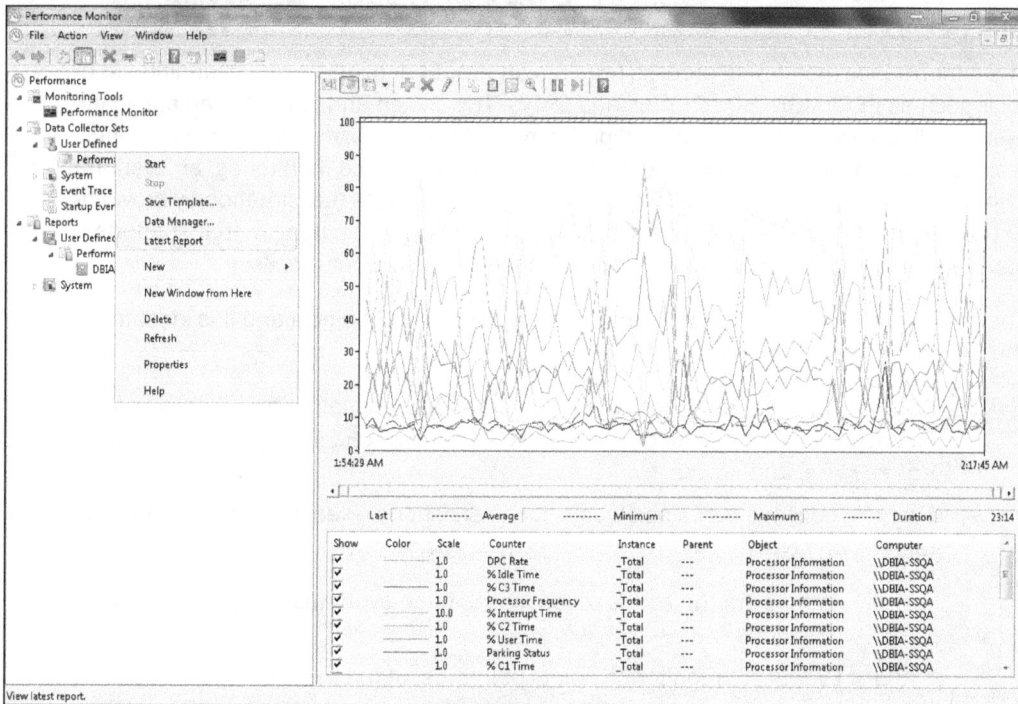

Also, the **SQLNexus** tool helps to load and analyze the performance data collected by the **SQLDiag** tool, which reduces the amount of time that we spend to manually analyze the collected data.

There's more.

SQL Server 2008 R2 has an internal feature called Management Data Warehouse that will perform the data collection and store the information as a data warehouse with extensive reporting functionality.

See Also

▶ The *Implementing Management Data Warehouse features* recipe highlights the relevant steps and automated methods to implement a performance baseline of data platform.

Monitoring resource usage with Extended Events

The performance monitoring process requires an event handling system in addition to existing tools such as PERFMON, SQL Profiler, and DMVs. The design and testing of an application system will always have unanticipated problems that require extensive troubleshooting techniques. To avoid any sort of interruption to the performance monitoring, an event-handling system for the server is essential. SQL Server 2008 addresses this situation by providing **Extended Events** (**XE**). The XE infrastructure is a lightweight mechanism that supports capturing, filtering, and action on events generated by the server process.

The process of events and data are managed by the internal objects and it is ideal to mention the Extended Events concepts.

▶ SQL Server Extended Events packages works as a container for XE objects such as package. The three kinds of XE packages are: `package 0` (XE system objects), `sqlserver`, and `sqlos`.

▶ Every XE package contains objects such as: actions, events, predicates, maps, targets, and types.

  ❑ Actions are the series of responses to an event that may have a unique set of actions

  ❑ Events are monitoring points of interest in the execution path of a program that can be used solely for tracing purposes or triggering actions

  ❑ Predicates works as a set of logical rules that will be used to evaluate events when they are processed

  ❑ A Map is an internal table that maps internal value to a string

  ❑ Targets are consumers that will process synchronous events on the thread that fires the event

  ❑ Types will hold the data for collection of bytes, length, and characteristics of the collection to interpret the data.

In this recipe, we will go through the steps that are included in monitoring the system resource usage using an Extended Events framework that can be utilized to help SQL Server monitoring in many ways. The process will help us to isolate excessive CPU utilization, monitor locking/deadlock, and identify long-running SQL queries.

Getting ready

Ensure that the following prerequisites are met before proceeding further:

▶ The underlying SQL Server version must be 2008 or higher

- Ensure that SQL Server Agent is started and running
- Ensure that MSDB system database has at least 100 MB free space available as all XE-based events are created in this system database
- Ensure that the login used to create XE must have CONTROL SERVER permission to manage the Extended Events objects
- Ensure that the login used to monitor XE has VIEW SERVER STATE permission to execute system catalogs and DMVs

There are a total of 258 events built-in with the database engine. The processes to monitor the SQL server instance using Extended Events is similar to creating an audit process to use CREATE or ALTER statements. XE follows these steps to create an Extended Events session. Alter it to start and stop the monitoring session, and then use the system catalogs and DMVs for monitoring and viewing the event information.

How to do it...

The following steps are required to set up monitoring resource usage with Extended Events using SQL Server 2008 R2.

1. To monitor using XE events setup, we will follow the process to set up and define a new extended events session object that includes operation system request and SQL Server channel.

2. In this recipe, we will monitor the long-running query events that occur in addition to non_yielding errors that occur from query execution.

```
--Chapter 8: Extended Events
--Long Running Queries execution demo
 DECLARE @db_id int
 set @db_id=DB_ID(N'AdventureWorks2008R2')
 select @db_id
```

3. In this recipe, we get the @db_id value for AdventureWorks2008R2 is 5.

```
CREATE EVENT SESSION LongRunningQueryExecution ON SERVER
ADD EVENT sqlserver.sp_statement_completed
( ACTION (sqlserver.sql_text)
WHERE sqlserver.database_id = 5 AND duration > 30000) ,
ADD EVENT sqlserver.error_reported (
        ACTION (package0.callstack, sqlserver.session_id,
sqlserver.sql_text, sqlserver.tsql_stack)
        WHERE ([severity] >= (20)
            OR ([error] = (17803)
            OR [error] = (701)
            OR [error] = (802)
            OR [error] = (8645)
```

```
        OR [error]=(8651)
        OR [error]=(8657)
        OR [error]=(8902))) ),
ADD EVENT sqlos.scheduler_monitor_non_yielding_ring_buffer_
recorded
add target package0.asynchronous_file_target
    (SET filename='c:\temp\page_split.xel', metadatafile='c:\temp\
page_split.xem')
```

If the SQL Server service account is not a member of the sysadmin group, then it must be a member of the group's Performance Monitor Users and Performance Log Users on the server.

Let us start the `LongRunningQueryExecution` event session:

```
-- START EVENT SESSION
ALTER EVENT SESSION LongRunningQueryExecution ON SERVER
STATE=start;
```

Now, let us run two queries that runs for more than five seconds to capture in extended events:

```
SELECT *
FROM AdventureWorks2008R2.Sales.SalesOrderDetail
ORDER BY UnitPriceDiscount DESC
GO
SELECT *
FROM AdventureWorks.Sales.SalesOrderDetail
ORDER BY UnitPriceDiscount DESC
GO
```

At this point, the event session needs to be altered to capture a `sp_statement_completed` value for a long-running query execution:

```
alter event session LongRunningQueryExecution
ON SERVER ADD TARGET package0.synchronous_bucketizer
(SET filtering_event_name = 'sqlserver.sp_statement_completed',
source_type=1, source='sqlserver.sql_text')
```

Capture the XML events to a view from the saved results:

```
CREATE VIEW dbo.Toread_xe_file as
select object_name as event, CONVERT(xml, event_data) as data
from sys.fn_xe_file_target_read_file('c:\temp\page_split*.xel',
'c:\temp\page_split*.xem', null, null)
go
```

Finally, parse the results from the `RAW` `XML` file to another table:

```
create view dbo.xe_Tofile_table as
select event
```

```
    , data.value('(/event/data[@name=''page_id'']/value)
[1]','int') as 'page_id'
    , data.value('(/event/data[@name=''file_id'']/value)
[1]','int') as 'file_id'
    , data.value('(/event/action[@name=''database_id'']/value)
[1]','int') as 'database_id'
    , convert(datetime, data.value('(/event/action[@
name=''collect_system_time'']/text)[1]','nvarchar(50)')) as 'time'
from dbo.Toread_xe_file
go


-- View results
select * from dbo.xe_Tofile_table
--drop event session Longrunningqueryexecution on server
```

This completes the required steps to set up monitoring resource usage with Extended Events using SQL Server 2008 R2.

How it works...

We have used the CREATE EVENT SESSION code that creates the event session to gather the sp_statement_completed value for a long-running query execution, in addition to the errors that are caused due to deadlocks on the specified server instance. Further, the event statement will gather related asyncIO requests and acquired locks on the objects that use a pre-defined target location that allows us to retrieve the results within SQL Server during execution.

Internally, the SQL Server threads generate operating system binaries (Win32 process and Win32 module) that are also called as **executable modules**. Each of these Windows process modules can contain one or more extended events packages that contain one or more extended events objects such as type, target, action, map, predicate, and event.

There's more

To obtain a list of Extended Events names from the existing SQL Server 2008 R2 instance, execute the following TSQL:

```
SELECT p.name, c.event, k.keyword, c.channel, c.description FROM
    (
    SELECT event_package = o.package_guid, o.description,
    event=c.object_name, channel = v.map_value
    FROM sys.dm_xe_objects o
    LEFT JOIN sys.dm_xe_object_columns c ON o.name = c.object_name
    INNER JOIN sys.dm_xe_map_values v ON c.type_name = v.name
    AND c.column_value = cast(v.map_key AS nvarchar)
```

```
    WHERE object_type = 'event' AND (c.name = 'CHANNEL' or c.name IS
NULL)
    ) c LEFT JOIN
    (
    SELECT event_package = c.object_package_guid, event = c.object_
name,
    keyword = v.map_value
    FROM sys.dm_xe_object_columns c INNER JOIN sys.dm_xe_map_values v
    ON c.type_name = v.name AND c.column_value = v.map_key
    AND c.type_package_guid = v.object_package_guid
    INNER JOIN sys.dm_xe_objects o ON o.name = c.object_name
    AND o.package_guid = c.object_package_guid
    WHERE object_type = 'event' AND c.name = 'KEYWORD'
    ) k
    ON
    k.event_package = c.event_package AND (k.event=c.event or k.event
IS NULL)
    INNER JOIN sys.dm_xe_packages p ON p.guid = c.event_package

ORDER BY name,event,keyword desc
```

This query will list out all the events based on packages, types, and predicates. In SQL Server 2008 R2, the row count is 258.

For more information on Extended Events internal methods, you may refer to `http://archive.msdn.microsoft.com/ExtendedEventManager`.

Implementing Management Data Warehouse features

The tools available for monitoring SQL Server performance are useful to obtain the information. However, on a larger scale they will be limited for automation. In order to carry out in-depth monitoring and analyzing the data in a graphical way, and in the form of reports, we may need traditional scripting methods to collect, monitor, and view the required information in a useful way.

Both the Windows operating system and SQL Server provide a number of tools that can be used to collect, analyze, monitor, and report performance-related data to some extent when they are used together. SQL Server 2008 includes the new performance monitoring warehouse feature called Data Collector and Management Data Warehouse (MDW). The Data Collector stands by its name to collect performance-related data from multiple sources and store in a central data warehouse to represent the data through reports in the SSMS tool. The collection process is performed as an automated administrative method using SQL Server Agent and SSIS packages.

In this recipe, we will implement the management data warehouse features on existing SQL Server 2008 R2 instance using SQL Server Management Studio tool. Before getting started with the recipe, it is essential to highlight the important components within Data Collector to store the management data, in conjunction to with the MSDB system database. They are:

- **Data collection sets**: They are definitions that are stored in the MSDB system database and use scheduled jobs for collecting performance data
- **Data Collector runtime component**: This is a standalone process that is used for loading and executing SSIS packages that are part of the collection set
- **Management data warehouse database**: This is a relational database where the collected data is stored having the pre-installed views and stored procedures for collection management
- **SSIS packages**: They are used to collect and update the data to the data warehouse database
- **MDW Reports**: These are pre-defined RDL files that are used to produce reports from SSMS for viewing the collected performance data and system information

Getting ready

The performance data collector feature is available in all server and specialized editions of SQL Server 2008 and 2008 R2 except SQL Server Express. For testing and development purposes, the Developer and Evaluation Enterprise editions can be used.

In order to use the data collector, we must ensure that the following tasks are completed:

- The SQL Server instance to host data collector data warehouse must be the 2008 version or higher
- Ensure that the SQL Server Agent is started and running with no errors reported
- Create and configure the management data warehouse
- Create the data collector login name MDW_Collector from **SSMS Object Explorer** to map them to data collector roles: dc_admin, dc_operator, and dc_proxy

> These data collector roles are stored in the msdb system database, and no user is a member of these roles except members of sysadmin. Fixed server role will have full access to SQL Server Agent objects and data collector views.

- Enable the data collection
- The data collector specific roles are required for the collection and storage of data for a single instance to a data warehouse

How to do it...

The following steps are to be followed to implement management data warehouse (MDW) features by enabling data collector store performance information to a data warehouse database:

1. On the host where MDW is stored using **SSMS** on **Object Explorer,** expand the server instance and expand the **Management** node for that server.

2. Right-click on **Data Collection,** click **Configure Management Data Warehouse** to open the **Configure MDW** wizard, and click **Next** to continue.

3. On the **Select configuration task** screen, choose **Create** or **upgrade** a management data warehouse radio button.

4. We will choose a new database to store MDW data by clicking on the **New** button on the **Configure Management Data Warehouse Storage** screen.

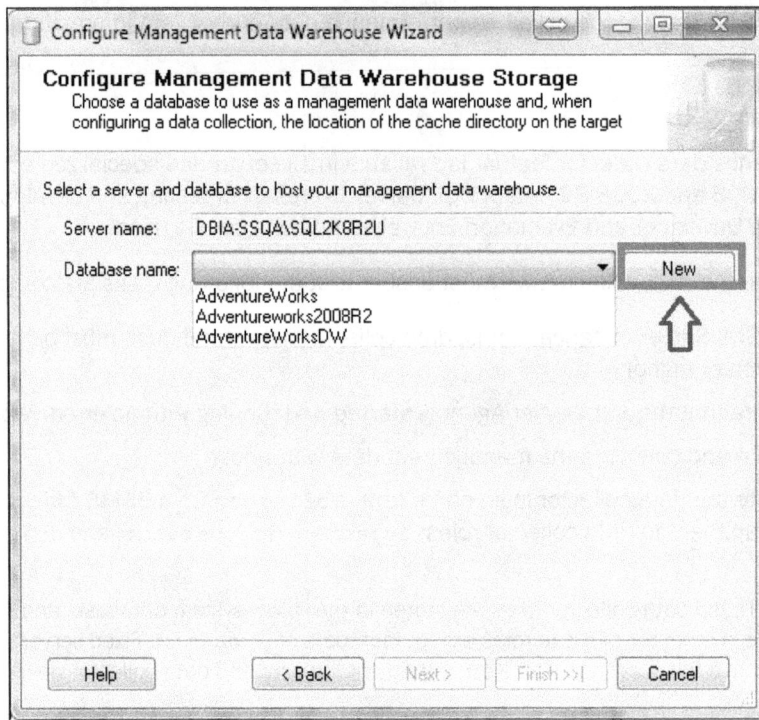

```
Configure Management Data Warehouse Wizard

Configure Management Data Warehouse Storage
    Choose a database to use as a management data warehouse and, when
    configuring a data collection, the location of the cache directory on the target

Select a server and database to host your management data warehouse.

Server name:      DBIA-SSQA\SQL2K8R2U

Database name:    [                          ▼ ]    [ New ]
                  AdventureWorks
                  Adventureworks2008R2
                  AdventureWorksDW


      [ Help ]          [ < Back ]   [ Next > ]   [ Finish >>| ]   [ Cancel ]
```

5. This will open the standard screen to create the **New Database** screen. For the recipe, we choose 1445_MDW as the name, leave all other selections as default, and click **OK** to continue.

6. On the **Map Logins and Users** screen, we will choose **MDW_Collector** at Users mapped to login, select `mdw_admin` database role membership for `1445_MDW` database, and then click **Next** to continue.

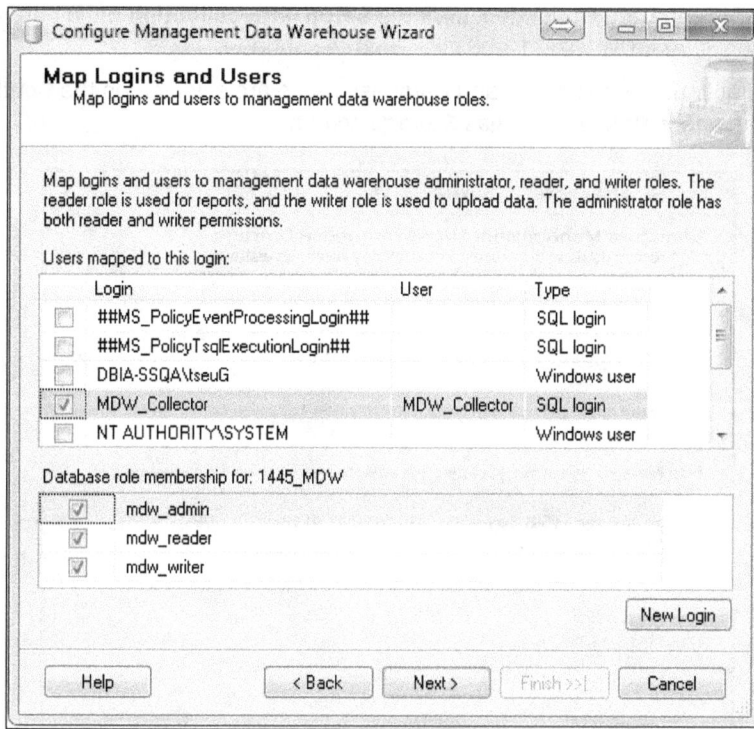

> If, a login is not available for data collection, we can click on the **New Login** button to create the login for the MDW database.

7. The next screen is an informational screen to complete the Wizard. Click **Finish** to perform the selected actions.

8. At the **Configure Data Collection Wizard** progress screen, the successful completion will present a **Success** status. Click on **Report** to save the actions to a file or **Send Report as Email**.

This completes the configuration to create a MDW database. Now, let us configure the instance to start collecting data to the existing MDW database by using the **Setup the data collection** option.

Depending on the task, the user must be a member of one or more of the fixed database roles for management data warehouse. The MDW roles are `mdw_admin`, `mdw_writer`, and `mdw_reader`.

1. Right-click on **Data Collection**, click the **Setup data collection** radio button to open the Configure MDW wizard, and click **Next** to continue.

2. By default, the Server name and Database name are selected on the **Configure Management Data Warehouse Storage** screen.

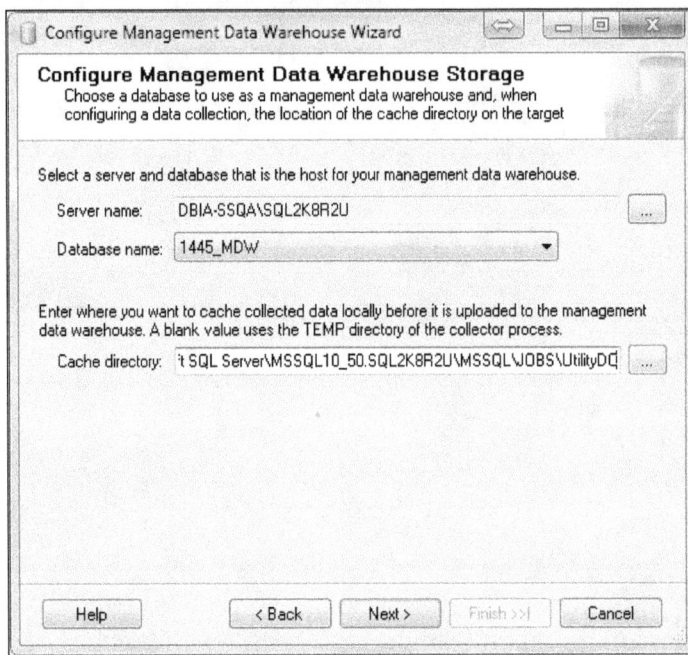

3. At the **Cache Directory** option, we will leave the defaults at this time to store under `%\Program files\SQL Server\ folder`. If a blank value is supplied then local server `C:\TEMP` folder will be used.

4. On the next screen, click **Finish** to complete the Wizard by using `1445_MDW` storage. Start system collection sets and enable the data collection.

5. Using the Configure Management Data Warehouse wizard, the three default system collection sets can be configured. Similarly, to create a user-defined collection set, we can use the `sp_syscollector_create_collection_set` procedure and create necessary `collection_items` to indicate what information the collection needs to collect.

6. The four different collector types are TSQL query, SQL Trace, Performance Counters, and Query activity.

This completes the set up of System Data Collections Sets to store the performance information in the `1445_MDW` database, which in turn completes the steps to implement management data warehouse (MDW) features.

> As best practice, the definitions of system collection sets can be scripted, for instance to script a Server Activity collection set using **Object Explorer** and right-click on **Server Activity** choose **Script Data Collection** as and select **CREATE To | New Query** window.

How it works...

The data collector configuration and components are stored in the MSDB system database and data collection information is stored on the user defined management data warehouse database. The storage components are the database where the configuration and collected data is stored, and execution components are used for data collection and storage. The required schemas and their objects for pre-defined system collection sets are created when we create management data warehouse; all the schemas that are created are classified as core and snapshots. When any user-defined data collection sets are created, a `custom_snapshots` that include collection items that use the generic TSQL query collector type. Internally, API components are used to enable interaction between the user interface and data collector.

When the MDW is configured, the `dcexec.exe` file is used by the data collector runtime component process. The data collection management is based on definitions provided in a collection set and the runtime component is responsible for loading and executing the SSIS package that are part of this collection set. There are two modes used by a collection set: non-cached mode and cached mode.

- ▶ **Non-cached mode**: It uses the same schedule for data collection and upload. The SSIS packages perform collection and upload of data as per the configured frequency; once the package execution is completed, they are unloaded from memory.

- ▶ **Cached mode**: It uses different schedules for data collection and upload. The package execution will collect and cache data until an exit from a loop control-flow task in the packages. This will perform the data flow repeatedly to enable the continuous data collection.

The important tasks for the SSIS packages are data collection and data upload, which are performed as a separate package execution. The data collector runtime component can only run data collection or data upload as it is not possible to run both of these tasks simultaneously.

The collection package gathers data and stores it in `Cache` Directory or in a temporary storage folder. The snapshot time and source of the data is appended by the SSIS package to the collected data.

The upload package reads the data from the temporary storage folder to process the data as required, and then uploads it to the management data warehouse database. All the insert operations are performed as `bulk-insert` operation to minimize the impact of server performance and reduce disk I/O.

> By default, the data capture will run every 15 seconds and upload will execute every hour.

There's more...

Once the management data warehouse feature is installed, we can obtain the initial information by performing the **Collect and Upload Now** action, as shown in the following screenshot:

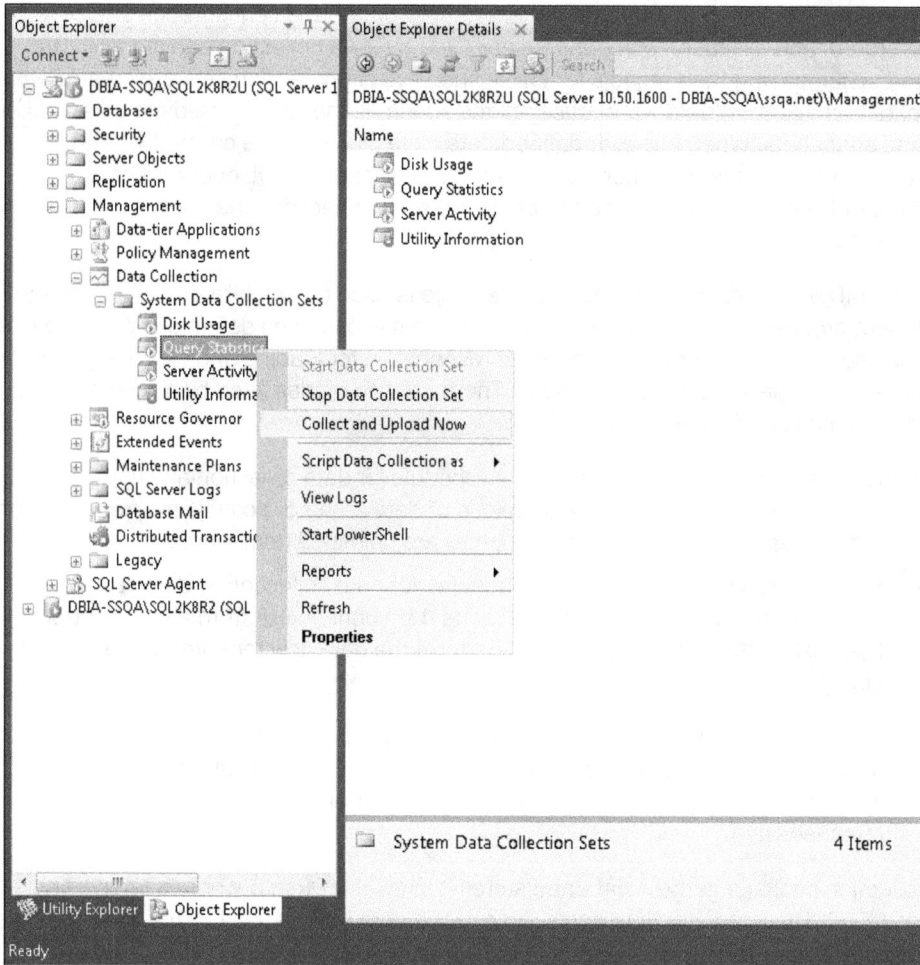

Designing maintenance tasks on a mission-critical environment

The key responsibility for a database administrator is to handle the data recovery strategy. There are varieties of tasks included in a Disaster Recovery (DR) plan that allows the restore of databases with minimum data loss The architecture and mechanics of backup and restore operations are fundamental to the maintenance task process.

SQL Server includes maintenance plans that provide various database maintenance tasks including backup, optimization, and integrity checks. There are multiple backup options available such as full database backup, differential backups, and transaction log backups. Similarly, the database optimization tasks - reorganizing and rebuilding of indexes-are essential to keep up the performance in addition to the integrity checks such as database consistency checks (DBCC). Database maintenance plans have been an integral part since SQL Server version 6.5 and are executed and scheduled using the SQL Server agent service. From SQL Server 2005, the maintenance plans are executed in the form of an SSIS package and scheduled using the SQL Server agent service.

In this recipe, we will work on steps in designing maintenance tasks on a mission-critical environment.

Getting ready

Ensure that the following prerequisites are followed in designing maintenance tasks on a mission-critical data platform:

- The account used to create the maintenance plans is a part of the `sysadmin` fixed server role group.
- The login used to schedule and execute the maintenance plan should have relevant permissions on the server and database.
- If the backups are stored on a network file server then the login must have write permissions on the file share.
- The recovery strategy for the user database is dictated by the recovery model; this property dictates the level of logging and log retention.
- In order to design a database maintenance plan to perform transaction log backups, the database recovery model must be `FULL`.
- The database maintenance plan strategy may vary depending upon the application functionality and time frame to perform maintenance tasks; as a reference, the typical maintenance plan strategy will be as follows:
  - Daily database backup—differential
  - Weekly database backup—full

- ❑ Transaction log backup—every 30 minutes

- ❑ Weekly database optimization tasks—defragmentation and removal of backup history

- ❑ Daily database optimization tasks—update statistics

- ❑ Checking database integrity—weekly

▶ Ensure to enable Agent XPs that in turn enables the SQL Server Extended stored procedure on the server using the following code:

```
sp_configure 'show advanced options', 1;
GO
RECONFIGURE;
GO
sp_configure 'Agent XPs', 1;
GO
RECONFIGURE
GO
```

▶ The SQL Agent service account must have read permission on Active Directory users.

▶ The SQL Agent service account must be a member of the local group Performance Monitor User.

Each of these tasks will have a separate plan and schedule to ensure that the database maintenance tasks are managed effectively. The maintenance plan wizard and features are available in all the editions of SQL Server 2008 R2 except Express editions (Express Edition, Express with Tools, or Express with Advanced Services).

For this recipe, we will create one maintenance plan with separate schedules for each to implement the maintenance tasks.

How to do it...

The following steps are to be followed in designing maintenance tasks on a mission-critical environment. All the steps are defined using the wizard:

1. Launch the Maintenance Plan wizard by expanding the **Management** node in **SSMS** and right-click on **Maintenance Plans** to open the **Maintenance Plan Wizard**.

2. The wizard will have sequential dialog boxes with an explanation, like every other Microsoft wizard. The initial screen presents an introduction on steps. Click **Next** to continue.

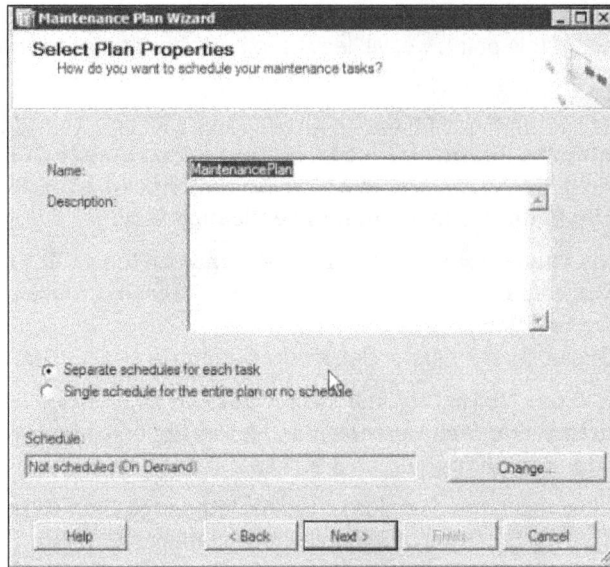

3. The **Select Plan** Properties allows specifying the **Name**, **Description**, and the **Schedule** for the maintenance plan.

4. Here, we will choose separate schedules for each task to ensure that they do not overlap the processes. Click **Next** to continue.

5. In the **Select Maintenance Tasks** screen, we will select more than one task for a given plan. Click **Next** to continue.

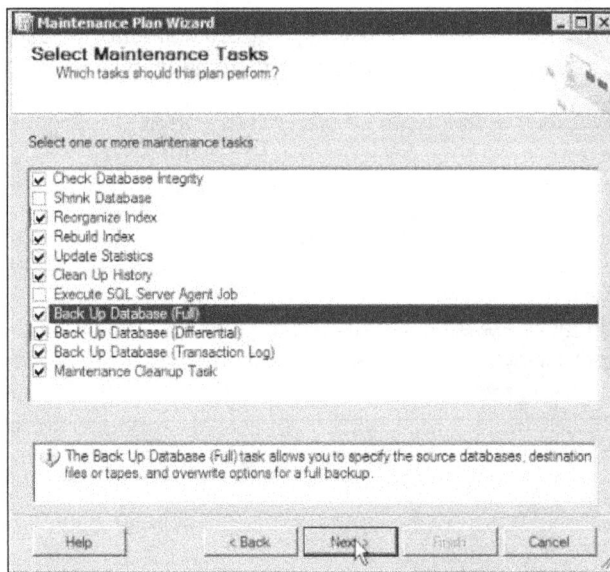

6. In **Select Maintenance Task Order,** we can choose the order should these tasks be performed. At this point, we will leave the defaults without changing the order of tasks.

7. The next set of screens will present individual tasks as per the selection: **Check Database Integrity, Reorganize Index, Rebuild Index, Update Statistics, Back Up Database (Full), Back Up Database (Differential), Back Up Database (Transaction Log), Clean Up History**, and **Maintenance Cleanup Task**.

8. At the screens **Check Database Integrity, Reorganize Index, Rebuild Index, Update Statistics, Back Up Database (Full), Back Up Database (Differential)**, and **Back Up Database (Transaction Log)** at the **Database(s)** selection drop-box, choose All user databases (excluding master, model, msdb, tempdb).

9. In the **Define Clean Up History** Task, select **Backup and restore history, SQL Server Agent job history**, and **Maintenance plan history** options, and choose the **Remove historical data older than** value as **3 Months**.

10. Once the task screens are completed, the **Maintenance Plan Wizard Progress** screen displays the process completion with a status as **Success**.

11. If there is a problem, it will be reported in the **message** column with a hyperlink. Click **Close** to close the wizard.

12. The newly created maintenance plan will be scheduled automatically, which can be viewed in the **SSMS | Management** folder **| SQL Server Agent | Jobs**.

This completes the steps to design maintenance tasks on a mission-critical environment.

How it works.

The maintenance plan tasks provide the required SSIS components for package deployment that act as elements to perform required database maintenance activities.

All the defined tasks within the maintenance plan will use an ADO.NET connection manager to connect. Then, the server instance will identify the relevant component based on the connection manager on each plan task against corresponding databases.

All the corresponding tasks within the plan can be viewed by clicking on the View T-SQL button on the maintenance task.

The maintenance plan tasks are executed using Execute Package Task within the SSIS packages that are stored in sysdtspackages90 table in the MSDB system database. Further, the following system-stored procedures are executed internally by the maintenance plan as per the schedule:

- ► `sp_clear_dbmaintplan_by_db`
- ► `sp_maintplan_close_logentry`
- ► `sp_maintplan_delete_log`

- `sp_maintplan_delete_plan`
- `sp_maintplan_delete_subplan`
- `sp_maintplan_open_logentry`
- `sp_maintplan_start`
- `sp_maintplan_update_subplan`

The **Execute Package** Task will execute the packages stored in the system database or on the file system. The execution will use the **File Connection Manager** or existing OLEDB Connection Manager to connect to the corresponding package.

Finally, the database maintenance plan tasks can be managed using own TSQL scripts using the SSIS packages where Execute SQL Task or SQL Task to execute the corresponding SQL script or stored procedure against the SQL Server. The SQL Task is commonly used to build tables, query metadata, execute DDL commands, and insert and delete data in preparation for other DDL or DML operations in data flow tasks. This will pass input and output parameters to SQL scripts and stored procedures to capture the results in variables.

Implementing Piecemeal restore strategies

The availability and recoverability is important for any database as that helps, at any point in time, to restore a database to a specific point-in-time. Also, to restore all file groups in that database to the same point-in-time requires the database design capable of implementing multiple file groups for a database. As the databases become larger and larger, the infrastructure and technology must support the availability strategy. In such cases, restoring an entire multi-terabyte database to a point-in-time could result in big outage. The online page restore feature from SQL Server 2008 R2 will build a best strategy of multiple database files availability in order to host very large databases and minimize the backup time.

Getting ready...

The following prerequisites are essential to use the online piecemeal restore feature:

- SQL Server 2008 R2 instance must be the DataCenter or Enterprise edition
- The SQL Server instance must be the 2005 version or higher
- The databases must contain multiple file groups that can be restored and recovered in stages through a process known as **piecemeal restore**
- The databases can use any of these recovery models: `SIMPLE`, or `BULK-LOGGED`, or `FULL`, but piecemeal restore is more flexible when `BULK-LOGGED` or `FULL` recovery model is used.
- Download and extract AdventureWorks2008R2 from the `http://msftdbprodsamples.codeplex.com/` site

Create a database with multiple file groups, tables, and insert data, and perform a full database backup using the following TSQL statement:

1. Create a sample PieceMeal database:

```
CREATE DATABASE [PieceMealDB] ON  PRIMARY
( NAME = N'PMDB_PRIMARY',
FILENAME = N'C:\Program Files\Microsoft SQL Server\MSSQL10_50.
SQL2K8R2U\MSSQL\DATA\PMDB_Primary.mdf' ,
SIZE = 3072KB , FILEGROWTH = 1024KB ),
FILEGROUP [Secondary]
( NAME = N'PMDB_Secondary',
FILENAME = N'C:\Program Files\Microsoft SQL Server\MSSQL10_50.
SQL2K8R2U\MSSQL\DATA\PMDB_Secondary.ndf' ,
SIZE = 1072KB , FILEGROWTH = 1024KB ),
FILEGROUP [Tertiary]
( NAME = N'PMDB_Tertiary',
FILENAME = N'C:\Program Files\Microsoft SQL Server\MSSQL10_50.
SQL2K8R2U\MSSQL\DATA\PMDB_Tertiary.ndf' ,
SIZE = 512KB , FILEGROWTH = 512KB )
LOG ON
( NAME = N'PMDB_log',
FILENAME = N'C:\Program Files\Microsoft SQL Server\MSSQL10_50.
SQL2K8R2U\MSSQL\DATA\PMDB_log.ldf' ,
SIZE = 1024KB , FILEGROWTH = 20%)
GO
--Make SECONDARY file group as default
ALTER DATABASE [PieceMealDB] MODIFY FILEGROUP [Secondary] DEFAULT
```

2. Get the physical location of the newly created database:

```
USE master
go
SELECT name,physical_name from sys.master_files where name like
'%PMDB%'
GO

CLONE 2 tables from AdventureWorks2008R2 database; the sample
database can be downloaded from CodePlex site www.codeplex.com.
Extract the AdventureWorks2008DBScriptsR2.msi package file that
will create %\folder name\AdventureWorks2008R2-Samples\% folder.
USE PieceMealDB
GO

CREATE TABLE [dbo].[Address](
    [AddressID] [int] IDENTITY (1, 1) NOT FOR REPLICATION NOT
NULL,
    [AddressLine1] [nvarchar](60) NOT NULL,
```

```
    [AddressLine2] [nvarchar](60) NULL,
    [City] [nvarchar](30) NOT NULL,
    [StateProvinceID] [int] NOT NULL,
    [PostalCode] [nvarchar](15) NOT NULL,
        [SpatialLocation] [geography] NULL,
    [rowguid] uniqueidentifier ROWGUIDCOL NOT NULL CONSTRAINT [DF_
Address_rowguid] DEFAULT (NEWID()),
    [ModifiedDate] [datetime] NOT NULL CONSTRAINT [DF_Address_
ModifiedDate] DEFAULT (GETDATE())
) ON [SECONDARY];
GO


CREATE TABLE [dbo].[BusinessEntity](
        [BusinessEntityID] [int] IDENTITY (1, 1) NOT FOR REPLICATION
NOT NULL,
    [rowguid] uniqueidentifier ROWGUIDCOL NOT NULL CONSTRAINT [DF_
BusinessEntity_rowguid] DEFAULT (NEWID()),
    [ModifiedDate] [datetime] NOT NULL CONSTRAINT [DF_
BusinessEntity_ModifiedDate] DEFAULT (GETDATE())
) ON [TERTIARY];
GO




PRINT '';
PRINT '*** Loading Data';
GO

PRINT 'Loading [dbo].[Address]';

BULK INSERT [dbo].[Address] FROM 'D:\SampleDbz\
AdventureWorks2008R2-Samples\AdventureWorks 2008R2 OLTP\Address.
csv'
WITH (
    CHECK_CONSTRAINTS,
    CODEPAGE='ACP',
    DATAFILETYPE = 'widechar',
    FIELDTERMINATOR= '\t',
    ROWTERMINATOR = '\n',
    KEEPIDENTITY,
    TABLOCK
);


PRINT 'Loading [dbo].[BusinessEntity]';
```

```
BULK INSERT [dbo].[BusinessEntity] FROM 'D:\SampleDbz\
AdventureWorks2008R2-Samples\AdventureWorks 2008R2 OLTP\
BusinessEntity.csv'
WITH (
    CHECK_CONSTRAINTS,
    CODEPAGE='ACP',
    DATAFILETYPE='widechar',
    FIELDTERMINATOR='+|',
    ROWTERMINATOR='&|\n',
    KEEPIDENTITY,
    TABLOCK
);
```

3. As best practice, perform a full database backup:

```
BACKUP DATABASE [PieceMealDB] TO  DISK = N'C:\Program Files\
Microsoft SQL Server\MSSQL10_50.SQL2K8R2U\MSSQL\Backup\
PieceMealFullDatabaseBackup.bak' WITH NOFORMAT, INIT,  NAME =
N'PieceMealDB-Full Database Backup', SKIP, NOREWIND, NOUNLOAD,
STATS = 10, CHECKSUM
GO
declare @backupSetId as int
select @backupSetId = position from msdb..backupset where
database_name=N'PieceMealDB' and backup_set_id=(select max(backup_
set_id) from msdb..backupset where database_name=N'PieceMealDB' )
if @backupSetId is null begin raiserror(N'Verify failed. Backup
information for database ''PieceMealDB'' not found.', 16, 1) end
RESTORE VERIFYONLY FROM  DISK = N'C:\Program Files\
Microsoft SQL Server\MSSQL10_50.SQL2K8R2U\MSSQL\Backup\
PieceMealFullDatabaseBackup.bak' WITH  FILE = @backupSetId,
NOUNLOAD,  NOREWIND
GO
```

4. Back up the `PieceMealDB` filegroup database as follows:

```
BACKUP DATABASE [PieceMealDB] FILEGROUP = N'PRIMARY',  FILEGROUP
= N'Secondary',  FILEGROUP = N'Tertiary' TO  DISK = N'C:\Program
Files\Microsoft SQL Server\MSSQL10_50.SQL2K8R2U\MSSQL\Backup\
PieceMealDB.bak' WITH NOFORMAT, INIT,  NAME = N'PieceMealDB-Full
Filegroup Backup', SKIP, NOREWIND, NOUNLOAD,  STATS = 10
GO
declare @backupSetId as int
select @backupSetId = position from msdb..backupset where
database_name=N'PieceMealDB' and backup_set_id=(select max(backup_
set_id) from msdb..backupset where database_name=N'PieceMealDB' )
if @backupSetId is null begin raiserror(N'Verify failed. Backup
information for database ''PieceMealDB'' not found.', 16, 1) end
RESTORE VERIFYONLY FROM  DISK = N'C:\Program Files\Microsoft SQL
Server\MSSQL10_50.SQL2K8R2U\MSSQL\Backup\PieceMealDB.bak' WITH
FILE = @backupSetId,  NOUNLOAD,  NOREWIND
GO
```

5. As best practice, perform a full database backup:

```
BACKUP DATABASE [PieceMealDB] TO  DISK = N'C:\Program Files\
Microsoft SQL Server\MSSQL10_50.SQL2K8R2U\MSSQL\Backup\
PieceMealFullDatabaseBackup.bak' WITH NOFORMAT, INIT,  NAME =
N'PieceMealDB-Full Database Backup', SKIP, NOREWIND, NOUNLOAD,
STATS = 10, CHECKSUM
GO


declare @backupSetId as int
select @backupSetId = position from msdb..backupset where
database_name=N'PieceMealDB' and backup_set_id=(select max(backup_
set_id) from msdb..backupset where database_name=N'PieceMealDB' )
if @backupSetId is null begin raiserror(N'Verify failed. Backup
information for database ''PieceMealDB'' not found.', 16, 1) end
```

6. Check the backup file consistency:

```
RESTORE VERIFYONLY FROM  DISK = N'C:\Program Files\
Microsoft SQL Server\MSSQL10_50.SQL2K8R2U\MSSQL\Backup\
PieceMealFullDatabaseBackup.bak' WITH  FILE = @backupSetId,
NOUNLOAD,  NOREWIND
GO
```

How to do it...

The process is two-fold:

▶ Using PARTIAL command with the RESTORE DATABASE command

▶ Restoring the corrupted pages (piecemeal restore)

The following steps are needed to implement the piecemeal restore strategies using the online page restore feature:

1. In this recipe, the PieceMealDB is used to restore from a full database using the PARTIAL keyword, and we will bring only PRIMARY filegroup online by leaving filegroups SECONDARY and TERTIARY.

2. Initially, we will perform a transaction log to capture the latest activities from the last database backup:

```
BACKUP LOG [PieceMealDB] TO  DISK = N'C:\Program Files\
Microsoft SQL Server\MSSQL10_50.SQL2K8R2U\MSSQL\Backup\PieceMeal_
TlogAfterBackup.bak' WITH NOFORMAT, NOINIT,  NAME = N'PieceMealDB-
Transaction Log  Backup', SKIP, NOREWIND, NOUNLOAD,  STATS = 10,
CHECKSUM
GO
```

3. Let us take down the `PieceMealDB` database that will simulate `OFFLINE` action as follows:

```
Use master
go
ALTER DATABASE [PieceMealDB] SET OFFLINE WITH ROLLBACK IMMEDIATE
GO
```

4. Also, there is another way to simulate the database corruption: shut down the SQL Server service and simulate a lost disk subsystem by deleting the primary file.

   ❑ Shut down SQL Server

   ❑ Delete the secondary datafile from `PMDB_Secondary.ndf` the `C:\ Program Files\Microsoft SQL Server\MSSQL10_50.SQL2K8R2U\ MSSQL\DATA\` folder for `PieceMealDB` database

   ❑ Restart the SQL Server service

   ❑ After restarting, the `PieceMealDB` database will not start up and the error log will represent the following error message:

   Error: 17207, Severity: 16, State: 1.

   FCB::Open: Operating system error 2(error not found) occurred while creating or opening file C:\Program Files\ Microsoft SQL Server\MSSQL10_50.SQL2K8R2U\MSSQL\DATA\. Diagnose and correct the operating system error, and retry the operation.

5. Now, we will perform a database `RESTORE`, recovering only `PRIMARY` filegroup and `LOG` file.

6. Initially, we will restore the database from a full database backup using the `NORECOVERY` option in order to allow the corresponding transaction log restore task:

```
RESTORE DATABASE [PieceMealDB]
FILEGROUP = 'PRIMARY'
FROM DISK = N'C:\Program Files\Microsoft SQL Server\MSSQL10_50.
SQL2K8R2U\MSSQL\Backup\PieceMealDB.bak'
WITH PARTIAL, NORECOVERY, REPLACE;
GO
```

7. Once the successful restore of the full database is completed, restore the transaction log using the following statement:

```
RESTORE LOG [PieceMealDB]
FROM DISK = N'C:\Program Files\Microsoft SQL Server\MSSQL10_50.
SQL2K8R2U\MSSQL\Backup\PieceMeal_TlogAfterBackup.bak'
WITH RECOVERY;
GO
```

8. For both restore database and restore log, the results will be as follows:

```
Processed 168 pages for database 'PieceMealDB', file 'PMDB_
PRIMARY' on file 1.
```

```
Processed 1 pages for database 'PieceMealDB', file 'PMDB_log' on
file 1.
```

```
RESTORE DATABASE ... FILE=<name> successfully processed 169 pages
in 0.206 seconds (6.409 MB/sec).
```

```
Processed 0 pages for database 'PieceMealDB', file 'PMDB_PRIMARY'
on file 1.
```

```
Processed 6 pages for database 'PieceMealDB', file 'PMDB_log' on
file 1.
```

```
RESTORE LOG successfully processed 6 pages in 0.076 seconds (0.533
MB/sec).
```

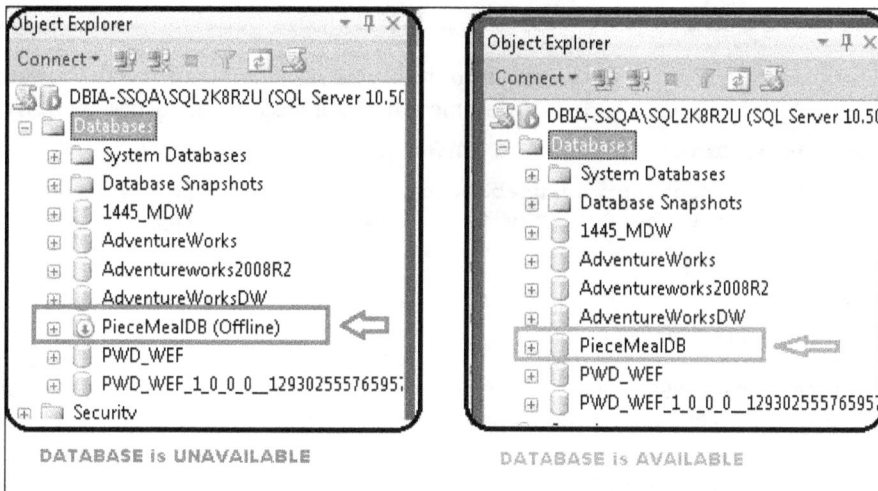

9. Let us verify the file status for the `PieceMealDB` database by querying system catalog:

```
use PieceMealDB
go
select name,state_desc,physical_name from sys.master_files where
name like '%PMDB%'
GO
```

It is also possible to obtain similar information using DATABASEPROPERTYEX system function. The statement will be: SELECT DATABASEPROPERTYEX ('PieceMealDB','STATUS');

10. The result will be as follows:

Name	State_desc	Physical_name
PMDB_PRIMARY	ONLINE	C:\Program Files\Microsoft SQL Server\MSSQL10_50.SQL2K8R2U\MSSQL\DATA\PMDB_Primary.mdf
PMDB_log	ONLINE	C:\Program Files\Microsoft SQL Server\MSSQL10_50.SQL2K8R2U\MSSQL\DATA\PMDB_log.ldf
PMDB_Secondary	RECOVERY_PENDING	C:\Program Files\Microsoft SQL Server\MSSQL10_50.SQL2K8R2U\MSSQL\DATA\PMDB_Secondary.ndf
PMDB_Tertiary	RECOVERY_PENDING	C:\Program Files\Microsoft SQL Server\MSSQL10_50.SQL2K8R2U\MSSQL\DATA\PMDB_Tertiary.ndf

10. Now, we have a `PARTIAL` availability of `PieceMealDB` database to verify execute `SELECT * from dbo.Address` statement that will present the following error:

    `Msg 8653, Level 16, State 1, Line 1`

    `The query processor is unable to produce a plan for the table or view 'Address' because the table resides in a filegroup which is not online.`

    Now, let us proceed to restore a PAGE to recover data pages that have become corrupted due to a disk problem.

11. The process for restoring specific pages is similar to restoring a filegroup or database or file. We can find the corrupted pages from the system database table `msdb.dbo.suspect_pages` or refer to `SQL Server error log` or a result from the `database consistency checks (DBCC)` process.

> It is highly recommended to execute the DBCC CHECKDB statement periodically and review results that will highlight all the irregular pages information.

12. To restore the page, we will use the full database backup file `PieceMealFullDatabaseBackup.bak` and transaction log backup file `PieceMeal_TlogAfterBackup.bak` that was created in earlier steps.

13. Using the following statement, let us restore database pages as a piecemeal process:

```
RESTORE DATABASE PieceMealDB
PAGE='1:18,2:24,3:36'
FROM DISK = 'C:\Program Files\Microsoft SQL Server\MSSQL10_50.
SQL2K8R2U\MSSQL\Backup\PieceMealFullDatabaseBackup.bak' WITH
NORECOVERY, REPLACE
GO
```

14. Now, restore the transaction log using the following statement:

```
RESTORE LOG PieceMealDB
FROM DISK= 'C:\Program Files\Microsoft SQL Server\MSSQL10_50.
SQL2K8R2U\MSSQL\Backup\PieceMeal_TlogAfterBackup.bak' WITH
RECOVERY;
```

15. Now, we have finished the process to restore a page to recover data pages.

This completes the required steps to implement piecemeal restore strategies using the online page restore feature.

How it works...

The piecemeal restore process involves a two-fold step—offline piecemeal and online piecemeal scenario.

- ▶ **Offline piecemeal scenario**: In the offline piecemeal restore scenario, the database is online after the partial restore sequence. The filegroups that have not yet been restored will remain offline and the relevant filegroups can be restored as and when they are required.

- ▶ **Online piecemeal scenario**: In the online piecemeal restore scenario, after the partial restore sequence, the database is online and the primary filegroup and all remaining filegroups are available. The filegroups that have not yet been restored will remain offline, but they can be restored while the database remains online.

In this recipe, the `PieceMealDB` database was restored from a full backup restoring the `PRIMARY` filegroup and the transaction logfile. We have used, `WITH` clause that includes, `PARTIAL` keyword and the `NORECOVERY` clause, which enables the transaction log backups to be restored. Once the transaction log restore step is complete, the database is partially available where the `PRIMARY` filegroup is available and all other objects that are stored in `SECONDARY` and `TERTIARY` filegroups. This process is very helpful to manage very large databases using the `PARTIAL` keyword during a data recovery operation that allows the users and application with initial database connectivity; while the DBAs prioritize the steps to load remaining filegroups that will have higher priority, making them available sooner.

In the next set of steps, we have successfully restored the single data-pages from a full database backup and corresponding transaction log backup files, which is similar to usual `RESTORE DATABASE` commands.

There's more...

It is best practice for very large databases (VLDB) to logically group and represent data in ways that form distinct parcels or subsystems. The piecemeal restore methods are helpful in procuring multiple data and filegroups partially that will essentially reduce the loss of one system that will not affect the availability of another system.

Planning and designing of a Disaster Recovery environment

As it stands, the disaster recovery (DR) is a recovery action, but in the real world it must be a proactive action where preparing to recover from potential disasters is important. The proactive actions must contain a well designed and tested restore plan for the data platform. The backup and restore plan should consider the disaster recovery planning with regard to particular environmental and business needs.

The ideal need for a disaster recovery plan will ensure that all the systems and data can be quickly restored to regular operation if a disaster occurs. In this recipe, we will work on the planning and design strategy of a disaster recovery environment for the SQL Server data platform. The planning and design of a DR environment involves a strategy and process rather than the physical steps to implement essentially a checklisted process.

Getting ready

The disaster recovery plan can be structured in many different ways that contain many types of information. There are various plan types that include the following:

- ▶ Specified hardware acquisition on standby environment
- ▶ Communication plan—written instructions
- ▶ List of people and escalation to be contacted if a disaster occurs
- ▶ High-level and detailed instructions for contacting people involved in the response to the disaster
- ▶ The authority and administration of the plan
- ▶ A checklist and checkpoint of required tasks for each recovery scenario
- ▶ All of these essential steps must be documented to dictate how long recovery will take and the final database state the users can expect

How to do it...

We will go through various scenarios that will help the DBAs and System Administrators to implement the planning and design steps of a DR environment.

The database recovery model affects the possibilities for disaster recovery of a database.

1. A SIMPLE recovery model will not allow transaction log backups, and all the changes since the most recent backup are unprotected. The point-in-time recovery is only possible to the end of a backup.

2. The required backup strategy for a SIMPLE recovery model must be FULL and DIFFERENTIAL backups, which contain just enough log data to recover the database.

3. The restore sequence starts with restoring a full database backup, followed by a corresponding differential backup.

4. A FULL recovery model requires a regular interval of transaction log backup, which can recover to an arbitrary point in time and all committed transactions can be recovered in the event of disaster.

5. Back up the tail of the log to capture the log records that have not yet been backed up. The tail-log backup is taken by using the BACKUP LOG database_name TO <backup_device> WITH NORECOVERY statement.

6. The typical restore sequence will be restoring to a point-in-time, recovering to a marked transaction and recovering to a log sequence number.

7. To perform point-in-time restores, an operation that involves full database backup and multiple log backups (performed every hour every day) are essential, such as restore a database to its state as of 15:00 hours on December 31, 2010. The steps are:

```
--Obtain list of backup file numbers
RESTORE HEADERONLY FROM AdventureWorks2008R2Backups
GO
--RESTORE from FULL database backup
RESTORE DATABASE AdventureWorks2008R2
FROM AdventureWorks2008R2Backups
WITH FILE=5, NORECOVERY;

--RESTORE from transaction log backup files
RESTORE LOG AdventureWorks2008R2
FROM AdventureWorks2008R2Backups
WITH FILE=14, NORECOVERY, STOPAT = 'Dec 31, 2012 14:00 PM';


RESTORE LOG AdventureWorks2008R2
FROM AdventureWorks2008R2Backups
WITH FILE=15, NORECOVERY, STOPAT = 'Apr 15, 2012 15:00 PM';
RESTORE DATABASE AdventureWorks2008R2 WITH RECOVERY;
GO
```

Recover to a marked transaction use `WITH STOPATMARK` or `WITH STOPBEFOREMARK` clause, assume that application code consist the naming of marked transactions using `BEGIN TRANSACTION <Name> WITH MARK`.

1. To perform marked transactions recovery, use the following TSQL statement:

```
RESTORE LOG AdventureWorks2008R2
    FROM AdventureWorks2008R2Backups
    WITH FILE = 14,
    RECOVERY,
    STOPATMARK = 'StockPricesat1500';
```

2. Now, let us work on recovering the transaction to a particular `Log Sequence Number (LSN)`, as follows:

```
--RESTORE the transaction log until a particular LSN
RESTORE LOG AdventureWorks2008R2 FROM DISK = 'G:\backups\Tlogs\
AdventureWorks2008R2_log.bak'
WITH STOPATMARK = 'lsn:12000000010000038'
GO
```

3. A `BULK-LOGGED` recovery model will work as an adjunct of a full recovery model that permits high-performance bulk operations by reducing log space usage with minimal logging for most bulk operations. The point-in-time recovery is not supported, but it can help to recover to the end of any backup. Now, we are at the point of managing backup media where the backup plans include provisions for managing backup media.

4. Prepare a schedule for overwriting backup media and use essential backup media. A backup device can be a disk, tape, or physical backup device that is provided by the operating system. To backup to a backup-file, perform the following TSQL steps:

```
--BACKUP to a specific physical location or default backup
location
BACKUP DATABASE AdventureWorks2008R2
    TO DISK = 'G:\Backups\DB_Backups\AdventureWorks2008R2.bak';


BACKUP DATABASE AdventureWorks2008R2
        TO DISK='AdventureWorks2008R2.bak';
--The default backup directory will be
--C:\Program Files\Microsoft SQL Server\MSSQL10_50.MSSQLSERVER\
MSSQL\Backup or
--user defined folder which is specific during the setup.


--BACKUP to a network file location using UNC (Universal Naming
Convention)
BACKUP DATABASE AdventureWorks2008R2
    TO DISK = '\\FileBackupServer\Backup\DB_backups\
AdventureWorks2008R2Data.Bak';
```

```
GO


--BACKUP to a TAPE device
BACKUP DATABASE AdventureWorks2008R2
        TO TAPE='\\.\tape0';
GO



--BACKUP to a logical device
--A logical device can be disk dump device/network disk backup/
tape backup device
--Use SP_ADDUMPDEVICE to define a logical device
--Here we will create the logical device and perform BACKUP
database
USE master
GO
EXEC sp_addumpdevice 'disk', 'AWorks2008R2DB',
'G:\Backups\DB_Backups\AdventureWorks2008R2-Data.bak';
GO
BACKUP DATABASE AdventureWorks2008R2
  TO AWorks2008R2DB
    WITH FORMAT;
GO
```

We are now ready to ensure the disaster readiness activities.

5. Test the entire backup and restore recovery procedures thoroughly.

> For additional checking on data and backups to increase the probability of error detection, use the RESTORE VERIFYONLY statement on the backup set.

6. Ensure that you define and document all the required steps to recover from various failures.

7. Ensure that you check the schedule of backup and restore jobs that include both system and user databases.

8. Always maintain the system logs intact. Archive windows operating systems event viewer logs for system, application, and security.

9. Keep a record of all required network libraries and the security mode used for all SQL Server instances.

10. Maintain a base-functionality script for a quicker assessment. Audit all important actions.

How it works...

The recovery process of copying data to a backup or restoring data from a backup is a multi-phase process. A differential backup contains sufficient log records to allow rolling forward the active transaction log records as part of restoring each backup. Each database will maintain a transaction log to roll back uncommitted transactions to bring the database into a transactional consistent and usable state, which is called **point-in-time**. The process of rolling forward any uncommitted transactions and bringing the database online is known as **recovery**.

A roll forward set is defined by restoring one or more full backups such as database backup or partial backup. In the case of differential backups, if files were added to the database as in the differential base, restoring a differential backup will overwrite pages in a roll forward set with data from the differential backup. The restore sequence operation corresponds to an individual phase such a data copy, redo (roll forward), and undo (roll back).

Implementing sustainable index maintenance practices for a VLDB & 24/7 environment

The index maintenance is one of the optimizing applications steps, and implementing sustainable index maintenance for a VLDB environment should be evaluated from several different perspectives. There are many cases for any performance hit will see on the databases, next to not having indexes or indexes that are very fragmented. Also, the issue will be multi-fold where fragmented indexes will take more space than to maintain the indexes alone impacting on all aspects of the database activities.

In this recipe, we will go through the strategy of implementing sustainable index maintenance practices for a very large database, and a database environment that must be available 24/7.

Getting ready

The process of implementing index maintenance practices includes the defragmentation of indexes by identifying the indexes that require maintenance activities, such as re-indexing or reorganizing.

In order to perform the ONLINE REBUILD method and DATA_COMPRESSION method, the SQL Server instance must be the DataCenter edition or Enterprise edition.

The sustainable index maintenance practice includes the list of indexes that is going for index scan and obtain a list of unused indexes on tables.

The instance must be SQL Server 2008 version or higher, and the database size must be over 250 GB in size.

How to do it...

The following steps are required in implementing sustainable index maintenance practices for a VLDB and 24/7 environment:

1. The first step in the index maintenance practice is to identify the indexes that require maintenance or indexes that are heavily fragmented.

2. SQL Server provides a data management view (DMV) `sys.dm_db_index_physical_stats` that is a multi-statement table-valued function that returns size and fragmentation information for data and indexes of a specified table or view.

3. Execute the following TSQL statement to obtain index fragmentation levels on `[Person].[Sales]` table in `AdventureWorks2008R2` database:

```
USE Adventureworks2008R2
GO
--Obtain DETAILED fragmentation information
select str(index_id,3,0) as indid,
left(index_type_desc, 20) as index_type_desc,
index_depth as idx_depth,
index_level as idx_level,
str(avg_fragmentation_in_percent, 5,2) as avg_frgmnt_pct,
str(page_count, 10,0) as pg_cnt
FROM sys.dm_db_index_physical_stats
(db_id(), object_id('person.sales'),null, 0, 'DETAILED')
go
```

4. The previous script gives the information of fragmented indexes on a specific table, and to obtain all the fragmented tables information, execute the following:

```
--Return the information index operational stats
--related to current low level I/O, locking, latching and access
method
SELECT * FROM sys.dm_db_index_operational_stats(NULL, NULL, NULL,
NULL);
GO

--DETAILED index fragmentation report for all the tables in the
database
--Ensure to change DB_ID value in below query as per the database
SELECT object_name(IdxPhyStat.object_id) AS [TableName],
    SysIdx.name AS [IndexName],
    IdxPhyStat.Index_type_desc,
    IdxPhyStat.avg_fragmentation_in_percent,
    IdxPhyStat.avg_page_space_used_in_percent,
    IdxPhyStat.record_count,
    IdxPhyStat.fragment_count,
```

```
      IdxPhyStat.avg_fragment_size_in_pages
  FROM sys.dm_db_index_physical_stats(db_
  id(N'AdventureWorks2008R2'), NULL, NULL, NULL , 'DETAILED')
  IdxPhyStat
      JOIN sys.tables SysTab WITH (nolock) ON IdxPhyStat.object_id =
  SysTab.object_id
      JOIN sys.indexes SysIdx WITH (nolock) ON IdxPhyStat.object_id =
  SysIdx.object_id AND IdxPhyStat.index_id = SysIdx.index_id
  WHERE SysTab.is_ms_shipped = 0
  ORDER BY TableName,avg_fragmentation_in_percent
  GO
```

5. The `Logical Fragmentation` is the percentage of out-of-order pages in the leaf pages of an index. The `Extent Fragmentation` is the percentage of out-of-order extents in leaf pages of a heap (no indexes). Now, we having the information on fragmented tables, and let us work on sustainable practices to reduce the fragmentation and maintain the index on these tables, assuming the tables row count is running several millions and the database is considered as a VLDB.

6. The frequency of how often to rebuild or reorg an index depends on the database size.

7. There are three choices for reducing fragmentation: drop and recreate the clustered index (`CREATE INDEX`), reorganize the index (`ALTER INDEX REORGANIZE`), and rebuild the index (`ALTER INDEX REBUILD`). To reduce the fragmentation on a heap, create a clustered index on the table and then drop the index.

> As best practice, it is essential to perform `REBUILD` operation if the physical fragmentation is between 15 percent and 20 percent. If the logical fragmentation is between 30 percent and 40 percent then performing `REORGANIZE` of indexes is ideal.

8. Perform the index reorganize job on every alternate night on all the tables that will have frequent insert, delete, and update transactions.

9. Perform the index rebuild job on every weekend on all the tables that will have frequent insert, delete, and update transactions.

10. Let us perform the different variations of rebuilding a specific index `PK_CreditCard_CreditCardID` and/or all the indexes on a table in `AdventureWorks2008R2` database:

```
--*****************************
-- Rebuild a specific index
ALTER INDEX PK_CreditCard_CreditCardID ON Sales.CreditCard REBUILD

-- Rebuild all indexes on a specific table
ALTER INDEX ALL ON Sales.CreditCard REBUILD
```

```
-- Rebuild an index, while keeping it available (Enterprise
Edition specific feature)
ALTER INDEX PK_CreditCard_CreditCardID
ON Sales.CreditCard REBUILD
WITH (ONLINE = ON, SORT_IN_TEMPDB = ON)

-- Rebuild an index with page-level data compression enabled
ALTER INDEX AK_CreditCard_CardNumber ON  Sales.CreditCard REBUILD
WITH (DATA_COMPRESSION = PAGE, SORT_IN_TEMPDB = ON)
```

11. Let us perform the multiple variations of index reorganize methods on `Person.BusinessEntity` table indexes:

```
--*****************************
-- REORGANIZE a specific index on BusinessEntity table
ALTER INDEX PK_BusinessEntity_BusinessEntityID
ON Person.BusinessEntity REORGANIZE

ALTER INDEX AK_BusinessEntity_rowguid
ON Person.BusinessEntity REORGANIZE

-- Reorganize all indexes for a table and compact LOB data type
ALTER INDEX ALL
ON Person.BusinessEntity
REORGANIZE WITH (LOB_COMPACTION=ON)
```

This completes the important steps in implementing sustainable index maintenance practices for a VLDB and 24/7 environment.

How it works...

In this recipe, we will use SQL Server DMVs and system catalogs in addition to INDEX modification DML statements.

Referring to DMV `sys.dm_db_index_physical_stats` determines the level of scanning performed to obtain statistical information based on a specified mode such as LIMITED, SAMPLED, or DETAILED. This DMV requires an Intent-Share (IS) table lock, regardless of the mode that is executed. The LIMITED mode is the fastest mode and obtains the information on the smallest number of pages. For a heap, the scanning will operate on PFS and IAM pages. The data pages of the heap are not scanned. The DETAILED mode is resource intensive, which will take a longer time than expected due to the nature of the scan performing size or fragmentation level of a table or index that scans all pages and returns all the statistics.

We have also used the DMV `sys.dm_db_index_operational_stats` that performs for a length of time that users or an application process must wait to read or write to a table or a partition. Any delay or lag on these processes is encountered due to significant I/O activity or hot spots. The important information for latching and locking contention refer to the values for `page_latch_wait_count` and `page_latch_wait_in_ms` columns. Also, the latch contention from row_lock_count and page_lock_count columns provides further information. To obtain additional information on how a row or page locks are obtained, refer to the row_lock_wait_in_ms and page_lock_wait_in_ms columns.

Coming to the index defragmentation and maintenance methods, we used `ALTER INDEX` statements that works on the rebuild of indexes on a specified table (clustered index), and the operation will not cause a rebuild of non-clustered indexes for that table. `ALTER INDEX` ...`REBUILD` statement execution will enable any disabled index and it does not rebuild any associated `nonclustered` indexes unless the keyword `ALL` is specified. In case the specified table is a heap (no index) then the rebuild operation has no effect on the table.

The keyword `SORT_IN_TEMPDB` option, as it refers the operation, is performed in `tempdb` database when it is specified. In this case, if `tempdb` is on a different set of disks than the user database then it will reduce the time needed to create an index as the operation is highly I/O intensive.

The keyword `ONLINE` has an advantage of not applying long-term table locks for the duration of the index operation. At the main phase of the index operation only Intent Share lock is held on the source table, and at the end of the operation the Shared lock is held on the source object and nonclustered indexes.

The keyword `LOB_COMPATION` will specify all pages that contain large object (LOB) data are compacted, by giving an advantage of compacting data can improve the usage of disk space and default setting is `ON`.

The index reorganize process, such as using `ALTER INDEX..REORGANIZE,` will specify the index leaf level to be reorganized, which is always performed `ONLINE`. This operation will reduce the fragmentation on the leaf level of an index (both clustered and nonclustered) causing the physical order of database pages to match the logical order. During this operation, the indexes are compacted based on the `fill-factor,` resulting in free space and smaller indexes.

> The rebuild operation can be minimally logged if the database recovery model is set to either bulk-logged or simple.

Configuring a manageable database consistency and integrity process for multiple databases and a VLDB environment

The data quality must be kept intact and the method to keep up is difficult to maintain for multiple databases and a VLDB environment too. The default response to recover the data from a disaster is to restore it from the backup tape of a file, but in cases where the source media such as a tape is crinkled or the backup file server disk has a problem, the recovery can be expensive. In this case, gigabytes of data might be lost just because of a hardware problem. There are few methods available in SQL Server to recover the data using the database consistency process, which involves a repair of corrupted data stored within the database.

As mentioned earlier, the data recovery will involve a REPAIR option that must be used as a last resort. Using this option might present a potential risk of losing database pages that will cause further data loss. However, if a nonclustered index is reported as corrupted then the ideal action is to drop and recreate the same index.

In this recipe, we will go through the strategic steps in configuring a manageable database consistency and integrity process for multiple databases and a VLDB environment. The recipe will cover the best practices in performing database consistency and integrity check steps to identify any internal errors to resolve in a proactive manner.

Getting ready...

There are no specific prerequisites to install or modify except the instance must be a SQL Server 2008 version or higher, having at least one user database to perform the steps defined in the recipe.

How to do it...

The recipe includes a multiple step approach by reviewing the important commands to validate and check for issues within the database. The steps involve checking database page usage and verifying allocation errors, and also include the integrity of database and database objects with a final touch-up to validate the integrity at the table and data validation level.

The following steps are required in configuring a manageable database consistency and integrity process for multiple databases and a VLDB environment.

1. The first step is checking the page usage and allocation. Use `DBCC CHECKALLOC` statement as follows:

   ```
   -- Check the current database.
   DBCC CHECKALLOC;
   GO
   -- Check the specific database.
   DBCC CHECKALLOC (AdventureWorks2008R2);
   GO
   --Just an estimation and no elaborated messages
   DBCC CHECKALLOC WITH ESTIMATEONLY,NO_INFOMSGS
   ```

2. When we execute the `CHECKALLOC` using `ESTIMATEONLY` and `NO_INFOMSGS`, the result will be as follows:

   ```
   Estimated TEMPDB space needed for CHECKALLOC (KB)
   -------------------------------------------------
   268

   (1 row(s) affected)
   ```

3. Running `DBCC CHECKALLOC` on the frequently updated table will help integrity verification and good maintenance practice.

4. Now, let us dive deep into checking the allocation and page structural integrity using `DBCC CHECKDB DBCC` and `CHECKFILEGROUP` statements.

   > The `DBCC CHECKALLOC` functionality is included in `DBCC CHECKDB`, so we do not have to perform `CHECKALLOC` separately when `CHECKDB` is executed.

5. Execute the following TSQL statements:

   ```
   --CHECK THE DATABASE ALLOCATION and PAGE STRUCTURE integrity
   -- Check the current database.
   DBCC CHECKDB;
   GO
   -- Check the AdventureWorks2008R2 database without
   --nonclustered indexes and extended logical checks.
   DBCC CHECKDB (AdventureWorks2008R2, NOINDEX) WITH EXTENDED_
   LOGICAL_CHECKS;
   GO

   --Extended Logical Checks and Physical Only cannot be used
   together
   --with physical only
   DBCC CHECKDB (AdventureWorks2008R2, NOINDEX) WITH PHYSICAL_ONLY;
   GO
   ```

The next series of steps will include DBCC commands to validate integrity at filegroup level, table level, and constraint level.

1. The DBCC CHECKFILEGROUP can be used to check allocation and structural integrity of all tables and views in a specified filegroup. The code is as follows:

```
--Check allocation and integrity in a specified filegroup of
current database
--CHECKS only PRIMARY filegroup
USE AdventureWorks2008R2;
GO
DBCC CHECKFILEGROUP;
GO


--CHECKS specific filegroup and integrity of the physical
structure of the page
USE AdventureWorks2008R2;
GO
DBCC CHECKFILEGROUP (2, NOINDEX) WITH PHYSICAL_ONLY;
GO
```

2. The data integrity for tables and indexed views can be checked using DBCC CHECKTABLE. The steps are simple and self-explanatory:

```
--Check data integirty for tables and views
DBCC CHECKTABLE ('Person.BusinessEntity') WITH ALL_ERRORMSGS

DBCC CHECKTABLE ('Person.BusinessEntity') WITH ESTIMATEONLY

DBCC CHECKTABLE ('Person.BusinessEntity', 1) WITH PHYSICAL_ONLY
```

> As a best practice, use the DBCC CHECKDB WITH DATA_PURITY option that will check the database for column values that are out of range. This option will check column-value integrity by default.

3. Finally, to alert on any CHECK or foreign key constraint violation, the DBCC CHECKCONSTRAINTS can be used. In order to alert the constraint violation, let us demonstrate the steps as follows:

```
--Check for constraints violation on specified table or indexed
view
--Obtain a pre update information
DBCC CHECKCONSTRAINTS ('Person.Address')

--CREATE a CHECK constraint on PostalCode column on the table
ALTER TABLE Person.Address ADD CONSTRAINT CHK_PostalCodeLength
```

```
CHECK (LEN(PostalCode) < 10)

--DISABLE the PostalCodeLength constraint
ALTER TABLE Person.Address NOCHECK CONSTRAINT CHK_PostalCodeLength
GO

-- Update the ModifiedData column for specific set of rows
UPDATE Person.Address
SET PostalCode = 980119801298013
WHERE AddressID <= 5
GO


--Enable the CHECK constraint on the table
ALTER TABLE Person.Address CHECK CONSTRAINT CHK_PostalCodeLength
GO

--Obtain post update information
DBCC CHECKCONSTRAINTS ('Person.Address')
```

This completes the multiple step approach in configuring the manageable database consistency and integrity process for multiple databases and a VLDB environment. These are essential in reviewing the important commands to validate and check for issues within the database.

How it works...

The process of checking and validation of database consistency and integrity will verify the allocation of data pages and internal structures of specified databases. All the verification and error messages are logged to SQL Server error log. Besides, setting up an alerting mechanism to pick up any warning messages that are generated with these DBCC commands will help solve the problem in a quicker way.

In this recipe, we have initially used the DBCC CHECKALLOC command to verify the allocation of data pages, which creates an internal database snapshot to maintain transactional consistency during the operation. Unless otherwise specified, the TABLOCK (table lock) will not be applied when the snapshot is created, until the operation is completed. The exclusive lock is applied for a consistency check. All the errors and warnings are generated with a state number and description.

The DBCC CHECKDB command will verify the checking of the integrity of the physical structure of the page and record hearers along with allocation consistency of the database. A complete run of the CHECKDB process will take longer depending upon the size of the database and data files. The default behavior will be comprehensive logical checks, where page structures are checked and new checks such as EXTEND_LOGICAL_CHECKS can be specified on indexed views, XML indexes, and SPATIAL indexes. The logical consistency checks will cross-check the internal index table of an object.

> DBCC CHECKDB statement with EXTEND_LOGICAL_CHECKS option is a resource intensive operation that must be performed only if there is a doubt of suspect index issues that are unrelated to physical corruption, or a page-level checksum is turned off on the database.

Configuring a server storage system for scalability

The scalability and performance is guaranteed when the reliable storage is configured at the hardware level. In general, the storage configuration and management is handled by the Storage Administrators and it is a compulsory exercise for an organization to involve DBAs at configuration level that will shape up a well-built database server on hardware perspectives.

The reliability characteristics and performance implications depend on the RAID configuration, and in this chapter we will go through the best practice layout in configuring a server storage system for scalability. When deploying a new SQL Server instance or performing a scale-out exercise of an existing SQL Server platform, it is important to have an overall understanding of the key file types that are essential for a database. The file type's workload along with the database type and size enables both storage administrators and DBAs to establish necessary storage requirements for the SQL Server environment. In this recipe, we will plan for and configure the SQL Server database storage in a SharePoint Server 2010 environment.

Getting ready...

Before we jump into how to accomplish the task, it is essential to touch up on essential database file considerations and configuration of a server storage system. These points will stand as a starting point too.

With the new features of SQL Server 2008, any type of data storage is possible:

- ▶ The OLTP database might include only a single database file, while those designed to support heavy transactional workloads or large schemas might use a variety of filegroup architectures to improve scalability, performance, operational convenience, or availability.

▶ It is also ideal to separate the multiple data files into separate disk partitions (physical).

▶ A database has at least one logfile to record all database modifications by each transaction-a critical component of the database for availability and data integrity. The active portion of a transaction log is required to bring the database back to a consistent state.

▶ The SQL Server temporary storage area, in other words using a `tempdb` database. This database is used for the storage of temporary data structures and is subject to intense and unpredictable I/O behavior. So, it is essential to locate the `tempdb` files on a separate RAID group with the fastest disks from the database files.

▶ FILESTREAM, which is a new feature from the SQL Server 2008 version. integrates the SQL Server database with the NTFS file system by storing `VARBINARY (BLOB)` data as files on the file system. This provides transactional consistency.

▶ The storage is managed as structured and semi-structured, such as images and rich media in the database, and uses the NT system cache for caching file data to reduce the performance issue.

▶ The underlying database server must be a SQL Server 2008 R2 version, and edition-wise it must be either DataCenter or Enterprise edition to host production data.

> SQL Server 2008 R2 Standard Edition also offers a similar database management solution for small organizations to run their applications with minimal IT resources.

How to do it...

To achieve a better scalability on the RAID types, the estimation of the number instances and configuration of storage/memory along with placement of database files will help on a larger scale. The following list comprises the best practice implementation in configuring server storage for scalability:

1. The content of application data must be considered to store the data in the database; estimating the content of database storage and calculating the number of documents will be determined by the SharePoint 2010 feature usage.

2. SharePoint 2010 server is designed to take advantage of database server scale out; the best practice is to host a dedicated SQL Server.

3. The guidance for 'when to deploy an additional server' will depend upon adding an additional database server when the existing web servers are running at full capacity.

4. Add an additional database server when the database storage exceeds five terabytes.

5. Configure the storage and memory L2 cache per CPU has a minimum of **2 MB** to improve memory.

> The next set of steps are essential to benefit the scalability by using the placement of data files.

6. Place the `tempdb` database data files on **RAID-1** or **RAID-1+0**, depending on their capacity requirement.

7. Select the appropriate RAID type for database files based on scalability. **RAID 1+0** or **RAID 6** will provide the best performance, but at a higher cost.

8. Place transaction logs on **RAID5** rather than **RAID1+0** for sequential workloads.

9. Create one **tempdb** file per **CPU core** and make all files equal in size.

10. Place `tempdb` files on a separate **RAID1+0** group from the database and logfiles with the fastest hard disk drives.

11. For **SharePoint server** data storage on the SQL Server database, do enable auto-create statistics as the **SharePoint Server** configures the required settings upon the provisioning and upgrade.

12. Create multiple data files equal in size for the content database. The number of data files must be less than the number of core CPUs.

13. To estimate the storage needs, the quicker way is to multiply the average row length by the number of records per month.

14. Multiply that result by the number of days', weeks', or months' worth of data that will be kept in the database to obtain the approximate amount of storage required. Add about 15 percent to this for database overhead.

How it works...

The scalability is addressed on a better scale when all the corresponding hardware configuration and tweaking is followed. Several SharePoint Server 2010 architectural factors influence storage design. The amount of content, features, and service applications used, number of farms, and availability needs are key factors.

Configuring SQL server storage architecture for quick recovery

In continuation of the previous recipe, the storage server configuration helps the data platform to keep up the scalability. Similarly, the storage architecture can also help to attain the quick recovery of data in case of failure.

Business-critical applications depend on SQL Server and its features maintain the data integrity as well as ensure data availability and performance, which requires the storage architecture to store data on high-performance and highly available storage resources.

In this recipe, we will go through the guidelines to be followed in configuring SQL Server storage architecture for quick recovery. The default features from Windows operating system Volume Shadow Copy Services (VSS) supports the SQL Server database backup and recovery to simply the data protection to ensure the high availability. The data protection strategy must be based on a recovery point and time objectives by keeping five 9s (99.999 percent) data availability with no single point of failure. The various vendors such as DELL, HP, EMC, and HITACHI can support high-end kind of enterprise-class hardware with their own provisioning software.

Getting ready

As we are configuring the storage architecture for quick recovery, the essential requirements for the server on the basis of the environment (X86 or X64) are: Windows operating system, SQL Server software, disks, and the hardware vendor's software. The following list comprises the requirements for this recipe:

- The operating system Windows 2008 X64 and Windows Server 2008 R2 versions have in-built virtualization technology called **Windows Hyper-V** for quick migration of hardware resources to provide high availability for SQL Server virtual machines.

- Ensure the use of SQL Server 2008 R2 DataCenter or Enterprise edition that provides enhanced scalability and high availability features to help the underlying operating system and hardware to accomplish the quick recovery.

- The storage platform must be available to host a dual-chassis system with up to six racks that will use the same type of logic boards and front-end port to access the back-end RAID group. The advantage with such a kind of system is to manage the storage levels up to PetaByte storage capacity.

- The Hardware vendor provisioning software will provide wide striping and thin provisioning functionalities. The disks can be managed with a feature for one or more pools of wide-striping process across many RAID groups within a Virtual Storage platform.

- Overall, the hardware components can be described for the storage system as follows:
    - 128 GB cache memory
    - 8 GB front-end ports (multiples of 2 is an ideal configuration)
    - SAS disks with 300 GB and 10K RPM
    - 4 x Quad Core Intel or AMD Opteron Processor with minimum 1.9 GHZ and 128 GB RAM equipped with 4 GB HBAs.

- The SAN configuration to use two-fiber channel switches for high availability, and servers can access the required LUNs that are mapped to the physical host.

How to do it...

The following process is essential in configuring the storage architecture for the quick recovery of data. To begin with:

1. Test the disks I/O and capacity growth for a specified configuration by using `SQLIO.exe` tool that is available from the Microsoft download center: `http://www.microsoft.com/downloads/details.aspx?familyid=9a8b005b-84e4-4f24-8d65-cb53442d9e19&displaylang=en`.

2. The disks that are presented to the SQL Server, referred to as LUNs, must be separated for each user database data and logfiles in addition to the `tempdb` system database files.

3. All the presented LUNs must be provisioned to the Provisioning tools as per the Vendor's software. The LUNs are to be divided as four redundant paths for the SQL operating system and Server 2008 binaries, user database data file, transaction logfile, and tempdb files.

4. As per the initial configuration, the two dual port host bus adapters (HBAs) must be installed for HA purpose.

5. All the LUNs are masked and zone to all four HBAs on each server as dedicated fiber channel ports on the storage platform.

6. For storage configuration, ensure that volume alignment (called sector alignment) is performed on the file system (NTFS) whenever a volume is created on a RAID device.

7. When a disk partition is formatted that will be used for SQL Server data files, it is mandatory to use a 64 KB allocation unit size for data, logs, and tempdb files.

8. When configuring HBAs on the host, ensure that the Queue Depth is set to an optimal value (depending upon the individual hardware vendor). For better scalability and performance, set the value to `64` with a discussion with the storage administrator.

9. The LUNs are catered to place database data and logfiles as separate provisioning pools in addition to tempdb files.

10. To achieve the best availability feature, it is ideal to choose RAID 1+0 for RAID groups to be presented for database and tempdb files.

11. The required disk capacity growth is calculated as 30 percent of the existing size to avoid any overhead of increase in file size during the database transactions operation.

12. Always have provisions for additional capacity to keep the backups for system and user databases, in line with the Service Level Agreement (SLA) as online availability for quicker data restores.

13. All the hardware must be hosted as 'hot-swappable' without causing any downtime to the SQL Server, where Windows Server 2008 (higher) and SQL Server Enterprise Editions support such a feature.

14. A fault-tolerant disk system such as RAID, mirrored disks, and SAN must be hosted to escalate the high availability feature for SQL Server.

This completes the essential steps in configuring storage architecture for quick recovery. These guidelines are required to build a scalable architecture that meets the performance and capacity requirements to keep up the highly available data platform.

How it works...

To validate the scalability and performance, the I/O stress tool is helpful. In addition to this tool, if the system is tuned optimally for SQL Server before the deployment, it helps us to identify hardware or I/O configuration-related issues.

The architecture reference described previously will stand as a building block-based storage solution for SQL Server data platform provision for a quick recovery. This feature provides the High Availability and flexible scalability that delivers performance by improving the resource utilization and reducing the hardware sprawl.

Managing a storage system for analyzing bottlenecks

The DBA will have a major influence for the design team given the deeper working knowledge of the SQL Server features beyond the core infrastructure. It is essential to understand the architecture for the storage system, hardware usage, and SQL Server abilities that will help us understand the business needs and design to meet the business requirements.

To reduce the bottle necks on the storage system, it is important to measure the disk throughput, which in turn helps the data transfer rate through an I/O subsystem. This is the main function for SQL Server scalability that manipulates data that resides in the memory or disk I/O, and any bottleneck on these areas will result in performance degradation of the SQL Server. There are many vendors available there to perform a certain level of benchmarking for their SAN products that can give us the benefit of required configuration for better performance.

In this recipe, we will go through the required practices in managing the storage system for analyzing bottlenecks. To provide a mission-critical platform delivery, understanding how to analyze the characteristics of I/O patterns in a data platform is useful in determining deployment requirements for any given workload.

Getting ready

It can be a challenging task to predict the hardware resources usage on a database server that doesn't exist; for the existing server there are many variables that can affect the utilization. The generic parameters/guidelines to analyze the system bottlenecks are as follows:

- ▶ 64-bit processors to address additional memory space.

- ▶ CPU-wise: L2 or L3 cache that will generally provide better performance and often play a bigger role than raw CPU frequency.

- ▶ Multi-core and multiple processors: doubling the number of CPUs is preferred to help SQL Server be efficient at parallelizing operations where the workload can be divided into multiple steps to provide increased performance on multiple CPUs.

> SQL Server 2008 R2 DataCenter edition supports up to 256 logical processors on the Windows Server 2008 R2.

- ▶ Memory: minimum at 4 GB and maximum can go up to 64 GB for better performance and reduce bottlenecks; this is ideal for OLTP applications 4 GB of memory per processor core.

- ▶ Disk subsystem: assign required storage space, take on I/O throughput per second (IOPS), and for SAN-related implementation ensure to include redundant host bus adapters and switches.

- ▶ Finally, use the network adapters and accompanying drivers from the hardware vendors to provide fault tolerance for increased throughput. It is ideal to equip the server with more than one Ethernet card. In such cases, one can be used for SQL Server traffic, one for heartbeat, and the other for operating system purposes.

- ▶ The operating system can be Windows Server 2003 R2, Windows 7, Windows Server 2008, and Windows Server 2008 R2.

- ▶ Required software for the tool to function: Microsoft Log Parser v2.2, Microsoft Office Web Components11 (OWC11), PowerShell v2.0 or higher, Microsoft .NET Framework 3.5 Service Pack 1, and Microsoft Chart Controls for Microsoft .NET Framework 3.5. Download these tools from:

    - ❑ Microsoft Log Parser v2.2 from `http://www.microsoft.com/ downloads/details.aspx?FamilyID=890cd06b-abf8-4c25-91b2- f8d975cf8c07&DisplayLang=en`.

    - ❑ Microsoft Office Web Components11 (OWC11) from `http:// www.microsoft.com/downloads/en/details. aspx?FamilyID=7287252c-402e-4f72-97a5- e0fd290d4b76&DisplayLang=en`.

    - ❑ Microsoft .NET Framework 3.5 Service Pack 1 from `http://download. microsoft.com/download/2/0/e/20e90413-712f-438c-988e- fdaa79a8ac3d/dotnetfx35.exe`.

    - ❑ Microsoft Chart Controls for Microsoft .NET Framework 3.5 from `http://www.microsoft.com/downloads/details. aspx?FamilyID=130f7986-bf49-4fe5-9ca8- 910ae6ea442c&DisplayLang=en`.

❑ PowerShell v2.0 from `http://support.microsoft.com/kb/968929`.

▶ Download Performance Analysis of Logs (PAL) tool from `http://pal.codeplex.com/releases/view/6759`.

▶ Additionally, we will use references to the `Performance Monitor` tool, which is a built-in tool in the `Windows Server` and desktop operating system.

How to do it...

The following are important steps that will help in managing storage systems for analyzing bottlenecks. These are essential to act in a proactive manner when a performance problem occurs:

1. Install the **PAL** tool by clicking on the `PAL_Setup_V2.0.6_x64.msi` file.

2. Gather the storage system-related counters using **PERFMON** (Performance Monitor) tool for the following counters:

   ❑ Physical Disk: percent Disk Time

   ❑ Physical Disk: percent Disk Read time

   ❑ Physical Disk: percent Disk Write time

   ❑ Physical Disk: Avg. Disk Queue Length

   ❑ Physical Disk: Avg. Disk sec/Transfer

   ❑ Physical Disk: Current Disk Queue Length

   ❑ Physical Disk: Disk Bytes/sec

   ❑ Physical Disk: Disk Transfers/sec

   ❑ Paging File: Paging File percent Usage and percent Usage Peak

3. Store these performance monitoring data in a `.blg` or `.csv` file in order to analyze the data for the **PAL** tool.

4. Copy the collected performance monitoring data to a folder where the **PAL** tool will be directed to extract the required information.

5. Run the **PAL** tool from the desktop and choose a `threshold` file to perform further analysis collection.

6. Click on the **Analysis** button to process the `threshold` file; the execution will be resource-intensive, which can take several minutes to complete.

7. Once the **PAL** analysis is completed, a HTML-based report will be displayed on the local browser. The report consists of an itemized table of contents that will show a number of alerts raised for each analysis.

8. Each of that analysis information will present a chart of collected performance counter, which contains analyses, description, references, and raised alerts.

9. Also, a chronological view show of alerts will help us correlate the symptoms of any storage-related problems. This is the best tool to perform any baseline and benchmarking procedures.

This completes the required steps to perform and manage a storage system for analyzing bottlenecks.

How it works...

The initial process of the tool is in sequential order—the `Relog.exe` from the Log Parser tool will filter the required performance-monitoring data that is being collected. Internally, this tool will break down the log into a smaller chunk that will analyze for `min`, `max`, `avg`, and `threshold` values. The alerts will be raised and reported when a default threshold is broken, where each analysis will contain zero or more thresholds, which is an internal mechanism to access. All the PAL-related threshold files will contain a large number of analyses to perform that will effectively analyze performance monitor logs to raise their importance and awareness of common.

> The GUI interface will help to perform batch processing of multiple perfmon logs, and the GUI editor is added to help with editing and creating a user-defined PAL threshold file.

The PAL core processing engine uses VBScript and .NET framework for GUI purposes. The tool will include all the new threshold files for IIS, Active Directory, MOSS/SharePoint, Biztalk, and SQL Server, which works with the operating system UAC control feature.

9
Troubleshooting

In this chapter, we will cover:

- ▸ Implementing systematized monitoring methods for data platform optimization

- ▸ Designing a filtered indexes and statistics feature

- ▸ Implementing table hints for advanced query tuning performance

- ▸ Implementing query hints for optimized performance

- ▸ Designing sustainable locking methods to improve concurrency

- ▸ Implementing parallel query processing methods

- ▸ Implementing the plan guide to enhance compile-time and runtime execution plans

- ▸ Configuring and managing storage system for optimized defragmentation processes

- ▸ Building best usage processes of Dynamic Management Views

- ▸ Implementing a benchmarking framework on multiple instances

Introduction

Troubleshooting is an important step in every database platform because RDBMS applications are self-tuned to some extent. Over a period of time, the data will be inserted and manipulated, then the performance will be degraded causing a slow response and sometimes unavailability of data. In such cases, we must ensure to build up processes and procedures to monitor SQL Server performance that can help optimize the required database objects, which lead to troubleshooting practices implementation.

In this chapter, we will go through highly-essential and most-required techniques using SQL Server 2008 and specific SQL Server 2008 R2 features. The troubleshooting will begin with monitoring methods and various available features such as filtered indexes, table hints, query hints, and perform parallel query processing methods by taking advantage of hardware and system resources.

Implementing systematized monitoring methods for data platform optimization

Optimization is a key level of achievement for every data platform, and SQL Server is not an exception. To accomplish performance optimization, it is essential to understand the aspects of SQL Server tuning and the approach is multi-layered. The process to keep up the optimization at sustainable levels is quite challenging and a continual activity. It is highly required to adopt the reliable methods for data platform optimization using SQL Server features.

There are different methods available in SQL Server. Using the tools and commands technique, we can help evaluate and troubleshoot the query performance. In order to achieve this, we must address the fragmented indexes and outdated statistics on the table that is suffering a performance loss. There are various best practices available and involved to evaluate query performance, which can be used as a checklist. But, these practices provide a basic level of query performance tuning guidelines.

In this recipe, we will go through a summarized view of major monitoring activities and methods that can have a demonstrable impact on fine tuning the optimization for the SQL Server data platform. The demonstration methods involve the usage of **Dynamic Management Views** (**DMVs**), server-side trace, obtaining an estimated query execution plan, and capturing performance statistics for cached query plans to evaluate query performance.

Getting ready

In order to simulate the performance optimization statistics, let us execute the following TSQL queries against `AdventureWorks2008R2` database:

Use the following TSQL statement to prepare the recipe and enable the monitoring methods:

```
--Use AdventureWorks2008R2 database and
--generate few long running queries to capture the information for
performance evaluation
USE Adventureworks2008R2
Go

SET SHOWPLAN_TEXT ON
GO
SET STATISTICS IO ON
GO
SELECT CreditCardID,CardType,CardNumber
FROM Sales.CreditCard
WHERE (CardType='Vista' and CreditCardID<>'' and
ModifiedDate>='2008-04-01')
GO
```

```
SET SHOWPLAN_TEXT OFF
GO


SET SHOWPLAN_TEXT ON
GO
SELECT CurrencyRateID,FromCurrencyCode,ToCurrencyCode,EndOfDayRate
FROM Sales.CurrencyRate
WHERE (CurrencyRateDate>'2005-06-30' and ModifiedDate<'2005-07-31')
GO
SET SHOWPLAN_TEXT OFF
GO


SET SHOWPLAN_TEXT ON
GO
SELECT BusinessEntityID,CreditCardID
FROM Sales.PersonCreditCard
WHERE (ModifiedDate>='2005-06-01' and ModifiedDate<='2007-07-31')
GO
SET SHOWPLAN_TEXT OFF
GO


SET SHOWPLAN_TEXT ON
GO
SELECT PersonType, FirstName,LastName,EmailPromotion,Demographics
FROM Person.Person
WHERE (ModifiedDate>'2003-01-01' and BusinessEntityID>4500)
GO
SET SHOWPLAN_TEXT OFF
GO
SET STATISTICS IO OFF
GO


--Currently executing queries
SELECT sqltext.TEXT,
der.session_id, der.status, der.command,
der.cpu_time, der.total_elapsed_time
FROM sys.dm_exec_requests der
CROSS APPLY sys.dm_exec_sql_text(sql_handle) AS sqltext
```

The preceding queries should generate the required information to evaluate the performance statistics.

How to do it...

The following steps are required in implementing systematized monitoring methods for data platform optimization to fine tune the queries:

1. Use the **SQL Server Management Studio** tool and right-click on SQL Server instance. Choose the **Activity Monitor** tool to open.

2. Overview the **% Processor Time**, **Waiting Tasks**, **Database I/O**, and **Batch Requests** status on the selected SQL Server instance.

3. Expand the **Recent Expensive Queries** tab to show the list of queries that are running slow.

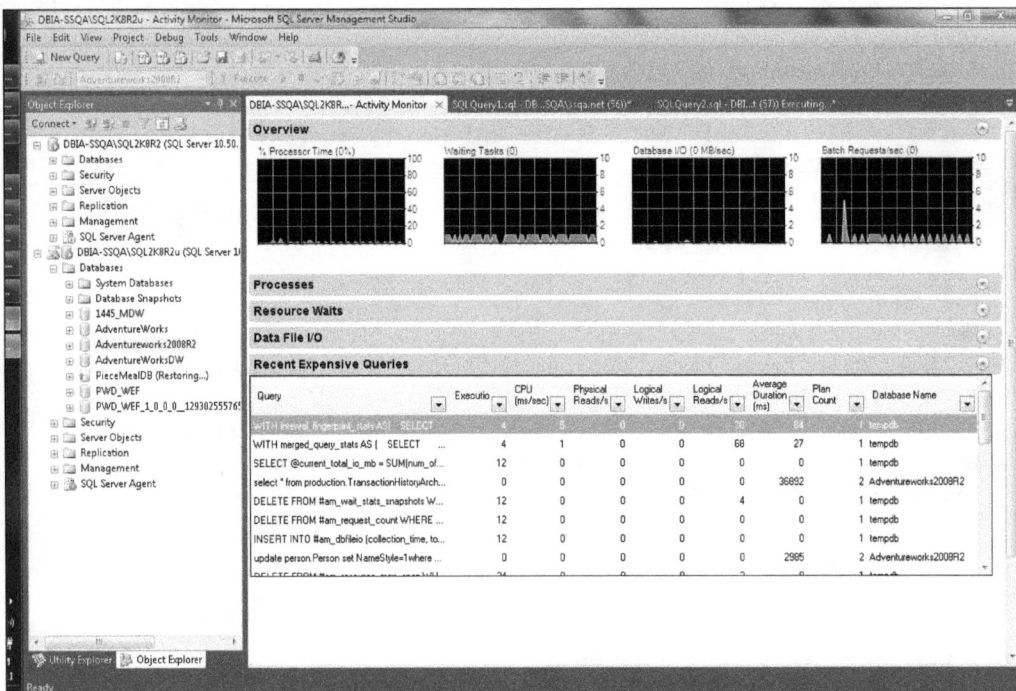

2. On the **Recent Expensive Queries** tab, select any of the queries against AdventureWorks2008R2 database to obtain the query execution plan. Right-click on any row and choose **Show Execution Plan**.

3. The show plan launches the graphical image that we get from a query editor from the query plan cache.

4. On the show plan window, we can observe the hint about **Missing Index (Impact %)** and suggestion to create an appropriate index displayed along with syntax to create that index.

5. The preceding information can also be obtained by using `sys.dm_exec_cached_plans` DMV along with the information about how many times the plan has been used during the query execution. Use the following TSQL:

```
SELECT * FROM
(SELECT user_seeks * avg_total_user_cost * (avg_user_impact *
0.01) AS
index_advantage, migs.* FROM sys.dm_db_missing_index_group_stats
migs) AS
migs_adv
INNER JOIN sys.dm_db_missing_index_groups AS mig
ON migs_adv.group_handle = mig.index_group_handle
INNER JOIN sys.dm_db_missing_index_details AS mid
ON mig.index_handle = mid.index_handle
ORDER BY migs_adv.index_advantage
```

6. Further, let us obtain more details on missing index information. Right-click in the **Execution plan** to select the **Missing Index Details** option to open a new **Query** window to execute the creation of new index.

7. Further, let us obtain the aggregated performance statistics based on the preceding query execution. To get the relevant information, execute the following TSQL:

```
SELECT t.text,
st.total_logical_reads
FROM sys.dm_exec_query_stats st
CROSS APPLY sys.dm_exec_sql_text(st.sql_handle) t
```

8. Also, execute the following TSQL to obtain additional query monitoring performance:

```
;WITH CTE([QExecCount], [Total Disk IO], [Avg Disk IO],
[QueryStmtText], [QPlan], [QueyHash], [QueryPlanHash])
```

```
AS
(
  SELECT TOP 20
    SUM(execution_count) AS QExecCount,
      SUM(total_physical_reads + total_logical_reads + total_
logical_writes) AS [Total Disk IO],
      SUM(total_physical_reads + total_logical_reads + total_
logical_writes) / SUM(execution_count) AS [Avg Disk IO],
      MIN(query_text) AS QueryStmtText,
      MIN(plan_handle) AS QPlan,
      query_hash AS QueryHash,
      query_plan_hash AS QueryPlanHash
  FROM
    (
    SELECT
      qs.*,
      SUBSTRING(qt.[text], qs.statement_start_offset/2, (
      CASE
        WHEN qs.statement_end_offset = -1 THEN
LEN(CONVERT(NVARCHAR(MAX), qt.[text])) * 2
        ELSE qs.statement_end_offset
          END - qs.statement_start_offset)/2
              ) AS query_text
          FROM
              sys.dm_exec_query_stats AS qs
              CROSS APPLY sys.dm_exec_sql_text(qs.[sql_handle])
AS qt
          WHERE qt.[text] NOT LIKE '%sys.dm_exec_query_stats%'
      ) AS query_stats
    GROUP BY query_hash, query_plan_hash
    ORDER BY [Avg Disk IO] DESC
)
SELECT
[dbid],[objectid],[QueryStmtText],[QExecCount],[Total Disk
IO],[Avg Disk IO], [query_plan]

--    TotalExecutions, [Total IO], [Avg IO],
   StatementTextForExample,
   tp.query_plan AS StatementPlan,
   QueyHash, QueryPlanHash
FROM
   CTE
   OUTER APPLY sys.dm_exec_query_plan(QPlan) AS tp
WHERE [dbid]>4
ORDER BY [dbid],[Avg Disk IO],[Total Disk IO] DESC;
```

This completes the required steps in implementing systematized monitoring methods for data platform optimization to fine tune the queries.

How it works...

We started using the SSMS tool to obtain the information and TSQL-based monitoring methods that will help to start optimizing the frequently running queries. The executed DMVs data is grouped at the instance level and subgrouped from the database level to collate the information required in performance troubleshooting. The information obtained here gives performance `waits` that indicate the actual problem on system resources such as disk, network, and memory. To talk about the process, we started with the SSMS tool by looking at the `Activity Monitor` and the `query execution plan`; these tools give high-level information on system resources usage with an explanation on the steps that are followed during a query execution. The monitor and query plan also help us to suggest the missing index for that query execution, which can be tested on the current database by retrying execution of the same query.

Further, we have used DMV to get information on how many times the query execution plan is used at the time of the query execution. The DMV started with the user-seeks from the `sys.dm_db_missing_index_group_stats` and joined with two other DMVs, `sys.dm_db_missing_index_groups` and `sys.dm_db_missing_index_details`, based on the handle condition. The DMV `sys.dm_db_index_usage_stats` gives us the information on what indexes are used on that instance since the last restart of SQL Server services. The `sys.dm_exec_query_stats` DMV is used to obtain metrics about what queries are running and how often; here, we used it to return aggregate performance statistics for cached query plans. Initially, this DMV might return inaccurate results if there is a workload currently executing on the server. Hence, it is executed within a **common table expression** (**CTE**). This recursive CTE is executed repeatedly to return subsets of data until the complete result set is obtained. SQL Server 2008 introduced a new column called `query_hash`, which gives the aggregated statistics on the query execution by using a common table expression function.

Designing a filtered indexes and statistics feature

Scalability and performance are the common buzzwords whenever we are dealing with large data sets, and to help further, indexes and statistics play an important role in query performance. A Database Administrator or Developer needs a good understanding of the indexing methods, which can result in efficient practices to return the required subset of data based upon the index key columns and their values.

Inside the database, the data is inserted, deleted, and updated frequently; to return subsequent results efficiently, indexes are helpful. However, NULL values are present in the data, and if it is likely that null values are stored in the data on a larger scale, the indexes will need efficient design for better performance.

In addition to the disk space required for Index DDL operations, temporary disk space is required for sorting (one new index at a time), unless the query optimizer finds the relevant execution plan that does not require sorting.

On the other hand, with the number of rows and column keys, the index will occupy large storage space, and having an index on every table is not sufficient. To filter the result's null values will have a heavy workload, and indexes must support the query optimizer to obtain a well-defined subset of data.

As and when data is inserted, the table size grows, and equally the index management is essential for query optimization. To manage such large indexes, SQL Server 2008 has introduced a new enhancement to scalability and performance by introducing the filtered indexes and statistics feature. In any case, keeping up the statistics on the table will offer a performance advantage.

Filtered index is an optimized non-clustered index, which means only a non-clustered index can be a part of a filtered index that is best suited for the query execution processes, which selects a small percentage of rows from a given table.

In this recipe, let us work on processes in designing a filtered indexes and statistics feature that will introduce the ability to create supportive indexes on a subset of rows without having a need to create an index on a large table.

Getting ready

The key point to designing effective filtered indexes is to understand what query the application is using and how the query execution relates to subsets of data. As database designers on the active tables in the databases, we must decide a better indexing strategy by selecting one column among the key columns as a primary key. By default, SQL Server creates a clustered index whenever a primary key is chosen.

A best reference for such a subset of data that can be related that have well-defined subsets are columns with mostly NULL values. For instance, a table `Production.Product` in `AdventureWorks2008R2` database consists of over 10,000 rows and 40 percent of data columns with heterogeneous categories of values such as `color`, `reorderpoint`, `listprice`, `weight`, and `style` with unique characteristics for each product category. Whereas the frequent queries are executed on a certain category of data, this is where we can improve the performance of queries for that data by creating a filtered index on the category.

How to do it...

The following steps are required in designing a filtered indexes and statistics feature using TSQL tasks:

1. In this recipe, we will use the `Production.TransactionHistoryArchive` table from the `AdventureWorks2008R2` database.

2. The table consists of one clustered index on the `TransactionID` column and one non-clustered index on the `ProductID` column, and holds more than 89,000 rows.

3. Assuming that we need to update the `ActualCost` column for a certain value on the `ProductID` column for a specified year—as a part of a year-end process—creating a full index on this table on the `ActualCost` and `ProductID` columns may be considered as an uneconomical method.

4. On the **SSMS** from **Query** option, select **Include Actual Execution Plan** and execute the following TSQL statement:

    ```
    SET STATISTICS IO ON
    GO
    SELECT TransactionID,TransactionDate,ProductID,ReferenceOrderID,Tr
    ansactionType,Quantity,ActualCost,ModifiedDate
    FROM Production.TransactionHistoryArchive
    WHERE ModifiedDate > '2006-01-01' and ModifiedDate < '2006-12-31'
    AND Quantity > 1
    SET STATISTICS IO OFF
    GO
    ```

5. Running the preceding query with query statistics presents the following information along with the execution plan:

    ```
    --Execution Statistics
    --(26499 row(s) affected)
    --Table 'TransactionHistoryArchive'. Scan count 1, logical reads
    622, physical reads 0, read-ahead reads 0, lob logical reads 0,
    lob physical reads 0, lob read-ahead reads 0.
    ```

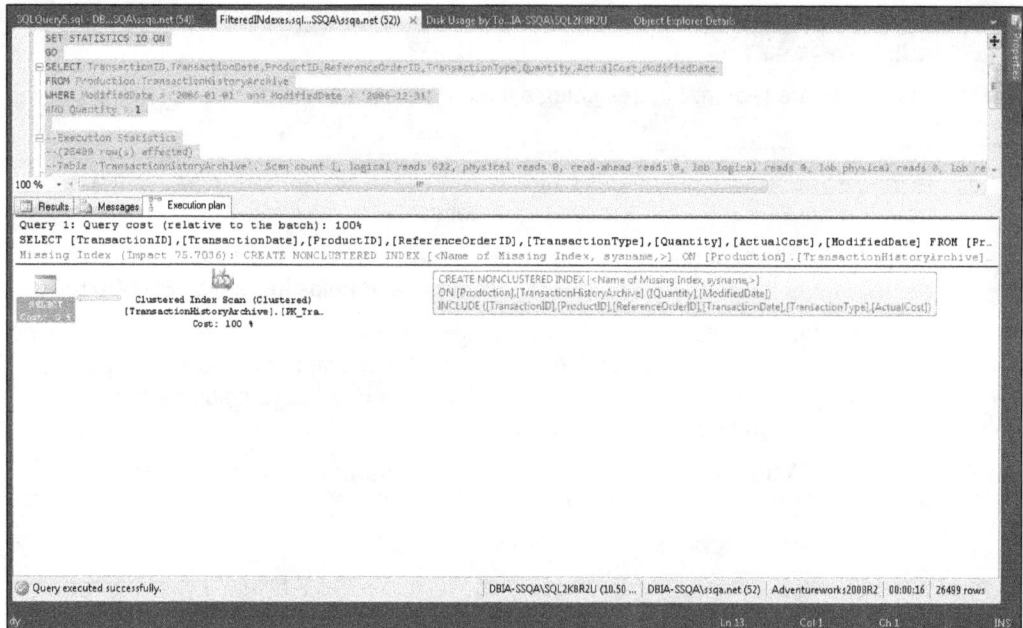

6. It is evident that the query is using a Clustered Index Scan on the `Production.TransactionHistoryArchive` table with the **scan count** and **logical reads** from the disk.

7. By selecting the actual execution plan during the query execution gives us information on the missing index too, where it is suggesting to create a `NONCLUSTERED` index on `Quantity`, `ModifiedData` by including `TransactionID`, `ProductID`, `ReferenceOrderID`, `TransactionDate`, `TransactionType`, and `ActualCost` columns.

8. So, to create the missing index as per the preceding information, on the query results window at the **Execution plan** tab, right-click and choose **Missing Index Details**. It will present a new query window with the following TSQL:

```
/*
Missing Index Details from FilteredINdexes.sql - DBIA-SSQA\
SQL2K8R2u.Adventureworks2008R2 (DBIA-SSQA\ssqa.net (52))
The Query Processor estimates that implementing the following
index could improve the query cost by 75.7036%.
*/

/*
USE [Adventureworks2008R2]
GO
CREATE NONCLUSTERED INDEX [<Name of Missing Index, sysname,>]
```

```
ON [Production].[TransactionHistoryArchive]
([Quantity],[ModifiedDate])
INCLUDE ([TransactionID],[ProductID],[ReferenceOrderID],[Transacti
onDate],[TransactionType],[ActualCost])
GO
*/
```

9. The improvement in the query execution cost is displayed as over 75%, which is a benefit when the query is executed frequently.

10. As per the suggested NONCLUSTERED index information and from the query text, let us replace [<Name of Missing Index, sysname,>] with [IX_ TransactionHistoryArchive_FilteredIdx_Quantity_ModifiedDate] and execute in the query window.

11. Again, execute the query from step 4. The results are presented as follows:

    --Post NONCLUSTERED suggested index creation results

    --Execution Statistics

    --(26499 row(s) affected)

    --Table 'TransactionHistoryArchive'. Scan count 1, logical reads 333, physical reads 0, read-ahead reads 0, lob logical reads 0, lob physical reads 0, lob read-ahead reads 0.

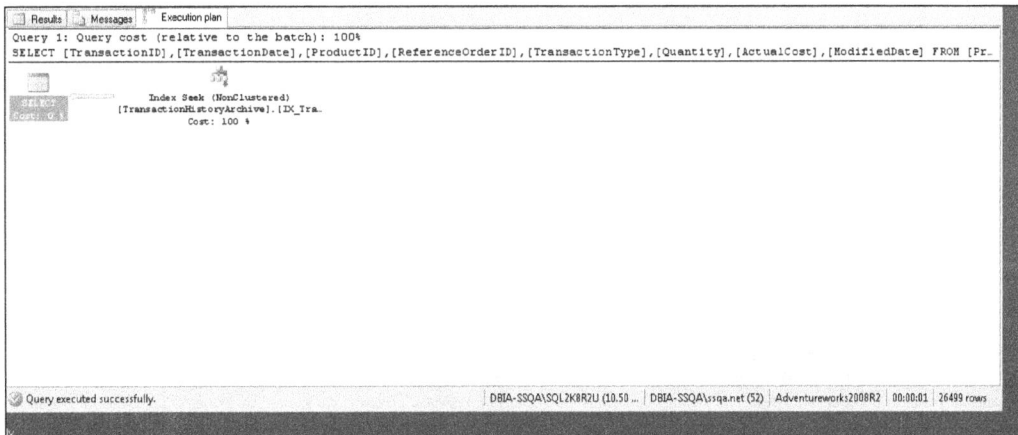

12. Continuing the discussion from step 3, proceed towards the creation of the new NONCLUSTERED index for the update query. Initially, we execute the update query without the supporting index as follows:

```
UPDATE Production.TransactionHistoryArchive SET
ActualCost=213.2999
WHERE ProductID >801 and ProductID<825 and
ModifiedDate>'2006-01-01' and ModifiedDate<'2006-12-31'
```

13. The execution results and execution plan are as follows:

```
Table 'TransactionHistoryArchive'. Scan count 1, logical reads
622, physical reads 0, read-ahead reads 0, lob logical reads 0,
lob physical reads 0, lob read-ahead reads 0.
(5222 row(s) affected)
```

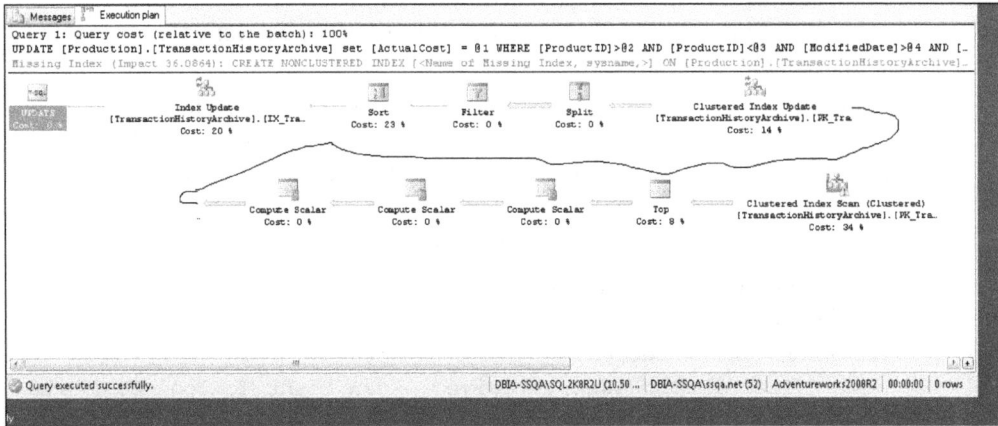

14. Create the required filtered index as follows:

```
USE [Adventureworks2008R2]
GO
CREATE NONCLUSTERED INDEX [IX_TransactionHistoryArchive_Upd_
ActualCost_ProductId]
ON [Production].[TransactionHistoryArchive]
([ModifiedDate],[ProductId]) where [ActualCost] IS NOT NULL
```

15. Once the preceding index is created, let us execute the update query from step 12. The execution plan results are presented as follows:

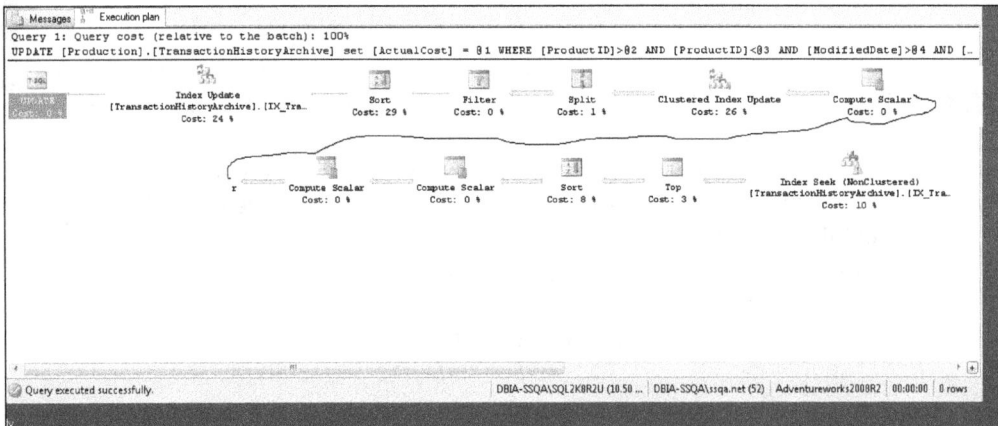

This completes the essential steps in designing a filtered indexes and statistics feature using TSQL tasks.

How it works...

The filtered index is an optimized nonclustered index especially suited to cover queries from a well-defined subset of data. The execution plan quality is more accurate than full table statistics because they cover only the rows in the filtered index. Also, when the filtered index contains only the frequently affected data with SELECT and UPDATE queries, the smaller size of index reduces the cost of updating the statistics.

In this recipe, we begin with a table having a large number of rows and a frequently executed query with the values such as:

```
ModifiedDate > '2006-01-01' and ModifiedDate < '2006-12-31'
AND Quantity > 1
```

Using the SET STATISTICS IO option and selecting **Include Actual Execution Plan** from the query editor obtains a detailed execution plan and statistics. The feature of the execution plan gives the hint of the missing index on that query and by creating a supportive index has improved the execution of the same query. Similarly, we select a subset of data to be updated for the ActualCost and ProductID columns and create supportive nonclustered index that helps the query optimizer to use an effective plan with this index.

In the filtered indexes, the filter predicate allows a logic using operators such as IN, IS NOT, =, <>, !>, and so on. The filtered statistics are created along with filtered indexes that will help the optimizer to use the same filter predicate to produce accurate results by taking the sampling from the statistics.

Implementing table hints for advanced query tuning performance

The table hints are similar to query hints that have been part of SQL Server since SQL Server 2000. The hints are useful to override query optimizer behavior during SELECT, INSERT, UPDATE, and DELETE execution tasks. Similarly, using the index hints in a TSQL query can reduce the query optimizer from choosing a specified execute plan. There are certain restrictions on using hints, such as both NOLOCK and HOLDLOCK cannot be used together.

SQL Server 2008 introduced a new feature called FORCESEEK table hint that will force seek over a scan during the query execution. Not all the time, query optimizer may choose an effective plan. Also, if the data platform is highly volatile, it requires the table statistics to be updated on a regular basis, otherwise a bad plan is generated during the frequently running query execution. The best place to provide table hints when the query intent to perform a single-time lookup with a specific value on a large table with more than a million rows, and by default the optimizer will scan the entire index before returning the value. In such cases, the disk IO costs from that index scan can prove costly, causing further slow response. In such situations, ensure that we manage to execute updated statistics on that table, then consider using the new table hint FORCESEEK. In this recipe, we will go through the demonstration of implementing table hints that will help the query performance tuning.

How to do it...

As the table hint is used during the duration of the DML statement's execution, the process is to use the TSQL statement. The following steps are required in implementing table hints for advanced query performance tuning:

1. In this recipe, we will use the Production.TransactionHistoryArchive table from the AdventureWorks2008R2 database.

2. The table consist of one unique clustered index, PK_TransactionHistoryArchive_TransactionID, on the TransactionID column, and two nonclustered indexes. The two indexes are a non-unique IX_TransactionHistoryArchive_ProductID on the ProductID column and non-unique IX_TransactionHistoryArchive_Upd_ActualCost_ProductId on the ActualCost and ProductId columns.

3. As a reporting requirement, we need to obtain the data pertaining to a specific product and product modified date.

4. On **SQL Server Management Studio** (**SSMS**) from Query, choose **Display Estimated Execution Plan** for the following TSQL statements:

```
SET STATISTICS IO ON
GO
USE Adventureworks2008R2
GO
SELECT TransactionID, ProductID,TransactionDate,ModifiedDate FROM
Production.TransactionHistoryArchive
WHERE   ProductID >710 AND
ModifiedDate >= '2007-01-01'
GO
```

5. The result is the graphical estimated execution plan that is as follows:

```
--Query statistics
/*

(31921 row(s) affected)
Table 'TransactionHistoryArchive'. Scan count 1, logical reads
622, physical reads 0, read-ahead reads 0, lob logical reads 0,
lob physical reads 0, lob read-ahead reads 0.
*/
```

6. The default choice of query optimizer has to verify the existence of a nonclustered index on the conditional columns.

   The optimizer has to choose either index on the ModifiedDate column to locate required rows and then look up the corresponding through the clustered index.

7. But, in this case, the graphical execution plan confirms the Clustered Index Scan PK_TransactionHistoryArchive_TransactionID and filters out the unmatched rows.

8. The query plan estimates the cost as 622 logical reads; one read per page of the table.

9. To help the optimizer, it has been decided to create a `nonclustered` index on the `ModifiedDate` column by including the `ProductID` column as follows:

```
--Create an additional NONCLUSTERED INDEX
USE [Adventureworks2008R2]
'GO
CREATE NONCLUSTERED INDEX [IX_TransactionHistoryArchive_
ModifiedDate]
ON [Production].[TransactionHistoryArchive] ([ModifiedDate])
INCLUDE ([ProductID])
GO
```

10. As we have created the `IX_TransactionHistoryArchive_ModifiedDate` index, let us check the execution plan of the query that is executed on step 4 without executing as follows:

```
--Check the execution plan without executing the query
SET STATISTICS IO ON
GO
USE Adventureworks2008R2
GO
SET SHOWPLAN_ALL ON
GO
SELECT TransactionID, ProductID,TransactionDate,ModifiedDate FROM
Production.TransactionHistoryArchive
WHERE  ProductID >710 AND
ModifiedDate >= '2007-01-01'
GO
```

11. Remember, we haven't executed the query, but we are able to obtain the query execution plan using the `SET SHOWPLAN_ALL` statement, and the result is as follows:

	StmtText	StmtId	NodeId	Parent	PhysicalOp	LogicalOp	Argument	DefinedValues	EstimateRows	EstimateIO	EstimateCPU
1	SELECT TransactionID, ProductI...	1	1	0	NULL	NULL	1	NULL	30458.89	NULL	NULL
2	I-Clustered Index Scan(OBJECT...	1	2	1	Clustered Index Sc...	Clustered Index Sc...	OBJECT:[[Adventurew...	[Adventureworks2008...	30458.89	0.4616435	0.0983353

AvgRowSize	TotalSubtreeCost	OutputList		Warnings	Type	Parallel	EstimateExecutions
NULL	0.5599788	NULL		NULL	SELECT	0	NULL
31	0.5599788	[Adventureworks2008R2].[Produ...		NULL	PLAN_ROW	0	1

12. The estimated show plan confirms the usage of the clustered index scan again, which is a costly affair in case of returning large number of rows. So, the optimizer has ignored the creation of a new `nonclustered` index on `SARGable` columns `ModifiedDate` and `ProductID`.

13. Now, let us use the required hint `FORCESEEK` on the preceding query to see the query execution difference that can reduce the resource usage.

14. Execute the following TSQL statement:

```
--Check the execution plan without executing the query
USE Adventureworks2008R2
GO
SET STATISTICS IO ON
GO
SET SHOWPLAN_ALL ON
GO
--Using FORCESEEK hint
SELECT TransactionID, ProductID,TransactionDate,ModifiedDate FROM
Production.TransactionHistoryArchive
WITH (FORCESEEK)
WHERE  ProductID >710 AND
ModifiedDate >= '2007-01-01'
GO
```

15. The query execution plan displays as follows:

	StmtText	StmtId	NodeId	Parent	PhysicalOp	LogicalOp	Argument	DefinedValues	EstimateRows
1	--Using FORCESEEK hint SELECT Transa...	1	1	0	NULL	NULL	1	NULL	30458.89
2	I-Nested Loops(Inner Join, OUTER REFE...	1	2	1	Nested Loops	Inner Join	OUTER REFERENCES:([Adventurew...	NULL	30458.89
3	I-Index Seek(OBJECT:([Adventurewor...	1	4	2	Index Seek	Index Seek	OBJECT:([Adventureworks2008R2].[...	[Adventureworks2008R2].[Producti...	30458.89
4	I-Clustered Index Seek(OBJECT:([Adv...	1	6	2	Clustered Index Seek	Clustered Index Seek	OBJECT:([Adventureworks2008R2].[...	[Adventureworks2008R2].[Producti...	1

EstimateIO	EstimateCPU	AvgRowSize	TotalSubtreeCost	OutputList	Warnings	Type	Parallel	EstimateExecutions
NULL	NULL	NULL	7.009999	NULL	NULL	SELECT	0	NULL
0	0.1273182	31	7.009999	[Adventureworks2008R2].[Production].[Transaction...	NULL	PLAN_ROW	0	1
0.06905092	0.0422232	23	0.1112741	[Adventureworks2008R2].[Production].[Transaction...	NULL	PLAN_ROW	0	1
0.003125	0.0001581	15	6.75305	[Adventureworks2008R2].[Production].[Transaction...	NULL	PLAN_ROW	0	30458.89

16. Observe the difference between the **EstimatedIO**, **EstimatedCPU**, and **TotalSubtreeCost** columns.

17. Also, let us execute the following TSQL to use the newly created `nonclustered` index by selecting **Include Actual Execution Plan** from the **Query** option in **SSMS**:

```
--Choose Include Actual Execution Plan option
--Using FORCESEEK hint
SELECT TransactionID, ProductID,TransactionDate,ModifiedDate FROM
Production.TransactionHistoryArchive
WITH (FORCESEEK ,INDEX (IX_TransactionHistoryArchive_
ModifiedDate))
WHERE  ProductID >710 AND
ModifiedDate >= '2007-01-01'
GO
```

18. The final result for the preceding TSQL along with table hints are displayed as follows:

This completes the required steps in implementing table hints for advanced query performance tuning.

How it works...

In this recipe, we started with a query that is used as a reporting requirement. We need to obtain the data pertaining to a specific product and the product modified date. We also checked the estimated execution plan for the query to obtain missing indexes information where a clustered index scan is shown, and also resource usage such as disk IO and CPU. In this process, as per the missing index information, we created a new `nonclustered` index, but the query optimizer still opted to choose `clustered index` scan. The new table hint `FORCESEEK` allows the query optimizer to force a query to use clustered or nonclustered index seek access. This hint is also helpful to forceseek when the predicate may not be getting a good cardinality estimate of data. In such cases, a seek is incorrectly calculated by the execution plan, which is treated more expensive than the usual data correlation.

At this point, we used the `FORCESEEK` hint; this hint can be used in the `FROM` clause of a DML statement by using a `WITH` keyword. This overrides the query optimizer's original choice of the clustered index scan access path and chooses the path of using the newly created index by using the `index seek` operation. In addition to the `FORCESEEK` hint, we used a query hint to use specific index to choose. The bottom line is only use this new table hint when you are in total control in your table design and data to perform the updated statistics on the table, otherwise the SQL Server query optimizer will choose the most optimal path to execute.

Implementing query hints for optimized performance

In continuation of the previous recipe, the query hints are useful when you are in control on table design and data, and not to mention about data distribution, which is a critical aspect to obtain optimized performance. However, the query hints implementation is not a compulsion to use at all times. The hints will always provide a short-term result – that satisfies the existing result set – which may not be efficient over a period of time due to the data changes on the table. A new enhancement has been added to the OPTIMIZE FOR UNKNOWN query hint to include new statistical data to determine values for local variables during the query optimization instead of default values. Similarly, if the data is spread across multiple tables (skewed data distribution), the OPTIMZIZE FOR clause could be used to optimize for a generic value. In such situations, this query hint might provide reasonable performance for a wide range of parameter values.

In this recipe, we will go through the high-level demonstration of implementing 'essential' query hints for the optimized performance of a data platform. The essential query hints used in this recipe are OPTIMIZE FOR UNKNOWN and RECOMPILE, which are enhanced in SQL Server 2008. We will use AdventureWorks2008R2 database in the code examples that are used to generate conditional basis queries.

How to do it...

In this recipe, we will use a query for a report to find names of employees who have sold a product. The following steps are required in implementing query hints for optimized performance:

1. Use the following TSQL statement along with the query statistics for the preceding requirement:

```
SET STATISTICS IO ON
GO
USE AdventureWorks2008R2;
GO
SELECT DISTINCT p.LastName, p.FirstName,e.LoginID
FROM Person.Person AS p
JOIN HumanResources.Employee AS e
    ON e.BusinessEntityID = p.BusinessEntityID
WHERE p.BusinessEntityID IN
(SELECT SalesPersonID  FROM Sales.SalesOrderHeader
WHERE SalesOrderID IN
(SELECT SalesOrderID FROM Sales.SalesOrderDetail
WHERE ProductID IN
(SELECT ProductID FROM Production.Product p
WHERE ProductNumber NOT like 'BK-R%')));
GO
```

2. The query result returns 17 employees and the statistics as follows:

```
Table 'Worktable'. Scan count 1, logical reads 16425, physical
reads 0, read-ahead reads 0, lob logical reads 0, lob physical
reads 0, lob read-ahead reads 0.
Table 'Product'. Scan count 1, logical reads 4, physical reads 0,
read-ahead reads 0, lob logical reads 0, lob physical reads 0, lob
read-ahead reads 0.
Table 'SalesOrderDetail'. Scan count 3806, logical reads 11499,
physical reads 0, read-ahead reads 0, lob logical reads 0, lob
physical reads 0, lob read-ahead reads 0.
Table 'SalesOrderHeader'. Scan count 290, logical reads 623,
physical reads 0, read-ahead reads 0, lob logical reads 0, lob
physical reads 0, lob read-ahead reads 0.
Table 'Person'. Scan count 0, logical reads 888, physical reads 0,
read-ahead reads 0, lob logical reads 0, lob physical reads 0, lob
read-ahead reads 0.
Table 'Employee'. Scan count 1, logical reads 9, physical reads 0,
read-ahead reads 0, lob logical reads 0, lob physical reads 0, lob
read-ahead reads 0.
```

3. Further to the preceding selection of product sales, let us instruct the query optimizer to use statistical data instead of initial data values. Use the following TSQL:

```
--Use the statistical data
DECLARE @LoginID NVARCHAR(250)
SET @LoginID='adventure-works\ranjit0'

SELECT TOP 5 * FROM HumanResources.Employee WHERE LoginID=@LoginID
OPTION (OPTIMIZE FOR UNKNOWN)
```

4. In addition to the preceding query hint OPTIMIZE FOR UNKNOWN, now let us instruct the query optimizer to use a particular value for the local variable by using the following TSQL:

```
--Use a particular data value
DECLARE @LoginID NVARCHAR(250)
SET @LoginID='adventure-works\ranjit0'

SELECT TOP 5 * FROM HumanResources.Employee WHERE LoginID=@LoginID
OPTION (OPTIMIZE FOR (@LoginId='adventure-works\ranjit0'))

SET STATISTICS IO OFF
GO
```

This completes the process for the OPTIMIZE FOR UNKNOWN hint. Let us work out the RECOMPILE hint.

5. In this recipe, we will obtain all the rows from the `Products` table by returning total sales and discounts for each production plus total revenue calculation for each product.

6. The required TSQL is shown as follows:

```
--The following examples return all rows from the Product table
based on the following condition:
--the first level query returns total sales and the discounts for
each product.
--in the second level query, the total revenue is calculated for
each product.
USE AdventureWorks2008R2;
GO
DECLARE @ProductName nvarchar(25)
SET @ProductName like'%Bike%'
SELECT distinct p.Name AS ProductName,
NonDiscountSales = (OrderQty * UnitPrice),
Discounts = ((OrderQty * UnitPrice) * UnitPriceDiscount)
FROM Production.Product AS p
INNER JOIN Sales.SalesOrderDetail AS sod
ON p.ProductID = sod.ProductID AND
p.Name = @ProductName
ORDER BY ProductName,Discounts ASC;
GO
```

7. The query returns 21 rows for the `@ProductName = 'Bike Wash – Dissolver'` value.

8. Now, let us obtain the information on the compiled plan in the memory:

```
--Obtain the information about a compiled plan in the memory that
is reused based on the number of executions
SELECT refcounts,cacheobjtype, objtype, usecounts,size_in_bytes
FROM sys.dm_exec_cached_plans
CROSS APPLY sys.dm_exec_sql_text(plan_handle)
WHERE text LIKE 'DECLARE @Product%'
```

9. The result is as follows:

```
refcounts   cacheobjtype   objtype   usecounts   size_in_bytes
2        Compiled Plan  Adhoc   1       81920
1        Compiled Plan  Adhoc   1       32768
```

10. Let us add the `RECOMPILE` hint to the query used in step 7:

```
--Use the RECOMPILE hint
DECLARE @ProductName nvarchar(25)
SET @ProductName='Bike Wash - Dissolver'
SELECT distinct p.Name AS ProductName,
```

```
NonDiscountSales = (OrderQty * UnitPrice),
Discounts = ((OrderQty * UnitPrice) * UnitPriceDiscount)
FROM Production.Product AS p
INNER JOIN Sales.SalesOrderDetail AS sod
ON p.ProductID = sod.ProductID AND
p.Name = @ProductName
ORDER BY ProductName,Discounts ASC
OPTION (RECOMPILE)
GO
```

11. Then, again execute the query used in step 9 to return the compiled plans in memory, as follows:

```
refcounts   cacheobjtype      objtype   usecounts   size_in_bytes
2           Compiled Plan   Adhoc   1         81920
1           Compiled Plan   Adhoc   1         32768
```

12. From the preceding result, we can see that there is no difference in the results when the RECOMPILE hint is used.

> We can also test the results by clearing the procedure cache from memory by using DBCC FREEPROCCACHE or DBCC FREESYSTEMCACHE ('ALL') WITH MARK_IN_USER_FOR_REMOVAL. The MARK_IN_USER_FOR_REMOVAL will remove the unused plan entries from the cache after they become unused.
>
> Ensure to execute these DBCC statements on a development platform, not recommended for use on a production server.

This completes the required process in implementing query hints for optimized performance.

How it works...

In this recipe, we followed a different alternative of using OPTIMIZE FOR UNKNOWN and RECOMPILE hints. There are two types of OPTIMIZE FOR hints: OPTIMIZE FOR UNKNOWN and OPTIMIZE FOR UNKNOWN. When the data is queried as many single TSQL statements and adhoc batches, the OPTIMIZE FOR UNKNOWN option is helpful to improve the efficiency of the plan cache for the defined workload.

> Using SP_CONFIGURE, setting the OPTIMIZE FOR UNKNOWN to 1 will affect the new plans, and the existing plans in cache are unaffected.

The OPTIMIZE FOR UNKNOWN hint directs the query optimizer to use the required algorithm to use the required parameter. However, specifying OPTIMIZE FOR causes the ParameterCompiledValue to be omitted from the showplan XML output, just as if parameter sniffing did not happen. The resultant plan will be the same regardless of the parameters passed, and may give more predictable query performance.

The optimizer goes through the statistical data to get a determination of values of local variables used that will generate a query plan instead of following the specific parameter values that were passed in the initial SELECT query.

> Using the `sys.dm_exec_cached_plans` DMV, the information on the compile plan stubs can be obtained; the `cacheobjtypes` is the key column.

Without the hint, the original query generates a cached query plan, which can be reused for the number of consecutive executions. By using the `RECOMPILE` hint, we have overridden the default optimizer behavior by forcing the query to compile each time when it is executed; that removes the requirement of storing query plans in cache.

It is essential to highlight the importance of table/query hints and understand how query plans can help to accomplish optimized performance. SQL Server 2008 (and higher) acknowledges that the `TABLE HINT` clause is introduced to allow the table-level hints as query hints in the `OPTION` clause of the queries. This feature is beneficial to provide the flexibility for a set of hints using a plan guide feature where the mere choice is to apply a query hint.

The plan guides feature is intended to *lock down* the supportive plans for all repeated queries against the databases, as opposed to a few queries alone. The inner-working for plan guides is: if the server handles a well-defined query and a repeated set of parameterized queries are executed then plan freezing will allow the DBA to pick a schedule when the system is running on expected levels. This will ensure that any subsequent compiles or recompiles do not pick a different (inefficient) plan to mix any unpredictability into the data platform performance.

Designing sustainable locking methods to improve concurrency

Every time a query is executed, the standard SQL defines four types of actions to maintain the concurrent transactions. They are dirty reads, non-repeatable reads, phantom reads, and lost updates. By default, SQL Server is efficient enough to use default locking mechanism behavior to control the task completion for simultaneous transactions. The locking behavior controls access to database resources and imposes a certain level of transactional isolation levels. The different SQL Server isolation levels are: READ COMMITTED, READ UNCOMMITTED, REPEATABLE READ, SERIALIZABLE, and SNAPSHOT—which is a SQL Server-specific isolation level implementation. In this recipe, we will go through the required steps in designing sustainable locking methods to improve concurrency on the data platform. By default, SQL Server allows using table hints for locking in SELECT, MERGE, UPDATE, INSERT, and DELETE statements to override the isolation level currently set at the session level. The default determination of locking is SHARED, UPDATE, and EXCLUSIVE on a resource depending upon the type of statement executed.

How to do it...

The following steps are required in designing sustainable locking methods to improve concurrency in the data platform:

1. We will begin with the HOLDLOCK hint that maintains the shared lock for the duration of the statement execution.

2. The HOLDLOCK hint is equivalent to the SERIABLABLE isolation level that will be used within a transaction.

3. Using the Production.Product table, we will obtain the results based on the condition between the ProductLine and DaysToManufacture columns.

4. Open a **New Query** window session on the **SSMS** tool and execute the following TSQL:

```
--Start a new query window session for this query

USE AdventureWorks2008R2;
GO
BEGIN TRAN
SELECT Name, ProductNumber, ListPrice AS Price,ProductLine,DaysToM
anufacture
FROM Production.Product
WITH (HOLDLOCK)
WHERE ProductLine = 'M'
AND DaysToManufacture between 2 AND 4
ORDER BY Name ASC;
GO
```

The preceding query returns around 38 rows that are matched as M for the ProductLine column.

5. Now, let us display the locking information by using the following TSQL:

```
SELECT resource_type, resource_associated_entity_id,
   request_status, request_mode,request_session_id,
   resource_description
FROM sys.dm_tran_locks
WHERE resource_database_id = DB_ID('AdventureWorks2008R2');
```

The locking information includes the shared range shared resource lock based on the serializable range scan and GRANT request status.

6. The sample lock information results are as follows:

resource_type	resource_associated_entity_id	request_status	request_mode	request_session_id
PAGE	72057594045595648	GRANT	IS	56
KEY	72057594045595648	GRANT	RangeS-S	53
DATABASE	0	GRANT	S	56

7. Again, open another **New Query** window and execute the following TSQL statement:

```
--Start a new query window session for this query on the same SSMS
SET TRANSACTION ISOLATION LEVEL READ UNCOMMITTED
GO
USE AdventureWorks2008R2;
GO
BEGIN TRAN
SELECT Name, ProductNumber, ListPrice AS Price,ProductLine,DaysToM
anufacture
FROM Production.Product
WITH (TABLOCK, HOLDLOCK)
WHERE ProductLine = 'M'
AND DaysToManufacture <2
ORDER BY Name ASC;
GO
```

8. Now, display locking information for this connection:

```
--Display lock information
SELECT resource_type, resource_associated_entity_id,
   request_status, request_mode,request_session_id,
   resource_description
FROM sys.dm_tran_locks
WHERE resource_database_id = DB_ID('AdventureWorks2008R2');
```

9. The sample lock information for the second query session is as follows:

resource_type	resource_associated_entity_id	request_status	request_mode	request_session_id	resource_description
DATABASE	0	GRANT	S	60	
KEY	72057594045595648	GRANT	RangeS-S	56	(8a73891e1f87)
PAGE	72057594045595648	GRANT	IS	53	1:819
OBJECT	1717581157	GRANT	S	59	

The queries are executed using transaction marks and the preceding statements are executed using `HOLDLOCK` and `TABLOCK` hints along with `SERIALIZABLE` and `READ UNCOMMITTED` isolated levels that create no additional locks on the key columns.

10. Now, use the optimistic locking method using `SNAPHOT ISOLATION` by using the `READ COMMITTED` isolation level and use the additional `UPDLOCK` hint.

11. Open a **New Query** window on **SSMS** tool:

```
USE master
GO
ALTER DATABASE AdventureWorks2008R2 SET ALLOW_SNAPSHOT_ISOLATION
ON
GO

SET TRANSACTION ISOLATION LEVEL SNAPSHOT
GO
USE Adventureworks2008R2
GO
BEGIN TRAN
SELECT Name, ProductNumber, ListPrice AS Price,ProductLine,DaysToM
anufacture
FROM Production.Product
WHERE ProductLine = 'M'
AND DaysToManufacture <2
ORDER BY Name ASC;
GO
```

The preceding query will return around 54 rows from the Production.Product table based on the ProductLine=M.

12. Open another **New Query** window session:

```
USE Adventureworks2008R2
GO
UPDATE Production.Product
WITH (UPDLOCK)
SET ListPrice=159.90
WHERE ProductNumber='ST-1401'
```

The preceding query will take a certain amount of time to update the rows based on the ProductNumber condition. The locking mode for this query will be Update Lock (LCK_M_U).

13. On the first query window (step 12), execute the following query:

```
--Once the second window session query is completed, execute the
following UPDATE query
USE Adventureworks2008R2
```

```
GO
UPDATE Production.Product
WITH (UPDLOCK)
SET ListPrice=159.99
WHERE ProductNumber='ST-1401'
```

The preceding query will take a certain amount of time to update the rows based on the ProductNumber condition. The locking mode for this query will be `Exclusive Lock` (LCK_M_X).

14. Both the queries on steps 12 and 13 are identified as slow updates for the rows based on the `ProductNumber='ST-1401'`. Without blocking each process, the update will succeed after a certain amount of time.

This completes the steps in designing sustainable locking methods to improve concurrency in the data platform.

How it works...

We started with the `TRANSACTION ISOLATION LEVEL` to `SERIALIZABLE` to use the `HOLDLOCK` hint by opening two separate query windows to execute the `SELECT` query. Executing or setting the isolation level to serializable may not be necessary if we use the default SQL Server isolation level, which is `READ COMMITTED`. As per the recipe, the isolation level will affect the connection until we explicitly change it. Then, we looked into using the `sys.dm_tran_locks` system catalog to obtain locking information for the relevant query sessions. This will display the information about the time of row or page locks held on the table that will allow the potential locking mechanisms on transactions to modify the query's rows while the original transactions remain open. While the data modifications is processing, whether or not the actual update is committed or rolled back at a later time, using the SERIALIZABLE isolation allows dirty reads that allows data reads in progress.

Later, we used scripts to see how to use optimistic locking using `SNAPSHOT ISOLATION` by referring to the `READ COMMITTED` option. The first process to hold the row version of `SELECT` and the next process of `UPDATE` statements are executed in different query windows. As per the settings, the `SELECT` statement will execute without holding any locks due to the snapshot isolation setting for that session. However, the second session will start updating the data using exclusive `UPDLOCK` until the update is executed that generates a new version of row. Another parallel operation of a similar update on another window will capture the automatic row versioning based on the snapshot isolation mode that is prevented by the first process from overwriting the update performed by the second process that will prevent any lost update.

Implementing parallel query processing methods

In recent times, the processing power of a hardware system has been increased. This helps speed up the processing of large data and data warehouse queries, which can be termed as **parallelism**. By default, SQL Server utilizes the power of a multi-core hardware platform for a large amount of data management chores. Specifically, in query processing, the CPU is used extensively to perform multiple threads simultaneously. CPU can be a logical process or hyper-threaded cores. In this recipe, we will work on required tasks in implementing parallel query processing methods that can enable database or application tuning to help improve the performance.

Getting ready

In order to set up and get the advantage of parallel query processing methods, the hardware plays an essential part. The minimum system requirements for parallel query processing is as follows:

- ► Processor type with a recommended `2.0Ghz` or faster:
    - ❑ Intel Xeon with Intel EMT64T support
    - ❑ Intel Pentium IV with EM64T support Pentium IV compatible
    - ❑ AMD Opteron 32-bit or 64-bit
    - ❑ AMD Athlon 64

- ► Operating system:
    - ❑ Windows Server 2008 SP2 64-bit
    - ❑ Windows Server 2008 R2 64-bit
    - ❑ Windows on Windows (WOW mode)

- ► Memory:
    - ❑ Minimum 2 GB or higher
    - ❑ Operating system maximum

- ► SQL Server Edition:
    - ❑ SQL Server 2008 R2 DataCenter
    - ❑ SQL Server 2008 R2 Enterprise
    - ❑ SQL Server 2008 R2 Standard
    - ❑ SQL Server 2008 R2 Web or Workgroup

▶ Hard disk space:

  ❑ Minimum 120 GB or higher

  ❑ Specific to database size maximum

  ❑ Data striping—RAID1 or Mirrored drive—RAID0

  ❑ Quick recovery and reliability—RAID 1+0

  ❑ Redundancy and high performance—RAID5

How to do it...

The following steps are required in implementing parallel query processing methods. By default, SQL Server controls provides flexibility to control parallelism by using the maximum degree of parallelism (MAXDOP) hint per query.

1. Use the default value of MAXDOP is 0 (zero). To supress parallel plan generation, the MAXDOP value can be set to 1.

2. Similarly, the max degree of parallelism option can be set as a server-side option using:

```
--Use 8 processors in a 12 CPU server
sp_configure 'show advanced options', 1;
GO
RECONFIGURE WITH OVERRIDE;
GO
sp_configure 'max degree of parallelism', 8;
GO
RECONFIGURE WITH OVERRIDE;
GO
```

3. Let us see how best the MAXDOP query hint can help in a frequently running or adhoc execution of queries. This can be achieved opening a **New Query** window on **SSMS**:

```
--Capture the query execution statistics and generate a showplan
for the query
SET STATISTICS IO ON
GO
SET SHOWPLAN_ALL ON
GO

--To generate PARALLELISM Physical Operation
Use Adventureworks2008R2
GO
SELECT * FROM Production.TransactionHistoryArchive ORDER BY
ProductID,Quantity
```

```
SET STATISTICS IO OFF
GO
SET SHOWPLAN_ALL OFF
GO
```

4. As we are gathering query execution statistics along with a query execution plan on the preceding query, the results are displayed as follows:

5. Again, let us execute the same query by using the MAXDOP hint:

```
--To avoid PARALLELISM Physical Operation and run on a SINGLE core
Use Adventureworks2008R2
GO
SELECT * FROM Production.TransactionHistoryArchive ORDER BY
ProductID,Quantity
OPTION (MAXDOP 1)
```

6. The query statistics and execution plan information are displayed as follows:

7. In addition to the MAXDOP hint, the **SQL Server Resource Governor** can be used to limit the amount of CPU resources for a workload request and the corresponding requests can be managed differently.

This completes the steps that are required in implementing parallel query processing methods.

How it works...

The SQL Server execution engine uses a plan that is generated during query parsing and the optimization phase for that query. By default, the MAXDOP value is 0, which means the query engine uses all the processor cores to parallelize a query depending upon the number of CPU cores available on that server.

Initially, in our case, we have set a server-wide maximum degree of parallelism to eight on a 12 CPU core system. Then, we have also chosen to use the MAXDOP query hint in a query by deciding a value of one, and the SQL Server query execution engine uses the explained route here. If a query explicitly uses a query hint of MAXDOP value that is greater than zero then the optimizer overrides the MAXDOP value configured for server-wide through the sp_configure statement.

Further, we remembered about **Resource Governor (RG)** where a similar operation can be accomplished. It is essential to highlight how MAXDOP and RG work inter-dependently. Let us assume that SQL Server instance resources are managed using the Resource Governor feature, and if a specified value in the MAXDOP query hint is lesser than the RG workload group's degree of parallelism limit value then the optimizer overrides the RG workload group setting. In case a server-wide MAXDOP setting is used along with RG enabled then the RG workload group degree of parallelism limit value is used by default.

The general conception of RG and MAXDOP is different from each other, and the MAXDOP option—OPTION (MAXDOP)—can be used as a query hint. However, this hint will override the default setting of MAXDOP that has been set up using the SP_CONFIGURE statement. Similarly, from SQL Server 2008 onwards, when MAXDOP exceeds the value that was configured by the RG, the database engine will use the RG MAXDOP value. This means the MAXDOP restricts the number of CPUs to be used within a query execution; however, the Resource Governor will not restrict the usage of the number of available physical and logical CPUs on the server.

There's more...

Further, if the server consist of 32 logical processors then by default the MAXDOP value will be 32 – unless a different value is explicitly specified using sp_configure statement. Also, if a server consists of 256 logical processors then MAXDOP uses the value as 64 unless a different value is specified server-wide.

> The maximum value for the degree of parallelism setting is controlled by the edition of SQL Server, CPU type, and the operating system. If a value greater than the number of available processors is specified, the actual number of available processors is used. If the server has only one CPU, MAXDOP value is ignored.

Refer to the recommendations and guidelines for the max degree of parallelism option from http://support.microsoft.com/default.aspx?scid=kb;en-US;2023536.

See also

For more information using Resource Governor capabilities, refer to the *Administer SQL Server workloads with Resource Governor* recipe in *Chapter 2, Administrating the Core Database Engine.*

Implementing the plan guide to enhance compile-time and run-time execution plans

SQL Server query optimizer is an efficient engine that plays an important role in producing an efficient query execution plan for a query. By default, the optimizer decides the eligibility for parallel operation by creating a parallel query plan. Many times, this may not be an efficient plan based on the optimization goals that are specific to an application; thus, using the plan guide process is a recommended method. In such cases, the query plan can be optimized or tailor-made based on the response time, disk IO, memory, and CPU.

The troubleshooting aspects of query performance involve the review of many areas such as design, table indexing, and query execution. In case of running a third-party application tool – where we are limited to modify or make any changes to queries that are causing performance problems – the plan guides are helpful as they allow applying hints to the query without having a need to change the actual query text that is generated from the application.

> The plan guides are also helpful within the upgrade of SQL Server from previous versions to a higher version scenario. Due to the nature of query execution, behavior between the versions may result as suboptimal plans; plan guides are helpful to restrict this behavior.

SQL Server 2008 introduces the plan guides concept where both query and table hints can be designated by using the `sp_create_plan_guide` statement within the stored procedures, triggers, functions, and adhoc queries. In this recipe, we will go through the process of implementing plan guides to enhance compile-time and run-time execution plans to help query optimization.

How to do it...

The following steps will stand out as the process of implementing plan guides to enhance compile-time and run-time execution plans to help query optimization (assuming that the following TSQL is generated from the application that has been captured using the **Activity Monitor** tool):

1. Use the **SSMS** tool to open a **New Query** window and execute the following TSQL:

```
SET STATISTICS IO ON
GO
SET SHOWPLAN_ALL ON
GO

USE AdventureWorks2008R2;
GO
SELECT Prod.Name AS ProductName,
NonDiscountSales = (OrderQty * UnitPrice),
Discounts = ((OrderQty * UnitPrice) * UnitPriceDiscount)
FROM Production.Product AS Prod
INNER JOIN Sales.SalesOrderDetail AS SODetail
ON Prod.ProductID = SODetail.ProductID
ORDER BY ProductName,Discounts ASC;
GO

SET STATISTICS IO OFF
GO
SET SHOWPLAN_ALL OFF
GO
```

2. The graphic execution plan is displayed as follows that shows an operation involving parallelism and scanning a nonclustered index, entirely on a range:

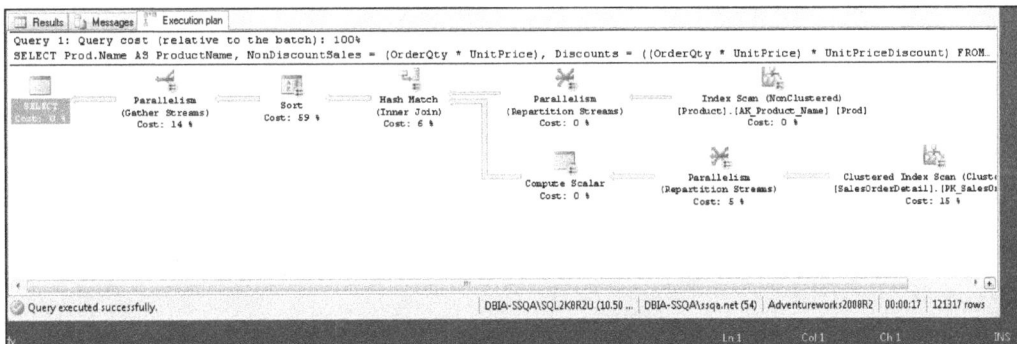

3. Only for this time, we need to avoid the parallelism without modifying the query text. So, how to accomplish this task without touching the actual query text? Let us create a plan guide as follows:

```
--Create a Plan guide to use MAXDOP hint
EXEC sp_create_plan_guide
@name = N'SalesOrderDetail_Product_Use_DegOfParallelism',
@stmt = N'SELECT Prod.Name AS ProductName,
```

```
NonDiscountSales = (OrderQty * UnitPrice),
Discounts = ((OrderQty * UnitPrice) * UnitPriceDiscount)
FROM Production.Product AS Prod
INNER JOIN Sales.SalesOrderDetail AS SODetail
ON Prod.ProductID = SODetail.ProductID ',
@type = N'SQL',
@module_or_batch = NULL,
@params = NULL,
@hints = N'OPTION (MAXDOP 2)'
```

4. To assure that the plan guide is created, let us query against a system catalog:

```
--Obtain the created plan guides on the SQL instance
SELECT * from sys.plan_guides
GO
```

5. The preceding query displays the newly created plan guide along with information about **create_date**, **scope_type**, and **hints** that are used.

6. Coming back to our requirement of repeating the execution of the same query without adding any hints can be done using the following code:

```
--Clearing the CACHE
DBCC FREEPROCCACHE
go
--Repeating the query execution with statistics
SET STATISTICS IO ON
GO
SET FORCEPLAN ON
GO

USE AdventureWorks2008R2;
GO
SELECT Prod.Name AS ProductName,
NonDiscountSales = (OrderQty * UnitPrice),
Discounts = ((OrderQty * UnitPrice) * UnitPriceDiscount)
FROM Production.Product AS Prod
INNER JOIN Sales.SalesOrderDetail AS SODetail
ON Prod.ProductID = SODetail.ProductID
ORDER BY ProductName,Discounts ASC;
GO

SET STATISTICS IO OFF
GO
SET FORCEPLAN OFF
GO
```

7. The query result execution statistics are displayed as follows:

```
(121317 row(s) affected)
Table 'Product'. Scan count 2, logical reads 10, physical reads 0,
read-ahead reads 0, lob logical reads 0, lob physical reads 0, lob
read-ahead reads 0.
Table 'SalesOrderDetail'. Scan count 3, logical reads 1356,
physical reads 0, read-ahead reads 0, lob logical reads 0, lob
physical reads 0, lob read-ahead reads 0.
Table 'Worktable'. Scan count 0, logical reads 0, physical reads
0, read-ahead reads 0, lob logical reads 0, lob physical reads 0,
lob read-ahead reads 0.
```

8. Also, the created plan guides can be disabled or enabled as follows (also, all the plans can be dropped):

```
--TO disable or drop the existing plan guides
EXEC sp_control_plan_guide N'DROP ALL';
EXEC sp_control_plan_guide N'DISABLE ALL';

--To Enable the disabled plan guide
EXEC sp_control_plan_guide N'ENABLE ALL';
```

This completes the set of processes in implementing plan guides to enhance compile-time and run-time execution plans to help query optimization.

How it works...

Initially, we had generated a query plan and statistics where the query optimizer picked up a plan for the query text that confirmed a parallelism operation. Then, we created a new plan guide based on the query text using the parameters `@stmt`, `@type`, `@hints`.

At this point, it is called a plan enumeration step where the query optimizer searches through the plan execution spare by considering different execution orders for operations such as scans and joins. At this level, the query optimizer assesses all the available plans in the cache and produces a suitable plan that is close enough to the optimum plan.

Additionally, without changing the query text, the plan guide is created based on the matching SQL text and hints that allows the optimizer to preserve the desired query plans for future reuse. Using the `sp_control_plan_guide` statement, we can control the usage of plan guides by dropping them altogether or disabling them temporarily.

Besides, the plan guides behavior has significant changes between SQL Server 2005 and SQL Server 2008 (higher) versions. Within SQL Server 2005, when the plan guide is applied as a hint—which results in a *no plan error 8722*—it will return to the client application and the query will not be executed. However, for SQL Server 2008, if the plan results in a no-plan error then the error is caught internally and the corresponding query is re-optimized without the hints. This behavior can be captured using the traditional tools, SQL profiler, or SYSMON (perfmon).

> To capture this behavior, SQL Profiler (server-side trace) is useful by bagging the `PlanGuideUnsuccessful` trace event. To capture the information using the Perfmon tool, use the `SQL Server: SQL Statistics\Misguided plan executions/sec` counter.

There's more...

If the plan guide cannot be honoured, the query optimizer compiles a different plan at compile time and no error is returned.

If we upgrade the SQL Server instance from 2005 version to SQL Server 2008 R2 then we should perform the plan guide validation by using `sys.fn_validate_plan_guide` function, which requires the plan guide to be passed as a parameter. This function is useful to see any errors associated because of the hints (*including USE PLAN hint*) that were applied.

The `sys.sp_create_plan_guide_from_handle system` stored procedure will enable the user to create a plan using USE PLAN hint on a statement based on the current cached plan. This feature is highly useful to make it possible to *freeze* plans for the complete database or system.

Also, it is not possible to script out the plan guides as the hints will behave the same way as an inline table or view, such as using INDEX or FORCESEEK table hints.

Configuring and managing storage systems for optimized defragmentation processes

The database fragmentation can be addressed by using native DBCC statements, and when it comes to physical storage system fragmentation then professional grade disk defragmentation software is essential. There is not much SQL Server-related technical details provided in this recipe, and most of the time the storage level tasks may not be a direct-responsibility for a DBA, where storage level administrators will manage the disk subsystem. In this recipe, we will go through the best practice process in configuring and managing the storage system for optimized defragmentation methods.

Getting ready

The following are the referred best practices to configure the storage for the database server to reduce any fragmentation.

▶ SQL Server 2008 R2 and Windows Server 2008 R2

▶ Using 64-bit operating system and software servers

▶ Using a dedicated server for SQL Server and application database

▶ The application requirement of processing large volumes of transactions and cater reporting needs to data warehouse systems requires substantial I/O system resources

How to do it...

The process defined here is essential in configuring and managing the storage system for optimized defragmentation processes.

We will go through a two-fold step here, initially looking at the storage configuration practices and then closing out the recipe by using the available tools.

1. For the high-end mission-critical application, it is always essential to use a SAN and RAID10 wherever possible.

> In recent times, the hardware vendor's implementation of SAN as RAID-DP (RAID Double Parity) or using a RAID6 setup platform will be a better choice based on application-specific and budgetary flexibility.

2. Perform disk volume alignment on NTFS volume by using the `diskpart.exe` program that is included as part of the Windows operating system.

3. In general, the hardware vendor will provide offset, otherwise it can be obtained through testing. A 64 KB offset (128 sectors) is a common value on many storage arrays.

4. It is ideal to set the offset value as 1024 KB (2048 sectors) for high-end application performance on the storage subsystem.

5. Set the NTFS allocation unit size as multiples of 64 KB (512 KB is minimum) allocation unit for the disks where data, log, and tempdb files will be installed.

6. When configuring **Host Bus Adapter** (**HBA**), choose the value as 16; that is ideal as a start-up value to cater for I/O intensive operations from SQL Server.

7. When designing the number **LUN** (**Logical Unit Number**), ensure to provide a mirrored drive in the event of disk failure. Keep the LUN volume structure and number of files as small as possible.

8. Always keep additional LUNs to cater to the future growth, where data will undoubtedly grow; in this case, it is essential to perform capacity testing on the database for the next two years to cater for the growth.

9. Separate the LUN and physical disk that is used for the backup of SQL Server databases. By default, the SQL Server backup operation uses one reader thread per volume and one writer thread per volume.

10. It is i deal to have a larger number of small drives by creating each LUN (Logical Unit Number) using drives from each bus to improve internal bandwidth.

11. Now, we are at the point using the freely available tools from the Windows Sysinternals site: `http://technet.microsoft.com/en-us/sysinternals/bb545046`.

12. On the Windows Sysinternals site, navigate to the **File and Disk Utilities** page. Here, let us download two tools: **Contig** from `http://technet.microsoft.com/en-us/sysinternals/bb897428` and **PageDefrag** from `http://technet.microsoft.com/en-us/sysinternals/bb897426`.

13. The **Contig** tool uses the internal defragmentation methods such as **Winternals Defrag Manager**. This tool is useful for performing a general defragmentation of disks.

14. On the Server, open a **Command Prompt utility** by choosing the **Run-As Administrator** option from **Start | Programs**. The general syntax for this tool is:

```
Usage: contig [-v] [-a] [-q] [-s] [filename]
```

-v	Use the -v switch to have Contig print out information about the file defrag operations that are performed.
-a	If you want to simply see how fragmented a file or files have become, use the -a switch to have Contig analyze fragmentation.
-q	The -q switch, which over-rides the -v switch, makes Contig run in "quiet" mode, where the only thing it prints during a defrag run is summary information.
-s	Use the -s switch to perform a recursive processing of subdirectories when you specify a filename with wildcards.

15. To use the tool on a specific directory, directly run: "`Contig -s D:\SQLDatabaseFiles\*.*`".

16. The **PageDefrag** tool provides the facility to defragment the **paging** files and **registry hives**.

17. The tool can be installed using **Administrator** privileges on the server that will present a list box confirming how many clusters make up the paging files on that server.

18. In addition to paging files, there is information about Registry hives (SAM, SYSTEM, SYSTEM.ALT, SECURITY, SOFTWARE, .DEFAULT), as well as how many fragments those files are in.

19. The command-line operation usage of **PageDefrag** is:

```
Usage: pagedefrag [-e | -o | -n] [-t <seconds>]
```

-e	Defrag every boot.
-o	Defrag once.
-n	Never defrag.
-t	Set countdown to specified number of seconds.

This completes the essential steps in configuring and managing the storage system for optimized defragmentation processes.

> It is highly essential to perform the preceding steps during the preferred maintenance window, which will work out as defragmentation activities.

How it works...

The storage level defragmentation needs to be addressed on a regular basis where many third-party tools are available in the market. In this recipe, we have used the Windows Sysinternals suite that offers many tools to accomplish the tasks. Initially, we overviewed the disk and storage configuration at the deployment level, then choosing two tools that are essential and helpful in defragmenting the storage level that is outside of the SQL Server environment.

> As a best practice, these methods must be followed whenever the fragmentation level is higher than 40 percent or half-yearly if the database system is highly transactional.

By default, the **Contig** tool uses the Windows NT defragmentation support that is introduced in NT 4.0 version; it will scan the disk collecting the locations and sizes of free areas. Then, it decides whether the file can be optimized based on the free areas and number of fragments the file currently consists of.

The **PageDefrag** tool can be used as a one-time operation to defragment the paging files and registry hives. It is recommended to test the tool in the development environment to ensure that no problems occur for SQL Server operations. Internally, the tool will use the Windows **chkdsk** operation on hard drives during the boot time startup of the server.

Building best usage processes of Dynamic Management Views

Dynamic Management Views (**DMV**) and functions are a useful resource for a DBA to obtain the server and database state information. The status of internal and implementation-specific data can be obtained along with the schemas. DMVs and functions are divided into two types: server-scoped and database-scoped. Further, each of them is organized into different categories such as Database mirroring, disk, CPU, Change Data Capture, Extended Events, SQLOS, Resource Governor, and many more. In this recipe, we will go through the recommended practices and best usage processes of DMVs in the SQL Server environment.

How to do it...

The following steps are formed as a guidance in building best usage processes of DMVs. For the record, there are a total of 136 DMVs and functions available in SQL Server 2008 R2.

> The number of DMVs will be changed based on the service pack releases and in future versions of SQL Server.

1. To obtain the list of DMVs and functions, let us execute the TSQL:

```
USE master
GO
SELECT name,type_desc,create_date,is_ms_shipped
FROM sys.system_objects WHERE name like 'DM[_]%'
ORDER BY name, type_desc
```

2. Once we obtain the list of all DMVs and functions, it is essential to group the essential DMVs that are used in day-to-day operations. Use the TSQL as follows:

```
--Get a list of grouped DMVs
SELECT name as [DMV/DMF Name],
type_desc as [Type],
[GroupName] =
CASE
  WHEN name LIKE 'dm_exec%' THEN 'Query/Session Execution'
  WHEN name LIKE 'dm_os%' THEN 'SQL Server Operating System'
  WHEN name LIKE 'dm_io%' THEN 'Disk I/O'
  WHEN name LIKE 'dm_tran%' THEN 'Database Transactions and locks'
  WHEN name LIKE 'dm_db_%index%' THEN 'Indexes'
  WHEN name LIKE 'dm_db%' THEN 'Database and database objects'
  WHEN name LIKE 'dm_db_mirror%' THEN 'Database Mirroring'
  WHEN name LIKE 'dm_resou%' THEN 'Resource Governor'
```

```
    WHEN name LIKE 'dm_clr%' THEN 'CLR based'
END
FROM sys.system_objects
WHERE name LIKE 'dm[_]%'
ORDER BY [GroupName] desc
```

3. Also, download the detailed system views map from Microsoft downloads: `http://www.microsoft.com/downloads/en/details.aspx?FamilyID=531c53e7-8a2a-4375-8f2f-5d799aa67b5c&displaylang=en`, which shows the key views involved and relationship between them.

4. In addition to obtaining the current system and database state with DMVs and functions, we can also use the **SSMS** tool that will produce standard reports that are essential in troubleshooting exercises.

5. To obtain server-scope-based reports:

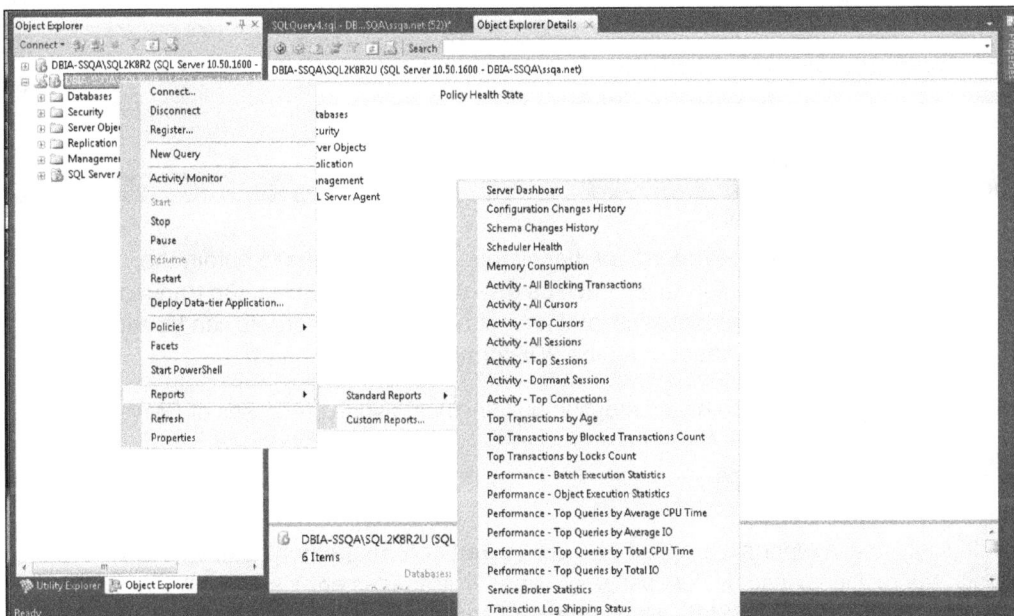

6. The server-scope reports are highly useful to obtain the server information based on configuration changes, memory consumption, activity, and top performing queries as a dashboard view. The reports can be exported as Microsoft Excel sheet or Adobe PDF formats.

7. To obtain database-scope reports:

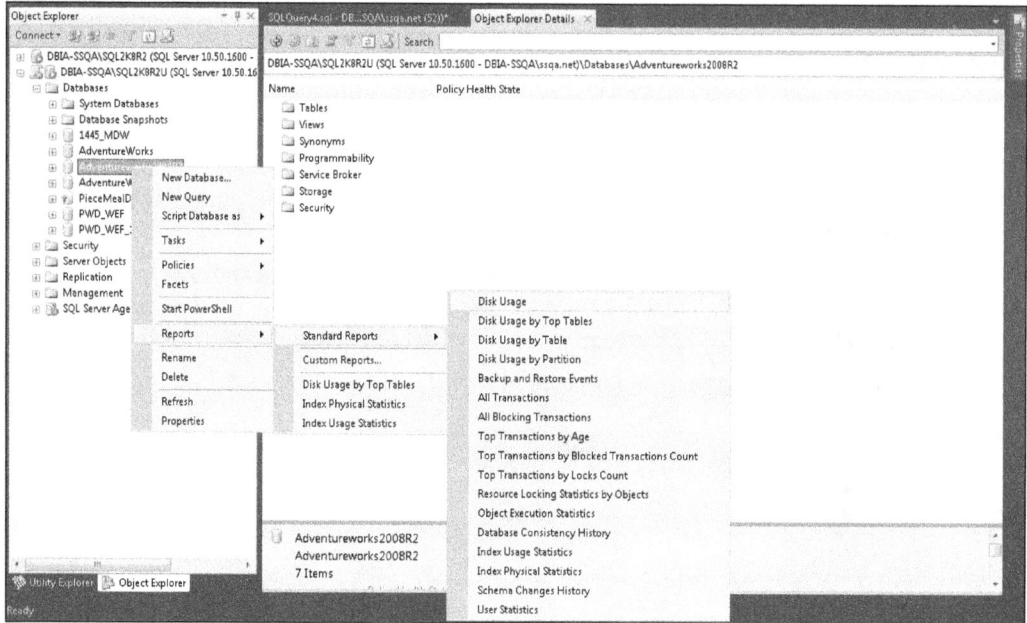

8. The database-scope reports are handy reports for the users to obtain the database-related information such as disk usage by the tables, top transactions activity, index usage statistics, and user statistics. These reports can be exported as Microsoft Excel sheet or Adobe PDF formats.

This completes the guidance-based steps in building best usage processes of DMVs.

How it works...

Traditionally, these reports are called as the **SQL Server Management Studio** (**SSMS**) reports. Though the recipe is titled as best usage of Dynamic Management Views (DMV), what we have seen is the usage of SSMS, which offers an advantage of not having any advanced TSQL programming knowledge.

The Management Studio reports are server-scope and database-scope, which provide the current snapshot of information on the server and database. Internally, the report executes the set of Transact-SQL statements and Dynamic Management Views (DMVs) that will correlate and aggregate information to present the data as a report. Internally, these reports will use the SQL Server Reporting Services (SSRS) components, but SSRS need not be installed on the desktop or the server.

Implementing a benchmarking framework on multiple instances

Benchmarking a platform is highly essential in order to keep up the **Service Level Agreements** (**SLA**) for your application and database environment. Also, the task will enable the service orientation behavior as a proactive manner that will avoid any unprecedented activity on the data platform.

The key result out of benchmarking is to find the problem with a consistent view of services, and familiarize with application operational behavior to streamline any issues that are persistent, not to mention about performance monitoring and troubleshooting. There are no technical details on how to implement this, but in this recipe we will go through a tool that will help in implementing a benchmarking framework on multiple instances of the data platform.

> **TPC** stands for **Transaction Processing Council**, which is a non-profit corporation founded to define transaction processing and database benchmarks to disseminate objective, verifiable TPC performance data to the industry.

Getting ready

The essential benchmarking requirements that are inline with SLAs are as follows:

- In the event of any failure, the database environment must be available within X minutes
- Data for the last six months must be available online
- The backups for the last eight years must be stored offsite and must be available within X hours during any requirement
- In the next two years, database size is expected to be (capacity)
- Obtain industry standards test such as TPC-C or TPC-H

How to do it...

In case the database platform is a highly transactional OLTP system then it is required to test the hardware and systems as per the industry standard TPC-C.

Every hardware vendor has his own standards implementation at his end; however, it is performed as high-level testing.

The following steps are required in implementing benchmarking a framework on multiple instances of the data platform:

1. A tool is available at `http://codeplex.com` called TPCCBENCH that can generate the TPC-C relevant benchmarking reports.

2. In addition to TPC-C-related reports, the tool can be used to perform testing a new database platform for throughput.

3. The command-line arguments for this tool are:

```
Commands are in \x:option format.
No spaces between the \x: and the option specified.
Valid command line arguements are:

\c:{1} number of clients you wish to run max 200

\s:{servername} name of the database server to benchmark

\d:{target database} the TPC database you wish to benchmark

\u:{username} login name to connect to server. For sql
authentication only
            ignored if \t option is used

\p:{password} login password to connect to server. For sql
authentication only
            ignored if \t option is used

\t use trusted connection notice no : or any following commands

\wh:{2} number of warehouses to use during tests.
        Depends on number of warehouses populated in test
database.

\m:{1} number of minutes to execute the test minimum 1 no maximum

\cs:{50} maximum number of delay between queries issued by the
Client.
        Any number between 0 and 50 is normal 0 for maximum
throughput
        50 for a standard tpc benchmark Client thinking delay

\sp used extended stored procedures instead of single issued
statements
```

```
\stl:{0} stagger Client load where {0} is the number of seconds to
delay each Client

\nl:{0} number of fixed loops to execute per Client. This
overrides the \m: switch

\hb Log to Heartbeat table to track replication latency.

Below is the work load mix switches all 5 must be used and must
equal 100.
\pno:{45} percent new order status
\pos:{43} percent order status
\pp:{4} percent Payment
\pd:{4} percent dilivery
\psl:{4} percent stock level

\? for help
```

4. Extract all the files from the downloaded file and execute the `tpccbench.exe` and `tpccdatabasegenerator.exe` files from the command-line prompt.

5. A new database is created by the tool to view the results from the generated tests for further reference. Once the results are satisfactory, the tool can be executed on multiple servers to obtain further information.

This completes the steps that are required in implementing a benchmarking framework on multiple instances of the data platform.

How it works...

The TPCCBench tool uses the default TPC benchmark system, which is a realistic database schema and measures the mainstream capability of data integrity. The TPC benchmarks will help the performance and price of a system by dividing the total system cost by the performance, which is measured in the transactions per second method.

Similarly, the TPC benchmarking system includes a suite of business-oriented adhoc queries with concurrent data modifications. These queries and corresponding data populating the database have been chosen to have a broad industry-wide relevance.

Such benchmark calculations will illustrate the decision support systems (DSS) to examine large volumes of data, query executions with high-degree of complexity. They will offer the answers to the mission-critical business questions that will measure the price and performance of a system by dividing the total system cost by the performance, which is measured in queries per hour.

There's more...

For more information on published TPC-E and TPC-H benchmark results on SQL Server 2008 R2 with hardware partners, refer to `http://www.microsoft.com/sqlserver/2008/en/us/benchmarks.aspx`.

10
Learning the Tricks of the Trade

In this chapter, we will cover:

- ▶ Automated administration across an enterprise
- ▶ Administrating resource health policies
- ▶ Administrating Analysis Services using Tools
- ▶ Managing events capture to troubleshoot problems

Introduction

Tools and Utilities are very useful for any data platform deployment, management, and administration. SQL Server includes a complete set of graphic tools and command-line utilities that are equipped with an impressive collection of management interfaces and services. These utilities allow all kinds of users to manage the day-to-day and essential tasks.

SQL Server Management Studio (SSMS) is the master of all the tools where many of the tools and utilities have been consolidated into SSMS. Also, the majority of the administrative tasks can be managed using a SQLCMD, PowerShell, and TSQL method, which requires SSMS to invoke these utilities. Inside the SSMS, we can invoke other tools such as SQL Server Profiler, Database Engine Tuning Advisor, or add other external tools in-house that are developed within the enterprise. During the installation of SQL Server, when we choose the **Shared Features** option, the setup will install various tools, such as Business Intelligence Development Studio (BIDS), Client Tools Connectivity, Integration Services, Client Tools Backwards Compatibility, Client Tools SDK, SQL Server Books Online, Management Tools Basic, or Management Tools Complete that will include SQL Server Management Studio (SSMS), SQL Server Connectivity SDK and Microsoft Sync Framework. For the configuration and management of SQL Server services, we will use the SQL Server Configuration Manager.

Let us classify the task as 'tools of the trade'; to cover all the SQL Server related tools and utilities it might require a separate book to explain. However, in this chapter, we will go through the important ingredients that are required to administer and manage the data platform. These important ingredients are:

▶ Managing automated administration using a multi-server environment

▶ Administering the resource health policies

▶ Administration of multiple analysis services using available tools

▶ Automating the event capture to troubleshoot problems

▶ Implementing DBA manageability practices

Automated administration across an enterprise

The automated administration of multiple SQL Server instances requires a pool of resources and multiple utilities to manage. Since SQL Server 2005 Service Pack 2 (SP2), the multiple instance management feature is introduced and using SQL Server agent services for the central administration of jobs. Managing multiple instances will increase the total cost of ownership (TCO) and software footprint. In this recipe, we will concentrate on the feature that will help in achieving automated administration across the data platform enterprise and manage multiple administrative scheduled jobs using Multiserver administration concepts.

Getting ready

To enable the Multiserver administration environment, we need more than one SQL Server instance that will stand as master server and target server. The Multiserver administration requires setup of a master server (MSX) and one or more target servers (TSX).

The Multiserver administration is possible between SQL Server 2008 R2 and lower versions, the least TSX version can only be until SQL Server 2000 SP3. The security settings for SQL Server and SQL Server agent services, which require a Windows domain account are an important requisite in Multiserver administration.

How to do it...

The implementation is a two-fold task that involves the setup of the master server and target servers. The following steps are essential to implement automated administration across an enterprise using the Multiserver administration concept:

1. Using **SSMS** in **Object Explorer**, connect to the SQL Server instance to expand and navigate to the **SQL Server Agent** folder.

2. Right-click on **SQL Server Agent** and point to **Multiserver Administration** and then choose **Make this as Master**, which opens the Master Server wizard to perform the process of making the master server and adding relevant target servers.

3. The initial screen presents **Master Server Operator** that will be created on the master server and each of the target servers. In order to send notifications for the Multiserver jobs, we can specify **E-mail address**, **Pager address**, and **Net Send address**. Click **Next** to continue.

4. **MSXOperator** is the only operator that can receive notifications for multiserver jobs.

5. The **Target Servers** screen will enable us to specify the servers to use as targets for SQL Server Agent jobs.

6. The existing registered servers will be presented on the left-hand side to add as **Target servers**. If there are any other SQL Server instances to be registered as target servers click on **Add Connection** to enter the **Server name** and the relevant **Authentication** (Windows Authentication or SQL Server Authentication). Click **Next** to continue.

7. Checking the **Server Compatibility** screen will process the addition of the master server and target servers. While checking server compatibility, if there are any errors, the **Status and Message** columns will display the relevant information.

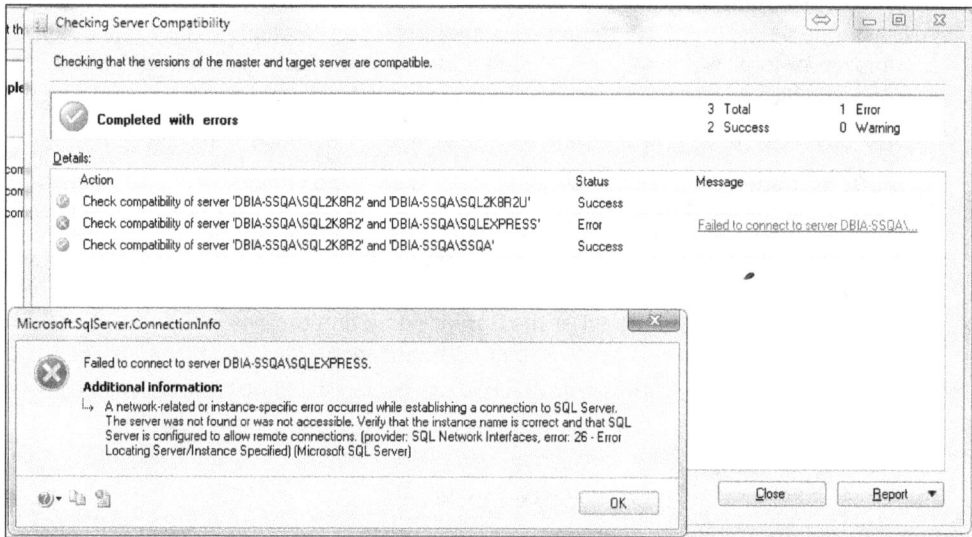

8. There is a problem in connecting to **DBIA-SSQA\SQLExpress** because the specified instance SQL Server service has not been started. To correct the Compatibility check failure for SQLExpress instance, the service has been started that completes the **Checking Server Compatibility** process.

9. Next, the **Master Server Login Credentials** screen is presented to specify the account that is used for the target server to connect to the master server. Click **Next** to continue.

> Ensure to select the option **Create a new login**, if necessary. Assign rights to the MSX, as it is essential to allow the target server to use Windows security to connect to the master server and download jobs for the **SQL Server Agent**.

10. The selection will enable the process to complete that will verify the choices made in the wizard. Click **Finish** to Enlist TSX Progress.

11. SQL Server **Books On Line** (**BOL**) documentation highlights the essential security settings for the distributed jobs. Make sure the following registry key is set so that job steps that are associated with a proxy will not be downloaded from the master server to the target server.

```
The master server registry sub-key: \HKEY_LOCAL_MACHINE\SOFTWARE\
Microsoft\Microsoft SQL Server\<instance_name>\SQL Server Agent\
AllowDownloadedJobsToMatchProxyName (REG_DWORD) is set to 1
(true). By default, this sub-key is set to 0 (false).
```

> The step mentioned earlier includes updates to the Windows registry; serious problems might occur if the process is followed incorrectly. For added protection, it is essential to backup the registry before modifying it. Follow the `http://support.microsoft.com/kb/322756` article about how to backup and restore the Windows registry.

12. At this point, if there are any errors, then the **Message** column will provide the relevant information as a hyperlink to review the information. Take relevant preventive action to correct the errors to complete the **MSX** and **TSX** progress.

13. To obtain information for all registered target servers, execute the following TSQL:

```
USE msdb;
GO


EXEC dbo.sp_help_targetserver;
GO
```

This completes the set up of the master server and target servers, and we now set up a scheduled job that will target multiple servers.

14. From **Object Explorer** right-click on **SQL Server Agent** and choose **New | Job** to open the **New Job** screen.

15. Navigate to the **Targets** section, which will present the option to schedule the job for the local server or multiple servers.

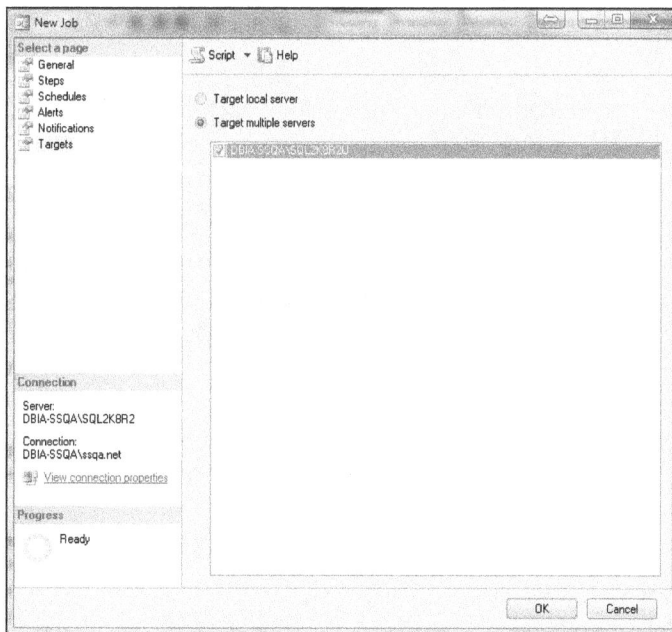

16. If, in case, a scheduled job is designed for multiserver jobs, which have been designed outside of SSMS, we must post the changes to the master server download list, so that target servers can download the updated job again.

17. To ensure the target servers have current job definitions, we must post an instruction on the master server using the following TSQL statement: `EXECUTE sp_post_msx_operation 'INSERT', 'JOB', '<job id>'`

18. The job ID context for that scheduled job can be obtained by the execution of the `sp_help_job` statement.

19. To resynchronize all multiserver jobs in the specified target server, execute the TSQL statement using `msdb` system database context: `EXEC dbo.sp_resync_targetserver N'<ServerName>';`

This completes the steps to implement automated administration across an enterprise using the Multiserver administration concept.

How it works...

The Master Server wizard plays an essential part in setting up automated administration on a Multiserver environment. Multiserver administration requires a master server and one or more target servers, so that the jobs will be processed on defined target servers. The wizard will perform the process to check the security settings for SQL Server Agent service and SQL Server service on all servers intended to become target servers. The process will create a master server operator (`MSXOperator`), which is required for Multiserver scheduled jobs to receive notifications for Multiserver jobs. Then the SQL Server Agent service will be started on the master server. Finally, the target servers will be enlisted based on the relevant service account permissions.

The concept of a Multiserver environment ensures that each target reports to only one master server and we must defect a target server from one master server by using the `msdb.dbo.sp_delete_targetserver @server_name = 'tsx-server', @post_defection = 0` statement. The default value for `@post_defection` will be 0, which indicates that no forced defection should occur and if the value is 1 then the forced defection of the target server will be implemented. When performing a change in the name of a target server, ensure to defect the TSX before changing the name and re-enlist it after the change. Finally, in order to remove all of the Multiserver configuration, we must defect all the target servers from the master server.

There's more...

For efficient multiserver administration, ensure that SQL Server Agent service is started, the service account must be a domain account and the account has rights to login as a target server.

Further, if there are a large number of target servers, then ensure to set up the Multiserver scheduled jobs on a server that is different from the current production server, because the target server traffic can affect the performance of the production SQL Server instance.

> To configure the appropriate level of security for a specific master server and target server's communication, set the target server SQL Server Agent registry subkey \HKEY_LOCAL_MACHINE\SOFTWARE\Microsoft\ Microsoft SQL Server\< instance_name> \SQLServerAgent\ MsxEncryptChannelOptions(REG_DWORD) to 1 or 2.

The default value for the SQL Server Agent registry subkey is 2, which enables the full SSL encryption and certificate validation between the target server and master server. As a best practice, unless there is a specific reason, do not attempt to change the value to anything other than 2.

See also

For more information on setting up new jobs, refer to the *Designing automated administration practices* recipe in *Chapter 2, Administration of the Core Database Engine.*

Administrating resource health policies

SQL Server Utility dashboard in SQL Server Management Studio helps monitoring multiple instances and policies for SQL Server instances and data-tier applications (DAC). Using the UCP, health policies can be configured for data-tier applications and managed instances of SQL Server; also, the policies can be defined globally or individually for that DAC or managed instance.

Many a time, over-utilization and under-utilization of policies for managed instances can be a long process. File space for storage volumes and database files together with server processor utilization can be obtained by using UCP resource policies, such as SQL server instance processor utilization. In this recipe, we will go through the important steps in administering the resource health policies using Utility Control Point (UCP).

Getting ready

The UCP and all managed instances of SQL Server must satisfy the following prerequisites:

▶ UCP SQL Server instance version must be SQL Server 2008 SP2 (and higher) or SQL Server 2008 R2

▶ The managed instances must be a database engine only

▶ UCP managed account must operate within a single Windows domain or domains with two-way trust relationships

▶ The SQL Server service accounts for UCP and managed instances must have read permission to Users in the Active Directory

To set up the SQL Server Utility, we must use SQL Server Management Studio:

▶ Create a UCP from the SQL Server Utility

▶ Enroll data-tier applications

▶ Enroll instances of SQL Server with the UCP

> Refer to *Chapter 3 Managing the Core Database Engine* for more information on the setup of SQL Server Utility.

How to do it...

The following steps are required to administer the resource health policies of managed instances and data-tier applications:

From **SSMS** click **View** and select the **Utility Explorer**.

1. Click on the **Utility Explorer**; populate the server that is registered as **utility control point**.

2. Click on **Utility Administration** to present **global policy settings** that will administer the resource utilization policy indicators.

3. Initially, set up the Global Policies on Data-tier applications for CPU and file space utilization specifically for data file and log file.

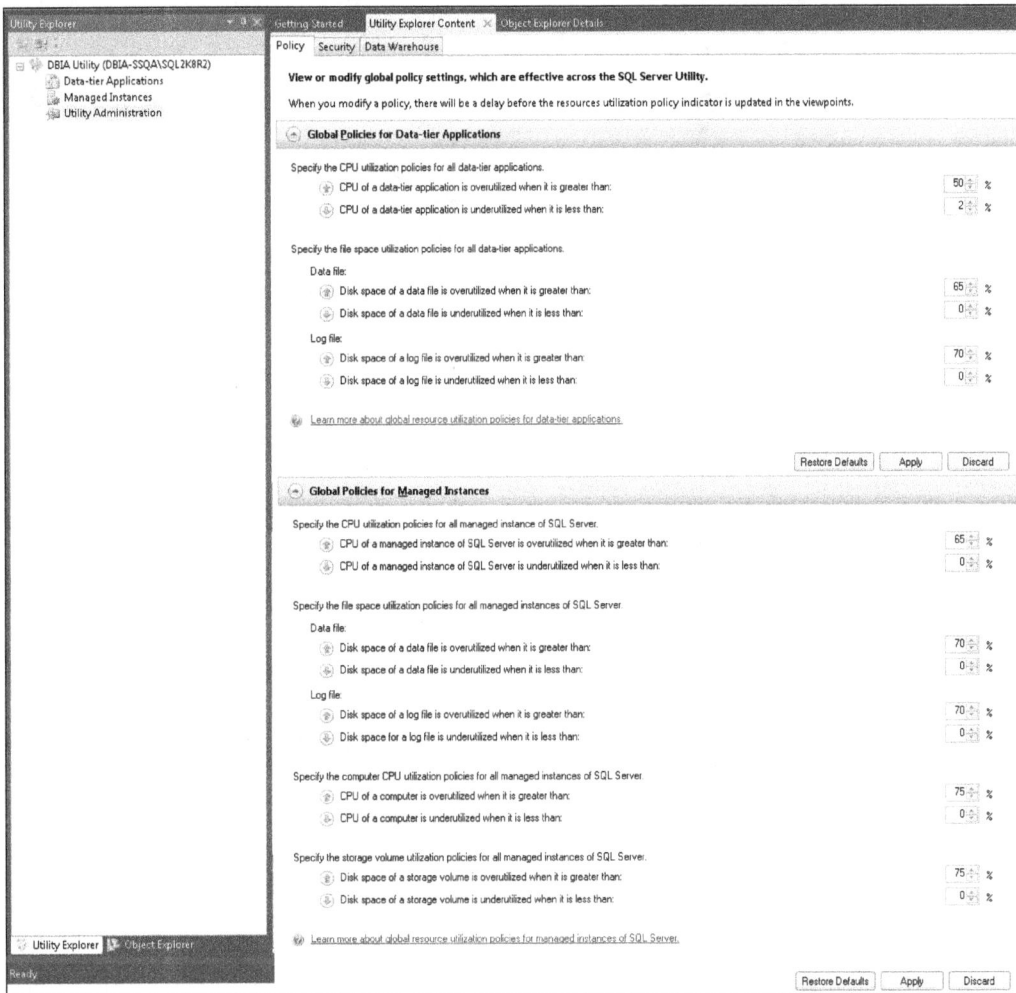

4. Make necessary changes as per the previous screenshot where the CPU utilization, file space utilization, and set storage volume utilization are presented with required values.

5. To identify how frequently a violation can be reported as over-utilized or under-utilized, we can use **Volatile Resource Policy Evaluation** under the **Policy** tab:

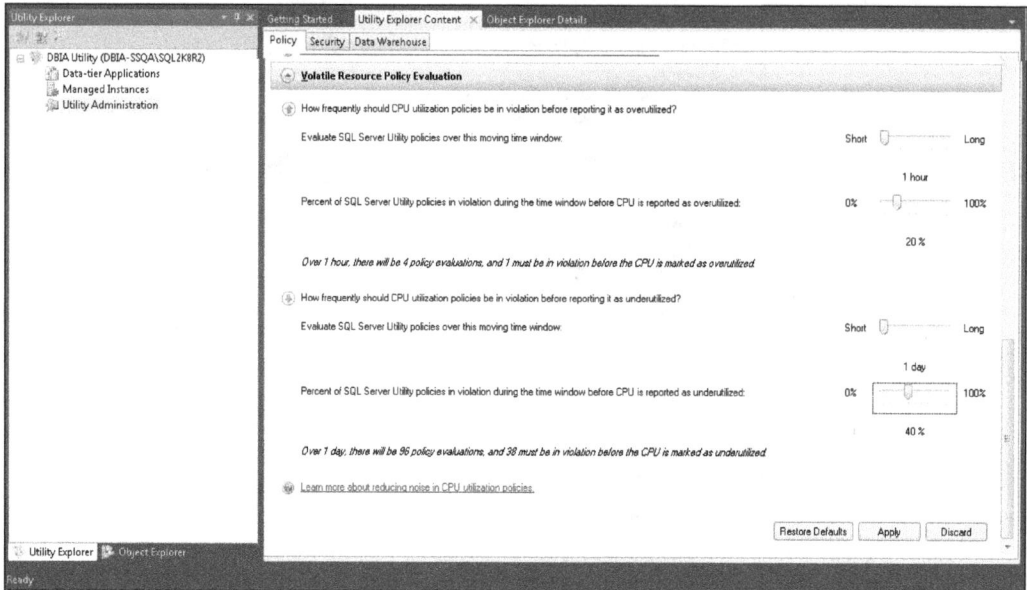

6. In this case, we choose the time to evaluate SQL Server Utility policies for every 1 hour and choose 20 percent of policies in violation during the time window.

7. In this selection, for over one hour there will be four policy evaluations and at least one must be in violation before the CPU is marked as over-utilized. This is a best practice setting to ensure that a highly transactional SQL Server instance is monitored for policy violation.

8. Click the **UCP** node to view summary data for the managed instances of SQL Server and data-tier applications (right-click to refresh). The Dashboard data is displayed in the **content** pane for **Managed Instances** and **Deployed Data-tier Applications**.

This completes the steps to administer the resource health policies of managed instances and data-tier applications.

How it works...

The Utility Control Point (UCP) is the main utility to administer any policy violations when the instances and data-tier applications are registered to manage. The evaluation time-period and tolerance for percent-violations are both configurable using the **Policy table settings** in **UCP administration** node.

Using Utility dashboard from SQL Server Management studio, the SQL Server health policies can be configured for data-tier applications and managed instances; the policies can be defined globally or individually.

The default data collection interval is 15 minutes, which cannot be changed and the default upper threshold processor utilization policy is 70 percent, which can be changed according to the usage of the SQL Server instance. Also, the default evaluation period for processor over-utilization is one hour, which can be configurable until one week based on the default percentage of data points in violation before a CPU violation is reported as over-utilization, which can be configurable between 0 percent and 100 percent.

In this recipe, as we set the four data points to be collected every hour, where the CPU utilization policy threshold is 20 percent, this means in a one-hour collection period 25 percent of data points are performed and report any violation of the CPU utilization policy threshold.

> As a best practice, to reduce any noise generated by a single or multiple violations, we can increase the evaluation period by another increment to six hours and the tolerance for percentage of violations by 30 percent.

Administrating multiple Analysis Services using Tools

Administering and managing Analysis Services includes managing all instances by maintaining optimal security, deployment, and data recovery that will process the data warehouse objects. The SQL Server tools can help the users and help the DBAs in automating tasks and monitoring activity within an Analysis Services instance. The service management tools can configure the server properties using SQL Server Management Studio and MMC snap-in makes it possible for users to configure Windows services. In this recipe, we will go through the important aspects and processes in the administration of multiple analysis services instances using the available tools.

Apart from sharing the same server hardware resources, every instance of SQL Server Analysis Services is completely independent, with independent executables, properties, security models, cubes, and so on.

How to do it...

The following are important points in administering and managing multiple instances of Analysis Services using SQL server tools:

1. Assume a scenario in a multiple instances of Analysis Services environment, such as:

    ❑ Set up of a communication channel using own port for each instance

❏ Remove BuiltIn\Administrator windows group as server admin and set Service accounts as server admin

❏ Set a server timeout and temporary directory for all compilations

❏ Enable a FlightRecorder and define a log file

❏ Set up a backup folder where the analysis services databases are stored

❏ Change a language and collation setting for an Analysis Services instance and assign a server administrator role to grant server-wide security privileges to a user or a group of users

2. Open an **Analysis Services** connection using **SSMS**, select **Connect** and choose **Analysis Services** to enter relevant **Server name** and **Authentication**.

3. Right-click on the opened Analysis Services instance and click on **Properties**.

4. By default, the **Analysis Services Properties** window will display only Basic category properties. On the **Analysis Services Properties** screen, select **Show Advanced (All) Properties** option to display all the properties of the server that are advanced.

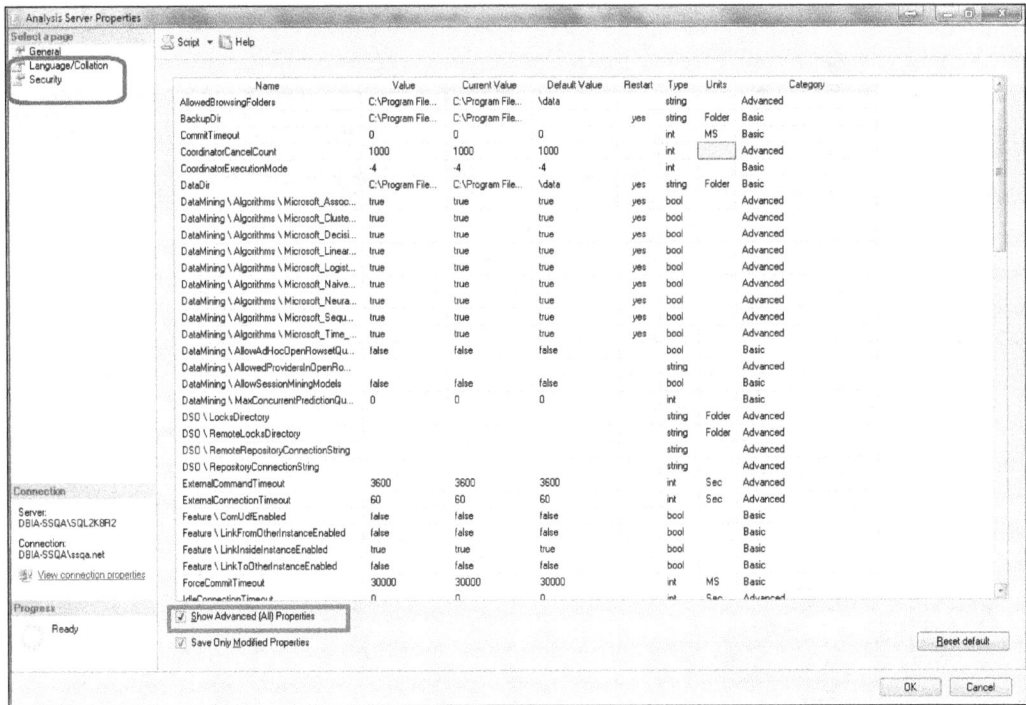

Taking into account these scenario points, the following process is defined to set relevant values on an Analysis Services instance where all the settings are sorted in an alphabetical order.

5. To set up a communication channel using your own port for each instance, scroll down to **Port** property and set the relevant value (for instance 2383) and we need to ensure that the defined port number has been added under the Windows firewall exceptions list to allow connections.

6. By default, the **Port** property value is **0**, which means the default port is **2383** used by an Analysis Services instance.

7. To set **BuiltIn | Administrator** windows group as server admin, scroll down to **Security | BuiltinAdminsAreServerAdmins** and choose **false** from the drop-down box in the **Value** column. To set Service accounts as server admin, choose **Security | ServiceAccountsIsServerAdmin** property and set it to **true**.

> The default value for **ServiceAccountsIsServerAdmin** property is **True**, which controls the SQL Server Analysis Services (SSAS) itself and is considered to have administrative privileges to the Analysis Server.

8. To set the server time, scroll towards **ServerTimeout** property and set relevant value in seconds, the default value is 3600 seconds. To set the **temporary** directory, scroll down to the **TempDir** property to set the directory, and the default folder for temporary analysis will be `%:\Program Files\Microsoft SQL Server\ MSAS10_50.SQL2K8R2\OLAP\Temp`.

> Many of these server settings are affected after the instance is restarted. All the settings as **Advanced** under **Category** and **'yes'** under **Restart** columns require a restart of the SSAS instance.

9. Click **OK** to effect all the selected changes and proceed to restart the SSAS instance using **SQL Server Configuration Manager** tool.

10. Finally, to change language and/or collation settings for the installed Analysis Services instance, click on the **Language/Collation** option on the **Select a page** pane. Similarly, to add a specific user or group of users as **Server Administrators for SSAS** instance, choose the **Security** option on the **Select a page** pane.

This completes the important points in administering and managing multiple instances of Analysis Services using SQL server tools.

How it works...

The important aspect of this recipe is setting up the port to enable an SSAS instance to accept the client connections. If the default port 2383 is changed on the SSAS instance, then unless an Analysis Services client specifies a port number, the connection will not be successful.

Similarly, if the SSAS client wants to connect to a named instance of Analysis Services (AS) that is listening on another port number, then the client either has to specify the exact port being used by the named instance, or it is directed to the Analysis Services redirector server on port 2382. The AS redirector service is part of the SQL Server Browser, which maintains a record of the port number for each instance of SSAS and SQL Server services on that server.

Managing events capture to troubleshoot problems

Performance slowdown is a common occurrence in any RDBMS platform and SQL Server is not an exception. The root cause can range from inadequate database design that is, improper configuration, to handling the application workload. The DBA must be able to identify the root cause in a pro-active manner to minimize the problem. Also, the essential task is to monitor when a simple query execution causes intermittent issues and take corrective measures to fix the problem. The Windows operating system and SQL Server have a flurry of tools and utilities to monitor the system activity and collect the required data, such as PERFMON (SYSMON), SQL Server Profiler, DBCC statements, Dynamic Management Views (DMVs), and Data Collector. From SQL Server 2008 version onwards, another diagnostic tool is added, which is SQL Server Extended Events (XEvents).

In this recipe, we will go through the methods on how to manage events captured in SQL Server troubleshooting scenarios, extended events with ETW-Event Tracing Windows. Extended Events are designed to configure, monitor, and capture different types of data (CPU, Memory, and Deadlocks), which includes performance data. ETW has been a built-in utility since Windows 2000 that enables the tracking of kernel and application events with minimal overhead. All the XEvents data collection processes are less-intrusive and provide a granular level of information for a wide range of monitoring and troubleshooting performance issues. It is helpful to take pro-active action when the server is experiencing severe performance issues causing client applications to timeout.

How to do it...

The following are the steps to go through the methods on how to manage events capture using Extended Events with ETW and TRACERPT tools:

1. From **Start | All Programs | Accessories |** right-click on the **Command Prompt** and choose the **Run As Administrator** to open a command prompt window to open a dedicated administrator console connection:

   ```
   SQLCMD -A
   ```

2. Using **SSMS** open a new query window and execute the following statements:

```
--CREATE XEVENT session to ETW File target
CREATE EVENT SESSION LongRunningQueryExecution_ETW ON SERVER
ADD EVENT sqlserver.sp_statement_completed
( ACTION (sqlserver.sql_text)
  WHERE sqlserver.database_id = 5 AND duration > 30000) ,
  ADD EVENT sqlserver.error_reported (
    ACTION (package0.callstack, sqlserver.session_id, sqlserver.
sql_text, sqlserver.tsql_stack)
      WHERE ([severity]>=(20)
      OR ([error]=(17803)
      OR [error]=(701)
      OR [error]=(802)
      OR [error]=(8645)
      OR [error]=(8651)
      OR [error]=(8657)
      OR [error]=(8902))) ),
ADD EVENT sqlos.scheduler_monitor_non_yielding_ring_buffer_
recorded
add target package0.ETW_CLASSIC_SYNC_TARGET
    (SET DEFAULT_ETW_SESSION_LOGFILE_PATH=N'D:\ENTZ\FS\ETW\SQLETW_
LongRunningQueries.etl')
```

3. From **Start | All Programs | Accessories |** right-click on the **Command Prompt** and choose the **Run As Administrator** to open a command prompt window to execute the following statements:

```
logman start "NT Kernel Logger" -p "Windows Kernel Trace"
(disk,file) -ets -o D:\ENTZ\FS\ETW\SQLETW_LongRunningQueries.etl
-bs 1024 -ct system
```

4. For a full list of options on LOGMAN utility, run logman /? in the command prompt window. Again, from the **SSMS Query** window, let us continue the Extended Events procedures:

```
-- START EVENT SESSION
ALTER EVENT SESSION LongRunningQueryExecution_ETW ON SERVER
STATE=start;
```

5. Now, let us run two queries that run for more than five seconds to capture the extended events:

```
SELECT *
FROM AdventureWorks2008R2.Sales.SalesOrderDetail
ORDER BY UnitPriceDiscount DESC
GO
SELECT *
FROM AdventureWorks.Sales.SalesOrderDetail
ORDER BY UnitPriceDiscount DESC
GO
```

6. At this point, the event session needs to be altered to capture the `sp_statement_completed` value for long running query execution:

```
alter event session LongRunningQueryExecution_ETW
ON SERVER ADD TARGET package0.synchronous_bucketizer
(SET filtering_event_name = 'sqlserver.sp_statement_completed',
source_type=1, source='sqlserver.sql_text')
```

7. Now, let us start the `EVENT SESSION`:

```
ALTER EVENT SESSION LongRunningQueryExecution_ETW ON SERVER
STATE=STOP;
```

8. As the query generates the events, at this point `STOP` the system `ETW` collection and Extended Events external ETW session from the command prompt that was opened in step 3.

```
logman update "NT Kernel Logger" -fd -ets
logman stop "NT Kernel Logger" -ets
logman update XE_DEFAULT_ETW_SESSION -fd -ets
logman stop XE_DEFAULT_ETW_SESSION -ets
```

9. Finally, let us combine the two `.etl` files using `TRACERPT` utility into a single `.csv` file on the command prompt window.

```
tracerpt D:\sqletwtarget.etl D:\ENTZ\FS\ETW\SQLETW_
LongRunningQueries.etl  -y -o SQLETW_LRQ.CSV
```

10. The newly created `.CSV` file can be opened using Microsoft Excel to obtain the collected trace events.

This completes the steps to go through the methods on how to manage events capture using Extended Events with ETW and TRACERPT tools.

How it works...

What we have used is Extended Events with ETW and TRACERPT tools to correlate data from the operating system and SQL Server engine. In a way, Extended Events is helpful to monitor and troubleshoot the long running queries on the server. This is helpful to take pro-active action when the server is experiencing severe performance issues causing client applications to timeout.

At this point, we have opened a Dedicated administrative Console (DAC) connection to perform the Extended Events process by directing the server related issues output to ETW. The output is written to a file that is created on a drive that does not use either the page file or SQL Server database files. Then, we allowed the traces to run for few minutes then closed both extended events and Windows Kernel trace. Now, we have used the `tracerpt.exe` file that will correlate both Windows trace and SQL Server ETW trace into one file for a better flow of information.

See also

For more information on Extended Events refer to the _Monitoring resource usage with Extended Events_ recipe mentioned in _Chapter 8, Maintenance And Monitoring._

More DBA Manageability Best Practices

I would like to present this final recipe of the book more like a list of best practices that I have collected and implemented during my DBA working years. I would like to stress that few may look elementary, but they is logical, which are overlooked most of the time. The following is the list of DBA manageability practices that are important to handle day-to-day tasks of the SQL Server 2008 R2 environment.

1. Design process: Determine the Project Scope and which roles will be required.

2. Design the SQL Server Database Engine infrastructure, Integration Services infrastructure, and wherever necessary SQL Server Analysis Services and SQL Server Reporting Services infrastructure.

3. Storage: Always perform a capacity planning exercise by compiling the amount of database storage that is needed for the next one or two years.

Required Information	Description
# Users Per Server	Total number of users hosted by that server.
% Concurrent Users	The percentage of users connected to the server during peak times.
Storage Capacity in Gigabytes	The calculated disk storage capacity needed.
% Buffer Factor (for growth)	The percentage of disk storage growth allowed by the system.
Read % of IOPS	The percentage of IOPS that are Read operations.
Write % of IOPS	The percentage of IOPS that are Write operations.
Disk Size (GB)	The drive size being considered for the storage system.

4. Ensure to choose appropriate RAID levels. For RAID 0, 1, or 1+0, calculate the number of drives necessary and divide the total storage by the actual drive size (round the value to the nearest and multiply by two).

5. Security: Analyze the required permission structure and make the necessary adjustments to ensure people have the rights they need to work, but not additional rights that may cause potential problems.

6. In addition to securing your database servers, make sure the system and user database backups and any external programs are also secure by limiting any physical access to storage media.

7. Ensure to include a backup strategy of transaction log backups every 15 minutes depending upon the SLA, daily differential backups, and weekly full database backup. This is to highlight the essentials of planning a Disaster Recovery (DR) strategy for the data platform.

8. Ensure that you have tested the backup files by restoring them to a standby server to ensure that there is no corruption on the backup media.

9. For highly transactional mission-critical databases, ensure to include a daily update on statistics schedule during the early hours of the working day and an alternative day schedule of index reorganization on volatile tables that will have numerous `INSERT/DELETE/UPDATE` operations.

10. Also include a re-index of highly transactional and volatile tables that will have numerous `INSERT/DELETE/UPDATE` operations.

11. Be sure to perform database integrity checks for the user databases.

12. Wherever possible, document the information pertaining to database, application usage, Service Level Agreement(SLA), data recovery, and escalation procedures.

> It is a best practice to validate the documentation by referring the steps to implement on a Virtual environment to simulate the actions. A similar approach can be followed when a SQL Server upgrade or Service Pack installation is planned.

13. Perform periodic disaster recovery – failover and failback – tests on the database platform.

14. For High Availability and Disaster Recovery purposes, it is ideal to consider Database Mirroring and Log Shipping on mission-critical databases. In case of high Recovery Point Objective, failover clustering is the best option.

15. Replace any redundant hardware by performing periodic checks on **server hardware | application, web**, and **SQL Server**. Be sure to involve the hardware vendor for any latest firmware updates on hardware resources such as CPU, Disk, and Network components.

16. Schedule the Log backup before the full backup. If you schedule the Log backup before the full backup, you will only have to restore the last full backup and one transaction log. Scheduling after the full backup will demand the restoration of the last full backup and two transaction logs backups.

17. Establish an Auditing Policy on the Backup Folder. Enabling file access auditing to the Backup Folder will monitor user access to the backups.

18. After the database is backed up in a file, compress and encrypt the files before moving the contents to tape backups or other forms of long-term storage.

Encrypting the backup files will help you protect the confidentiality of the information if somebody gains physical access to the media.

Index

[PACKT] enterprise 器
PUBLISHING
professional expertise distilled

Thank you for buying
Microsoft SQL Server 2008 R2 Administration Cookbook

About Packt Publishing

Packt, pronounced 'packed', published its first book "*Mastering phpMyAdmin for Effective MySQL Management*" in April 2004 and subsequently continued to specialize in publishing highly focused books on specific technologies and solutions.

Our books and publications share the experiences of your fellow IT professionals in adapting and customizing today's systems, applications, and frameworks. Our solution-based books give you the knowledge and power to customize the software and technologies you're using to get the job done. Packt books are more specific and less general than the IT books you have seen in the past. Our unique business model allows us to bring you more focused information, giving you more of what you need to know, and less of what you don't.

Packt is a modern, yet unique publishing company, which focuses on producing quality, cutting-edge books for communities of developers, administrators, and newbies alike. For more information, please visit our website: www.PacktPub.com.

About Packt Enterprise

In 2010, Packt launched two new brands, Packt Enterprise and Packt Open Source, in order to continue its focus on specialization. This book is part of the Packt Enterprise brand, home to books published on enterprise software – software created by major vendors, including (but not limited to) IBM, Microsoft and Oracle, often for use in other corporations. Its titles will offer information relevant to a range of users of this software, including administrators, developers, architects, and end users.

Writing for Packt

We welcome all inquiries from people who are interested in authoring. Book proposals should be sent to author@packtpub.com. If your book idea is still at an early stage and you would like to discuss it first before writing a formal book proposal, contact us; one of our commissioning editors will get in touch with you.

We're not just looking for published authors; if you have strong technical skills but no writing experience, our experienced editors can help you develop a writing career, or simply get some additional reward for your expertise.

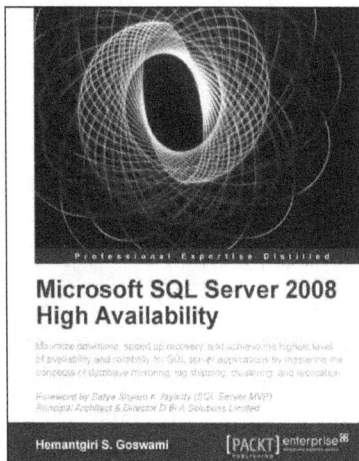

Microsoft SQL Server 2008 High Availability

ISBN: 978-1-849681-22-3   Paperback: 308 pages

Minimize downtime, speed up recovery, and achieve the highest level of availability and reliability for SQL server applications by mastering the concepts of database mirroring,log shipping,clustering, and replication

1. Install various SQL Server High Availability options in a step-by-step manner

2. A guide to SQL Server High Availability for DBA aspirants, proficient developers and system administrators

3. Learn the pre and post installation concepts and common issues you come across while working on SQL Server High Availability

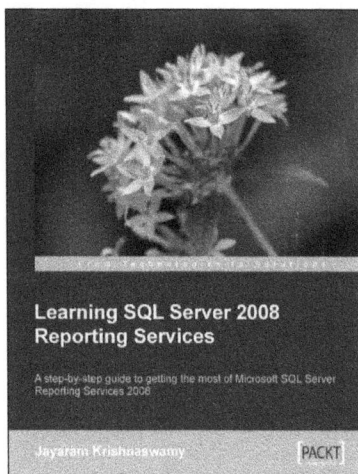

Learning SQL Server 2008 Reporting Services

ISBN: 978-1-847196-18-7   Paperback: 512 pages

A step-by-step guide to getting the most of Microsoft SQL Server Reporting Services 2008

1. Everything you need to create and deliver data-rich reports with SQL Server 2008 Reporting Services as quickly as possible

2. Packed with hands-on-examples to learn and improve your skills

3. Connect and report from databases, spreadsheets, XML Data, and more

4. No experience of SQL Server Reporting Services required

Please check **www.PacktPub.com** for information on our titles

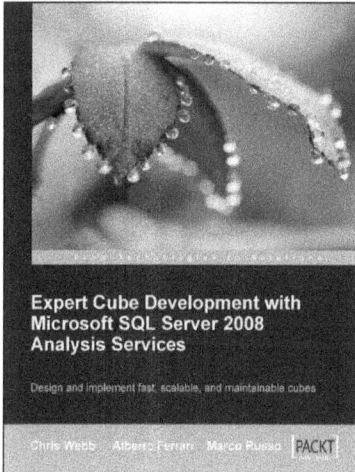

Expert Cube Development with Microsoft SQL Server 2008 Analysis Services

ISBN: 978-1-847197-22-1   Paperback: 360 pages

Design and implement fast, scalable and maintainable cubes

1. A real-world guide to designing cubes with Analysis Services 2008

2. Model dimensions and measure groups in BI Development Studio

3. Implement security, drill-through, and MDX calculations

4. Learn how to deploy, monitor, and performance-tune your cube

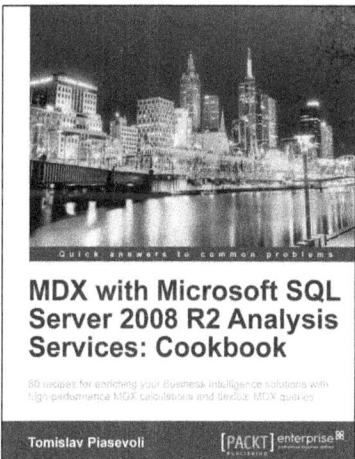

MDX with Microsoft SQL Server 2008 R2 Analysis Services Cookbook

ISBN: 978-1-849681-30-8   Paperback: 400 pages

80 recipes for enriching your Business Intelligence solutions with high-performance MDX calculations and flexible MDX queries

1. Enrich your BI solutions by implementing best practice MDX calculations

2. Master a wide range of time-related, context-aware, and business-related calculations

3. Enhance your solutions by combining MDX with utility dimensions

Please check **www.PacktPub.com** for information on our titles